"From the Great Desire of Promoting Learning":

Thomas Hollis's Gifts to the

Harvard College Library

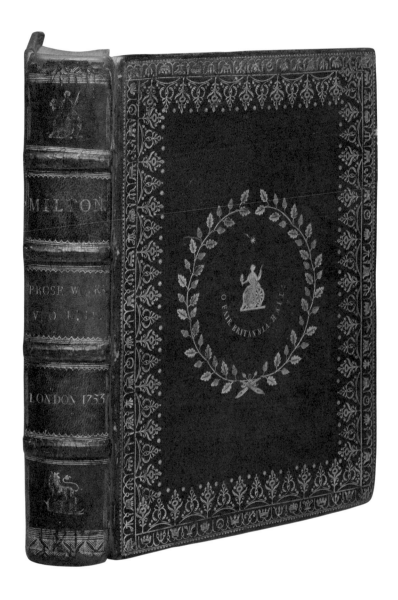

Figure 1. John Milton, *The Works* [in prose] (London, 1753 [i.e., 1756]). Bound in green morocco covers and brown morocco spine. On the printed Hollis bookplate in this two-volume set of Milton's prose, an early Harvard librarian has written: "Relato 28 Dec., 1759. This splendidly bound copy of the writings of Mr Hollis's favorite author was among the earliest books he gave, and escaped the fire of Jany 24, 1764." See Checklist, p. 133. f *EC75.H7627.Zz756m2 2 v. 30 cm.

"FROM THE GREAT DESIRE OF PROMOTING LEARNING": THOMAS HOLLIS'S GIFTS TO THE HARVARD COLLEGE LIBRARY

William H. Bond

Introduction by Allen Reddick
Preface by William P. Stoneman

HOUGHTON LIBRARY OF THE HARVARD COLLEGE LIBRARY 2010

Distributed by Harvard University Press
Cambridge, Massachusetts and London, England

A Special Issue of the *Harvard Library Bulletin*
Volume 19: Numbers 1-2

HARVARD LIBRARY BULLETIN
VOLUME 19: NUMBERS 1-2 (SPRING-SUMMER 2008)
PUBLISHED FEBRUARY 2010
ISSN 0017-8136

Editor
William P. Stoneman

Coordinating Editor
Peter X. Accardo

The Harvard Library Bulletin *is published quarterly by Houghton Library of the Harvard College Library. Annual subscription $35 (U.S., Canada, and Mexico), $41 (foreign); single issue $15.*

Editorial correspondence should be addressed to William P. Stoneman, Houghton Library, Harvard University, Cambridge, MA 02138, email stoneman@fas.harvard.edu; claims and subscription inquiries should be addressed to Monique Duhaime, Houghton Library, Harvard University, Cambridge, MA 02138, email duhaime@fas.harvard.edu.

Publication of the Bulletin *is made possible by a bequest from George L. Lincoln '95, and by a fund established in memory of William A. Jackson.*

The paper used in this publication meets the minimum requirements of the American National Standard for Information Sciences—Permanence of Paper for Printed Materials, ANSI z39.49-1984.

Contents

Figure 2. Giovanni Battista Cipriani, *[Double Portrait drawing of TH]* (London, 1767). In pencil and ink.
MS Typ 576 (31) 32 cm.

Preface

BILL BOND PERFORMED THE SAME FUNCTION FOR BILL JACKSON which I, a third Bill, now gladly but sadly, perform for him, namely placing in context work unfinished at his death. In the concluding paragraph of his Introduction to the posthumous publication of *Records of a Bibliographer* (Cambridge, Mass.: Belknap Press of Harvard University Press, 1967) William Henry Bond wrote that "a librarian and bibliographer of [William Alexander] Jackson's caliber occupies very nearly the position of a public utility in the scholarly world." The same can surely be said of Bond himself. His work on the *Supplement to the Census of Medieval and Renaissance Manuscripts in the United States and Canada* (New York: Bibliographical Society of America, 1962) is comparable to Jackson's work on the second edition, revised and enlarged, of *A Short-Title Catalogue of Books Printed in England, Scotland & Ireland and of English Books Printed Abroad, 1475-1640* (London: Bibliographical Society, 1976-1991). Both efforts built on the work of a previous generation of bibliographers and resulted in standard reference works which continue to be cited and have been used in the creation of electronic tools that have carried their purpose forward to a new generation of users.

Bill Bond succeeded Bill Jackson as Librarian of Houghton Library in 1965 and on his retirement Bond was elected Sandars Reader in Bibliography at Cambridge University in 1982. His Sandars Lectures later became *Thomas Hollis of Lincoln's Inn: A Whig and his Books* (Cambridge: Cambridge University Press, 1990). With Hugh Amory, Bond was the author of *The Printed Catalogues of the Harvard College Library, 1723-1790* (Boston: Colonial Society of Massachusetts, 1996). Both of these works led Bond to the present work and he clearly enjoyed this last retirement project. He was well aware of how this work would alter radically our understanding of Thomas Hollis and we all regret he did not live to see the impact his work would have.

Our collective thanks go to Nancy and Sally Bond for their leading role in advancing their father's final project; to Professor Allen Reddick for writing an excellent introduction to Bond's checklist; to Sarah Stewart who worked with Bill on this project in 2002-2003 and acted as his legs and his eyes in the finishing of the checklist and tying up thousands of loose ends; to Peter Accardo and Dennis Marnon who have helped to polish the final product; to Karen Nipps and David Whitesell for their bibliographic contributions; to Roger Stoddard for his guidance; and to Duncan

Todd who has shaped the checklist into a published product of which we all hope Bill would be proud. In making his extensive gifts to Harvard College Library, Thomas Hollis acted "from the great desire of promoting learning." That was Bill's hope as he prepared this checklist and that has also been our hope as we have seen the present work into publication.

William P. Stoneman
Florence Fearrington Librarian
of Houghton Library of the Harvard College Library
February 2010

Introduction[1]

Allen Reddick, University of Zürich

I

ON FEBRUARY 8, 1764, PRESIDENT EDWARD HOLYOKE of Harvard College sent a letter to Thomas Hollis of Lincoln's Inn, London, describing a celebration and a disaster that had taken place during the preceding month.[2] The account of the celebration honoring the Hollis family gives no warning of the catastrophe and subsequent appeal to follow.

> Sir,
>
> I received your kind letter of May 17, together with the case of books, which (according to your usual goodness) you sent therewith; for which our corporation, in a grateful sense of your beneficence, send you their thanks, as in the enclosed vote. I had wrote you long before this time; but waited till I could inform you of the name of a new building added by our general court to those we have already. The account of which is as followeth:—Our college hath been of late so much increased by the number of students (at present 184 undergraduates) that we applied to our general court, that they would make us such a grant as would enable us to build such a house as we wanted; which grant, viz. £ 400. sterling, they readily made us; accordingly, we immediately proceeded upon the affair, and erected a very fair building, much more beautiful and commodious than any we had before, which was finished the last summer, and contains two-and-thirty chambers. About which time, I being in company (on a certain occasion) with a large number of our ministers, when (speaking of said building) it was moved by one of the company, since

1   William H. Bond did not write a preface to his checklist, although he left brief notes and commentary towards one, generously shared with me by his daughters, Nancy and Sally Bond. I have endeavored to incorporate these into this introduction. I am grateful to the Bonds and to William Stoneman for encouragement, and of course to the memory of Bill Bond himself for his inspiration and friendship.

2   Printed as Appendix LXX in Francis Blackburne, *Memoirs of Thomas Hollis*, 2 v. (London, 1780), 2:730-732. No holograph of the letter occurs in the correspondence of Hollis and Holyoke preserved in the Massachusetts Historical Society or the Harvard University Archives.

the house is now finished, what will the name of it be? I answered, that as Mr. Thomas Hollis, of London (your bountiful uncle) was by far our greatest benefactor, I thought it ought to have the name of Hollis, on which they all manifested their hopes it would be so called.

The overseers agreed "it would be a most proper name for it," but thought it right that the Governor, Francis Bernard, should make the final decision. To him, Holyoke

shewed the great obligations we had been under to do honour to the name of Hollis, first with respect to Mr. Thomas Hollis, who was our greatest benefactor, as he had established with us two professorships and ten scholarships, besides gave us a great number of books, and a most valuable philosophic and mathematical apparatus; and with respect to Mr. Nathaniel Hollis, who established two scholarships, and others of the name who sent us an orrery, armillary sphere, &c. &c. &c. And further with respect to Mr. John Hollis, who sent us a large number of most valuable books; to which I added your own almost annual benefactions. I added, moreover, That though there was one of our towns which, for the honour of that family, was named Holliston, yet the reason of that name would not long be remembered; but if one of the colleges was so named it would perpetuate the memory of our great benefactor, and the honour of his house. Upon which I told the governor I requested that the new building at the college might be named HOLLIS. To which he readily answered, With all his heart.

On January 13, the Governor and Council, with the lower house, met in Cambridge (in Holden Chapel) with the express purpose of viewing the new building.

And when they were well seated . . . I rose up and said: "As there are here present his Excellency the Governor, the Honourable his Majesty's Council, and the Honourable House of Representatives, who by their vote gave to the College the new building in our view, it cannot therefore be an improper time to ask a name for it: wherefore I apply to your Excellency to give the name."

Upon which the Governor, standing up, said:— "I now give to this new building the name of HOLLIS-HALL."

After this there was a gratulatory oration in English, given by one of the students, and that in a handsome manner. And after an agreeable entertainment of the whole court (who dined in the College-hall) they went to take a view of the new-named building; and then returned to Boston.

Holyoke concludes this portion of the letter to the point: "Sir, I write you this very particular account of the whole affair, that you may see how very desirous we are to do honour to your worthy and munificent family."

Holyoke's combination of straightforwardness, transcription, flattery, and genuine gratitude transparently sets the stage for the dramatic report that follows.

> But, however I rejoice in all I have said above, as done in honour of your generous and charitable house, the holy providence of GOD calls me to bewail the great, and, in some regards, irreparable loss, we have sustained by fire, since the 13th of January above-mentioned.
>
> The small-pox coming to Boston, and beginning to spread, the general court were much alarmed (for that the greatest part of them, by far, had never had it); and therefore desired the Governor to adjourn them to Cambridge; which he did; and they came up and sat here on Jan. 18. The Governor and Council in the Library and the Representatives in the Hall underneath, till the 24th, when it being very cold, they made large fires, and that in the library had (it is thought) in the day-time fired a beam which run under the hearth, which in the dead of night set fire to the library and the whole house, which was so increased when discovered, that no single thing could be saved, and was so raging, as to baffle all attempts to stop it, the wind having been, and then continuing, very strong. The other three buildings, viz. Massachusetts, Hollis and Stoughton, were much endangered, the fire catching upon them several times, but having a good engine, and well tended, none (by the good providence of GOD) but Harvard was lost; but then the treasure therein was vastly worth more than the building; viz. the whole library, which at least consisted of 5000 volumes; of which near 3000 were quartos and folios, every thing also in the apparatus, procured by the munificence of your family. It is true the general court immediately made us a grant for rebuilding the house; but at present we have no provision made for obtaining a library and apparatus, wherefore we are greatly at a loss what we shall do in that respect; and I am afraid must despair of those losses being made up, unless it be from your side of the water; but cannot have the face to ask your assistance, having continually received great benefactions from your bountiful hand; but this you will give us leave to hope for, that you would be pleased to move any gentlemen of your acquaintance, who are charitably disposed to assist us in the repair of these our great losses. There are others of our corporation who will write you on this matter, to beg your assistance, as above, with whose motions I know you will readily comply, whereby you may be a means of greatly serving us . . .

In the postscript, Holyoke informs Hollis that "the only ornament of our Hall was our benefactor's picture," and asks him, if he has one, to send a copy for the hall, along with "an escutcheon of the arms of the family, which also was lost in the library." With all of this dreadful news, Holyoke is able at least to reassure him "that the last parcel of books you sent, with your letter of May 17, have escaped destruction, as it remained in my house for want of boxes, and fitting a place for them in the library."

II

President Holyoke's pains to lead Thomas Hollis through the stages of building, proposing, viewing, naming, and celebrating not only convey the drama but also re-stage baptismal and commemorative rituals. Holyoke summarizes so explicitly the Hollis family's previous benefactions, of course, in order to remind him of the great lineage of patronage by the Hollises, now materially disrupted and virtually erased, except for the shell of the new building. His description of the hall as a temple-monument in honor of his ancestor, bare except for portrait and family arms, might appeal to the recipient's vanity, as well as a sense of paternal responsibility. Yet Thomas Hollis was not a vain man, nor eager to have his name celebrated; he did believe, however, in the power of material objects to hold iconic significance and symbolic meaning, whether intellectual, political, or social. Such significance and meaning were usually accrued and imparted through gift or exchange between members of a like-minded network, both contemporary and cross-generational. In his appeal to Hollis, Holyoke must have sensed Hollis's commitment to such a system of significance. The loss of the gifts from, and the remembrances of, the benefactor from the mother country exposed the institution and its students to a vacuum of identity and heritage. While the naming of a building in his honor certainly pleased him, the materials of study, consultation, and ownership—of identity formation—were Hollis's committed interests. Thomas Hollis was uniquely positioned to compensate Harvard for the crippling loss, one which effectively made it impossible to continue a proper educational mission. As we shall see, he was just the person to call upon, and he was already actively gathering books to send.

The fire constituted a great tragedy. The library was the largest in the British colonies, possibly anywhere in North America. "An Account of the Fire at Harvard-College," a long, articulate, and detailed notice, was published as a broadsheet in Boston the following day, and it was picked up by the *London Chronicle* for March 20-22, 1764.[3] The London version includes two alterations that reveal the likely intervening hand of Thomas Hollis. Following the notation in the account that many of the destroyed items had been given "by our great benefactor the late worthy Thomas Hollis, Esq; of London," it removes the comment, "Some of the most considerable additions that had been made of late years to the library, came from other branches of this generous Family." Doubtless he considered the remark too fulsome and personal; however, he

3   Vol. XV, No. 1131, pp. 273-74. Peter X. Accardo brought this reprinting to my attention.

allows the subsequent passage to stand: "the other [donation], of 56 volumes, by the present worthy Thomas Hollis, Esq; F.R.S. of London, to whom we have been annually obliged for valuable additions to our late library." While he may not have wanted his enemies in London to know that he was sending books to the American colonies (though soon this did not seem to concern him in his efforts for Harvard, whereas it did in his activities of donations elsewhere in the world), nevertheless the example which he set for others could be useful in these circumstances, especially as the notice contains a factual, straightforward account of items sent and deliveries made in service to the institution. The *Chronicle* also adds one sentence, following the inventory of scientific apparatus lost in the fire, an addition Thomas Hollis was in the best position to make: "The value of the whole apparatus could not be less than 300l. sterling:", inserted before the broadsheet's "All destroyed!" Whether or not President Holyoke's letter arrived in London before the broadsheet account reached Hollis is unknown; whenever he read it, Hollis quickly had it republished to sound the alarm for assistance.

The disaster prompted Hollis to increase several-fold his shipments to Harvard, determining the books to which the young men should be exposed and (both implicitly and explicitly) helping to design their education and curriculum. Furthermore, the library's collection was also available to members of the public, which Hollis clearly recognized in his inscriptions to the "publick" library of Harvard College. The surviving eighteenth-century records show many members of the public withdrawing books.[4] In other words, Hollis's books were also intended to educate a full contingent of (primarily) men from the colony, beyond the Harvard community proper. Most of these books and authors had never before been read on the shores of North America. Hollis's response to the fire also enabled a vigorous connection to the leaders of Harvard and important colonial divines, especially in Boston and New England, which would prove influential, both in North America and in England, through the tumultuous decade following the Seven Years' War and the build-up to the American Revolution. Reflecting later upon "the Plan adopted by me in regard to Books intended to be presented to that College," Hollis would write to Edmund Quincy, in Boston, on October 1, 1766:

> I confess to bear propensity, affection toward the People of North America; those of Massachuset's and Boston in particular, believing them to be a good and brave People. Long may they continue such, and the Spirit of Luxury, now consuming Us to the very marrow here at home, kept out from them!
>
> One likeliest means to the End will be, to watch well over their Youth, by bestowing on them a reasonable, manly education; and selecting thereto the wisest, ablest, most accomplished of Men, that art or wealth can obtain: for Nations rise and fall by Individuals not Numbers, as I think all History proveth.

4   Kenneth Carpenter, *The First 350 Years of the Harvard University Library* (Cambridge, Mass.: Harvard University Library, 1986), 14-15, 32, 33.

With Ideas of this kind have I worked for the Public Library at Cambridge in N. England; neither caring too exactly to remember, how the last, best Library in all America was lost there; nor, a sober, retired Person, without a by-view, not long to be unearthed, acting surely from Vanity; nor sparing toward it Expence, Labor or Time.

It is certain the last winter I passed in Town, against Inclination, Health and Conveniency, on account of the Stamp-act; and this Summer, with much preceeding time, time the most valuable of all things, on account of that Library.[5]

III

Hollis's aims for Harvard College have received careful attention from historians and bookmen, but have never been examined or delineated in the detail they deserve, principally because the actual books have never before been located and an inventory published.[6] With the publication of W. H. Bond's comprehensive checklist, such an examination can now be undertaken, briefly in this introduction, and more fully by contemporary scholars. But before we examine Thomas Hollis's program, we should attempt to understand something of the man himself and the origins of and reasons for his extraordinary connection to Harvard College, which neither he nor his ancestors ever even saw.

Much has been illuminated about Thomas Hollis's history in recent decades through the research of W. H. Bond.[7] The Hollis family had been successful cutlers and later amassed a considerable fortune as manufacturers and merchants. They were an

5   W. H. Bond, ed., *Letters from Thomas Hollis of Lincoln's Inn to Andrew Eliot* (Cambridge, Mass.: Houghton Library, 1988), 92-93.

6   In addition to Bond's work, most notable among existing studies are those by Caroline Robbins, esp. "Library of Liberty—Assembled for Harvard College by Thomas Hollis of Lincoln's Inn," *Harvard Library Bulletin* 5 (1951), 5-23, 185-96, reprinted in her *Absolute Liberty*, ed. Barbara Taft (Hamden, Conn.: Archon, 1982); and Annabel Patterson, *Early Modern Liberalism* (Cambridge: Cambridge University Press, 1997), passim. Much of Bond's work of assembling the information in the checklist and gathering information concerning these efforts required a thorough examination of the accession lists in the Harvard University Archives, correspondence (much unpublished) between Hollis and his contacts at Harvard and in Boston, and, of course, his unpublished diary from the years 1759-70, at Houghton Library. I have relied on Hollis's diary in my description of his activities and aims throughout this introduction.

7   W. H. Bond, *Thomas Hollis of Lincoln's Inn: a Whig and His Books* (Cambridge: Cambridge University Press, 1990), esp. ch. 1.

old Dissenting family and predictably "Real" or "Old" Whig in politics.[8] From early on, they supported Dissenters' charitable and educational causes, and Dissenting worship in general. The first Thomas Hollis prospered as a whitesmith and cutler in Rotherham in the West Riding of Yorkshire. He founded the Sheffield Hospital, a charity to maintain sixteen poor cutlers' widows, and was a leader in the Upper Chapel in Sheffield before his death in 1663. His son Thomas the second (1634-1718) was apprenticed to a cutler and was eventually sent to London, where he became an independent merchant. In Bond's words, "He and his wife, Anne (Thorner), worshipped at Pinner's Hall, London's leading Independent Meeting House, and in 1679 he secured a ninety-nine-year lease of the Hall, which was served during most of the eighteenth-century by a line of distinguished Dissenting ministers including Isaac Watts and Caleb Fleming, all closely associated with the Hollis family" (30). While in London he met Increase Mather, who had come there in 1688 to negotiate a new charter for the Massachusetts Bay Colony. Mather was at this time Rector of Harvard College, which was in considerable danger of collapse, its governing boards having been eliminated and with no charter that explicitly protected its rights and existence. Thus began the Hollises' connection to Harvard, as Increase Mather actively sought out leading Dissenters in London to support the struggling young Dissenting institution in the American colonies. Thomas the second's brother-in law, Robert Thorner, who also became acquainted with Mather, left a sizable bequest to Harvard. This Thomas Hollis also generously founded and supported Dissenter interests and charities in Sheffield. Thomas the third (1659-1731), eldest son of Thomas the second, established the Hollis Professorships in Divinity and in Natural Philosophy, the oldest chairs in North America, and gave them donations totaling at least £5,000. He gave other gifts, including books, and Hollis Hall was chiefly, as we have seen, named in his honor. Along with his brothers Nathaniel (d. 1738) and John (d. 1735), Thomas Hollis the third was also very active in supporting charities in England, including Baptist and Independent religious societies. John Hollis also gave books to Harvard. Nathaniel was the father of Thomas the fourth (d. 1735), a supporter of charitable causes himself. Thomas the fifth (1720-1774, the Thomas Hollis who concerns us here) was the son of Thomas the fourth and his wife, Sarah (d. before 1735).

Thomas the third had amassed a considerable fortune, which he left at his death to his brother Nathaniel and son Thomas the fourth. Thomas Hollis (the fifth) was heir of both these brothers and came into his fortune at an early age: his father died when he was only fifteen, his uncle when he was eighteen. Immensely wealthy, Thomas the fifth

---

8   On this designation, see, e.g., John Sainsbury, *Disaffected Patriots: London Supporters of Revolutionary America, 1769-1782* (Kingston and Montreal: McGill-Queens's University Press, 1987), 7-12, 125-9, passim; Caroline Robbins, *The Eighteenth-Century Commonwealthman* (Cambridge, Mass.: Harvard University Press, 1959), 1-18; Colin Hayden, *Anti-Catholicism in Eighteenth-century England, c. 1714-80* (Manchester: Manchester University Press, 1993), 184-97, passim.

now had options open before him other than the commercial career for which he had been educated (partially in the Low Countries); having received his father's bequest when he was still in his minority, he was no longer obliged to make money. "A career in public service," writes Bond, "seemed to open before him, and a liberal education was now to be added to the practical training he had already acquired" (6). Thomas Hollis was reoriented by his guardians to a classical education; he studied Greek and Latin with his tutor, John Ward, Professor of Rhetoric at Gresham College.

As a Dissenter, Hollis would not be groomed for Oxford or Cambridge, but he seems to have found his educational model early on in John Milton's remarkable prescriptions for education written in his letter to Samuel Hartlib, published as *Of Education*. Milton's precepts are intended to fit "a man to perform justly, skillfully, and magnanimously all the offices, both private and public, of peace and war."[9] Milton sets out the requirements for education into a moral life of public service, acting deliberately and tirelessly to support religious and political freedom (concerning what to read, what languages to learn, what sciences, what travels and formal studies, and so on, and in what order). Hollis's career followed Milton's plan (Hollis always referred to it as the "MASTER tract") with remarkable consistency; the most significant divergence is an important one, however: Hollis always insisted on remaining a private subject rather than a public figure (despite his constant intervention in public causes behind the scenes).

When he came of age, he bought extensive farmland in the southwest of England (Milton had advised his reader to study agricultural science), some thousands of acres, five or six farms, and he would eventually farm them or have them farmed by tenants. Beginning at age twenty, Hollis read law (as prescribed in Milton's letter) in Lincoln's Inn for around six years, after which, as Milton had insisted should be the culmination of a proper education, he embarked on two grand tours, traveling throughout Europe, from Scandinavia to Malta and as far east as Poland and Vienna. While in Italy, where he spent many months, he met numerous members of the intelligentsia, as well as book dealers and collectors and amateurs in art, and he began purchasing coins, medals, classical antiquities, and books, collecting for himself and as gifts for others. It was in Italy where he seems to have developed his interest in and commitment to the distribution of objects connected with political, religious, and moral positions he valued. The importance of objects as signifying allegiance and as conveying and performing a commitment became nearly obsessive for Hollis all his adult life.

Hollis was an ardent republican, as well as Dissenter, yet this designation requires some refining. Hollis was not necessarily anti-monarch and actively promoted "Revolution" (i.e., 1688) values. Hollis believed that the will of the people and the constitution should be protected more forcefully from corrupt powers within the

9   Blackburne, 1:84; J. G. Nichols, *Literary Anecdotes of the Eighteenth Century*, 6 vols. (London, 1812), 3:20.

government and the Crown. He looked back to Lord Molesworth, Milton, and Algernon Sidney for his justifications for the protecting of the rights of subjects and institutions. Hollis republished several classic prose texts of the seventeenth century (concerning law, the state, the church, and liberty) and had them specially bound and distributed to destinations and individuals all over Europe and some in the colonies. He gave most of these to Harvard and also, in the colonies, to Princeton (his first donation appears to have been ten guineas to "the newly erected college at Prince's-town, in New Jersey" in 1754), Columbia, Yale, and the University of Pennsylvania.[10] He also gave them to individuals whom he wanted to support and to win to his causes, in America and throughout Europe, where many remain in libraries to this day. Besides Harvard, the most frequent recipients, who retain the books in their collections, were the Zentralbibliothek Bern, Switzerland, with a magnificent collection of nearly 400 remarkably pristine volumes, including Hollis's "canonical" books; the Zentralbibliothek Zürich, with a unique collection of anti-Jesuit publications; Christ's College, Cambridge, with books including spectacular copies of *Paradise Lost* and Locke's own copy, with annotations, of his *Two Treatises on Government*; and Dr. Williams's Library, London, the famous Dissenting institution.

Harvard's collection is the largest, especially because of efforts following the fire. Yet there were other reasons as well. Hollis was motivated by the strong historical tie between members of his family and Harvard College, by the unique role of Harvard as the premier institution in the English-speaking world for training Dissenting preachers and leaders, by its increasing importance in the colonies, and by its centrality to the sovereignty and religious issues so close to his heart and, no doubt eventually, to its geographical importance to the growing struggle with the home country. Furthermore, as he increasingly lost confidence in the mother country's ability to resist the forces of arbitrary authority that would constrain freedom and (one of his recurrent words, following Milton) "manliness," Hollis appears to have thought that the English colony in the New World, educated in the right spirit, might be the only remaining hope to perpetuate the spirit of English liberty. That Hollis intended his gifts to establish a great library for Dissenting young men, one which should continue to educate generations for years after his death, is demonstrated by his bequeathing of £500 in his will to establish Harvard's oldest endowed book fund, still active today.

IV

Hollis had already begun giving many books before the fire, as we have seen. He seems to have given important books including a first edition of Vesalius and books on classical architecture and a variety of subjects (unlike the strictly theological books given by his ancestors), many of which were destroyed. The library had outgrown its quarters in

10   Blackburne, 1:60.

Cambridge and therefore when a shipment of books arrived late in the year before the fire, the packing cases, as Holyoke confirms, were stored apparently unopened in the President's house so they survived the fire. Furthermore, some other books that Hollis had given to Harvard earlier, such as the Vesalius, were so beautiful that the President kept them in his house too, so some important things survived.

By the time news of the fire arrived in London, Hollis was already collecting books and raising money for the college. He knew the booksellers in London intimately and canvassed them for their cooperation in donating books to the college, which some of them did. As we can trace in his diary, Hollis gathered books from all over the place for a year or more. He made a daily round of all the bookshops that he knew in London and picked up books that would be good for the college to have. By examining Hollis's diary, Harvard library records, and the books themselves, we can estimate that Hollis sent at least thirty shipments across the Atlantic at various dates. Some of them were undated and must be inferred.

Hollis's activities in preparing and shipping books can be summarized from W. H. Bond's thorough descriptions in his *Thomas Hollis of Lincoln's Inn*.[11] The great majority of the books Hollis gave to Harvard after the fire, unless they were in fine or sound bindings already, he had rebound in London by two binders, John Matthewman and John Shove (his earlier master-binder was Richard Montagu, who executed beautiful bindings on books, such as Hollis's edition of Milton's *Works* [in prose], some of which are still preserved at Harvard). It is hard to imagine that these binders could have done much work for anyone else at these times. Several other binders did a very few of the volumes. In some cases, books in fine or simply sound bindings would be "vamped" by inserting new endpapers, headbands, and other details, structural and decorative, including adding Hollis's own emblematic tools to any existing decoration. Some of the books Hollis sent have fine emblematic bindings, and many are well preserved. Most are relatively plain and simply decorated, if at all; these are often well-worn, some with readers' annotations, showing they were actually taken down and consulted. As he prepared his books, another catastrophe of fire struck, this time in London. Hollis books were once again destroyed in June 1764, when a fire devastated Matthewman's shop, destroying a large number of books as well as the beautiful tools designed by Cipriani. On June 6, Hollis records:

> Lamented this misfortune on many accounts; but cheered Mathewman all I could. I have lost by it a large and very fine collection of books, relating chiefly to Government, which were there for binding, and were intended to be sent to Harvard College in N. E.; besides much time and thinking. I will not be discouraged, however, but begin collecting a finer parcel for that College; and I

11   Esp. ch. 2.

thank God, that it was not my own house that was consumed; a Calamity that would have mastered my poor Philosophy!

He immediately began to collect books that had been lost and submitted want-lists to dealers. Eventually new tools were cut, in late 1764 and early 1765, and the stamping continued again.

V

Hollis's donations to Harvard represent what must be the largest gift of books to one destination during the eighteenth century; his efforts far exceed those of any other private individual. In fact, when we consider the entire program of distribution, to sites in Europe and North America, it becomes clear that his network of gifts has perhaps never been matched by an individual. In total, he must have given at least four thousand volumes, many of them rare and valuable, many comprising multiple pamphlets and other fugitive pieces bound together. The full nature of the propaganda campaign is resembled only by the mass production and distribution of books in more recent history.

Analyzing the individual gifts, their contents, binding, and inscriptions, together with any relevant comments by Hollis himself, we can trace a map of Hollis's intentions and beliefs concerning the donations to Harvard. One particularly fascinating glimpse into one aspect of Hollis's project—virtually an epitome of it, debating, then resolving, his beliefs concerning the power of books and scholarship—can be found within the volume of John Ray's *Select Remains* (1760). The flyleaf contains the following quotation, apparently in the handwriting of previous owner and editor George Scott, from Samuel Johnson's *Rasselas, the Prince of Abyssinia*:

> The Life that is devoted to knowledge passes silently away, and is very little diversified by Events. To talk in publick, to think in Solitude, to read and to hear, to inquire, and answer Inquiries, is the Business of a Scholar. He wanders about the World without Pomp or Terrour, and is neither known or valued but by Men like Himself.—Prince of Abyssinia Vol. i. p. 43.

Hollis adds the note: "written by Mr. Johnson." On the back flyleaf, Hollis responds, with a quotation from Hobbes:

> "Desire of praise disposeth to laudable actions, such as please them whose judgment they value; for of those men whom we contemn, we contemn also the praises. Desire of praise [Fame] after death does the same. And though after death, there be no sense of the praise given Us here on Earth, as being

joyes, that are either swallowed up in the unspeaka[ble] joyes of Heaven, or extinguished in the extreme torments of Hell; yet is not such praise vain: Because men have a present delight therein, from from [*sic*] the foresight of it, and of the benefit that may result thereby to their Posterity, which though they now see not yet they imagine, & any thing that is pleasure in the sense, the same also is pleasure in the Imagination." Leviathan, 1651, in folio, p. 48.

The quotations do battle over the memory and the soul, as it were, of John Ray and like-minded erstwhile scholars. Johnson (with whom Hollis is happy to disagree) proposes the first position, Hobbes the second. The quotation from *Rasselas* alludes to Ray's scholarly life, at Cambridge and afterwards as tutor, emphasizing the slow, modest, narrowly effective life of words. The quotation from Hobbes stakes out the territory of the scholar as inspired by self-belief and the power of pleasing worthy successors and readers, of consciousness of the world and the effects of one's efforts within it, and the power of words before and after the death of the author. Ray's work is his "Remains," that which is left, especially the accounts of his travels through Britain ("Mr. Ray's Itineraries," pp. 105-319). Hollis insists—as against George Scott's invoking of Johnson's deflating image of the scholar—that "actions" of authors, specifically their words, retain a life, and that praise of authors—one of Hollis's activities, praising those in his Pantheon, giving them fame—incites them to bold and great deeds that live on after the author's death. (Ray's work in natural theology would notably influence later scientists; he is sometimes considered the father of British natural history.) Therefore, it is important to praise them and hold them up to public worth. Hollis is also concerned about the legacy of the books themselves, which continue to do their author's work, as living things—*pace Areopagitica*—even after his or her death. Note his care to cite the location of the passage in the specific edition of Hobbes, the folio edition which he, of course, had already sent to Harvard in 1764; on p. 48 of that book, Hollis has written in the margin, "Love of Vertue, from Love of Praise." Hollis is always interested in the network of, and dialogue and connections between, books; in this regard, he frequently points the reader to a particular truth on a particular page to be gleaned from a volume. In this case, the dialogue is pursued among Johnson, Hobbes, Ray, and ultimately Hollis himself, who choreographs it. The significance of the quotation taken from Hobbes's *Leviathan* to Hollis's own practice is clear: Hollis was apparently pleased to receive praise from those in Harvard and Boston, who knew he was engaged in a grand donation. It is part of his intention to maintain a public and celebrated connection between the colonies and the old country, one that would have mutual political, religious, and intellectual benefit, and would establish an example for others. In the course of donation or exchange, and of publishing and financing other works, the political, moral, and intellectual allegiances are established. In this regard, he is concerned about his own legacy and that of his family for what they represent, as much as anything. (In the great majority of donations in Europe, especially to Bern and Zürich, he preferred to work anonymously and assiduously protected his anonymity.)

Hollis transcribes the same quotation from *Leviathan* (with minimal variations) onto the back flyleaf of John Ward's *A System of Oratory* (1759), underlining the phrases "yet is not such fame [*sic*] vain" and "and of the benefit which may redound thereby to Posterity." Ward was Hollis's unassuming tutor. On the first flyleaf, Hollis quotes from "Lycidas":

> Fame is the spur, that the clear spirit doth raise,
> (That last infirmitie of noble mind)
> To scorn delights & live laborious days;
> But the fair guerdon where we hope to find,
> And think to burst out into sudden blaze,
> Comes the blind Furie with th'abhorred shears,
> And slits the thin-spun life; But not the praise
> Phebus repli'd, and
> Milton's Lycidas[12]

See the Note at the end of this book. [i.e., the passage from Hobbes]

On the second flyleaf, in Hollis's hand:

> The free and ingenuous sort of men were evidently born to study and love learning for itself, not for lucre or any other end, but the service of God & of truth, and perhaps that lasting fame & perpetuity of praise, which God & good Men have consented shall be the reward of those whose publish'd labours advance the good of mankind.
> Milton's Areopagitica.

Hollis's appeal to these quotations and the qualities of "praise," "fame," and "reward" has implications both for Hollis's own activities and for the role the books and authors will play in succeeding generations, as indeed for the students who are reading the works and preparing for their own lives. "Praise" in this context involves attention and attributed value, attributed specifically by those who come afterward; this is what gives the words life. Citing them publicly, presenting the book as gift, adorning it appropriately physically, remembering, through a kind of litany, other workers laboring for similar causes—all these acts give value to the object and enable

---

12   Hollis copied the same passage from "Lycidas" onto the flyleaf of a copy of Milton's *Works* [in prose] he donated to Geneva, plus the three previous lines of the poem: "Were it not better done as others do,/To sport with Amaryllis in the shade,/Tied in the tangles of neera's [*sic*] hair?"

the object to express and demonstrate its value through its "fame." Milton's words even imply a quasi-sainthood for those who would write in such service. In the passage from Hobbes, "praise" also involves a sense of self-worth. Ward is an important figure in this regard, as a man who lived modestly and made few claims for himself, but who influenced—again, in a modest manner—the debates of the day, especially concerning the relation between science and religion. As Hollis's tutor, Ward imparted his own spirit, knowledge, and commitment through intellectual exchange. Hollis further points, embraces, usurps, and sends along the accumulated font of wisdom and a sign of solidarity.

When Hollis has the books of which he approves vamped, rebound, or otherwise altered at his direction, he takes over the books—their contents as well as materials themselves—for his own purposes. In such a way, he recruits or dragoons the work to his own efforts of propaganda and influence, as if it has been written to the cause, to the minute. Yet the archaic or otherwise old-fashioned quality of some of the books— their lettering, for example, or their paper, or layout—is also rhetorically useful for communicating to the recipient and reader (especially when old and new elements are juxtaposed) the message that the causes are the same over time, and that current crises and concerns were anticipated by the great writers of the past, from Aristotle to Cicero, to Algernon Sidney, John Milton, or John Locke. Hollis's vamping is his own form of creation and collaboration, enlisting in the ranks of great men and their causes. In symbolic terms, Hollis creates a kind of shrine in which the spirit of the author and his cause is handed over for preservation and inspiration. The work is itself treated as if it were a living being, resurrected or enlivened for new life. Hollis's traces (gilt-stamps, smoke prints, special endpapers and ribbons, as well as annotations and inscriptions) partake of a ritual syncretism between creators—of the original work and the re-created work. Thus, the volumes enact a collaboration between like minds, a type and model for what occurs during the donation to a specific source. The exchange and transformational aspects of the books are thus visible on and within the books themselves. Even anachronistic aspects of the book decoration inscribe the collaboration.

Furthermore, Hollis was inspired by Milton's stirring words in *Areopagitica*, words he copied into several books given to Harvard and elsewhere: "For books are not absolutely dead things . . . They are as lively, and as vigorously productive, as those fabulous dragon's teeth; and being sown up and down, may chance to spring up armed men."[13] The intent for the colonists was clear, and perhaps more successful than Hollis could have imagined or, indeed, would have hoped (he would have been devastated to know of the outbreak of war with the mother country). Hollis is concerned about the Bostonians and actively seeks word of and from them, often in the New England Coffee

13   Richard Baron, ed. *The Works* [in prose], 2 v. (London, 1753 [i.e., 1756]), 1:151; this edition of Milton's prose is one of Hollis's favorite "liberty books," sent to many destinations.

House in London and from ships' captains after transatlantic voyages, and he attempts to support their grievances against the mother country. The diary documents his concerns and activities for the colonists, with something done on their behalf virtually every day over more than ten years.

In a most evident way, Hollis is involved in promoting a kind of "identity formation," as Benedict Anderson phrases it, based on writing, reading, and ownership.[14] The identity of the American colonists was, in a manner of speaking, still immature and unformed, in the process of being formed, even while its character was more or less set. We are reminded of Edmund Burke's great "Speech on Conciliation with the Colonies," in which he turns his attention to the American character and spirit, concluding with rhetorical force that this spirit is set and is fierce, proud, unbending, and accustomed to confrontation. There was a great deal to fight over, and Hollis enters the lists.

VI

Hollis's activities as educator and propagandist, as distributor and publisher of books and pamphlets for the Americans' concerns, should be seen as part of a larger program of propaganda and influencing public opinion. Hollis's monitoring of news and opinions in the printed press was a daily affair, as we know from his diary, and he very often inserted for anonymous publication articles, letters, or notices reflecting his interests. The diary is full of references to his journalistic and pamphlet publications, and the scholar can identify hundreds of likely published pieces from his hand, though it is impossible to be certain of all of them. Every act was intended to influence public opinion towards the causes he cared about. He also distributed in England works published in the American colonies, most of them unavailable and controversial, sent him by American friends. Many of these are tracts written in the midst of controversies raging in the colonies concerning British policies towards them. Some of them he sent back to Harvard with his own binding and notes. He also arranged for republication in England of colonial tracts, some of them incendiary. And as we can see from the checklist, Hollis sent the Americans copies of British tracts concerning American affairs almost as soon as they were written.

Hollis's "transatlantic patronizing"[15] may be observed in the case of John Adams, who probably encountered Hollis's "liberty canon" (Milton, Sidney, Harrington, Locke, et al.) while on a Hollis scholarship (funded by Thomas Hollis the third) as a student at Harvard College in the 1750s. His *A Dissertation on the Canon and Feudal Law* (1765) praised Hollis's core writers for establishing and protecting religious and

14   Benedict Anderson, *Imagined Communities: Nationalism. Reflections on the Spread and Origin of Nationalism* (London: Verso, 1983).

15   John S. Tanner and Justin Collings, "How Adams and Jefferson Read Milton and Milton Read Them," *Milton Quarterly* 40 (2006): 210.

political principles. Hollis arranged to publish the tract in England, though ignorant of its author. As recent scholars have claimed, Hollis's donations of "liberty books" to Harvard

> had supplied the Whig view of British history adopted by Adams in the *Dissertation*. Thus, Hollis had in effect disseminated seeds of liberty to America, from which sprang Adams's *Dissertation*, and then transplanted fruit from the American tree of liberty back on English soil . . . He placed republican texts, Milton's biography [by Toland] and prose foremost among them, in the hands of extraordinary readers such as Jefferson and Adams. They in turn spread these libertarian ideas in the Colonies and eventually back to England and the Continent, and ultimately forward into history.[16]

Adams writes of these authors and their effect on him in his *Thoughts On Government: Applicable to the Present State of the American Colonies*:

> A man must be indifferent to the sneers of modern Englishmen, to mention in their company the names of Sidney, Harrington, Locke, Milton, Nedham, Neville, Burnet, and Hoadley. No small fortitude is necessary to confess that one has read them. The wretched condition of this country, however, for ten or fifteen years past, has frequently reminded me of their principles and reasonings. They will convince any candid mind, that there is no good government but what is Republican.

In an earlier version of the *Thoughts* (a letter to William Hooper) he affirms that "In my early Youth, the Works of [these writers] were put into my hands."[17] Not only does Adams credit these writers (Hollis's liberty canon) with value, he also implies the scarcity of works. Adams invokes their unfashionable names, saved from complete ignorance in the colonies by Hollis, in order to strike back at the political realities he was encountering and attempting to resist.

Similarly, Andrew Eliot writes to Hollis in 1767, upon receiving a shipment of books destined for Harvard, as follows:

> Harrington, Sydney, Locke, almost any man may study his whole life to advantage. I am particularly obliged to you for Milton's prose works. They who consider that very great man only as a poet of the first rank, know less than half his character. He was every thing. I have often read detached pieces of his,

---

16   Tanner and Collings, 210.

17   Robert. J. Taylor, et al., *Papers of John Adams*, 14 v. (Cambridge, Mass.: Harvard University Press, 1977-2008), 4:87, 74.

and shall never be weary of his Defensio Populi Anglicani . . . I blush to own that I have never gone through the whole of these prose works. I have lost a great deal. Perhaps my pleasure is the greater now . . . His sentiments are so just, and his attachment to liberty so firm, that he ought to be open to every Englishman.[18]

Milton had been the test case for political freedom, and the battle over his reputation and his actual works could take the form of his case for rebellion. The prose, which was kept out of print in England and only through Hollis's efforts republished and copies sent to North America—these very volumes at Harvard read by many influential figures— is uncompromisingly concerned with the right and duty of the individual to protect individual rights even if it means rebelling against the monarch. The importance of Hollis's success in introducing these volumes of republican writing, Sidney, Locke, and others, but especially Milton, cannot be overestimated in relation to the development of the ideas in the colonies that lead to the break with England, the founding of the United States, and the early years of Federalism.[19]

Not everyone was, or would have been, pleased with Hollis's transatlantic activities. It seems likely that such an important publication as Samuel Johnson's *The Patriot*, for example, is intended to answer Hollis and his activities (in addition to Wilkes et al.) as much as anyone else. (Hollis's book distribution activities became known in England, despite his efforts to keep them anonymous, and he was considered suspect and perhaps dangerous to the authorities in London. James Boswell had discovered republican books Hollis had sent all over Europe, especially to Bern, describing and ridiculing them in his journal account on November 30, 1764, and had probably written to Johnson about them, although the donor was not yet known to him. Soon thereafter, it would appear, they put two and two together.) Johnson's pamphlet answers Hollis's positions on several points without mentioning his name: it calls the accusations concerning the activities of the Catholics in Canada lies and intolerance; the accusations against bishops in the colonies unfounded; the penalties exacted by the British against all Bostonians, despite the innocence of some, justified; and so on. This pamphlet appeared in 1774, and second and third editions were printed in November 1774 and May 1775. The piece was collected in Johnson's *Political Tracts* of 1776. In other words, an effort was made to keep the physical pamphlet circulating.

On the title page of *The Patriot*, quoting from Milton's sonnet that begins "I did but prompt the age to quit their clogs," Johnson usurps the following lines in an

18   *Letters from Andrew Eliot to Thomas Hollis*, in *Massachusetts Historical Collections*, 4th series, 4 (Boston, 1858), 412-13.

19   For an account of attempts to control Milton's reputation in the 18th century and the ideological uses to which Milton and other authors could be put, see Allen Reddick, "Johnson Beyond Jacobitism: Signs of Polemic in the *Dictionary* and the *Life of Milton*," *ELH* 64 (1997): 983-1005.

incendiary and ironic use of Milton's words against the "patriot" champions of Milton: "That bawl for freedom in their senseless mood,/And still revolt when Truth would set them free./Licence they mean when they cry Liberty;/For who loves that must first be wise and good" (ll. 9-12, with "They" for "That" (l.9), and "Yet" for "And" (l. 10)). It is no coincidence that John Adams implicitly answers Johnson and his rhetoric with lines from the same poem ("those lines of the immortal John Milton"), placed rhetorically at the conclusion of his famous tract, *Thoughts On Government: Applicable to the Present State of the American Colonies*, published as a pamphlet in Philadelphia in April 1776, reprinted immediately thereafter in Boston: "I did but prompt the age to quit their clogs/By the known rules of ancient liberty,/ When straight a barbarous noise environs me/Of owls and cuckoos, asses, apes, and dogs" (ll. 1-4). Both Johnson and Adams knew how to use Milton to insult the opposition, and insult it they did. Adams repossesses and reifies Milton's text as a claim for the rights of the colonists and the "clogs," or defenders, of the British government. There is clearly a battle over the use of Milton; and Hollis and his books were the source of Milton in the colonies. The battle over Milton's significance and alliance was waged through Hollis. In the words of two recent scholars of this subject, "Hollis was midwife to the knowledge of republican Milton not only for both Adams and Jefferson but for the eighteenth century generally, and on both sides of the Atlantic."[20]

VII

With the checklist before us, it is possible to consider in some detail the kinds of books Hollis sent to Harvard College. It is possible, as well, to examine Hollis's intentions as revealed through his attention to the book as a physical object and the importance of its publishing history and availability. Hollis's attention to the physical nature of the book is especially obvious when we see that he had most, or many, of the books sent to Harvard bound in quality bindings. Some of them are the famous emblematic bindings, often in beautiful morocco, decorated with his extraordinary symbols. These tools are often reproduced within the book on the flyleaves as well, usually as smoke-prints. The educational program concerning the symbols will be discussed below, but the emphasis on acquiring and sending the best editions is worth considering here. He is preoccupied with keeping crucial books in print (especially those considered politically contentious, such as Milton's *Works* [in prose], Algernon Sidney's *Discourses concerning government*, and John Locke's *Letters on Toleration*, among many others) and with distributing them and making sure that specimens of earlier printings, if they are the only ones surviving, are preserved. If we note the frequency with which he inscribes a comment such as "it is very scarce," "libro raro," "very scarce," "very rare," "becoming more scarce," we perceive that Hollis is not only taking cognizance of

20   Tanner and Collings, 208.

the bibliographical detail and of the value of the book, but also of the entropy which causes books as well as the other creations of human beings to decay; furthermore, he is cognizant of the forces of destruction or control that would destroy such books and documents.

His note in the splendid copy of Henri Estienne's *Thesaurus graecae linguae* provides both an example and a *précis* of his efforts in this regard:

> T·H has been looking out, above two Years, for a fine copy of Harry Stephens Greek Thesaurus for Harvard College. At length he purchased one out of the Library of the late learned Dr. Samuel Chandler. It is hardly to be imagined, what difficulty there is, even when money & industry are not wanting, to secure good Copies of the Old & best Editions of Classical & prime Authors. Time has consumed many of them. And many others, by common agreement of all our principal Booksellers, have been returning back for Years past, as they came on sale, to the European Continent from our Island. So much for the Dissipation, Ignorance of the times!

Time, laxness, "Dissipation, Ignorance"— the battle in Britain is virtually lost. It is in the New World, among liberty-loving freemen, that Hollis hopes for proper education, wisdom, and morality. On several occasions, Hollis notes in his diary that he spent time perusing the books from Chandler's library, searching for books to send to Harvard College, having them vamped and bound, then crated and sent away.

While Hollis is particularly interested in providing the basis, guidance, and materials for the proper education of young men in public morality, another reason he sends the books to Harvard, it seems probable, is that the New World was far enough away from England that the forces threatening liberty, which he saw everywhere, were less likely to destroy them in the colonies. Through scattering of the books—his motto, of course, being "ut spargam," from *Areopagitica*—they would be more likely to survive, if scattered widely enough, as all locations would be less likely to be overrun or fall into the hands of enemies. The apocalyptic character of his concerns for the state of human liberties should not be underestimated. Hollis's optimism for the improvement and education of society—owning and reading the right books will enable men and women to know the truths and to uphold them—should be seen as the counterpart of his suspicions, eventually verging on paranoia, of darker forces of destruction. These two partially contradictory sentiments powered his extraordinary activities throughout his adult life.

But the inhabitants of British dominions were also in danger. In particular, the Treaty of Paris (1763), ending the Seven Years' War, was seen by Hollis and his sympathizers as confirmation that not only would Catholics now be tolerated, but that the way was prepared for them to take over, in North America if not in Great

Britain itself. Hollis was furious at the allowance of the Crown that the "Papists" could keep a bishop in Quebec, as well as the enfranchisement of Catholics in the colonial legislature of Grenada. Even the plan (considered the brainchild of Archbishop Secker and the Society for the Propagation of the Gospel) of establishing Anglican bishops in the colonies—unwelcome and resisted by Hollis and his friends who assumed that the bishops would be used to further the powers and interests of the Crown and government ministers, and would disenfranchise the Dissenters—was in turn melded together as part of the plan for Catholic hierarchy as well. It was to be assumed that a covert plan for bringing popery into the colonies was underway. The cost to personal liberties, it was argued, would be enormous, and Hollis filled the popular press in London with outrage against these plans. As he would put it, "Popery is always the same,"[21] the snake that never dies, and so writers against the "Papist religion" are to be resurrected to carry on in the never-ending campaign. Consequently, he sends many anti-Catholic books and pamphlets to Harvard, to warn them against the true aims of Catholics and of High Church Tories. His largest anti-Catholic shipment was to the library in Zürich, to which he sent a remarkable collection of anti-Jesuit books and pamphlets, collected throughout Europe. The activities of the Catholics, and especially the Jesuits, in North America, prompted a loud cry of alarm, which he replayed throughout his contacts.

His notes in the volumes of William Prynne's *An exact chronological vindication* (known as *Prynne's Records*) demonstrate his fears of Catholic forces in England. Prynne's own note, explaining the rarity of the volumes, that "not 70 of them being rescued from the" Great Fire of 1666, seems to encourage Hollis's suspicions of "papists" in his own day. As his inscriptions make clear, and the diary entries from September 20 and November 13, 1766, indicate, Hollis believed that a "papist" had stolen and disposed of the missing pages, pp. 848-993, from Prynne's books when they were being rebound in John Matthewman's bindery. He writes alarmingly: "It is supposed, that there are not six copies of this valuable work, at this time, in Britain!" Hollis suspects the infiltration of Catholics, especially Jesuits, throughout society, seeking to sabotage the work of ideas and information. In 1761, he offered the British Museum "a rare and master-print against the Jesuits" which the Trustees declined to display, Hollis's condition for the gift, as likely to cause offence. He considered their behavior "strange, very strange," i.e., suspicious and therefore monitory. The print he sent to Christ's College, Cambridge, and the enormous collection of anti-Jesuit materials originally intended for the library of the museum, to Zürich.

---

21   Cf. *London Chronicle*, August 13-16, 1768; Blackburne, 1:395.

VIII

Hollis is unusually concerned with what books are in print, where the copies have been acquired (see e.g., Hollis's notes in the copies of Giggeo and Ange), and how they should be appreciated. Harvard men should understand where certain books fit in the controversies and understand the correct positions. Hollis is determined that the record of past heroics and arguments from classical times through the Middle Ages and Elizabethan period to the seventeenth century and the present, not be lost and that they be presented as a coherent part of a curriculum for young men preparing themselves for public service and public morality. There is a certain archival emphasis in many cases, as he assembles a record of publications and especially disputations. Hollis is trying to keep in front of the eyes of his readers and recipients arguments of the past, which are, in a way, the arguments of the ages: religious toleration for Protestants, the dangers of the Catholics, the abuse of arbitrary power through the monarchy and the Established Church, etc. These voices are resurrected or kept alive by Hollis to do battle in the present and future ages. As Caroline Robbins points out, he sent the catalogue of the library of Anthony Collins in part because it identified the authors of so many useful pamphlets.[22] Classical writings concerning tyranny were given, such as Caesar's commentary, with Hollis's clear call to its future readers: "Very Rare, Very Curious, Very useful, it might be, to the Trained Bands of Massachusetts." He even concerned himself with evidence concerning the proper way to die and the understanding of the nature of the soul and its existence after death. This is, of course, a predictable concern for a Dissenter and a topic often debated, especially with Catholics and High Churchmen; but in Hollis's activities, it is joined with an admiration of anti-tyrannical Stoical writings concerning the relation between body and soul.

It is astonishing that Hollis was able to shape such a coherent list of books with such a coherent project. Many books and their arguments were long forgotten. It must have been through discussions with like-minded people in London and elsewhere in Great Britain that he assembled a list of books worthy and consistent with his work. He wrote to Jonathan Mayhew in May 1766, "The effigies which you desire, may be seen at this time on the library of Harvard College, feature by feature; though indeed it would require an exact eye and some time to cull out and put those features together."[23] An example of an unlikely candidate might be Arthur Wilson's *History of Great Britain*, which covers the reign of James I, and particularly the entanglements of the Crown with foreign concerns. There is no obvious indication from the book's title that it would be useful to Hollis: *The History of Great Britain, being The Life and Reign of King James the First, relating To what passed from his first Access to the Crown, till his Death.* Published in 1653, the history is a critical documentary of James I, aiming to rely upon

22   Robbins, "Library of Liberty," 17.

23   Blackburne, 1:322.

records and to steer a middle course between praise and damnation. In the process, it makes clear his mistakes, leading to present and future trouble, and the dangers posed by foreign interests, Jesuits, and so on. A book apparently little known or discussed, Hollis found it, perused it, had it bound, and sent it, a testimony to the importance of a careful scrutiny of kings and the dangers lurking for monarchs and the government and people.

Few if any of Hollis's contemporaries concerned themselves so with the physical details of a book, including illustrations, especially rare and/or specially-commissioned portraits, sometimes tipped-in. For Hollis, the book was a complete educational tool, emphasizing a community of like-minded believers. The publication record, as well as provenance and responsibility, form networks of connection and implication. Hollis "objectified" the book, reifying its significance, as well as preserving it for posterity, even if it is *not* read. The value added to a text through its "encrustation" provides an objectified presence, valued as physicalization of a kind of belief and a community of believers. It should be said, however, that the great majority of these Harvard books and pamphlets were to be *read*, not simply *preserved*, in counter-distinction to many books sent throughout Europe, in particular Switzerland, which give the impression of being representative possessions. The books are by no means all "precious" as objects (whatever their worth as useful and/or rare volumes), rather, except for those intended to make a symbolic statement (such as the beautiful Montague-bound green morocco, extra-illustrated volumes of Milton's *Works* [in prose]—sent before the fire— or the large paper edition of Sidney's *Discourses concerning government*, with proofs of Sidney's portrait tipped in, all bound in stunning, gold-embossed red morocco), the volumes are intended for student use and understanding.

The remarkable tools for gilt-stamping, which have been well described by W. H. Bond, but on which further research should be fruitful, were first designed by Giovanni Battista Cipriani, probably in early 1759.[24] The tools include the seated owl and the owl with wings spread with a palm branch in its talons, the cock, the Roman goddess Libertas, the harpy with a severed head, the liberty cap known as the pileus, the dagger, the lyre, the wand of Aesculapius, the club of Hercules, the trident of Neptune, and several others. These emblems can also be found as exquisite smoke prints inserted into volumes, usually among the front or back binder's leaves.

IX

In the copy of *Bibliotheca Literaria* (1722-1724) Hollis sent to Harvard, inscribed "palmal, aug. 1, 1767," Hollis writes a short inventory and narrative of his furious gift-giving activities to that point:

24   Bond, *Thomas Hollis*, 40-77.

T·H· has had the honor to send one Copy of this work to the Library of Harvard College, already. But the work is so curious, valuable, especially for The Memorial concerning the Desiderata in Learning; that he could not forbear sending another copy of it to the College. In the beginning, He sent Books on Government, beside stray Books, to Harvard College; for, if Government goeth right, ALL goeth right. Then, He sent Grammars, Dictionaries of Root and other Languages, with critical Authors; in hope of forming first rate Scholars, the NOBLEST of all Men! Now, he dribblets out the like. And thinks, to take his leave.

In an attempt to characterize more fully Hollis's donation, I have isolated several general categories into which most of the books in W. H. Bond's checklist may be divided. The categories are fluid and overlapping; others could have been isolated. The category headings in some cases are general and contain works in some ways different from one another. They are not intended to be exhaustive or conclusive. The great majority of books sent were in English, but a few were in other modern languages as well as in Latin.

1. CONTROVERSIAL PUBLICATIONS CONCERNING GOVERNMENT, ITS BASIS, AND INDIVIDUAL FREEDOMS (e.g., Bodin, 1577; Trenchard; Priestley, 1768, *Liberty*, 1769, *Remarks*, 1769; including many 17th-c. works, e.g., Hobbes, 1651, 1682; Prynne; Neville, 1681, 1698, 1763; Nedham; *State Tracts* [justifying the revolution of 1688-89], 1692-93; Sidney; Campbell, 1747; [Wilkes controversy, e.g., Wilkes, *Complete collection of the genuine papers*, 1769; Tooke, 1770])

2. HISTORIES OF ENGLAND (especially Whig, illustrating ancient liberties, e.g., Arthur Wilson, 1653; Adam, ed. Hearne, 1727; White Kennet, ed., *Complete History of England*, 1706; Oldmixon, 1735-39; Ralph, 1744; Macaulay, 1763-65, 1766, 1767, 1768; Walpole, 1768)

3. ON THE AMERICAN QUESTION (e.g., Cumberland, 1724; Eliot, 1765; Mayhew, 1763, 1764, 1766; Chauncy, 1767, 1768; Jenyns, 1765; Pownall, 1766; Tucker, 1766; *An Appeal to the World*, 1770, published from colonial sources; *Horrid massacre*, 1770)

4. ANTIQUITIES (Classical: mainly Greek, Roman, Egyptian; medieval English; e.g., Gamucci, 1580; Basil Kennet, 1746; Marliani, 1622, 1544; Reinesius, 1682; Vaslet, 1732; Edward Stillingfleet, 1685; Malcolme, 1738; Venuti, 1749; Pancrazi, 1751; Pignoria; Piranesi; Philip Webb, 1756, 1760; Wise)

5. DESIGNS, ESPECIALLY MEDALS, COINS ("illustrating and upholding liberty"), civic architecture, prints (e.g., Vetruvius, 1521, 1584, 1590; Palladio, 1581, 1767; Savot, 1627; Patin, 1663, 1672, 1683; William Clarke, 1767; Caracci; Ames, 1748, 1749; Folkes, 1756, 1763; Wren, 1749; Christ, 1750; Jennings, 1764; Piranesi)

6. HISTORIES OF OTHER NATIONS AND THEIR DYNASTIC STRUGGLES (e.g., Contarini, 1591, and Limojon de St. Didier, 1680, on the Republic of Venice; Interiano (Genoa), 1551; Joseph Hill (Dutch and United Provinces, especially against the French), 1673)

7. ROMAN AND CLASSICAL HISTORY (e.g., Nicetas Choniates, 1562, Major, 1768; Edward Montagu, 1760)

8. LINGUISTIC/PHILOLOGICAL BOOKS (especially English [e.g., John Wallis, 1653, 1678]; but also, e.g., Accademia della Crusca, *Vocabolario*, 1746-1748, Perrin, 1767; and Latin, Greek, Persian, Syriac, Egyptian, Hebrew [e.g., George Ollyffe, 1750; Otho, 1675], Turkish [Megiserus, 1612], Chaldean [Münster, 1527], Celtic [Cleland, 1768, 1768?]; bilingual or English dictionaries, e.g., Baretti, *A dictionary of the English and Italian languages*, 1760; Edward Phillips, 1720, Martin, 1748, 1749, 1762, 1766; Ephraim Chambers, 1751-53)

9. BRITISH LAW AND LEGAL HISTORY (e.g., Daines Barrington, 1766, 1769; Bracton, 1640; Bonnaire, 1751; Coke, 1738; Hale, 1739; Simpson, 1765)

10. RELIGION (especially confession, religious toleration, establishment, nature of God and trinity, e.g., Whichcote, 1698; Tindal; Jeremiah White, 1712; Chubb; Nye, 1701, 1715; Collins; Woolston; Sykes; Hoadley, *Civil government* and *Submission*, 1710, 1719; Clayton; Chandler; Blackburne; Rotheram, 1767)

11. DEATH AND NATURE OF THE SOUL (e.g., Woolner, 1655; Baxter, *An enquiry into the nature of the human soul*, 1745; Layton; John Reynolds, 1725; Samuel Clarke, 1760; Broughton, 1766)

12. THE ENGLISH REFORMATION (e.g., Burnet, 1681-85; Benjamin Bennet, 1721, 1723; Bendlowes, 1768; Bowman, 1768)

13. THE DISSENTERS AND DISSENTING CHURCHES (e.g., Bastwick, 1646; Defoe, 1703; Calamy, 1703-1705, 1718; Fleming; Towgood, 1752, 1753, 1755)

14. WRITINGS AGAINST JESUITS AND/OR CATHOLICS (e.g., Bale, 1543; Perrault, 1667; Morton, 1679; Wake, 1688; Prynne; Barker 1735; Joshua Bayes, 1735; Earle, 1735; Chandler, 1745; Baron, 1752, 1768; *Authentic memoirs concerning the Portuguese inquisition*, 1769; Geddes, 1715)

15. AGAINST THE EARLY STUARTS, KINGSHIP, PRETENDER, CIVIL WAR, GLORIOUS REVOLUTION, EXCLUSION OF STUARTS (e.g., George Buchanan, 1689; Sherlock, 1691; Welwood, 1689; Calamy, 1718)

16. LIBRARY AND SALE CATALOGUES, BOOKS, COINS, MEDALS (e.g., Stadtbibliothek Bern, 1764; Biblioteca Medicea Laurenziana, 1764; *Harleian miscellany*, 1744-46; Bridges, 1725; Anthony Collins, 1730/1; Haym, 1741; Fairfax, 1751; Dingley, 1753; Mead; Selbye, 1755; Perry, 1762; Clarendon, 1764; Letherland, 1765)

17. "LIBERTY" POETS (e.g., Milton; Marvell; Akenside, 1738; Thomson, 1752; Glover, 1760)

18. BOOKS ON LITERATURE, INCLUDING LITERARY CONTROVERSIES (e.g., Orrery, 1698; Milner, 1698; Bentley, 1699; Richardson, 1734; Pemberton, 1738; Trapp, 1742; John Mason, *Poetical composition*, 1749, *Prosaic numbers*, 1749; Daniel Webb, 1762, 1769, 1769; Hugh Blair, 1763; Lowth, 1763; James Macpherson, 1763, 1765; Percy, 1767; Elizabeth Montagu, 1769)

19. POETRY (e.g., Waller, 1711; Gay, 1712, 1721?; Philips, 1720; Shakespeare, 1728; Smart, 1752; William Mason, 1764)

20. SCIENTIFIC DISCOVERIES, SCIENCES, MEDICINE AND MATHEMATICS (e.g., Roger Bacon, 1659; Hooke, 1606, 1670, 1677, 1678; Digby, 1664; Cheyne, 1724; Harvey, 1766; Wallerius, 1759, 1768; Cornaro, 1768; Franklin, 1769; Isaac Barrow, 1670; Newton)

21. VOYAGES TO PRIMITIVE PLACES (e.g., Sandys, 1673; Cooke, 1712; Dobbs, 1744 [advocating settling of colonies to thwart the French]; Charlevoix, 1744, 1756; Casas, *Tears of the Indians*, 1756, [detailing massacres by the Spaniards in Mexico, West Indies, etc.; used as propaganda in England to support English supplanting the Spanish]; Ulloa, 1760; Griffith Williams, 1765; Alexander Dalrymple, 1767, 1770; Adanson, 1769 [translated into English for use, now that the British arms have reduced French influence in Senegal; also with natural and cultural history and description])

22. NATURAL HISTORIES (especially of America, e.g., *America, or an exact description of the West-Indies*, 1655; or with political implication, e.g., Borlase, 1754, 1758; Adanson, 1757)

23. MEMOIRS OR BIOGRAPHIES OF HEROIC FIGURES (e.g., Plutarch, 1758; Aretino, 1628, 1636; Anglesey, 1693; *A short . . . life . . . of Mr. Chubb*, 1747; Strype; Ludlow, 1751; Middleton, 1757)

24. CANONICAL PHILOSOPHICAL AND POETICAL WRITINGS, ESPECIALLY CLASSICAL (e.g., Plato, 1602, 1763; Aristotle, 1619; Cicero; Avicenna, 1609; Boethius, 1671; Longinus, 1694; Lucretius, 1725; Marcus Aurelius, 1749; Montaigne, 1759; Pascal, 1734; Petrarca, 1560; Tasso, 1737; Virgil, 1741)

25. EDUCATION (e.g., Milton; Priestley, 1765; Ainsworth, 1736; Rollin, 1735; Boswell, 1738; Sheridan, 1769, 1769; Smith, 1770)

26. SKEPTICAL AND EMPIRICAL PHILOSOPHICAL WRITINGS (e.g., Bayle; Descartes, 1749; Locke, 1752; Price, 1769)

27. PUBLIC ECONOMY AND COMMERCE (e.g., Petty, 1662; Gee, 1729; John Law, 1750; George Gordon, 1753; Beccaria, 1769; Mildmay, 1765)

28. EUROPEAN REFORMERS (e.g., Calvin, 1550; Beze, 1554; Luther, 1652; Erasmus, 1645; Jortin [on Erasmus], 1758-60)

29. PAINTING (e.g., Caracci; Du Fresnoy, 1716; Piles, 1708, 1715)

30. SYSTEMS OF MORAL PHILOSOPHY (e.g., Harte, 1736; Grove, 1749; Hutcheson)

31. CLASSIC ENLIGHTENMENT WRITERS, ESPECIALLY FRENCH (e.g., La Mettrie, 1748; Diderot, 1749; Montesquieu, 1758; d'Alembert, 1764-1767; d'Holbach, 1767)

Some of these titles we might think of as predictable considering Hollis's republican and Dissenting leanings and his intellectual pedigree: Milton, Sidney, Locke, Blackburne, Hoadley, as well as classical writings against tyranny, for example. Anti-Catholic works, especially pamphlets, are to be expected, along with anti-Stuart writings. But there are many surprises, especially at first glance, though few of these works are disinterested. The natural histories, for example, tend to pertain to current politics, such as lands falling into British hands, whose natural history will prove useful to a strong and free Britain or America. Similarly, the works of history (whether of England or of other countries) tend to confirm particular versions of history useful for Hollis's aims. Even the volumes from the *Ökonomische Gesellschaft des Kantons Bern* (The Economic Society of the Canton of Bern) on rural economy (*Recueil de memoires concernants l'oeconomie rurale*, 1760-61) are intended to draw attention to the activities of a model society based on free republican values, the city and Canton of Bern, as Hollis's note intimates: "But the liberal deviseth liberal things, and by liberal things shall he stand," etc. (Hollis sends several books to Harvard pertaining to Switzerland.) In short, whatever their independent worth, virtually all of Hollis's gifts pursue a purpose, a coherent and wide-ranging plan. Nevertheless, it is clear from this list that Hollis intended Harvard men to be exposed to a wide variety of history, culture, and thought, despite being tailored towards a particular kind of intellectual leaning: Republican, tolerant in view of religious doctrine and practice (as always, with the exception of the Catholics), awareness of graphic representation for the perpetuation of certain beliefs and behaviors, from ancient Rome to the present. Furthermore, his dispersing of catalogues and booklists indicates that 1) he wanted the recipients to know the record of books published on certain subjects and existing in certain collections, and 2) he wanted to inspire them to collect or at least read the many extant books. Hollis is working for the present and the future, and he is attempting to leave a record of important works in preparation for troubled times.

The intricate relation between content, physical details (such as lettering or decoration), and annotations may be traced by examining any of a large number of books in the Hollis donation. A particularly eloquent example is the volume bound in red morocco stamped with startling gold emblems: the sermon tracts by Andrew Eliot (*A Sermon [for] the Anniversary for the Election of His Majesty's Council for the Province*, 1765) and Jonathan Mayhew (*The Snare broken . . . occasioned by the repeal of the Stamp-Act*, 1766) is a magnificent complete sign or compendium of signs. As W. H. Bond puts it, the volume "fully exploits its emblematic possibilities."[25] First, Eliot's sermon, delivered before the colonial governor, His Majesty's Council, and the Massachusetts Bay House of Representatives, is stately, measured, glancing at and criticizing the Stamp Act as the author carefully delineates the virtues important to a good and Christian monarch and his government, and the rights and responsibilities of the governed. It sets the stage, in a way, for Mayhew's characteristically direct and blunt tract, which speaks more to the moment of the repeal of the despised Stamp Act and embodies a warning against the forces of tyranny (Bond refers to Eliot as "a trifle cooler in his rhetoric than Mayhew"[26]). Eliot's sermon was printed—by Hollis?—in London, a more refined printing production than Mayhew's, published in Boston: the pamphlets unite the centers of the communities, London and Boston, and unite causes between like-minded men—Eliot's urbane, moderate address to the monarch and the governed, with a less-guarded, more personal and triumphant sermon of defiance, characteristic of Mayhew. These men were also Hollis's main contacts in Boston and the conduit through which his books reached Harvard: first Mayhew, succeeded, at his early death in 1766 (not long after *The Snare Broken* was delivered), by Eliot. The volume therefore binds together successive Dissenting figures in the cause for religious and political liberty, Hollis's own contacts and the conduits through which he sent books to Harvard, the two lands of England and American colonies, and the traditions of justification of monarchy and its abuse.

The exceptionally elegant volume belies the apparent humility of the tract format—although Mayhew's is dedicated to Pitt—and is more pristine because there are no Hollis inscriptions. The "message" and paratextual information is provided through descriptive and graphic signs. On the spine are four imprints of the seated owl. A motto adapted from Sallust's *Bellum Iugurthinum* x.6, is begun on the back cover: "DISCORDIA RES MAXIMAE DILABVNTVR" (Great communities fall to pieces through discord.); the front cover concludes it: "CONCORDIA RES PARVAE CRESCVNT" (Small communities grow great through harmony.). Above the first ("DISCORDIA") part of the motto on the back is the short sword point downward,

25   Bond, *Thomas Hollis*, 60 (illustration of binding on p. 61).

26   Bond, *Letters*, 79.

signifying conflict; below it, the owl and palm inverted, signify the end of peaceful pursuits. On the front cover ("CONCORDIA") the owl and palm are in normal position over the Latin motto and the sword is point upward (inverted) beneath.

The message of the covers is intricate. "CONCORDIA" is of course associated with the American colonies and Boston as well as their people. But it also refers to Harvard and its connection with Hollis. The volume begins with the images of concord on the front cover, opening the way to Eliot's temperate sermon, published in London, signifying both an example and a warning. It continues, around the column of wise, adjudicating owls on the spine, to the back cover, with the clearer warning signified by the dagger and the inversion of natural peace. The back cover (with "DISCORDIA") is contiguous with the second tract, Mayhew's hot sermon. Mayhew and others believed that the Stamp Act was prelude to a larger design of tyranny instigated from the crown and government ministers. Therefore, the progression incorporates a threat, from moderation (Eliot) to outspoken and general opposition (Mayhew). The clauses from Sallust are reversed from their usual order, thus drawing attention to the two parts of the rhetorical whole. Furthermore, the "great community," with its discord and subsequent disintegration (a typical Hollis preoccupation), certainly glances at Britain, while the "small community" refers to the colonial settlements.

XI

After the fire, the books were kept together in the old library in special alcoves devoted to Hollis's gifts. They filled almost two large alcoves, each consisting of four large bookcases. Some of the very large books, such as a set of Piranesi prints of Rome, were kept in cupboards, which had shelves big enough to hold large sheets of paper.[27] Some earlier books bore Hollis's letterpress book labels: small capitals with full stops placed at hyphen height, in the manner of classical inscriptions: EX DONO/THOMAE HOLLIS, ANGLI,/HOSPIT · LINCOLN · /REG · ET ANT · SS · LOND · /SODALIS" (an Englishman, a member of Lincoln's Inn, and a Fellow of the Royal Sociey and the Society of Antiquaries). Books were customarily marked upon their arrival in Cambridge by the insertion of an engraved college bookplate designed and cut by Richard Hurd of Boston, with the donor identified in manuscript. Hollis sent Harvard a metal plate with a finer engraved imitation of Hurd's bookplate, incorporating Hollis's letterpress book label, to discourage manuscript additions.[28] All books not already in the Library (with the exception of those kept in the President's house for his perusal), and most duplicates as well, were apparently placed on the shelves, although interestingly some were restricted. Kenneth Carpenter notes that, "The list, begun in 1765 and in use up to

27   W.H. Bond and Hugh Amory, *The Printed Catalogues of the Harvard College Library 1723-1790* (Boston: Colonial Society of Massachusetts, 1996), xvi.

28   Bond, *Thomas Hollis*, 89-90 (illustrations on p. 90).

1789, that records gifts of Thomas Hollis in the order in which they stood on the shelves noted that P meant "absolute prohibition" and that an * designated a book prohibited "to undergraduates." . . . There seem to be three absolute prohibitions and of them only one book that would have been considered dangerous, Francis Hutcheson's *Moral Philosophy* . . . . Many more were prohibited to Undergraduates."[29] Of these, the Hollis gifts of Bolingbroke, Shaftesbury, and Mandeville may be examples. Hollis would not have approved of such scruples.

Eventually, the library exceeded its space once more, at which time (1838) Harvard built Gore Hall solely for the purpose of a new library. But the Hollis books would be irredeemably dispersed. The college had already begun expanding into a proto-university, with a medical school, law school, and other divisions. Medical books (including Hollis's gifts) went into the medical library, law books to the law library, and so on. After the building of Widener Library in 1915, the Hollis books were simply dispersed to the Widener stacks. Eventually, appropriate books found their way to the Fine Arts Library, the Map Collection, and the other libraries and collections where, for the most part, they remain. By tracking the distribution of these books, we can mark the change that came over the college as it became a university: from a college aimed primarily at producing more Dissenting ministers to the establishing of separate schools appropriate to a university. Hollis's books denote the various interests necessary for a complete education; their eventual (and current) distribution exemplifies the multi-faceted aspect of the great university Hollis prefigured. The collection shows what a well-educated man (with substantial resources and a particular turn of mind, devoted to liberty causes!) would have collected in the eighteenth-century, as well as an index to the great change in the Harvard Library and Harvard College. Hollis, however, would neither have imagined, nor approved of, the departmentalizing of a person's education into separate schools. He would have insisted on a liberal and broad education for a life of intelligent and informed service and public morality.

Hollis sent a copy of James Harris's *Hermes* to Harvard, from an edition he designed and sponsored for publication in 1765. In the entire text of this book, he marks only one passage, the penultimate paragraph:

> In truth, each man's Understanding, when ripened and mature, is a composite of *natural Capacity*, and of *super-induced Habit*. Hence the greatest Men will be necessarily those, who possess *the best* Habits. Hence also moderate Capacities, when adorned with valuable Science, will far transcend others the most acute by nature, when either neglected, or applied to low and base purposes. And thus for the honour of CULTURE *and* GOOD LEARNING, *they are able to render a man, if he will take the pains, intrinsically more excellent than his natural Superiors.*

29   Carpenter, 28.

Hollis writes in the margin, in his clear, tireless hand, a message to these faraway students: "Mark, Youth, mark well, the justness, beauty of this closing Passage!"

***

Thomas Hollis's importance to eighteenth-century British culture and the dissemination of "liberty" throughout the world is being uncovered to an extent never before possible, even in his own lifetime. This checklist is a crucial step in the process of discovery. Hollis's donations to Harvard College form a cornerstone of his activities, and the inventory and description of these books will allow scholars to piece together the extensive network of activities, institutions, individuals, and ideas, to which Hollis was dedicated. It should, for example, considerably augment efforts to assemble a reliable list of books Hollis sponsored and in some cases designed. With the current checklist in print, the descriptive and analytical catalogues of the donations to Bern, Zürich, and other destinations—being carried out by the present author, to be published as subsequent volumes by Harvard—can contextualize and cross-list their material more comprehensively and intelligently. These volumes will in turn open up one of the largest and most important international networks of republican ideas, iconography, and thinking in modern history. Hollis's interest in forming or influencing the political mind should be considerably illuminated: through contributing to periodicals, dispersing propaganda through gifts and iconographic images, developing arts and sciences, circulating ideas, texts, artifacts, and books between countries and communities, participating in the communities of the London coffeehouses, and corresponding with recipients within Great Britain, Continental Europe, and the American colonies. The immense task of editing Hollis's unpublished diary now at Harvard should be made easier, many of the references illuminated through the information contained in Bond's Harvard checklist.

Once we are attuned to the presence of Hollis, he seems to be everywhere, in eighteenth-century British culture, American colonial culture, and even on the Continent. We even find him in the foreground of two paintings by Canaletto, whom Hollis supported during his extended stay in England with six important commissions. Hollis's friend Joseph Smith, the British Consul in Venice, presumably initiated the arrangement.[30] In turn, Smith (and others) channeled publications from the continent to Hollis: he specifically exploited Smith as a source for collecting books and pamphlets against the Jesuits (a part of the collection now in Zürich). The links among Great Britain, the American colonies, Switzerland, the Republic of Venice, and other

---

30   See Bond, *Thomas Hollis*, 14, including n. 1. Hollis, his traveling companion Thomas Brand, and Hollis's servant are apparently the conspicuous figures in the foreground of Canaletto's "The Piazza del Campidoglio" and "Old Walton Bridge."

European centers of Protestantism or republicanism allow further insight into the circulation of ideas and the notions of identity formation within these societies. Hollis distributes the graphic and printed record for his causes and places books in lands where they were previously unknown, hoping they will "spring up armed men." For no place were his efforts more energetic than for Harvard College. W. H. Bond's great accomplishment illuminates the way.

Legend

Sample entries

Jackson, John Baptist, 1701-1780?

>   ‡*An enquiry into the origin of printing in Europe* (London, 1752). Inv. 7.3 (part); 2.2.4.32;
>   C9 <651010, h> On flyleaf: "John Baptist Jackson, Artist. an ingenious irregular."
>   B 4507.52*
>
>   *An essay on the invention of engraving and printing in chiaro oscuro* (London, 1754).
>   Inv. 7.3 (part); 2.2.4.32; C9 <651010, h> B 4507.52*

Entries begin with AUTHOR, title *in italics*, and place of publication and date in parentheses.

>   † identifies books in Hollis's emblematic bindings.

>   ‡ indicates the presence of annotations by Hollis.

Inv. 7.3: the book is identifiable in the manuscript inventories of books received by Harvard (Harvard University Archives, unpublished: UA III.50.27.61 VT) as the third item in inventory number 7. Only about half of the books in this checklist appear in these inventories. "Part" indicates that the inventory entry lists more than one item.

2.2.4.32: the shelfmark of the book in the library room in the rebuilt (1765) Harvard Hall, as recorded in the Alcove Lists (ca. 1765), (Harvard University Archives UA III.50.15.31.5 VT). See W. H. Bond and Hugh Amory, *The Printed Catalogues of the Harvard College Library 1723-1790* (Boston, 1996), *Publications of the Colonial Society of Massachusetts* LXVIII, p. xvii. There were ten alcoves, each centered on a window, each originally containing four bookcases. Hollis's gifts, with few exceptions, were kept in Alcoves 2 and 4. This sample shelfmark locates the book in Alcove 2, case 2, the 32nd book on shelf 4. The shelves were numbered from the bottom up, with folios on the lowest shelves, quartos above them, and smaller formats at the top. See Bond and Amory, p. xvi.

C9: the book is listed on page 9 of the printed catalogue of 1790. Books also found in the printed catalogue of 1773 are identified by a page number following the letter B. See Bond and Amory.

<651010, h>: the date of receipt ("nd" if not known and ".." for unknown month or day); in this case, 1765, October 10, followed by some specific information about the binding: "h" for bindings commissioned by Hollis, "v" for books bound in vellum (for Hollis during his stay in Italy), "r" for subsequently rebound volumes, and "xt" for titles bound in tract volumes.

If the book contains annotations by Hollis, those annotations are given locations and follow in quotation marks. A few books (Milton's *Works* [in prose], for example) are too heavily annotated to permit full quotation; these instances are so indicated in the entry.

B 4507.52*: the modern call number of the book. The asterisk (*), with a few exceptions fully noted, locates the book in Houghton Library. STC call numbers are also located in Houghton. Call numbers are subject to change when books are recataloged and consequently may vary from those recorded here. Individual libraries maintain files of changed call numbers.

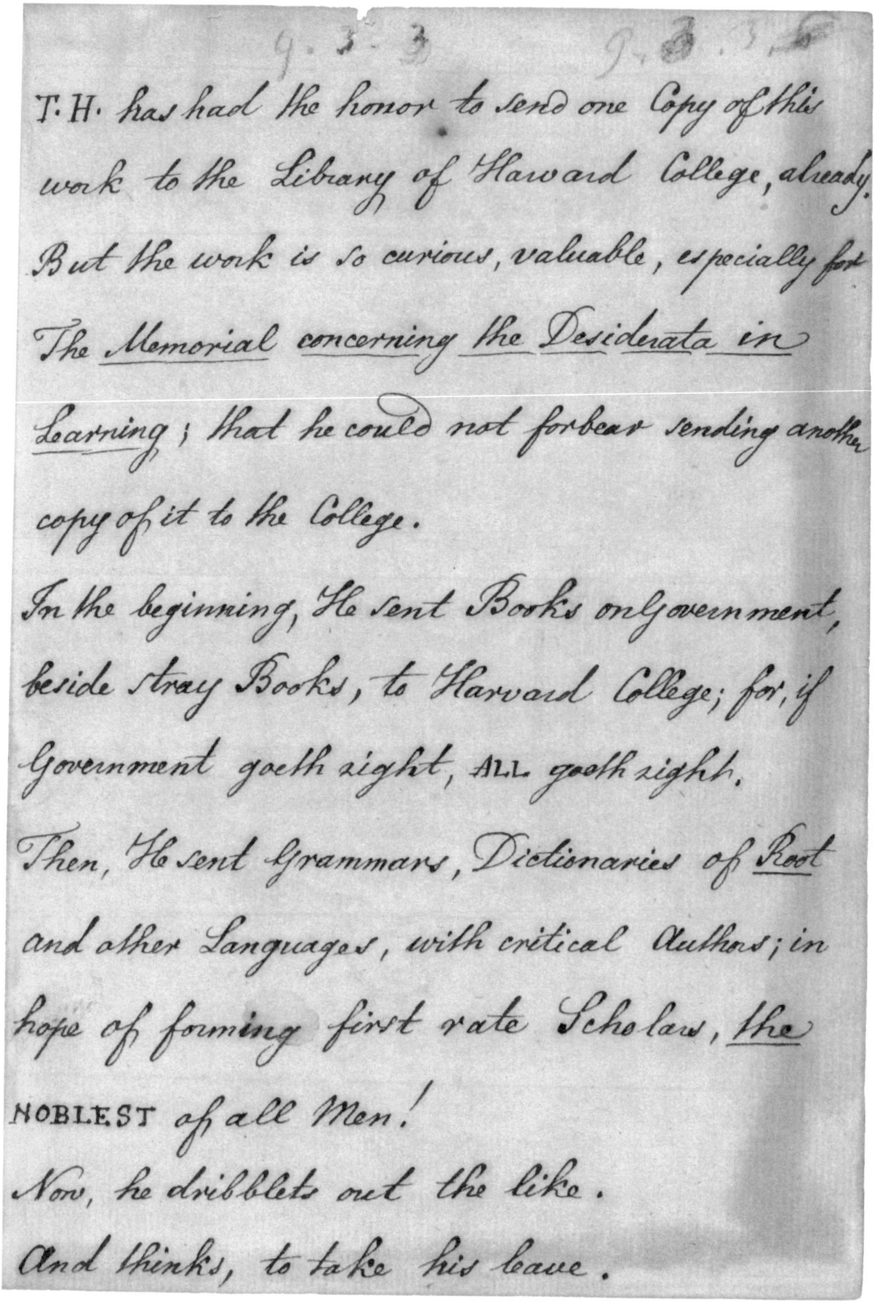

q. 3. 3 *q. 3. 3. 6*

T. H. has had the honor to send one Copy of this
work to the Library of Harvard College, already.
But the work is so curious, valuable, especially for
The _Memorial_ concerning the _Desiderata in_
Learning; that he could not forbear sending another
copy of it to the College.

In the beginning, He sent Books on Government,
beside stray Books, to Harvard College; for, if
Government goeth right, ALL goeth right.

Then, He sent Grammars, Dictionaries of _Root_
and other Languages, with critical Authors; in
hope of forming first rate Scholars, _the_
NOBLEST of all Men!

Now, he dribblets out the like.
And thinks, to take his leave.

Figure 3. *Bibliotheca Literaria* (London, 1722-1724). On the front flyleaf of a book given in 1767, TH provides a modest overview of his gifts on different subjects. See Introduction, pp. 22-23, and Checklist, p. 49.
*EC75.H7267.Zz722b 23 cm.

Checklist of Thomas Hollis's Gifts to the Harvard College Library

A

ABBATI OLIVIERI-GIORDANI, ANNIBALE DEGLI, 1708-1789. *Marmora Pisaurensia* (Pesaro, 1738). Inv.4.2; 2.3.2.12; C7 <641212?, h> f*IC7.Ab196.738m

ABELA, GIOVANFRANCESCO, 1582-1655. ‡*Della descrittione di Malta … libri quattro* (Malta, 1647). 4.3.4.18; C48 <nd, v> On flyleaf: "The ever-warring, lounging Maltese!" On half title: "Libro raro T·H." f*EC75.H7267.Zz647a

ABU AL-FARAJ, *see* Bar Hebraeus, *Specimen historiae Arabum*

ACADÉMIE DES JEUX FLORAUX (France). *Receuil de plusieurs pièces d'éloquence* (Toulouse, [n.d.]). Inv.4.110; 2.2.7.15; not in C <641212?> Original Hollis gift not located.

ACCADEMIA DELLA CRUSCA. *Vocabolario* (Naples, 1746-1748). 4.1.1.11-15; C202 <nd, h> f*IC6.Ac121CV.1746 6 v. in 5

ACCIARDI, MICHELE. *Mustapha Bassi di Rodi schiavo in Malta* (Naples, 1751). Inv.4.11; 2.4.4.13; C59 (under Mustapha) <641212?, v> Ital 5554.1*

ACHERLY, ROGER, 1665?-1740. *The Britannic constitution* (London, 1747). Inv.16.52; 2.4.2.13; C92 <670511, r> f*EC7.Ac458.727baa

Actiones et monumenta martyrum ([Geneva?], 1560). Inv.3.89; not in C <641208, h> C 7516.60*

ADAM, OF DOMERHAM. *Historia de rebus gestis Glastoniensibus*, ed. Thomas Hearne (Oxford, 1727). 4.1.6.9; C5 <nd, h> Br 5187.92.13* 2 v.

ADAMS, SAMUEL, 1722-1803, *see An appeal to the world*

ADANSON, MICHEL, 1727-1806.
Histoire naturelle de Senegal, coquillages (Paris, 1757). Inv.5.10; 2.2.4.30; C71 <6506.., r> MCZ Special Collections copy 2

Voyage to Senegal (London, 1759). C73 <nd, r (original spine label preserved)> Bookplate wrongly identifies donor as the State of New Hampshire. Afr 5180.2*

ADDISON, JOSEPH, 1672-1719. *A discourse on ancient and modern learning* (London, 1739). 4.2.5.22; C104 <nd, r> 16434.23.5*

An address to their Graces the Archbishops of Canterbury and York (London, 1767). 4.4.6.27; C219 <nd, h (marbled boards)> *EC75.B5628.752s

ÆPINUS, FRANZ ULRICH THEODOR, 1724-1802. *Cogitationes de distributione caloris per tellurem* (St. Petersburg, [1761]). 6.1.3.29; C215 <nd, h (marbled boards)> *EC75.H7267.Zz769t

AGIO DE SOLDANIS, GIOVANNI PIETRO FRANCESCO, ca. 1710-1760.
‡*Della lingua punica* (Rome, 1750). Inv.3.134; C53 (under Soldanis), C235 (under De Soldanis) <641208, v> On flyleaf (author's hand?): "Donato dal'Autore al Sr. Hollis Caualiere Inglese in Malta il disette Novembre 1752." *IC7.Ag498.750d

[Another issue] 4.4.7.31; C53 (under Soldanis), C235 (under De Soldanis) <nd, r> *IC7.G6754.749s

AGOSTINI, ANTONIO. *Dialoghi intorno alle medaglia* (Rome, [1592?]). Inv.3.15; 2.2.3.12; C129 <641208, h> Plates on p. 11, 82-83 are sources for some of TH's emblems. Arc 1350.2 F*

AGOSTINI, LEONARDO, 1593-ca. 1670. *Gemmae et sculpturae antiquae depictae* (Franeker, 1694). Inv.8.35; 4.4.6.30 (under Gronovius); C129 <661001, r> Fine Arts X Cage XFA 4623.5.5.2

AINSWORTH, ROBERT, 1660-1743.
De clypeo Camilli antiquo (London, 1734). Inv.10.18; 6.3.5.7; C4 (under Dissertatio) <680712, marbled boards> *EC7.Ai665.734d

†‡*The most natural and easy way of institution* (London, 1736). Inv.2.86; 2.4.7.2; C219 (under Institution) <6410.., h> On flyleaf: "This a scarce and <u>curious</u> collection. See on the same subject the divine Milton, and Mr. Locke. Milton, like Michael Angelo in statuary, per vie <u>terribile</u>, in a <u>wonderful</u> manner, has <u>outlin'd</u> the whole subject, in ONE sheet in quarto. T·H." On title page of first tract: "very scarce." *EC75.H7267.Zz734e

Robert Ainsworth's dictionary, English and Latin (London, 1773). Inv.16.27; 6.3.20.12-13; C202 <670511, r> HD KG 13192

Thesaurus linguae latinae (London, 1752). 2.2.1.15-16; C202 <670511, h> 5231.11 F* 2 v.

See also Kemp, John

AKENSIDE, MARK, 1721-1770.
‡*Odes on several subjects. The second edition* (London, 1760). C237 <nd, xt> On title page: "By Dr. Akinside [*sic*]." *EC75.Ak347.745oc

The voice of liberty, or, A British philippic (London, 1738). 4.2.3.22; C238 <nd, h> f*EC75.H7267.Zz740p

ALAMANNI, LUIGI, 1495-1556.
Opere Toscane ([Leiden], 1532). Inv.3.147 (part); 2.4.8.18; C140 <641208, v> *IC5.Aℓ116.B532ob

Opere Toscane [vol. 2] (Leiden, 1533). Inv.3.147 (part); 2.4.8.18; C140 <641208, v> *IC5.Aℓ116.B532ob

ALBERTI, LEANDRO, 1479-1552. *Descrittione de tutta l'Italia* (Venice, 1577). 4.4.5.25; C48 <nd, r> Ital 2145.50.10*

ALEMBERT, JEAN LE ROND D', 1717-1783. *Mélanges de litterature* (Amsterdam, 1764-1767). 4.1.8.44-47; C123 (under Rond) <nd, h> 39574.26* 5 v.

ALEXIS DE SOMMEVOIRE, 17ᵗʰ cent. *Tesoro della lingua greca-volgare* (Paris, 1709). 4.1.4.14-15; C205 <nd, h> 4281.22* 2 v.

ALGAROTTI, FRANCESCO, CONTE, 1712-1764.

†*Il congresso di Citera* (Londra [i.e., Leghorn], 1765). Not in C <68…., h> Bound as part of Algarotti's *Opere.* *EC75.H7267.Zz764a

An essay on the opera (London, 1767). 4.4.8.25; C104 <nd, h> TH designed the title page and probably translated the dedication to Pitt the elder. *EC75.H7267.Zz767a

†‡*Opere* (Leghorn, 1764-1765). Inv.17.22; 4.3.8.5-12; B5, C104 <68…., h> On flyleaf of v. 2: "The greatest weakness of the learned, accomplished Algarotti, was his biass to one Person." (The first item in v. 2, "Saggio sopra l'Accademia di Francia," is dedicated to Signor Tommaso Hollis.) In the margin of pp. 8-9: "Allusion to the inscription under the Mezzotinto of Newton; an impression of which, was long since sent to Harvard College." *EC75.H7267.Zz764a 8 v.

ALMON, JOHN, 1737-1805.

‡*A collection of the most interesting tracts: lately published in England and America* (London, 1766-67). 4.1.7.19-21 <67…., r> On title page of speech by William Pitt: "Added by direction of T·H." A reprint of 17 tracts concerning the colonial crisis; most of them supplied by Jonathan Mayhew and Andrew Eliot to TH, who transmitted them to Almon. *EC75.Aℓ682.766c 3 v.; most entered in C as if individual tracts.

A complete collection of the Lord's protests (London, 1767). 4.4.6.21-22; C148 <nd, r> Br 130.4* 2 v.

The history of the late minority (London, 1766). 4.1.7.11; C146 <nd, r> Br 2060.369*

America, or an exact description of the West-Indies (London, 1655). Inv.9.30; 4.4.8.45; C48 <680711, h> *EC75.H7267.Zz655p

The American gazette (London, 1768-1770). Inv.12.21; 6.1.5.1; C145, C243 <690818 & 70….?, h> Part 6 is in a pamphlet binding, with notes by Andrew Eliot on the title page. US 2812.26* 2 v.

AMES, JOSEPH, 1689-1759.

A catalogue of English heads: or, An account of about two thousand prints (London, 1748). Inv.4.182; 2.1.6.8; C32 <641212?> Declared lost, 1986.

‡*Typographical antiquities* (London, 1749). Inv.16.37; 2.2.4.26; C3 <670511, h> On flyleaf: "Mr. Joseph Ames was a worthy and a courteous Man, & a laborious Antiquarie. T·H." B 5170.139*

AMORY, THOMAS, 1691?-1788? ‡*An antiquarian doctor's sermon* (London, 1767). 4.4.6.27; C255 (under title) <nd, h (marbled boards)> On title page: "By John Buncle Esq." *EC75.B5628.752s

Ampliation du discours intitulé: Histoire véritable des choses passées ([n.p.], 1589). 2.1.8.26; C245 (under Charles) <671209?, h (half calf and marbled boards)> Fr 1232.3.10*

ANDERSON, GEORGE, 1676-1756. *An estimate of the profit and loss of religion* (Edinburgh, 1753). Inv.4.128; 2.1.5.28; C189 (under Religion) <641212?, h> *EC7.An233.753e

ANDERSON, WALTER, 1723-1800. *The history of France* [in the reigns of Francis II and Charles IX] (London, 1769). Inv.12.5; 6.1.2.18-19; B5, C54 <690818, h> Fr 1202.7* 2 v.

ANGE DE SAINT-JOSEPH, 1636-1697. ‡*Gazophylacium linguae Persarum* (Amsterdam, 1684). 3.1.2.15; C202 <670121, h> On flyleaf: "The Note in the Giggeius notwithstanding, I have since, most unexpectedly obtained this Book, &, as times go, at a cheap rate too, for 55 shillings. It was sold in a public auction of no great Account; was probably unknown to the East India Buyers; and the Booksellers, who know I wish well to them & to the Press, Guard it North Americans! would not bid against me. T·H Pall Mall, jan. 21, 67." 3261.8 F*

See also Giggeo, Antonio

ANGLESEY, ARTHUR ANNESLEY, EARL OF, 1614-1686. *Memoirs* (London, 1693). Inv.3.133; 2.2.6.39; C29 <641208, 18th c. calf> *EC65.An464.693m

Anglica, Normanica, Hibernica, Cambrica, a veteribus scripta (Frankfurt, 1603). 4.4.3.5; not in C Original Hollis gift not located.

ANGLO-SAXON CHRONICLE. *Chronicon saxonicum,* ed. Edmund Gibson (Oxford, 1692). 4.2.5.16; C48 <nd, h> Br 1055.122*

Annual miscellany for the year 1694 (London, 1708). B11, C141 (under Dryden) <nd, r> *EC65.D8474.B709m v. 4

Another estimate of the manners and principles of the present time (London, 1769). C246 <nd, r> *EC75.A100.769a2

The answer at large to Mr. P—tt's speech (London, 1766). 4.1.7.20; C250 <nd, xt> *EC75.A100.766a2

An answer to Mr. Peirce's Western inquisition (London, 1721). Inv.5.29 (part); 2.3.7.6; C323 (under Peirce) <6506.., h> *EC7.P3551.720w

An answer to the letter from Amsterdam ([London?], 1678). 2.4.5.19; C244 <nd, xt> *EC65.A100.678a

An appeal to the world (London, 1770). Inv.13.71; 6.1.6.6; C145 (under Boston, Vindication) <700926, h> *AC7.Ad196.769ab

APPIANUS, OF ALEXANDRIA. *Historia delle guerre civili de' Romani* (Verona, 1730). Inv.4.19; 2.4.4.30-31; C12 (wrongly dated 1630) <641212?, v> KE 30177* 2 v.

APTHORP, EAST, 1733-1816. *A review of Dr. Mayhew's Remarks on the answer* (London, 1765). 2.4.6.2; C256 <nd, h> *AC7.M4537.B766m v. 2

AQUINO, CARLO D', 1654-1737. *Lexici militaris* (Rome, 1724). 4.4.2.3-4; C 202 <nd, h> War 137.24 F* 2 v.

ARBUTHNOT, JOHN, 1667-1735. *Tables of ancient coins* (London, 1727). Inv.16.79; 2.2.4.1; C129 (under Arbuthnot, Charles) <670511, h> f*EC7.Ar197.727t

ARETINO, PIETRO, 1492-1556.
Vita di S.Caterina vergine (Venice, 1628). Inv.3.168; 2.4.8.25; C27 (under Etiro, Partenio) <641208, v> *IC5.Ar345.540ve

Vita di San Tomaso d'Aquino (Venice, 1636). Inv.3.166; 6.4.7.47; C27 (under Etiro, Partenio) <641208, v> *IC5.Ar345.543vd

Argonautica, Hymni, et De lapidibus, ed. A. C. Eschenbach, H. Estienne, and J. Scaliger (Utrecht, 1689). 4.2.8.29; C17 (under Orpheus) Original Hollis gift not located.

Argumentum anti-normannicum (London, 1682). Inv.2.90 (under Argument); 2.2.6.21; not in C <6410.., h> *EC65.C7746.682a

ARINGHI, PAOLO, *see* Bosio, Antonio

ARISTOPHANES. *Il Pluto* [Greek and Italian] (Florence, 1751). Inv.3.91; C12 <641208> Original Hollis gift not located.

ARISTOTLE. †*Opera omnia quae extant* (Paris, 1619). 4.2.1.19-29; C12 (wrongly dated 1691) <nd, h> Ga 112.117 F* 2 v.

ARNAUD, GEORGIUS D', 1711-1740. *Specimen animadversionum criticarum* (Haarlem, 1728). 4.3.7.7; not in C <nd, h> Class 9618.2*

ARPE, PIERRE FRIEDRICH, 1682-1740. †‡*Apologia pro Jul. Caesare Vanino* ([Rotterdam], 1712). Inv.7.10; 2.2.7.27; C126 <651010, h> On title page: "Rariss." Phil 4265.1.90*

ARRIAN. *Dei fatti dei magno Alessandro* (Verona, 1730). Inv.4.24; 2.4.4.31; C12 <641212?, v> KE 30272*

Art de verifier les dates (Paris, 1750). 4.3.4.20; C34 (under Benedictins) <nd, h> H 1907.50 F* 2 v. in 1

The art of governing (London, 1722). 2.3.7.38; C247 (under Government) <641208, h> *EC75.H7267.Zz735t

ASCHAM, ANTHONY, d. 1650.
‡*A discourse upon government* (London, 1648). Inv.10.41; 4.8.3.37; C82 <680712, h> On title page: "very curious"; a long bibliographical note at the end. *EC65.As230.648d

‡*Of the confusions and revolutions of governments* (London, 1649; 3rd ed. of *A discourse*). Inv.12.36; 6.2.8.9; not in C <690818, h> On flyleaf: "This is the best edit. of a curious & rare book. Concerning the unfortunate author of it, see A. Wood's Ath. Oxon. Vol. 2, p. 385. T·H." *EC65.As230.648dc

ASCHAM, ROGER, 1515-1568.
‡*The English works* [with biographical preface by Samuel Johnson] (London, [1761]). 4.4.4.14; C104 <nd, r> On p.[i]: "+ Written by Mr. Johnson [Dictionary Johnson]." *EC75.J6371.A761aa

A report and discourse (London, [1570?]). Inv.4.59 (part); 2.2.6.19; C104 <641212?, h> STC 830

The scholemaster (London, 1571). Inv.4.62; 2.1.7.7; C104 <641212?, r> STC 835 (B)

Toxophilus (London, 1589). Inv.4.59 (part); 2.2.6.19; C219 <641212?, h> STC 830

ASGILL, JOHN, 1659-1738.
‡*An argument proving that according to the doctrine of eternal life* ([London], 1700). Inv.9.26 (part); 4.3.7.33; C 257 <680711, xt> On title page: "Very rare" *EC7.As295.700ab

The assertion is … (London, 1710). Inv.9.26 (part); 4.3.7.33; not in C <680711, xt> *EC7.As295.710a

‡*The metamorphosis of man* (London, 1727). Inv.9.25; 4.3.8.1; C153 & 257 <680711, h> On title page: "very rare." *EC7.As295.727m

Mr. Asgill's extract (London, 1714). Inv.9.26 (part); 4.3.7.33; C244 <680711, xt> *EC7.As295.713aa

The Pretender's declaration (London, 1713). Inv.9.26 (part); 4.3.7.33; not in C <680711, xt> *EC7.As295.713p

The Pretender's declaration transpos'd (London, 1716). Inv.9.26 (part); 4.3.7.33; C244 <680711, xt> *EC7.As295.716p

The succession of the House of Hannover vindicated (London, 1714). Inv.9.26 (part); 4.3.7.33; C244 <680711, xt> *EC7.As295.714s

ASH, JOHN, 1724?-1779. *The easiest introduction to Dr. Lowth's English grammar* (London, 1766). 4.2.8.51; C51 <nd, h> EducT 20757.66.2*

Assedio di Vienna d'Austria (Modena, 1684). Inv.3.159; not in C <641208> Original Hollis gift not located.

ASSEMANI, STEFANO EVODIO, 1711-1782, *see* Biblioteca Medicea Laurenziana

ASSER, JOHN, d. 909. *Annales rerum gestarum Ælfridi Magni* (Oxford, 1722). Inv.17.10; 4.4.5.18; C54 <68….> Original Hollis gift not located.

ASTELL, MARY, 1668-1731. *An impartial inquiry into the causes of rebellion* (London, 1704). Inv.4.38 (part); 2.3.5.33; not in C <641212?, xt> *EC7.As824.704i

ATAVANTI, PAOLO. *De origine ordinis servorum b. Mariae dialogus* (Florence, 1741). C64 <nd, v> C 462.6*

ATHENAEUS, OF NAUCRATIS. *Deipnosophiston biblia pentekaideka*, ed. Isaac Casaubon (Leiden, 1657). Inv.8.19; 4.2.2.19; C12 <661001, h> Ga 121.15 F*

ATKEY, ANTHONY, fl. 1725-1733. ‡*Letters written, in MDCCXXV, to the Rev. Dr. Samuel Clarke* (London, 1745). Inv.2.97; 2.1.6.11; C257 <6410.., h> On title page: "By Mʳ. Atkey Dissenting Minister." *EC75.H7267.Zz743m

ATWOOD, WILLIAM, d. 1705?
†‡*Jani anglorum facies nova* (London, 1680). Inv.17.15; 4.3.8.17; C82 <68…., h> On title page: "Believe by Mr. Attwood of Gray's Inne. See 'Plato Redivivus,' by the ingenuous Harry Neville." Br 166.80*

‡*Jus anglorum ab antiquo* (London, 1681). Inv.17.26; 4.3.8.21; C82 <68…., h> On title page: "Believe by Mr. Attwood." *EC65.At968.681j

AUGUSTUS, EMPEROR OF ROME, 63 B.C.-14 A.D. *The Emperor Augustus his two speeches in the Senate-House at Rome* (London, 1675). 2.4.5.19; not in C <nd, xt> *OGC.D620.Eg675

Austin, and the monks of Bangor (London, 1713). 4.2.3.22; C237 <nd, h> f*EC75.H7267.Zz740p

‡*Authentic memoirs concerning the Portuguese inquisition* (London, 1769). Inv.12.78; 6.1.7.10; C121 <690818, r> On back flyleaf: "First published by W. Sandby Anno 1761." C 5482.6.2*

AVERANI, NICCOLO, d. 1727. *Dissertatio de mensibus Aegyptiorum* (Florence, 1737). 4.4.5.12; C34 <nd, v> Eg 807.37*

AVERY, BENJAMIN, d. 1764. *The old Whig* (London, 1739). Inv.7.17; 2.1.5.37-38; C120 <651010, h> *EC7.Av373.735ob 2 v.

AVICENNA, 930-1037. *Kitab al-Thani min Qanum al-Qanum l'Ibn Sina*, tr. Peter Kirsten (Breslau, 1609). 4.2.3.24; not in C <nd, h> 3231.22 F*

AZZIO, TOMMASO. *De ludo scacchorum* (Pisauri, 1583). 4.2.6.25; C104 (under Actius) <nd, h> SG 3615.83*

B

BACON, SIR FRANCIS, 1561-1626. *The works* (London, 1753). Inv.16.7; 2.2.2.23-25; C104 <670511, h> Phil 1850.2 F* 3 v.

BACON, NATHANIEL, 1593-1660. *An historical and political discourse of the laws and government of England* (London, 1760). Inv.1.14; 2.3.3.30; C82 <631024, r> Br 306.47.5 F*

BACON, ROGER, 1214?-1294. *Frier Bacon his discoveries* (London, 1659). Inv.4.104; 2.2.8.43; C104 <641212?, h (rebacked)> 24215.2*

BAÏF, LAZARE DE, 1496?-1547. *De re vestiaria* (Paris, 1553). Inv.4.195; 2.1.8.21; C3 <641212?, h> *FC5.B1494.B553d

BAILLIE, JOHN, d. 1743. *An essay on the sublime* (London, 1747). 2.1.6.13; not in C <6410.., h> *EC7.St932.731d

BAILLIE, ROBERT, 1599-1662.

‡*An historical vindication of the Church of Scotland* (London, 1646). Inv.4.60; 2.1.7.6; C64 <641212?, h> A short bibliographical note by TH. *EC65.N1583.646h

‡*Ladensium αυτοκατακρισισ, the Canterburians self-conviction* ([Amsterdam, 1640]). Inv.4.55; 2.1.7.18; not in C <641212?, h> Bibliographical notes byTH facing title page. STC 1206 (B)

‡[Another edition] ([London], 1641. 2.1.6.35; C220 (under Canterburian) <nd, h> On flyleaf: "See also 'LADENSIVM AYTOKATAKPIΣIΣ. The Canterburians self conviction.' in 2°. printed 1640, by Mʳ. Robert Bailey. See also 'An historical Vindication of the Government of the Church of Scotland, by Robert Baylie. Minister at Glasgow; printed in 2°. at London 1746.'" *EC65.B1583.640ℓca

‡*The life of William [Laud]* (London, 1643). Inv.4.46; 2.1.6.35; C25 & 207 <641212?, h> A short bibliographical note by TH. *EC65.B1583.640ℓca

BAKER, SIR RICHARD, 1568-1645. *A chronicle of the kings of England* (London, 1684). Inv.5.8; 2.1.3.10; C54 <6506.., h> Br 306.43.7 F*

BAKER, ROBERT, fl. 1770. *Reflections on the English language* (London, 1770). Inv.14.39; 6.1.8.8; C136 <700926, h> 9266.5*

BALE, JOHN, 1495-1563. *Yet a course at the Romish fox* ([Zurich, 1543]). Inv.4.152; 2.2.8.19; C173 (under Harryson) <641212?, h> STC 1309

BALGUY, THOMAS, 1716-1795. *A letter concerning confessions of faith* (London, 1768). Inv.11.14; 6.1.4.25; C275 (under Confessional) <6809.., h> *EC75.R4375.B768t

BANDINI, ANGELO MARIA, 1726-1803, *see* Biblioteca Medicea Laurenziana for commentary

BANDURI, ANSELMO, ca. 1670-1743. *Numismata imperatorum Romanorum* (Paris, 1718). Inv.5.55; 2.3.1.22-23; C129 <6506.., h> Arc 1475.2 F* 2 v.

BARBERINI, MAFFEO, *see* Urban VIII, Pope

BARBEYRAC, JEAN, 1674-1744.
Histoire des anciens traitez (Amsterdam, 1739). 4.2.1.14; C145 <nd, r> Harvard Depository Int 187.26.3 F

Traité de la morale des pères de l'église (Amsterdam, 1728). 4.4.4.21; C46 <nd, h> C 527.28*

BARCLAY, JOHN, 1582-1621. *Argenis* (Venice, 1656). Inv.3.161; C105 <641208, v> MLb 176.33*

BARCLAY, ROBERT, 1648-1690. †*An apology for the true Christian divinity* (London, 1736). Inv.2.117; 2.3.7.22; C153 <6410.., h> *EC65.B2354.Eg678aha

BARDI, GIOVANNI DE', CONTE DI VERNIO, 16th cent. *Memorie del calceo fiorentino* (Florence, 1688). Inv.3.37; 2.4.4.19; C6 (under Memoire), C105 (under Bini) <641208, r> Typ 625.88.194

BARETTI, GIUSEPPE, 1719-1789. *A dictionary of the English and Italian languages* (London, 1760). Inv.4.7; 2.2.4.27-28; C202 <641212?, h> The preface was written by Samuel Johnson. *EC75.B2377.760d 2 v.

BAR HEBRAEUS, 1226-1286.
Historia compendiosa dynastiarum (Oxford, 1663). 4.2.7.29-30; C132 (under Abul-Pharajio) <nd, h> Sem 1001* 2 v.

Specimen historiae Arabum, ed. Edward Pococke (Oxford, 1650). C134 (under Pocock) <nd, h> OL 21120.1*

BARKER, JOHN, 1682-1762. ‡*Popery the great corruption of Christianity* (London, 1735). Not in C <6506.., h> Inside front cover: "Ut spargam. T·H." *EC75.H7267.Zz735s2

BARNES, JOSHUA, 1654-1712. ‡*The history of … Edward III[d]* (Cambridge, 1688). 4.1.3.1; C25 <nd, h> On flyleaf: "Good copies of our Old English Historians, and Writers of the Lives of our antient Kings, are becoming very scarce. But they shall be sent, 8 or 10 more it may be, great & small, besides those now sent, to Harvard College. T·H." On the portrait frontispiece: "A tired Impression from an ordinary Ingraving. But T·H is always glad to preserve the Effigies of Authors of any tolerability." Br 1480.30 F* (A)

BARON, RICHARD, d. 1768.
The pillars of priestcraft shaken (London, 1752). Inv.2.71; 2.1.8.22-23; not in C
<6410.., h> *EC7.B2687.752p 2 v.

†‡[Another edition] (London, 1768). 4.4.7.34-37; not in C <nd, h> On back flyleaf in
v.1: "The late Rev. Richard Baron was born at Leeds, in Yorkshire and was educated at
Glasgow, in Scotland, under the late Professor Hutcheson, who gave him an honorable
Testimonial in writing, on his leaving that University. ap. 14, 1768 T·H." Identical
inscription and date in the copy given by TH to Andrew Eliot. *EC7.B2687.753pb (A)
4 v.

BARONIO, CESARE, CARDINAL, 1538-1607. *Critica historico-chronologica in universos
annales ecclesiasticos* (Antwerp, 1705). 4.4.1.20-23; C35 (under Pagi) <nd, r>
C 1822.5.50 F* 4 v.

BAROZZIO, GIACOMO, *see* Vignola, Giacomo Barozzio

BARRIÈRE, DOMINICUS, ca. 1620-1678. *Villa Aldobrandini Tusculana* (Rome, 1647).
4.4.2.9; not in C Original Hollis gift not located.

BARRINGTON, DAINES, 1727-1800.
‡*Observations on the statutes* (London, 1766). 4.1.4.21; B6, C79 <nd, h> On flyleaf: "By
Mr. Barrington, Brother to Lord Viscount Barrington. A Lawyer by profession. A
respectable Gentleman." *EC75.B2772.766o

Observations on the more ancient statutes (London, 1769). Inv.12.12; 6.1.3.6; C79
<690818, h> Br 67.12*

BARRINGTON, JOHN SHUTE BARRINGTON, VISCOUNT, 1678-1734.
A letter from a lay-man, in communion with the Church of England (London, 1714).
2.1.6.14; C219 (under A letter in favour of the dissenters) <671209?, h>
*EC65.C5614.681c

Miscellanea sacra (London, 1770). Inv.14.16; 6.1.5.8-10; B6, C154 <700926, h>
C 1108.91.17* 3 v.

BARROW, ISAAC, 1630-1677.
‡*Lectiones geometricae* (London, 1670). Inv.4.44; 2.4.7.5; C50 <641212?, h> On flyleaf:
"This Book was originally given as a present by Dr. Barrow to Mr. Locke; and Mr. Locke
gave it to Mr. Maurice Ashley, Brother to the Characteristicks Earl of Shaftesbury. T·H."
Tipped in, slips in the handwriting of Locke and Ashley. *EC65.L7934.Zz670b

Opuscula (London, 1687). 4.2.3.21; C106 <nd, h> C 1109.1 F*

A treatise of the pope's supremacy (London, 1680). 4.1.7.41; not in C <nd, h>
C 4155.12.3*

Works (London, 1722). Inv.5.4; 2.4.1.28; B6, C154 <6506.., h> C 1109.4 F* 2 v.

BARROW, JOHN, 17th cent. *The Lord's arm stretched out* (London, 1664). 4.4.6.18; C259
<680930?, h> *EC75.H7267.Zz698r

BARTHELEMY, JEAN JACQUES, 1716-1795. *Reflections on the ancient alphabet and language
of Palmyra* (London, 1755). Inv.3.1; not in C <641208, r> 3224.106 PF*

BARTHOLIN, CASPAR, 1655-1738. *De inauribus veterum syntagma* (Amsterdam, 1676). Inv.3.58 (part); 2.1.7.48; C3 <641208, h> *QDC6.B2838.B675da

BARTHOLIN, THOMAS, 1616-1680.
Antiquitatum veteris puerperii syntagma (Amsterdam, 1676). Inv.3.58 (part); 2.1.7.48; C3 <641208, h> *QDC6.B2838.B675da

De armillis veterum schedion (Amsterdam, 1676). Inv.3.58 (part); 2.1.8.49; C3 <641208, h> *QDC6.B2838.B675da

BARTOLI, PIETRO SANTI, 1635-1700.
Admiranda romanorum antiquitatum (Rome, 1693). 6.3.1.33; C3 <641208?, v> p*IC6.B2857.685ab

Li antiche lucerne sepolcra (Rome, 1729). 4.1.3.14; C3 <nd, h> f*IC6.B2857.671aca

Gli antichi sepolchri (Rome, 1727). 4.1.3.15; C3 <nd, h> Arc 1010.202*

Médailles ... du cabinet de la reine Christine (The Hague, 1742). Inv.5.60; 2.2.1.14; not in C <6506.., h> Arc 1455.2 F*

See also Virgil

BARTOLOMMEI GIA SMEDUCCI, GIROLAMO, 1584?-1662. *L'America, poema eroico* (Rome, 1650). Inv.8.27; 2.4.3.2; C140 (under Bartholomaeus) <661001, r> f*IC6.B2858.650a

BARTOLUCCI, GIULIO, 1613-1687. *Bibliotheca magna rabbinica* (Rome, 1675-1685). 4.2.3.9-12; C132 (under Bartolucius) <67....?, calf> f*IC6.B28574.675b (B) 4 v.

BARTON, PHILIP, 1718 or 19-1796. *A sermon preached in Lambeth chapel* (London, 1766). 6.1.3.29; C259 <nd, h> *EC75.H7267.Zz769t

BARWICK, PETER, 1619-1705. *The life of the reverend Dr. John Barwick* (London, 1724). Inv.14.63; 6.1.6.46; C25 <700926, h> Br 1852.16.5*

BASTWICK, JOHN, 1593-1654.
Flagellum pontifici & episcoporum Latialium ([n.p.], 1635). Inv.2.120; 2.2.8.34; C154 <6410.., h> *EC65.B2985.634fb

[Another edition] (London, 1641). Inv.4.192; 2.2.8.42; C154 <641212?, h> *EC65.B2985.634fc

Praxeis ton episkopon, Apologeticus ad praesules Anglicanos ([n.p.], 1636). Inv.4.171 (under Apologeticum); 2.2.8.17; C154 <641212?, h> STC 1576

The utter routing (London, 1646). Inv.2.44; 2.2.6.6; not in C <6410.., h> *EC65.B2985.646u

BATE, GEORGE, 1608-1669. *Elenchus motuum nuperorum in Anglia* (London, 1676). 4.4.8.19; C54 <nd, h> Br 1820.139.2*

BAUDELOT DE DAIRVAL, CHARLES CÉSAR DE, 1648-1722. ‡ *De l'utilité des voyages* (Rouen, 1727). Inv.16.41; 2.2.7.2-3; C105 <670511, h> On flyleaf: "A pretty book, full of useful, ingenious & elegant ideas. T·H." Arc 386.14.5* 2 v.

BAXTER, ANDREW, 1686?-1750.

An appendix to the first part of the enquiry (London, 1750). Inv.5.21 (part); 2.4.5.7; not in C <6506..?, h> *EC75.H7267.Zz750b2

An enquiry into the nature of the human soul (London, 1745). Inv.5.21 (part); 2.4.5.5-6; C93 <6506.., calf> *EC75.H7267.Zz745b

Matho; sive, Cosmotheoria puerilis (London, 1736). 4.1.7.28; C10 <nd, h> Phil 282.5*

Matho: or, The cosmotheoria puerilis (London, 1745). 4.1.7.29-30; B6, C10 <nd, h> Phil 282.5.5* 2 v.

BAXTER, WILLIAM, 1650-1723.

Glossarium antiquitatum britannicarum (London, 1719). 4.1.6.13; C3 <nd, r> *EC7.B3375.719g

Reliquiae Baxterianae (London, 1726). 4.1.6.12; C3 <nd, h> *EC7.B3375.726r

BAYES, JOSHUA, 1671-1746. ‡*The Church of Rome's doctrine* (London, 1735). Not in C <6506.., h> Inside front cover: "Ut spargam. T·H." *EC75.H7267.Zz735s

BAYES, THOMAS, d. 1761. ‡*Divine benevolence* (London, 1731). 2.1.6.11; C259 (under Bayes, Joshua) <6410.., h> On title page: "By Mr. Bayes, Dissenting Minister at Tunbridge." *EC75.H7267.Zz743m

BAYLE, PIERRE, 1647-1706.

Dictionnaire historique et critique (Rotterdam, 1720). Inv.2.2; 2.3.1.11-14; C25 <6410..> Original Hollis gift not located.

Histoire de Mr. Bayle et de ses ouvrages (Amsterdam, 1716). 4.4.8.6; C29 (under Monnoye) <nd, h> 38563.22.55*

Miscellaneous reflections, occasioned by the comet (London, 1708). Inv.5.37; 2.2.6.28; C105 <6506.., r> Marked "Duplicate for sale. C. Folsom, Librn." 24281.8* A second copy, 2.2.6.29, Andover-Harvard OLD DIV 124 Bayle, declared lost.

Œuvres diverses (The Hague, 1727-1731). Inv.5.66; 2.2.2.1-4; C105 <6506.., r> 38561.4 F* 4 v.

Pensées diverses ... à l'occasion de la comête (Amsterdam, 1749). Inv.2.107; 2.1.8.28-31; C105 <6410.., h> 24281.6* 4 v.

‡*A philosophical commentary* (London, 1708). Inv.5.38; 2.2.6.30-31; C155 <6506.., h> On flyleaf: "A curious tract, tho' all to one side." C 1108.77.5* 2 v.

BAYLY, ANSELM, d. 1794. *Introduction to languages, literary and philosophical* (London, 1758). Inv.17.21; 4.3.6.34; B6, C135 <68...., r> 1222.16*

BEACH, PHILIP. *A letter to Thomas Burnet* (London, 1736). Inv.4.138 (part); 2.2.5.23; C213 (under Burnet) <641212?, h> *EC65.B9343.S736t

BEACH, THOMAS, d. 1737. *Eugenio, or, Virtuous and happy life* (London, 1737). 4.2.3.22; C238 <nd, h> f*EC75.H7267.Zz740p

BEATTIE, JAMES, 1735-1803. *An essay on the nature ... of truth* (Edinburgh, 1770). Inv.14.41; 6.1.4.13; B6, C93 <700926, h> *EC75.B3806.770e

BEATTIE, CHARLES, 1715?-1772. *The journal of a two months tour* (London, 1768). 6.1.6.35; C219 <nd, h (sheep and marbled boards)> Tr 405*

BECCARIA, CESARE, MARCHESE, 1738-1794.
‡*Del delitti e delle pene, edizione sesta* (Harlem, 1766). 4.2.8.19; B7, C82 <nd, r> TH identifies the author. Soc 3511.1.4*

A discourse on public œconomy and commerce (London, 1769). Inv.12.90; 6.1.8.7; C37 <690818, h> Econ 302.1.5*

†‡*Traité des délits et des peines* (Lausanne, 1766). 4.1.8.41; C82 <nd, h> TH identifies the author. Soc 3511.2.2*

BECCARIA, JOHANN. *Refutatio cuisdam libelli ... De iure magistratum* ([n.p.], 1590). 2.1.8.4; C82 <671209?, r> Tr 501*

BEDE, THE VENERABLE, SAINT, 673-735. *Historiae ecclesiasticae ... libri quinque* (Cambridge, 1722). Inv.5.64; 2.4.1.3; C64 <6506..?, h> Br 1055.25 F*

BEGER, LORENZ, 1653-1705. *Thesaurus Brandenburgicus selectus* (Brandenburg, 1696). Inv.11.2; 6.1.1.2-4; C129 <6809.., russia > Arc 1455.1 F* 3 v.

BEHRENS, GEORG HENNING, 1662-1712. ‡*The natural history of Harts Forest* (London, 1730). 4.4.7.15; C71 <nd, 18th c. calf> On back flyleaf: "The institution of a Professorship of Chemistry, Botany, and Minerallogy [sic] at Cambridge in N.E. would, it is apprehended, promote more the wealth & ingenuity of the North Americans, with preservation to them of their INDUSTRY and MANLINESS, than any other measure that could be taken there." NH 1257.30*

BELL, JOHN, 1745-1831. *Bell's common place book* (London, 1770). Inv.14.42; 6.1.1.5; C105 <700926, v> Based on John Locke's system for a commonplace book. Many of Bell's examples were furnished by TH. Educ 7300.1 F*

BELLARMINO, ROBERTO FRANCESCO ROMOLO, SAINT, 1542-1621. *Dichiarazione della dottrina Cristiana* (Lucca, [1590?-1610?]). Inv.3.158; C155 <641208, v> Andover-Harvard, Safe 686 R.C. Bellarmino

BELLE-ISLE, CHARLES LOUIS AUGUST FOUQUET, DUC DE, 1684-1761. ‡*Lettres* ([n.p.], 1759). 2.2.3.20; C219 <nd, h> On flyleaf: "For the public library of Harvard College in New England From the Committee for cloathing French Prisoners of war." f*EC75.H7267.Zz759b (A)

BELLERS, FETTIPLACE, 1687-1750. *A delineation of universal law* (London, 1754). Inv.16.88; 2.2.4.21; C82 <670511, r> *EC7.B4165.740ac

BELLORI, GIOVANNI PIETRO, 1615?-1696.
Descrizione delle immagini dipinte da Raffaelle (Rome, 1751). Inv.17.30 (under Vasari); 4.4.8.16; C105 <68...., v> *IC6.B4174.695db

Picturae antiquae cryptarum Romanorum (Rome, 1750). 6.3.1.23; not in C <nd, v> Fine Arts Arc 750.22 PF

Veteres arcus Augustorum triumphis insignis (Rome, 1690). 6.3.1.26; C33 <nd, v> p *EC75.H7267.Zz690b

BENDLOWES, PHILIP, d. 1769.

Animadversions on an essay [by John Rotheram] (London, 1769). 6.1.4.28; C259 (under Bendlow) <nd, h> *EC75.H2448.767o (A)

An inquiry into the cause which obstructed the reformation (London, 1768). 6.1.4.28; C259 (under Bendlow) <nd, h> *EC75.H2448.767o (A)

BENEDICTUS, ABBAS PETROBURGENSIS. *De vita & gestis Henrici II. et Ricardi I.*, ed. Thomas Hearne (Oxford, 1735). Inv.17.34; 4.4.5.15-16; C25 <68...., h> Br 1345.9* 2 v.

BENNET, BENJAMIN, 1674-1726.

A defence of the memorial of the reformation (London, 1723). Inv.4.179; 2.1.6.47; B7, C64 <641212?, h> *EC7.B4891.723d

A memorial of the reformation (London, 1721). Inv.4.74; 2.1.6.20; B7, C64 <641212?, h> Br 327.17*

BENNET, JOHN, d. 1686. *Constantius the Apostate* (London, 1683). 4.3.8.4; C207 <nd> Original Hollis gift not located.

BENSON, THOMAS, b. 1678 or 1679. †*Vocabulario anglo-saxonicum* (Oxford, 1701). 2.3.6.2; not in C <nd, h> 9286.6.15*

BENTHAM, EDWARD, 1707-1776, ed. *Ton palaion ... epitaphioi* (Oxford, 1768). Inv.13.61; 6.1.6.10; C13 <700926, h> Harvard Depository KE 30670

BENTIVOGLIO, GUIDO, 1577-1644. *Relationi ... in tempo delle sue nuntiature di Fiandria* (Antwerp, 1629). 4.4.4.2; C55 <6410.., v> Neth 282.1*

BENTLEY, RICHARD, 1662-1742.

Dissertation upon the epistles of Phalaris (London, 1699). Inv.17.18; 4.4.7.39; C105 <68...., r> *EC75.H7267.Zz699b

The present state of Trinity College (London, 1710). Inv.9.23 (part); 4.3.7.25; not in C <680711, h> *EC65.B4465.B710b

Remarks on a late discourse of free-thinking (London, 1714). Inv.5.32 (part); 2.3.8.1; B7, not in C <6506.., h> *EC65.B4465.B715f

Remarks on a late discourse ... part the second (London, 1715). Inv.5.32 (part); 2.3.8.1; B7?, not in C <6506.., h> *EC65.B4465.B715f

See also A short account

BENTLEY, RICHARD, 1707-1782. *Philodamas, a tragedy* (London, 1767). 6.3.2.14; C229 (under title) <nd, xt> *EC75.B4467.767p

BERGIER, NICOLAS, 1563-1623. *Le dessein de l'histoire de Reims* (Reims, 1635). Inv.4.25; 2.3.5.39; C3 <641212?, v> *FC6.B4543.635d

BERNARD, EDWARD, 1638-1696, *see* Smith, Thomas

BERNARD, SIR FRANCIS, 1712-1779. *Letters to the ministry* (London, 1769). Inv.13.7; 6.1.6.2; C147 <700926> Original Hollis gift not located.

BERNARD, JEAN FRÉDÉRIC, d. 1752. †‡*Dialogues critiques et philosophiques* (Amsterdam, 1730). Inv.4.94; 2.2.7.16; C105 <641212?, h> On flyleaf: "Par Bernard, Libraire a Amsterdam." *EC75.H7267.Zz730b

BERNBERCH, PAUL. *Tyrannus* (Jena, 1675). Inv.4.49; 2.1.6.32; C82 <641212?, h> Gov 512.11*

BERTIUS, PETRUS, 1565-1629. ‡*Theatrum geographiae veteris* ([Leiden, 1618]). Inv.12.1; 6.1.2.2; C49 (under Ptolemy) <690818, h> On front flyleaf: "A fine copy of a very rare work. It was purchased out of the late Duke of Newcastle, and intended to be forwarded to Harvard College, at Cambridge, in New England. It cost four Guineas. ap. 14, 1769." Map Collection, Pusey Library, Mp 2.1618

BERTOLI, GIANDOMENICO. *Le antichità d'Aquileja* (Venice, 1739). 4.4.3.23; C3 <nd, calf> Typ 725.39.205 F (B)

BERTRAM, CHARLES, 1723-1765, *see Britannicarum gentium historiae antiquae scriptores tres*

BETHEL, SLINGSBY, 1617-1697. *The world's mistake in Oliver Cromwell* (London, 1668). 2.4.5.19; C245 (under Cromwell) <nd, xt> *EC65.B4654.668wc

BEVERIDGE, WILLIAM, 1637-1708.
De linguarum orientalium (London, 1658). Inv.14.69; 4.1.8.2; C132 <700926, h> 3224.13*

‡[Another edition] (London, 1664). Inv.10.33; 4.3.8.16; <680712, h> On title page: "rare." 2255.16*

BÈZE, THÉODORE DE, 1519-1605.
De haereticis puniendis ([Geneva], 1554). Inv.4.140; 2.1.7.22; C155 <641212?, h> *FC5.B4694.554d

Poemata (Leiden, 1757). Inv.15.24; 6.2.8.41; C140 <691129> Original Hollis gift not located.

Tractatio de polygamia (Geneva, 1568). Inv.1.35 (part); 2.2.8.14; C155 <631024, r> *FC5.B4694.568t

Tractatio de repudiis et divortiis (Geneva, 1569). Inv.1.35 (part); 2.2.8.14; C155 <631024, r> *FC5.B4694.568t

BIBLE. English. Purver. 1764. *A new and literal translation of all the books of the Old and New Testament* (London, 1764). Inv.5.3; 2.3.2.13-14; C22 <6506.., h> Andover-Harvard SCR Folio 306.24 Purver c1-2

BIBLE. Polyglot. Walton. 1657. ‡*S. S. Biblia sacra polyglotta … edidit Brianus Walton* (London, 1657). 2.1.1.1-12; C23 <64...., 17th c. blue morocco> On flyleaf of v. 1: "Thomas Hollis, an Englishman, a Lover of Liberty, civil & religious, Citizen of the World, is desirous of having the honor to present this set of books, (a gift, originally, of the author of it, to Edward Hyde, Earl of Clarendon, Chancellor of England,) to the public Library of Harvard College, at Cambridge, in New England. Pall Mall, aug. 24, 1764." A "loyal" copy, on royal thick paper. TH's Diary, August 11, 1764, states that it was bought specifically for Harvard College. The set included a 13th v. containing Edmund Castell's *Lexicon heptaglotton* (London, 1769), *q.v.* Sem 1353 PF* 6 v. in 12

BIBLE. O.T. Latin. Le Clerc. *Veteris Testamenti libri historici* (Amsterdam, 1708). Inv.10.5 (misdated 1735); 4.2.4.4-7 <680721> Original Hollis gift not located.

See also Codex preudepigraphus Veteris Testamenti

BIBLE. O.T. Psalms. English. *A new English translation of the Psalms,* by Thomas Edwards (Cambridge, 1755). Inv.13.12; 6.1.5.21; C40 <700926, h> Bi 68.28.755*

BIBLE. N.T.
Coptic. *Novum testamentum aegypticum vulgo copticum,* ed. David Wilkins (Oxford, 1716). Inv.12.10; 6.1.3.16; C24 <690818, h> Sem 386.4*

Gaelic. ‡*Tiomnadh nuadh* (Dunedin [*i.e.,* Edinburgh], 1767). Inv.14.62; 6.1.5.17; C46 <700926, h> On flyleaf: "This Galic [*sic*] or Erse New Testament, was printed at Edinburgh, at the expence of the Society instituted in Scotland for the propagation of Christian Knowledge." On a slip, tipped in: "It is said, a Dictionary of the Gallic or Erse language is printing in Scotland. Had it been actually printed a copy of it would have been sent to Harvard College." Annotations at the end of the book concern a French and an English Gaelic dictionary. Celt 3030.1.7*

Latin. Vulgate. *Novum Testamentum ... auxit Joannes Clericus* (Frankfurt, 1714). Inv.10.6; C41 <680712, h> Andover-Harvard S.C.R. folio 332 Bible 2 v.

BIBLE. N.T. Gospels. Gothic.
Quatuor d. n. Jesu Christi evangeliorum (Dordrecht, 1665). 4.3.5.27; C23 <nd, h> On title page: "Suum cuique Tho: Hearne 1716." 8267.81*

Sacrorum evangeliorum versio gothica, ed. Edward Lye (Oxford, 1750). Inv.12.9; 6.1.2.17; C223 <690818, h> 8267.82.5.5*

Fragmenta versionis Ulphilanae, ed. Johan Ihre (Uppsala, 1763). Inv.13.65; 6.1.3.34; C116 <700926, h> 8267.82.6*

BIBLE. N.T. Acts.
Greek & Latin. *Acta apostolorum,* ed. Thomas Hearne (Oxford, 1715). 4.1.6.11; C22 <nd, h> Bi 42.715*

See also Codex apocryphus Novi Testamenti; Fabricius, Johann Albert

BIBLIOTECA MEDICEA LAURENZIANA.
Catalogus codicum manuscriptorum bibliothecae Mediceae Laurentianae (Florence, 1764). 4.2.1.1; C32 <nd, h> C 507.64 F* v. 1 only

Codici MMS. Orientalium catalogus (Florence, 1742). 4.2.1.2; C32 (under Assemanus) & C132 <nd, r> Sem 1503.9 F*

Bibliotheca Fratrum Polonorum ([Amsterdam], 1656-1692). 4.4.3.15-21; C170 <nd, early sheep> Andover-Harvard Safe folio 656 Unit P778b 1656, copy 1, 9 v.

‡*Bibliotheca literaria* (London, 1722-1724). 4.2.5.38; C87 <670801, h> On flyleaf: "T·H· has had the honor to send one Copy of this work to the Library of Harvard College, already. But the work is so curious, valuable, especially for <u>The Memorial concerning the Desiderata in Learning</u>; that he could not forbear sending another copy of it to the College. In the beginning, He sent Books on Government, beside stray Books, to Harvard College; for, if Government goeth right, ALL goeth right. Then, He sent

Grammars, Dictionaries of Root and other Languages, with critical Authors; in hope of forming first rate Scholars, <u>the</u> NOBLEST of all Men! Now, he dribblets out the like. And thinks, to take his leave." On facing flyleaf: "Palmal, aug. 1, 1767." On title page: "UT SPARGAM T·H" *EC75.H7267.Zz722b Second copy not located.

BIELFIELD, JAKOB FRIEDRICH, FREIHERR VON, 1717-1770. *Institutions politiques* (The Hague, 1760-1762). 4.1.4.14-16; C82 <nd> Original Hollis gift not located.

BINET, ÉTIENNE, 1569-1639. *Essay des merveilles de nature* (Rouen, 1657). Not in C <nd, contemporary calf> *FC6.B5125.620em

Biographica britannica (London, 1747-1766). 4.4.2.10-16; C26 <nd, r> Br 196 F* 7 v.

Biographica classica (London, 1750). 4.2.8.17-18; B7, C26 <nd, h> *EC75.H7267.Zz750h 2 v.

BIRCH, THOMAS, 1705-1766.

    An account of the life of John Ward (London, 1766). Inv.14.10; 6.1.7.6; C26 & C207 <700926, h> *EC7.B5315.766a

    ‡[Another copy] 4.2.7.16; C26 & C207 <nd, h> TH identifies the editor. *EC75.H7267.Zz740m

    An historical view of the negotiations between the courts of England, France, and Brussels (London, 1749). Inv.8.39; C55 <661001> Original Hollis gift not located.

    The history of the Royal Society (London, 1756-1757). Inv.2.29; 2.2.4.3-4; B7, C137 <6410.., r> f *EC7.B5315.756h 4 v. in 2

    Inquiry into the share which … Charles I had … in the transactions of the Earl of Glamorgan ([London, 1756]). Inv.4.69; 2.2.5.11; C55 <641212?, h> Br 1815.154*

    See also Thurloe, John

BIRINGUCCI, VANNOCCHIO, 1480-1539? *De la pirotechnia* ([Venice], 1540). 4.3.6.21; not in C <nd, h> Typ 525.40.213

BLACKBURNE, FRANCIS, 1705-1787.

    †‡*The confessional* (London, 1766). 2.4.6.7; C156 <nd, h> On flyleaf: "By the Rev. Thomas [*sic*] Blackburne Arch-deacon of Richmond in Yorkshire. Reader, bestow Honor on so accomplished, excellent a Personage!" Sponsored and designed by TH, who secured the text in MS. for publication. *EC75.H7267.Zz766b

    †‡[Another edition] (London, 1767). 4.3.6.18; C156 <670414, h> On flyleaf: "By the incomparable Francis Blackburne, Arch-deacon of Richmond in Yorkshire. Thomae Hollis et Populorum. 14 Ap. 1767." Sponsored and designed by TH. *EC75.H7267.Zz767b (A)

    †*Considerations on the present state of the controversy* (London, 1768). 4.3.6.20; C156 <nd, h> *EC75.H7267.Zz768b (B)

    †‡*A critical commentary on Archbishop Secker's letter* (London, 1770). Inv.14.56 (part); 6.1.6.22; not in C <700926, h> On title page: "By Mr. A.D.B." *EC7.Se243.B767b (B)

    Occasional remarks upon some late strictures on The confessional (London, 1768). 6.1.4.28; C261 (under Blackburne, Tho.) <nd, h> *EC75.H2448.767o (A)

Occasional remarks ... Part II (London, 1769). Inv.12.79; 6.2.5.7; C156 <690818, h>
*EC75.B5628.769o

Remarks on the Rev. Dr. Powell's sermon (London, 1758). 2.4.5.4; not in C <nd, h>
*EC75.H7267.Zz725m

‡*A serious enquiry into the use and importance of external religion* (London, 1752).
4.4.6.27; C328 (under Religion external) <nd, h (marbled boards)> TH identifies
Blackburne and the Bishop of Durham on title page; at the foot: "very scarce."
*EC75.B5628.752s

‡*A short historical view of the controversy* (London, 1765). Inv.5.19; 2.4.5.3; C156
<6506.., h> On flyleaf: "By the very learned & excellent Arch Deacon Blackburne, of
Richmond, in Yorkshire." *EC75.H7267.Zz765b

BLACKMORE, SIR RICHARD, d. 1729. *Prince Arthur* (London, 1696). 4.2.3.30; C140 <nd>
Original Hollis gift not located.

BLACKSTONE, SIR WILLIAM, 1723-1780. *A reply to Dr. Priestley's remarks* (London, 1769).
6.1.7.20; C244 <nd, xt> *EC75.B5677.769r

BLACKWELL, THOMAS, 1701-1757. †*Memoirs of the court of Augustus* (Edinburgh, 1753).
Inv.1.15; 2.2.4.14-16; B7, C55 <631024, h> *EC7.B5683.753m 3 v.

BLAIR, HUGH, 1718-1800. ‡*A critical dissertation on the poems of Ossian* (London, 1763).
Not in C <nd, xt> TH identifies author. *EC75.B5754.763c

BLAIR, JOHN, d. 1782. *The chronology and history of the world* (London, 1756). Inv.16.50;
2.2.1.8; C34 <670511, h> H 1907.56 F*

†‡[A Blank book] Inv.7.23; 4.2.5.19; not in C <651010, h> On flyleaf: "This book was bound,
long since, to have served a noble purpose. It may still serve some noble purpose, at
Cambridge, in New England. Pall Mall, june 24, 1765. T·H." TH's inserted note, on the
proper care of newly bound books, is preserved in the Manuscript Department, March
1992. Briefly employed at Harvard as a guest book. A 1455.5*

BLEWITT, GEORGE. *An enquiry whether a general practice of virtue tends to the wealth or
poverty* (London, 1725). Inv.12.63; 6.1.7.33; C46 (under Enquiry) <690818, h>
*EC7.M3125.T725b

BLOMER, THOMAS, 1679 or 80-1764. *A full view of Dr. Bentley's letter to the Lord Bishop of
Ely* (London, 1710). Inv.9.23 (part); 6.1.8.14; C220 <680711, h> *EC65.B4465.B710b

BLOUNT, CHARLES, 1654-1693.
†*The miscellaneous works* ([London], 1695). Inv.4.197; 2.1.8.53; C106 <641212?, h>
*EC65.B6236.695m

A summary account of the deists religion (London, 1745). 4.2.7.15; C279 <nd, h>
*EC75.H7267.Zz746t

BLOUNT, SIR THOMAS POPE, BART., 1649-1697.
Censura celebriorum authorum (London, 1690). Inv.1.8; 2.3.3.10; not in C <631024, h>
*EC65.B6239.690c

De re poetica (London, 1694). Inv.14.6; 6.1.6.40; C106 <700926, h>
*EC75.H7267.Zz694b

BOCCACCIO, GIOVANNI, 1313-1375. *Libro … delle donne illustri* (Venice, 1645). Inv.3.145; 2.4.8.24; C26 (under Boccaccius) <641208, v> *IC5.B6308.Ei545b

BODMER, HEINRICH, PRINTER, ZURICH, *see* Hottinger, Johann Heinrich

BODIN, JEAN, 1530-1596. *Les six livres de la republique* (Paris, 1577). Inv.17.5; 4.4.3.9; C82 <68…., r> f*FC5.B6324.576sb

BOETHIUS, d. 524. *Consolationis philosophiae libri V* (Leiden, 1671). Inv.10.35; 4.2.7.40 & 4.3.7.32; C106 (3 copies listed) <680712> Original Hollis gifts not located.

BOILEAU-DESPRÉAUX, NICOLAS, 1636-1711. *Oeuvres* (Geneva, 1716). Inv.4.8; 2.3.4.30-31; B7, C140 <641212?, h> *FC6.B6364.B716o (B) 2 v.

BOLD, SAMUEL, 1649-1737. ‡*A collection of tracts publish't in vindication of Mr. Lock's Reasonableness of Christianity* (London, 1706). Inv.10.36; 4.3.8.22; C156 <680712, r> A nonce collection with special printed title page; individual tracts are dated 1697-1705; TH notes on title page: "rare." *EC7.B6376.B706c

BOLINGBROKE, HENRY ST. JOHN, VISCOUNT, 1678-1751. *The works*, ed. David Mallet (London, 1754). Inv.16.76; 2.1.4.21-25; C106 <670511, r> f*EC7.B6385.C754w 5 v.

BOLLAN, WILLIAM, d. 1776.
  †*The ancient right of the English nation to the American fishery* (London, 1764). Inv.16.39; 2.2.4.23 & 4.1.4.7; C244 <670511, h> *AC7.B6382.764a

  †*Coloniae anglicanae illustratae* (London, 1762). 2.2.4.19 & 4.1.4.7; C145 <nd, h> *AC7.B6382.B766t

  Continued corruption, standing armies, and popular discontents considered (London, 1768). 6.3.2.14; C244 <nd, xt> US 2880.5* (A)

  An epistle from Timoleon (London, 1768). Inv.10.17; 4.3.5.3; C148 <680712> Original Hollis gift not located.

  ‡*The freedom of speech and writing* (London, 1766). 6.3.2.19; B7, C145 & C244 <nd, h> On title page: "Ut spargam. T·H." *AC7.B6382.766f

  †[Another copy] 4.1.5.2; B7, C145 & C244 <nd, h> *AC7.B6382.B766t

  †*The mutual interest of Great Britain and the American colonies* (London, 1765). 4.1.4.7; C244 <nd, h> *AC7.B6382.B766t

BOLLETTI, GIUSEPPE GAETANO, 1709-1769. ‡*Dell'origine e de'progressi dell'instituto delle scienze di Bologna* (Bologna, 1751). Inv.4.141; 2.3.8.12; C106 <641212?, v> On flyleaf: "Bought at Bologna in September 1752, by TH, then upon his Travells." Typ 725.51.225

BOLTON, ROBERT, 1697-1763.
  On the employment of time (London, 1751). Inv.12.86 (part); 6.1.5.29; C261 (under Boulton) <690818, r> *EC75.F8754.B751p

  [Another edition] (London, 1754). Inv.11.9; 6.1.5.29; C261 (under Boulton) <6809.., h> *EC7.B6395.750oc

BONNAIRE, LOUIS DE, 1680-1753.
  ‡*L'esprit des loix, quintessencié* ([Paris], 1751). Inv.7.12; 2.2.7.21-22; C83 <651010, r> On flyleaves: "Bought at Paris, in May 1753, by TH, on his Travells. Mem: When I was first

at Paris, upon the coming out of Monsr. De Montesquieu's Book, 'De l'Esprit des Loix', Labbé — gave Me a Copy of the following Verses, which certainly came from some one of the Sett of Abbé Debonnaire's Friends." 44 lines of French verse, beginning "Vous connoissez l'Esprit des Loix, | Que pensez Vous de cet Ouvrage?" ending "Ce n'est point un Esprit critique | Qui me sert ici d'Apollon. | Voila toute la politique | De notre moderne Solon." 39594.3.23* 2 v.

‡*Les leçons de la sagesse* (Paris, 1750-1751). Inv.7.6; 2.2.7.37-39; C46 (under Debonnaire) <651010, h> Front flyleaves, 21-page life of the author in TH's hand; "This Book was bought by Me upon my Travells, at Paris in May 1753. TH. The preceding account of the Author was sent Me in June 1753 from Paris, by my old & worthy Friend L'Abbé — at my particular Request." *EC75.H7267.Zz750b 3 v.

BONNET, CHARLES, 1720-1793. *Contemplation de la nature* (Amsterdam, 1769). Inv.13.13; 6.1.4.6-7; C71 <700926, h> *FC7.B6437.764cd 2 v.

BORCH, OLE, 1626-1690. *Cogitationes de variis Latinae linguae aetatibus* (Copenhagen, 1675). 4.3.7.10; C135 (under Borrichius, Olaus) <nd, v> 5275.10*

BORLASE, WILLIAM, 1695-1772.
‡*The natural history of Cornwall* (Oxford, 1758). Inv.16.74; 2.4.2.1; B7, C71 <670511, h> On flyleaf: "Books of this kind, well considered, may be of singular use, benefit to Colonists; and so it is hoped they will prove, especially, to the Good and ingenuous People of New England! T·H." On title page: "The knowledge, sense, method, beneficence, of this Book is extraordinary!" f*EC75.H7267.Zz758b

‡*Observations on the antiquities … of … Cornwall* (Oxford, 1754). Inv.16.73; 2.1.2.18; C3 <670511, h> On flyleaf: "— Antiquaries, whose labors are useful & laudable — John Milton of Ref[ormation]." Br 3809.9 F*

BOSCOVIC, RUDYER JOSIP, 1711-1787. *De solis ac lunae defectibus libri v* (London, 1760). Inv.5.71; 2.2.4.6; C141 <6506.., h> *ZSC7.B6522.760d (B) A second copy, Inv.16.81; 2.2.4.11 <670511?>, not located.

BOSIO, ANTONIO, 1575-1629. ‡*Roma subterranea* (Rome, 1651). Inv.17.1; 4.3.1.9-10; C3 (under Aringhi) <68…., v> On title page of v. 1: "It is apprehended, the very learned, excellent Nathaniel Lardner D.D. travelled with G. Treby, as his Governor. T·H." The book once belonged to Sir George Treby, 1644?-1700. Arc 1015.202 F* 2 v.

BOSSE, ABRAHAM, 1602-1676. ‡*Sentimens sur la distinction des diverses manières de peinture* (Paris, 1649). Inv.5.73; 2.4.8.25; C9 <6506.., v> On flyleaf: "An ingenious, useful book." Typ 615.49.230

BOSWELL, JOHN, 1698-1757. *A method of study* (London, 1738). 4.3.7.11-12; B7, C106 <nd, h> Educ 7337.38* 2 v.

BOULANGER, NICOLAS ANTOINE, 1722-1759.
L'antiquité dévoilée (Amsterdam, 1766). Inv.9.39; 4.3.8.25-27; C106 <680711, h> *FC7.B6637.766ab 3 v.

[Another copy] Inv.17.16; C106 <68…., h> *FC7.B6637.766a 3 v.

Dissertations sur Elie et Enoch ([Amsterdam, 1764]). Inv.17.28; 4.4.8.27; C106 <68…., h> *FC7.B6637.764d (B)

Recherches sur l'origine du despotisme ([Paris?], 1763). Inv.2.81; 2.1.8.38; C82 <6410.., h> *FC7.B6637.761rd

[Another edition] ([Amsterdam?], 1766). Inv.17.27; 4.4.8.12; C82 <68...., h> *FC7.B6637.761rh

BOULTER, HUGH, 1672-1742. *Letters written by His Excellency* (Oxford, 1769, 1770). Inv.13.1; 6.1.7.1-2; C145 <700926, h> *EC7.B6656.770ℓ 2 v.

BOWEN, EMANUEL, d. 1767. *A complete system of geography* (London, 1747). 4.1.1.8-9; B8, C33 & C248 <nd, v.1 rebound (1986), v.2 h (rebacked)> Map Collection, Pusey Library, MAP-LC G114.C77 F* 2 v.

BOWMAN, THOMAS. *A review of the doctrines of the reformation* (Norwich, 1768). Inv.14.36; 6.1.6.45; C157 <700926, h> C 6367.68*

BOWYER, WILLIAM, 1699-1777, *see* Trapp, Joseph

BOYLE, CHARLES, *see* Orrery, Charles Boyle, earl of

BOXHORN, MARCUS ZUERIUS, 1612-1653.
De majestate regum principumque ac praerogativa (Leiden, 1699). Inv.3.116; 2.3.8.2; C244 <641208, v> *EC65.M6427.R652d

‡*Metamorphosis Anglorum* ([The Hague?], 1653). Inv.2.111; 2.2.8.51; not in C <6410.., h> On flyleaf: "Salus Populi suprema lex esto T·Hollis." Br 306.53.3*

BOZE, CLAUDE GROS DE, 1680-1753. *Explication d'une inscription antique* (Paris, 1705). 4.4.7.26; C3 <nd, h> AH 8514.5*

BRACTON, HENRY DE, d. 1268. *De legibus et consuetudine Angliae* (London, 1640). Inv.16.89; 2.3.5.13; C79 <670511, r> On flyleaf: "T·H was glad to give a guinea unbound for this copy; yet hopes to see, before it is long, all our antient and noble Law-writers reprinted." On title page: "Ut spargam. T·H." *EC75.H7267.Zz640b

BRADY, ROBERT, 1627?-1700. ‡*A full and clear answer* (London, 1681). Inv.17.29; 3.8.24; C83 <68...., h> TH identifies author. *EC65.B7298.681f

BRAMSTON, JAMES, 1694?-1744. *The art of politicks* (London, 1731). Inv.14.22; 6.1.7.17; C238 <700926, h> *EC7.M6942.727t

BRAMSTON, SIR JOHN, 1574-1655. *Articles of accusation* [concerning ship money] ([London], 1641). Inv.10.50 (part); 4.4.7.2; not in C <680712, h> *EC65.G798P.B641t

BRANDT, GEERAERT, 1626-1685.
The history of the Reformation [in the Low Countries] (London, 1720-1723). Inv.1.1; 2.2.1.1-4; C65 <631024, h> Neth 2251.1 F* 4 v.

An abridgement of ... [the] history of the Reformation (London, 1725). Inv.4.81; 2.1.6.30-31; B8, C65 <641212?, h> *NC6.B7343.Eg725ℓ

BRAUN, JOSEF ADAM, 1712-1768. *De admirande frigore artificiali* (St. Petersburg, [1760]). 6.1.3.29; C215 <nd, h> *EC75.H7267.Zz769t

Brevis ad artem cogitandi introductio (London, 1770). Inv.14.35; 6.2.8.13; C88 <700926, h> *EC75.P4288.770b

BRICE, ANDREW, 1690-1773.

The grand gazetteer, or topographic dictionary (Exeter, 1760). Inv.3.69; 2.4.1.10; C48 <641208, r> Title page wanting; title derived from C. Widener Geog 577.60 F

An Exmoor scolding (Exeter, [1763?]). Not in C <nd, 1847 pamphlet binding> *EC7.B7613.727ef

BRIDGES, JOHN, 1666-1724.

†*Bibliothecae Bridgesianae catalogus* (London, 1725). Inv.2.94 *or* Inv.13.16; 2.1.6.30; not in C <6410.. *or* 700926, h> *EC75.H7267.Zz725c Second copy not located.

‡*A brief account of many of the prosecutions of the people call'd Quakers* (London, 1736). Inv.4.83; 2.4.7.3; C68 (under Quakers) <641212?, h> On flyleaf: "In 'The Pillars of Priestcraft shaken' is preserved a master tract in behalf of the Quakers & of Liberty; which was written by the late Lord Hervey, in answer to an artful tract of the late Dr. Sherlock's, then B. of Salisbury, intitled 'The Country Parson's Plea.'" C 8307.36.50*

A brief dissertation on funeral solemnities (London, 1745). Inv.2.65 (part); 2.1.6.13; C224 (under Funeral) <6410.., h> Sometimes attributed to Matthew and Micaiah Towgood. *EC7.St932.731d

BRIET, PHILIPPE, 1601-1668. *Parallela geographiae veteris & novae* (Paris, 1648). 4.5.10-12; C48 <nd, h> Geog 3106.48* 3 v.

BRINDLEY, JAMES, 1716-1772. *The history of inland navigations* (London, 1766). 2.4.6.5-6; C119 Declared lost.

BRISSON, BARNABÉ, 1531-1591. *Opera minora* (Leiden, 1749). 4.3.3.13; C77 <nd, h> 7137.49 F*

Britannicarum gentium historiae antiquae scriptores tres, ed. Charles Bertram (Copenhagen, 1757). 4.1.8.5; C3 <nd, h> The text is a forgery by Bertram. *EC75.H7267.Zz758b2 (A)

[Another copy] Inv.4.125; 2.1.8.3; C3 <641212?, h> *EC75.H7267.Zz758b2 (B)

†*British liberties* (London, 1766). 4.1.7.10; C84 <nd, h> Br 67.25*

Britton. The second edition (London, 1640). Inv.16.43; C79 <670511, h> STC 3804

BROOKE, FULKE GREVILLE, BARON, *see* Greville, Fulke, baron Brooke

BROUGHTON, THOMAS, 1704-1774. *A defence of the commonly-received doctrine of the human soul* (Bristol, 1766). Inv.8.43; 2.3.7.19; C138 <661001, h> C 1134.81.35*

BROWN, JOHN, 1715-1766.

‡*An estimate of the manners* (London, 1758). Inv.2.67; 2.3.7.3; C107 <6410.., r> On title page: "iohn brown d.d." *EC75.B8136.757eℓ

‡*On religious liberty* (London, 1763). 4.1.4.13; not in C <nd, h> Heavily annotated. *EC75.R4375.763ℓ

†‡*Thoughts on civil liberty, on licentiousness and faction* (London, 1765). 2.4.6.36; C107 <nd, h> The tools are inverted on this binding, indicating disapproval. On title page: "By Dʳ Brown, Vicar of Newcastle." Gov 512.21.2*

BROWNE, ISAAC HAWKINS, 1705-1760.
A pipe of tobacco (London, 1736). Inv.14.24; 6.1.7.17; C238 <700926, h>
*EC7.M6942.727t

[Another edition] (London, 1744). 4.2.7.16; C238 <nd, h> *EC75.H7267.Zz740m

Poems upon various subjects (London, 1768). Inv.10.21; 4.3.5.20; C141 <680712, r>
*EC7.B8168.768pb (B)

BROWNE, SIR THOMAS, 1605-1682. *Christian morals* [with biographical preface by Samuel
Johnson] (London, 1756). Inv.4.120; 2.1.8.24; C156 <641212?, r> *EC75.J6371.A756c

BROWNE, THOMAS, 1654?-1741. *Miracles work's* [*sic*] *above and contrary to nature* (London,
1683). Inv.4.42; 2.4.7.15; C182 (under title) <641212?, h> *EC65.B8186.683m

BRUCKNER, JOHN, 1726-1804. *A philosophical survey of animal creation* (London, 1768).
6.2.8.16; B6 & C104 (under Animal creation) <nd, h> KC 17879*

BRUZEN DE LA MARTINIÈRE, ANTOINE AUGUSTIN, 1662-1746. *Le grand dictionnaire
géographique* (The Hague, 1726-1739). Inv.8.3; 4.1.2.11-20; C49 <661001, h (v.1,5,6 r)>
Geog 577.26 F* 10 v.

BRYANT, JACOB, 1715-1804. *Observations and inquiries relating to various parts of ancient
history* (Cambridge, 1767). 4.1.4.17; C107 <nd, h> *EC75.B8411.767o

BUCHANAN, GEORGE, 1506-1582.
Appendix to The history of Scotland [Probably a fragment of a larger volume; missing title
page supplied] ([London?], 1721). 4.2.7.21; not in C <nd, r> Br 8540.30.5* (A)

De jure regno apud Scotos, or, A dialogue (London, 1689). 2.2.5.16; C245 <671209?, h>
*EC75.H7267.Zz691t

A detection of the actions of Mary Queen of Scots ([London?], 1721). 4.2.7.21; C213
<nd, r> TH may have given two copies. Br 8540.30.5* (A)

Opera omnia, ed. Thomas Ruddiman (Leiden, 1725). Inv.2.26; 2.3.4.11-12; C107
<6410.., h> KG 11696* 2 v.

‡*Rerum Scoticorum historia* (Edinburgh, 1582). Inv.3.83; 4.3.4.21; C55 <641208, 16th-17th c.
armorial binding> On title page: "Ut spargam." STC 3991

BUCHANAN, JAMES. *Plan of an English grammar-school education* (London, 1770). C220
<nd, r> Gutman Library Educ 2268.3

BUCKLEY, SAMUEL, 1674?-1741.
A letter to Dr. Mead, concerning a new edition of Thuanus's History (London, 1728).
2.3.8.8; C107 <nd, r> H 706.04.13*

A second letter to Dr. Mead (London, 1728). 2.3.8.8; C107 <nd,r> H 706.04.13*

A third letter to Dr. Mead (London, 1730). 2.3.8.8; C107 <nd, r> H 706.04.13*

BULIFON, ANTONIO, 1649-ca. 1707. ‡*Lettere memorabili* (Pezzoli & Naples, 1698 & 1697).
Inv.6.11; 2.2.7.40-43; C107 <650817, r> On flyleaf of v. 4: "Lettere curiossis. rariss. T·H."
*IC6.B8723.693ℓba 4 v.

BULLET, JEAN-BAPTISTE, 1699-1775. *Mémoires sur la langue celtique* (Besançon, 1754-1760). Inv.17.3; 4.4.1.17-19; C135 <68…., h> *FC7.B8742.754m 3 v.

BULSTRODE, SIR RICHARD, 1610-1711. *Miscellaneous essays* (London, 1715). Inv.13.25; 6.1.7.21; C107 <700926, r> 15492.50*

BUNON, ROBERT, 1702-1748. ‡*Expériences et demonstrations faites à l'Hôpital de la Salpêtriere* (Paris, 1746). 4.1.8.34; C97 <nd, h> On flyleaf: "A singular and rare book." *EC75.H7267.Zz756b

BUNYAN, JOHN, 1628-1688. *The pilgrim's progress,* "22^d ed." (London, 1728). 4.1.7.38; C158 <nd, h> 15492.44*

BUONAMICI, CASTRUCCIO, CONTE, 1710-1761. ‡*Commentariorum de bello italico* (Leiden, 1750-1751). Inv.3.115; 4.1.7.36-38; C55 <641208, v> On flyleaf: "T·H bought at Naples the 15th. March 1752." Ital 457.1* (A) 3 v.

BUONANNI, FILIPPO, 1638-1725. *Numismata Pontificum Romanorum* (Rome, 1699). C129 <nd, r> Arc 1485.1 F*

BUONARROTI, FILIPPO, 1661-1733. †*Osservazioni sopra alcuni frammenti di vasi* (Florence, 1716). Inv.2.17; 2.2.4.2; 6 (under title) <6410.., h> The apparent source of TH's Psyche tool: plate xxviii and p.196-197. Typ 725.16.246 (B)

BUONMATTEI, BENEDETTO, 1581-1647. ‡*Della lingua toscana libri due* (Venice, 1735). 4.3.5.23; C51 <nd, v> On flyleaf: "T·H bought at Naples in July 1751" ; "This book is highly esteemed among the learned in Italy." 7281.6*

BURGES, CORNELIUS, 1589?-1665. ‡*The Presbyterians not guilty* (London, 1713). 2.1.7.20; C221 (under Charles I) <671209?, h> At the end: "N.B. The Notes are both clever & useful." *EC65.W4574.653cb (B)

BURGHLEY, WILLIAM CECIL, BARON, 1520-1598.
A collection of state papers, ed. Samuel Haynes (London, 1740). Inv.16.5; 2.4.2.14-15; C145 <670511, r> Br 1635.14 F* 2 v.

La copie d'une lettre envoyée d'Angleterre à Dom Bernardin de Mendoze ([London?], 1588). 2.1.8.26; C249 (under Mendoze) <671209?, h> Fr 1232.3.10*

BURIGNY, JEAN LEVESQUE, 1692-1785. *Histoire de la philosophie payenne* (The Hague, 1724). Inv.12.37; 6.1.8.49; C120 <690818> Filmed by "Harvard College Library Imaging"; the original Hollis gift not located. Master Microforms: Film Mas 2557

BURKE, EDMUND, 1729-1797.
Observations on a late state of the nation (London, 1769). 6.3.2.14; C250 (under Nation) <nd, xt> Annotation by Amos Adams, Harvard College Librarian: "N:B. The State of the Nation on which these Observations were made is contained in a Volume of Pamphlet[s]. Octavo. Letter'd Colonies Vol: 1…." *EC75.B9171.769o

A philosophical enquiry into the origin of our ideas of the sublime and beautiful (London, 1761). 4.1.7.43; C93 <nd, r> Harvard Depository Phil 8402.14.2

Storia degli stabilimenti europei in America (Venice, 1763). 4.4.7.6-7; not in C <nd, h> US 2002.15.15* 2 v.

BURLAMAQUI, JEAN JACQUES, 1694-1748. *Principes du droit naturel* (Geneva, 1748). Inv.4.123; 2.1.8.14; C83 <641212?, r> *FC7.B943.741pc

BURMAN, PIETER, 1668-1741. *Vectigalia populi Romani* (Leiden, 1734). 4.4.4.23; C3 <nd, r> AH 7107.34*

BURN, RICHARD, 1709-1785.

‡*Ecclesiastical law* (London, 1763). 4.1.4.9-10; B8, C78 <nd, r> Note at end on the author, the dedication, and a passage on the preceding page seen but not recorded by C. N. Greenough, probably discarded in rebinding. Br 327.63* 2 v.

The history of the poor laws (London, 1764). 4.1.7.9; C29 <nd, r> Soc 2115.56*

The justice of the peace, and parish officer (London, 1766). 4.1.7.2-5; C79 <nd, r> Law School: Rare UK 997.7 BUR 4 v.

BURNET, GILBERT, 1643-1715.

‡*The history of the reformation* (London, 1681-1683-1685). Inv.16.33; 2.2.3.1-3; C65 <670511, h> On title page: "Ut spargam T·H." *EC65.B9343.679hb 3 v.

The history of the rights of princes (London, 1682). 6.1.7.47; C107 <nd, h> *EC75.H7267.Zz682b

‡[Another copy] Inv.4.181; 4.7.7.48; C107 <641212?, h> On title page: "Ut spargam T·H." C 11323.6*

‡*Some letters* [*Travels in France*] (Rotterdam, 1686 [i.e., Lyons? 1687]). Inv.4.139; 2.3.8.5; C73 <641212?, v> On flyleaf: "Given me at Naples, 1752, by Don Francesco Valetta, an accomplished, excellent Gentleman, a friend of the Characteristic Earl of Shaftesbury." *EC65.B9343.687s2f

Three letters concerning the present state of Italy ([London], 1688). Inv.4.117; 2.4.7.40; C73 (under Supplement to ditto.) <641212?, h> *EC65.B9343.688t

BURRIDGE, EZEKIEL.

‡*Historiæ nuperæ rerum mutationis in Anglia* (London, 1697). Inv.9.42; 2.2.6.18; C55 <680711, h> On title page: "Ut spargam. T·H." *EC75.H7267.Zz697b (A)

‡[Another copy] Inv.5.39; 4.3.7.40; C55 <6506.., h > On title page: "Ut spargam. T·H." *EC75/H7267.Zz697b (B)

BURROUGHS, JOSEPH, 1685-1761. *The popish doctrine of auricular confession* (London, 1735). Not in C <6506.., h> *EC75.H7267.Zz735s

See also Enty, John

BURTHOGGE, RICHARD, 1638-ca. 1700.

Christianity a revealed mystery (London, 1755). Inv.4.99 (part); 2.2.6.27; C265 <641212?, h> *EC65.B9528.694c

An essay upon reason (London, 1694). Inv.4.99 (part); 2.2.6.27; C265 <641212?, h> *EC65.B9528.694c

Of the soul of the world (London, 1699). Inv.4.99 (part); 2.2.6.27; C265 <641212?, h> *EC65.B9528.694c

Organum vetus & novum (London, 1678). Inv.4.93 (part); 2.2.8.2; C265 <641212?, h>
*EC65.B9528.678o

Tagathon, or, Divine goodness explicated (London, 1672). Inv.4.93 (part); 2.2.8.2; not in C
<641212?, h> *EC65.B9528.678o

BURTON, EDMUND, fl. 1763. *Antient characters deduced from classical remains* (London,
1763). Inv.14.38; 6.1.8.1; C108 <700926, h> Class 2027.63*

BURTON, JOHN, 1696-1771. ‡*Ad amicum epistola* (Oxford, 1768). Inv.14.55 (part; under
Commentariolus); 6.1.6.22; C207 <700926, h> TH lists contents of tract volume on
flyleaf. *EC7.Se243.B767 (B)

BUTLER, JOSEPH, 1692-1752. *The analogy of religion* (London, 1736). 2.4.3.24; B8, C159
<nd, h> *EC75.H7267.Zz736b

BUXTORF, JOHANN, 1564-1629.

‡*Grammaticæ chaldaicæ et syriacæ libri III* (Basel, 1615). 4.2.8.35; C51 <nd, h> On title
page: "Ut spargam. T·H." 3225.15*

De abbreviaturis Hebraicis (Basel, 1613). 4.2.8.21; C132 (misdated 1636) Original Hollis
gift not located.

Liber Cosri, ed. Buxtorf (Basel, 1660). 4.2.7.25; C132 (under Cosri) <nd, h>
*GC6.B9866.660ℓ (B)

Synagoga Judaica (Basel, 1661). 4.3.8.35; C69 <nd, v> *GC6.B9865.Ef541ℓb (B)

BYROM, JOHN, 1692-1763. *A full and true account of a horrid and barbarous robbery*
(London, 1728). 4.2.3.22; C238 (under Cambridge coach) <nd, h>
f*EC75.H7267.Zz740p

BYTHNER, VICTORINUS, 1605-1670.
Amir qesar rav, Manipulis messis magnae (London, 1639). 4.2.8.34; not in C <nd, r>
STC 4259

Leshon imudim, Lingua eruditorum (Oxford, 1638). 4.2.8.34; C51 <nd, r> STC 4259

C

Cabala, sive Scrinia sacra (London, 1691). Inv.16.68; 2.2.3.19; C145 <670511, r>
f*EC65.A100.654cc

CÆSAR, JULIUS. ‡*Commentari di C.Giulio Cesare*, tr. Andrea Palladio (Venice, 1575).
4.4.5.26; C120 (under Palladio) <nd, h> On flyleaf: "Very Rare, Very Curious, Very
useful, it might be, to the Trained Bands of Massachusetts." *OLC.C116.Ei575

CAIUS, THOMAS, d. 1572. *Vindiciae antiquitatis academiae Oxoniensis*, ed. Thomas Hearne
(Oxford, 1730). 4.1.6.27-28; C5 <nd, h> Educ 4030.6* 2 v.

CALAMY, EDMUND, 1671-1732.
A defence of moderate non-comformity (London, 1703-1705). Inv.12.82; 6.1.7.39-41; C159
<690818> Original Hollis gift not located.

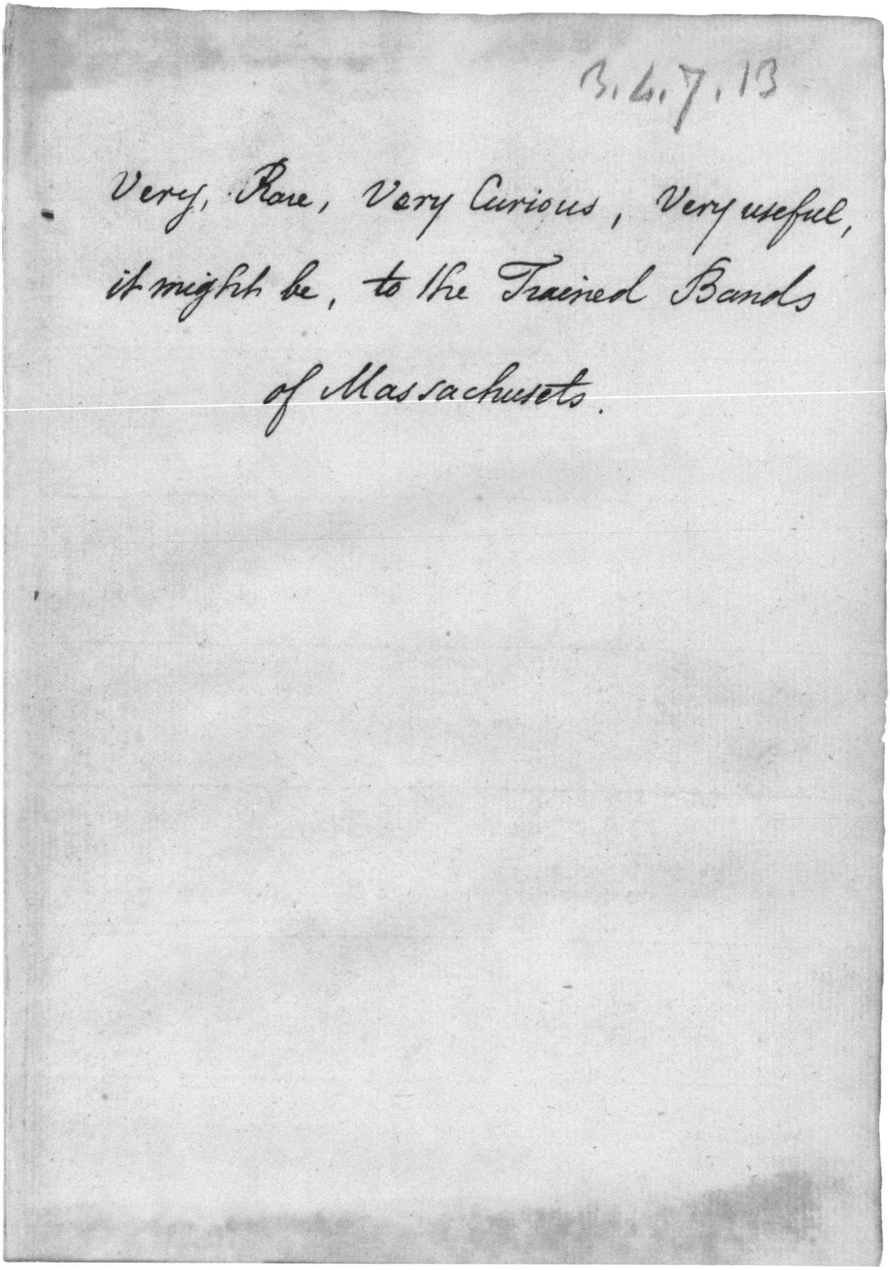

3.4.7.13

Very, Rare, Very Curious, Very useful,
it might be, to the Trained Bands
of Massachusets.

Figure 4. Julius Caesar, *Commentari* (Venice, 1575). On the front flyleaf, TH describes the value of his gift to Harvard students and to Massachusetts citizens. See introduction p. 21, and Checklist, p. 59. *OLC.C116.Ei575 22 cm.

‡*A letter to Mr. Archdeacon Echard* (London, 1718). Inv.12.81; 6.1.6.42; C213 <690818, r> On flyleaf: "Books of this kind, however curious and important, are becoming every day more scarce — for many reasons. T·H." *EC7.C1253.718ℓ

CALDWELL, SIR JAMES, BART., d. 1784. *Debates relative to the affairs of Ireland: in the years 1763 and 1764* (London, 1766). Inv.9.20 *or* Inv.17.24; not in C <68…. *or* 680711, h> Br 12020.3* 2 v. Second copy not located.

CALVIN, JEAN, 1509-1564. *Epistle both of godly consolacion* (London, 1550). 2.2.8.28; C266 <nd, h> STC 4407.5

CALZOLARI, FRANCESCO, fl. 1622, *see* Ceruti, Benedetto

CAMDEN, WILLIAM, 1551-1623.
Britannia (London, 1607). Inv.16.58; 2.1.3.1; C48 <670511, r> STC 4508 F (A)

[Another edition] tr. by Edmund Gibson (London, 1722). Inv.16.32; 2.2.2.18-19; B8, C48 <670511, h> Br 3615.90.8 F* 2 v.

Epistolae (London, 1691). 4.4.7.8; C108 <nd, h> Br 3615.90.9*

Remaines (London, 1629). 2.1.7.12; C7 (under title) <nd, calf> STC 4524

CAMPBELL, JOHN, 1708-1775.
‡*Liberty and right* (London, 1747). 4.2.7.11; C249 <nd, r> On title page: "very rare. By Dr. Campbell." *EC75.C1527.747ℓ

‡[Another copy] 2.3.7.29; C249 <6410.., h> On title page: "very curious, very rare." *EC75.H7267.Zz759m

CANINI, GIOVANNI ANGELO, 1617-1666. ‡*Iconografia* (Rome, 1669). Inv.4.4; 2.3.3.11; C3 <641212?, h> On flyleaf: "The original Manuscript & Designs for this Book were bought by my most ingenious & worthy Friend Laurence Natter, at Lord Oxford's Sale, & were given to Me by Him April 14, 1755, being my Birth Day. TH." Four of the engravings bear annotations by TH concerning subject or provenance. Typ 625.69.259 F (B)

CAPACCIO, GIULIO CESARE, 1552-1634.
Balnearum, quae Neapoli, Puteolis, Baiis, Pithecusis … extant virtutes (Naples, 1604). Inv.3.98 (part); 4.4.6.6; not in C <641208, h> Ital 4101.1*

Neapolitanae historiae (Naples, 1607). Inv.3.99; 2.3.5.18; C4 <641208, r> Ital 3823.1* v. 1 only

Puteolana historia (Naples, 1604). Inv.3.98 (part); 2.3.5.19; C4 <641208, h> Ital 4101.1*

CARACCI, ANNIBALE, 1560-1609. *Scuola perfetta per imparare a disegnare tutto il corpo humano* (Rome, [n.d.]). 4.4.3.4; C33 <nd, r> FA 6470.201 F*

CARO, ANNIBALE, 1507-1566. *Rime* (Venice, 1572). Inv.3.117; 4.4.6.11; C141 <641208, v> *IC5.C2200.569rb

CARPENTIER, P., 1697-1767. *Glossarium novum* (Paris, 1766). 4.2.1.9-12; C202 <nd, h> 5291.10 F* 4 v.

CARPZOV, JOHANN BENEDIKT, 1639-1699. *Dissertatio de vaca rufa* (Leipzig, 1692). 4.4.6.24; C266 (under Carpzovius) <nd, v> *GC6.W1235.B692d

CARRINGTON, JOHN, d. 1701. *The Lancashire Levite rebuk'd* (London, 1698). 4.4.6.18; C306 (under title) <680930, r> *EC65.C2355.698ℓ

CARTARI, VINCENZO, b. ca. 1500. ‡*Imagini delle dei de gl'antichi* (Venice, 1574). 4.3.5.24; C4 <nd, v> On flyleaf: "TH bought at Naples in Feb: 1752 of p. Pancrazi." *IC5.C2418.556ia

CASAS, BARTOLOME DE LAS, 1474-1566. *The tears of the Indians* (London, 1656). Inv.4.166; 2.2.7.31; C61 (under Phillips, John) <641212?, h> US 2522.2.105*

CASAUBON, MERIC, 1599-1671.
De quatuor linguis commentationis (London, 1650). Inv.4.198; 2.2.8.29 *or* 4.2.8.37; C135 (misdated 1750) <641212?, h> *EC65.C1648.650d Second copy not located.

Of credulity and incredulity (London, 1670). Inv.4.188; 2.1.8.40; C160 <641212?, h> *EC65.C2648.670o

‡*A treatise concerning enthusiasme* (London, 1656). Inv.3.137; 2.1.7.38; C160 <641208, r> On title page: "cited and recommended by Lord Shaftsbury in his Characteristics." *EC65.C2648.654tb

The case of non-residency (London, 1706). 2.1.6.14; C227 (under Non-residency considered) <671209?, h> *EC65.C5614.681c

The case of America and Great Britain (London, 1769). 6.1.6.30; C242 (under The case of Great Britain and America) <nd, h> US 2812.10*

CASSIUS DIO COCCEIANUS.
Delle guerre de romani (Venice, [1548]). Inv.3.152; 2.4.8.20; C14 (under Dio Cassius) <641208, v> *IC5.L55435.533dc

Historiae romanae qui supersunt (Hamburg, 1750-1752). 4.2.1.17-18; C14 <nd, r> Gd 22.15 F*

See also Augustus, Emperor of Rome

CASTELLION, SÉBASTIEN, 1515-1563. †‡*Contra libellum Calvini* ([Amsterdam?, 1612?]). Inv.4.153; 2.2.8.25; C160 (under Calvin) <641212?, h> On flyleaf: "Vide de libro hoc rarissimo, et vero ejus authore, Mosheimium in Historia Serveti p. 155; et Reimannum in catalogo bibl. theologicae p. 1043. Multo in hoc libello continentur de Serveto et Calvino, quae alia frustra quaerimus." C 1346.37*

CASTELL, EDMUND, 1606-1685. *Lexicon heptaglotton* (London, 1669). Inv.16.48; 2.2.1.5-6; C202 <670511, h> 2251.5 F* 2 v.

[Another copy] 2.1.1.13; C202 <64…., 17th c. blue morocco> On royal thick paper; presentation copy to Edward Hyde, 1st earl of Clarendon (1609-1674), with a matching set of Bishop Brian Walton's Polyglot Bible, *q.v.* 2251.10 PF*

CASTELLI, GABRIELE LANCILOTTO, PRINCIPE DI TORREMUZZA, 1727-1794. ‡*Siciliae et objacentium insularum veterum inscriptiorum nova collectio* (Palermo, 1769). Inv.15.1; 6.3.1.2; C7 (under title) <691129, h> On title page: "Princeps Torremuzzae"; at end: "The Prince of Torremuzza, who is excellent as accomplished, is the great Patron, of English, Scottish & Irish Travellers in Sicily. Palmal, aug. 12, 1769 T·H." Class 4887.69 F*

CATALANI, GIUSEPPE, 1698-1764. *Prefazioni … a gli Annali d'Italia* (Milan, 1756).
Inv.4.87; 2.4.7.48; not in C <641212?, boards with vellum spine> The 1790 catalogue
includes this with Muratori, *q.v.* *IC7.M9335.744ad v. 18

†‡*Catalogue des livres de la bibliothèque des … jesuites du Collège de Clermont* (Paris, 1764).
2.3.7.11; C32 (under Clermont) <nd, h> A sale catalogue, March 19, 1764. The tools are
inverted on this binding, indicating disapproval. On flyleaf, a quotation from Milton, *Of
reformation touching church-discipline*, concerning Loyola and the Jesuits.
*EC75.H7267.Zz764c

CATENA, GIROLAMO. *Vita del Papa Pio quinto* (Rome, 1587). 2.3.8.45; C26 <641208, v>
C 4489.6*

CATHOLIC CHURCH.
Breviarium Romanum (Paris, 1739). Inv.4.142-145; 2.3.8.27-30; C189 <641212?, black
morocco> C 9312.739* 4 v.

La constitution Unigenitus, avec des remarques ([n.p.], 1739). Inv.4.164; 2.1.8.36; C198
(under Unigenitus) <641212?, h> C 5567.39*

‡*Index librorum prohibitorum* (Rome, [1752]). Inv.2.105; 2.3.8.44; C116 <6410.., v> On
flyleaf: "Bought at Rome, ap. 14. 1752, by T·H then upon his Travels." B 7267.52*

Missale ad usum atque consuetudinem insignis ecclesiae saxonicae (Paris, 1515). Inv.8.54;
C182 <661001, h> C 9712.12*

Missale Romanum (Paris, 1739). Inv.4.147; 2.3.89.31; C189 <641212?, black morocco>
C 9401.739*

Pontificale Romanum (Venice, 1740). Inv.4.146; 2.3.8.26; C189 <641212?, black morocco>
C 9397.40*

Rituale Romanum (Leiden, 1726). Inv.4.148; 2.3.8.34; C189 <641212?, black morocco>
C 9443.726*

CATULLUS. *Epithalamio nelle nozze di Peleo i Teti* (Siena, 1751). Inv.3.120 (under Palermo;
part); 2.4.7.12; C238 <641208, h> *IC7.A100.B752h

CAVE, WILLIAM, 1637-1713. *Scriptorum ecclesiasticorum historia literaria* (Oxford, 1740-
1743). 4.1.2.21-22; C65 <nd, h> C 536.88.5F* 2 v.

CELLARIUS, CHRISTOPH, 1638-1707.
‡*Geographia antiqua* (London, 1731). Inv.3.121; 4.2.5.8; C48 <641208, h> On front flyleaf:
"T. Hollis 1737/8." Wanting the atlas volume. An early acquisition by the seventeen-
year-old Hollis. Map Collection, Pusey Library, MAP-LC G1033.C44 1731*

Isagogæ in linguam arabicam (Zeitz, 1686). 4.3.7.8; C51 <nd, h> 3234.38*

‡*Notitia orbis antiqui* (Cambridge, 1703-1706). Inv.8.31; 4.1.5.29-30; C48 <661001, v>
On front flyleaf of v. 1: "This is a valuable copy of a curious Work, on account of the
learned notes with which it abounds. These notes were written, it is believed, by the late
excellent Dr John Ward, Professor of Rhetoric at Gresham College etc. etc. etc. T·H."
Map Collection, Pusey Library, MAP-LC DE28.C3 1703 2 v.

CELSI, MINO. ‡*De haereticis capitali supplicio non afficiendis* ([n.p.], 1584). Inv.4.98;
2.1.8.43; C161 <641212?, h> On first front flyleaf: "Liber Thomae Hollis, Angli, Hospitii

Lincolniensis, Regalis et Antiquariorum Societatum Sodalis; libertatis, patriae, praestantistque eius constitutionis laudatissimo anno 1688 recuperatae amatoris studiosissimi." On second flyleaf: "Ex lib. Johann. Ward, LLD. Rhet. Prof. Gresh. Reg. et Ant. SS. Sodal. Mus. Brit. Cur." *EC75.H7267.Zz584c A second copy, Inv.12.40; C161 <690818>, not located.

CERRI, URBANO. ‡*An account of the state of the Roman-Catholic religion* (London, 1715). Inv.8.52 (under Steele); 2.4.7.19; C68 (under Steele, Sir Richard) <661001, h> On flyleaf: "There is reason to believe, that the Dedication was written by the accomplished, humorous, active, beneficent Sir Richard Steele, & not by Bishop Hoadly, as some late Writers have supposed. T·H   Pall Mall, may 26, 66." *EC7.H6502.715a

Certain ancient tracts concerning the management of landed property (London, 1767). 4.3.6.28; C1 & C125 (under Tracts, certain ancient) <nd, h> Agr 912.25*

CERUTI, BENEDETTO, d. 1620. *Musaeum Franc. Calceolari Iun.* ([Verona, 1622]). Inv.3.23; 2.1.4.26; not in C <641208, h> NH 346.22*

CHALONER, SIR THOMAS, 1521-1565. *De rep. anglorum instauranda libri decem* (London, 1579). Inv.3.123; 2.1.6.36; C83 <641208, h> STC 4938

CHAMBERLAYNE, JOHN, ed. ‡*Oratio Dominica* (Amsterdam, 1715). 4.2.6.2; C108 & C135 <nd, r> Formerly owned by William Bohun (signature on title page, with "Che trae l'uom del Sepolcro, ed in vita il serba. Petrarca." by TH. On flyleaf: "William Bohun Esq. was descended from an antient Family; bred a Lawyer; variously learned, active to extreme age; singular in his manners; but, mark Youths of Cambridge in New England! at all times, like his Brethren the English Lawyers, State Hacks many excepted, a strenuous Advocate for civil and religious Liberty. He published several things. Among them, that curious Tract, preserved since in the 'Cordials' by Rev. Mr. Baron, intitled, 'A Brief View of Ecclesiastical Jurisdiction in England.' In the Year 1742, he read private Lectures in English Law, at Lincoln's Inne, to the Writer of these Anecdotes, who has been willing to set them forth, in preservation to his Memory." *EC7.C3555.715o

CHAMBERS, EPHRAIM, 1680 (ca.)-1740. *Cyclopaedia, or, An universal dictionary of arts and sciences* (London, 1751-53). Inv.16.26; 2.2.1.10-13; B9, not in C <670511, h> Cyc 255 F*

CHAMBERS, SIR WILLIAM, 1726-1796. *A treatise on civil architecture* (London, 1759). Inv.2.1; 6.3.1.15; C8 <6410.., h> Fine Arts X Cage XFA1552.447.2 PF

CHANDLER, SAMUEL, 1693-1766.
Great-Britain's memorial against the Pretender (London, [1745]). 2.1.6.19; C229 (under Pretender) & C245 (under Britain) <67…., xt> *EC7.C3617.745gh

The history of persecution (London, 1736). Inv.16.95; 2.2.5.24; C65 <670511, h> C 2057.36*

The notes of the church considered (London, 1735). C267 <6506.., h> *EC75.H7267.Zz735s2

A second treatise on the notes of the church (London, 1735). Not in C <6506.., h> *EC75.H7267.Zz715s2

See also Estienne, Henri

CHANUT, PIERRE MARTIAL, *see* Council of Trent

CHAPPELOW, LEONARD, 1683-1768. *Elementa linguae arabicae* (London, 1730). 4.2.7.7; C51 <nd, h> 3234.24*

CHARLES I, KING OF ENGLAND.
A large declaration concerning the late tumults in Scotland (London, 1639). Inv.14.1; 6.1.2.20; C145 <700926, h> STC 21906

The kings most gracious messages for peace ([London], 1648). 2.2.8.3; C252 (under Symmons) <nd, h> *EC65.Sy653.647vb

‡*A true copy of the journal* [of his trial] (London, 1684). 4.2.3.3; C145 <661001, h> On engraved frontispiece portrait: "Vae Patriae casus Rex 'profanum vulgus' est! Floreat Libertas, Pereat Tyrannis! T·H." *EC75.H7267.Zz684g

‡*The works* (Aberdeen, 1766). Inv.11.11; 4.4.6.46-47; C108 <6809.., h> On front flyleaf of v. 1: "Floreat Libertas! Pereat Tyrannis! T·H." *EC.C3804E.73 2 v.

See also Tragicum theatrum actorum; Tryal of King Charles I; The speeches and prayers

CHARLEVOIX, PIERRE-FRANÇOIS-XAVIER DE, 1682-1761.
‡*Histoire et description générale de la Nouvelle France* (Paris, 1744). Inv.8.6; 4.1.4.25-27; C73 <661001, h> Laid down on back flyleaf of v.1, newspaper cutting from *St. James's chronicle* signed "Liberius" and annotated by TH: "April 5, 1766." Can 160.5* 3 v.

Histoire du Paraguay (Paris, 1756). 4.2.4.3-5; C73 <nd, h> Harvard Depository KG 108 3 v.

CHARPENTIER, JACQUES, 1524-1574. *Platonis cum Aristotele in universa philosophiae, comparatio* (Paris, 1573). Inv.15.7; 6.1.6.26; C93 <691129, r> Gp 83.235*

The charters of the following provinces [Virginia, Maryland, Connecticut, Rhode Island, Pennsylvania, Massachusetts Bay, and Georgia] (London, 1766). 4.2.5.23; C145 (under America) <nd, h> US 230.6*

CHAUNCY, CHARLES, 1705-1787.
‡*A letter to a friend* (London, 1767). Inv.9.50 (under Landaff); C269 <680711, calf (bound in Cambridge, Mass., 1768, by J. Smith, Jr.)> A long footnote printed on pp. 40-41 tells of Harvard College and the Hollis benevolence to it, but confuses several of the Thomas Hollises. *EC75.Ew367.767s

[Another edition] (London, 1768). 4.4.6.3; C269 <nd, h> Includes a Supplement by Caleb Fleming. Designed by TH and dated April 14, 1768. *AC7.C3954.767ℓb

[Another copy] Formerly bound in Tr 405*; rejected as a duplicate.

CHEYNE, GEORGE, 1673-1743. *An essay of health and long life* (London, 1724). 4.4.6.43; B9, C97 <nd, h> *EC7.C4294.724e

CHICOYNEAU, FRANÇOIS, 1672-1752. *A succinct account of the plague at Marseilles* (London, 1721). 4.2.7.16; C29 (under Plague) <nd, h> *EC75.H7267.Zz740m

CHIESA, LODOVICO DELLA, CONTE, 1568-1621. *Dell'historia di Piemonte* (Torino, 1608). Inv.3.53; 2.4.7.7; C55 <641208, r> *IC6.C4347.608h

CHILD, SIR JOSIAH, 1630-1699. *A new discourse of trade* (Glasgow, 1751). Inv.4.91; 2.2.8.7; C37 <641212?, r> Econ 213.3*

CHILLINGWORTH, WILLIAM, 1602-1644. *The works* (London, 1742). Inv.16.51; 2.4.2.8; C162 <670511, r> C 1155.9 F*

CHIMENTELLI, VALERIO, d. ca. 1670. *Marmor Pisani* (Bologna, 1666). Inv.3.94; 2.3.4.3; C4 <641208, v> Arc 1093.1*

CHIOCCO, ANDREA, d. 1634, *see* Ceruti, Benedetto

CHISHULL, EDMUND, 1671-1733. *Antiquitates asiaticæ; christianam æram antecedentes* (London, 1728). Inv.2.6, Inv.5.61; 2.2.1.18; C4 <6410.. *or* 6506.., h> f*EC7.C4476.728a Three sets recorded in the 1790 catalog; only one located.

CHONIATES, NICETAS, ca. 1140-1213.
Historia degli imperatori greci, tr. Giuseppe Horologgi (Venice, 1562). Inv.3.40; 2.3.5.22; C60 (under Niceta) <641208, calf> *MGC.Ac722.Ei562d (B)

Historia de gl'imperatori greci, tr. Lodovico Dolce (Venice, 1569). Inv.4.26; 2.4.4.37; C60 (under Niceta) <641212?, r> *MGC.Ac722.Ei569d

CHRIST, JOHANN FRIEDRICH, 1700-1756. *Dictionnaire des monogrammes* (Paris, 1750). Inv.9.24; 4.4.6.38; C108 <680711, h> Typ 715.50.279

‡*Christi servus etiam in summa captivitate liber* (London, 1653). 4.4.4.11; not in C <661001, h> A broadside concerning the imprisonment of William Prynne. On broadside: "This Print rare. T·H." f*EC65.P9567.644bb (A)

CHUBB, THOMAS, 1679-1747.
A collection of tracts (London, 1730). 4.1.5.16; C162 <nd, r> f*EC7.C4705.B730c

A discourse on miracles (London, 1741). 4.2.7.35; C271 <nd, r> *EC7.C4705.B747t

An enquiry concerning redemption (London, 1743). 4.2.7.35; C271 <nd, r> *EC7.C4705.B747t

An enquiry concerning the grounds and reasons ... on which two of our anniversary solemnities are founded (London, 1732). 4.3.7.24; C270-271 <nd, calf> Andover-Harvard S.C.R. 621 Chubb copy 2

An enquiry into the ground and foundation of religion (London, 1745). 4.2.7.35; C271 <nd, r> *EC7.C4705.B747t

Four dissertations (London, 1746). 4.2.7.35; C271 <nd, r> *EC7.C4705.B747t

The ground and foundation of morality (London, 1745). 4.2.7.35; C271 <nd, r> *EC7.C4705.B747t

The true gospel of Jesus Christ (London, 1739). 4.2.7.35; C270 <nd, r> *EC7.C4705.B747t

See also A short and faithful account of the life

CHURCH OF ENGLAND. *Codex juris ecclesiastici anglicani*, comp. Edmund Gibson (Oxford, 1761). Inv.6.4; 2.3.1.7-8; C78 <650817, h> C 11307.13.3 F* 2 v.

CHURCH OF SCOTLAND. *Canons* (Edinburgh, 1769). 6.1.3.18; not in C <700926, h> *EC75.H7267.Zz769d

CICERO.

The epistles of M. T. Cicero to M. Brutus, tr. Conyers Middleton (London, 1743 [i.e., 1742]). 4.4.6.5; C13 <nd, h> *EC75.H7267.Zz742m

The letters of Marcus Tullius Cicero, tr. William Melmoth (London, 1753). Inv.13.36; 6.1.4.16-18; C13 <700926, h> KPE 927* 3 v.

Opera, ed. Robert Estienne (Paris, 1538-1539). Inv.8.2; 4.2.2.2-3; C13 <661001, h> f*OLC.C485.538 (A) 4 v. in 2

†‡*Opera* (Paris, 1740-1742). Inv.8.25; 2.4.3.14-22; C13 <661001, h> On back flyleaf v. 1: "From the Library of the Jesuits, Professed, Ipsists at Paris, to that of Harvard College! And by the Intrigues of a Courtezan, not the Wisdom of a State! O strange uncertainty of human matters! Man of New England, Student, Read the curious account, of Mons. D'Alembert, 'Sur la destruction des Jesuites en France'; imitate the Learning, Temperance, Gravity, Diligence, Ingenuity, Politeness of the Jesuits; study, practice Virtue; & assert, at all times, with the noblest of Antiquity & the Author of these works, in sober stedfastness, even unto blood, salvs popvli svprema lex esto! Pall Mall, april 14, 1766. T·H·." *OLC.C485.740 (B) 9 v.

Tully's three books of offices, tr. Thomas Cockman (London,1732). 4.2.8.9; C13 <nd, r> Lc 39.607*

See also Middleton, Conyers

CIPRIANI, GIOVANNI BATTISTA, 1727-1785, *see Liberty prints*

CLAGETT, WILLIAM, 1646-1688. †*The present state of the controversie* (n.p., n.d.). Inv.12.17 (part); 6.1.5.26; not in C <690818, h> *EC7.W1377.B688c

CLARENDON, EDWARD HYDE, EARL OF, 1609-1674.

A catalogue of a collection of manuscripts (London, [1764]) Not in C <nd, marbled wrappers> Note (unidentified hand) on lot 102 (the first draft of Clarendon's History of the Rebellion): "This was bo't for the Ratcliffe (as were most of the M.S.) library Oxon, for 100 Guineas." B 1827.288*

‡*The history of the rebellion* (Oxford, 1702-1704-1759). 4.3.2.1-4; B9, C55 & C159 <67....?, calf > On half-title of v.1: "Edward Hyde, at length Earl of Clarendon, in the opinion of the writer, so far as he can judge, a hack Lawyer of commendam, of working, but not first-rate abilities; a wordy, partial Historian. See the Prose-works of his opposite, the man, who || in no respect, || would subscribe slave, the matchless John Milton. T·H aug. 7. 1767." *EC65.C5417.702h 4 v.

State papers collected by Edward, earl of Clarendon (Oxford, 1767). Inv.10.10; 4.3.1.14; C145 <680712, h> Br 1800.45.2 F* v. 1 only

CLARKE, JOHN, 1687-1734. *An essay upon study* (London, 1737). 4.3.8.28; B9, C108 <nd, h> Educ 7317.37*

CLARKE, SAMUEL, 1675-1729. *An essay towards demonstrating the immateriality ... of the soul* (London, 1760). 4.2.7.15; C234 (under Soul) <nd, h> *EC75.H7267.Zz746t

CLARKE, WILLIAM, 1696-1771. ‡*The connexion of the Roman, Saxon, and English coins* (London, 1767). 4.2.3.27; C129 <67...., h> On flyleaf: "T·H devotes, cheerfully on the perusal of it, this curious, valuable, and singularly learned Book, purchased for his own small Library, to the Public Library at Harvard College, in Cambridge, in New England. Palmal, june 2, 67." Arc 1538.1 F*

CLARKSON, DAVID, 1622-1686. *The case of protestants in England* (London, 1681). 2.1.6.14; C221 <671209?, h> *EC65.C5614.681c

CLAYTON, ROBERT, 1695-1758.
    The Bishop of Clogher's speech … on Monday, February 2, 1756 (London, 1757). 2.1.6.9; C273 (misdated 1756) <6410.., h> *EC7.C5797.B755t

    †[Another edition] (London, 1758). 2.1.5.39; C273 (not differentiated from the 1ˢᵗ edition) <6410.., h> *EC75.H7267.Zz752t

    A defence of the Essay on spirit (London, 1753). C272 <700926?, h> *EC75.J7285.753f

    The doctrine of the Trinity, as usually explained, inconsistent with Scripture and reason (London, 1754). 2.1.6.9; C273 <6410.., h> *EC7.C5797.B755t

    An essay on spirit (London, 1752). 2.2.5.6; C272 <6410.., h> *EC7.C5797.751ec

    Letters which passed between the Bishop of Clogher and Mr. William Penn (London, 1756). 2.1.6.9; C273 <6410.., h> *EC7.C5797.B755t

    Some thoughts on self-love (London, 1753). Inv.2.56; 2.1.6.9; C272 <6410.., h> *EC7.C5797.B755t

    A vindication of the histories (London, 1753). Inv.2.57; 2.2.5.5; C163 <6410.., h> C 1161.32*

CLELAND, JOHN, 1709-1789.
    ‡*Institutes of health* (London, 1761). Inv.12.91; 6.1.7.49; C108 <690818, h> On title page: "By Mr. Cleland!" *EC75.C5895.761i

    Specimen of an etimological vocabulary (London, 1768). 6.1.4.31; C135 (under Celtic. Specimen) <nd, h> 3274.5*

    ‡*View of a literary plan, for the retrieval of the antient Celtic* ([London, 1768?]) Inv.13.58 (misdated 1746); C235 (under Celtic) <700926, r > On flyleaf: "It is very doubtful whether this ingenious, learned, valuable wo[rk] will get published, the subscription of it proceeding slowly. T[H] has subscribed for a copy of it, with the hope of sending it to Harvard College, a help to those ingenuous, first-rate students, scholars, who, he makes no doubt, are forming there. The Celtic seems, clearly, To be the root of our own mother tongue, if not of every other." *EC75.H7267.Zz768c

    The way to things by words (London, 1716). 6.1.4.31; C135 (under Celtic) <nd, h> 3274.5*

    [Another copy] 4.2.6.26; C135 (under Celtic) <nd, r> 1233.25*

CLEONIDES. *Harmonicum introductorium* , ed. Georgio Valla ([Venice, 1497]). Inv.1.12 (under Vitruvius); 2.3.3.24; C109 <631024, v> The sole incunable among TH's gifts. An omnibus volume, including Vitruvius Pollio, *De architectura libri decem*; Sextus Julius Frontinus, *De aquæductibus*; and Angelo Poliziano, *In priora analytica prælectio.* Inc 5404

CLIFFORD, MARTIN, d. 1677.
‡*A treatise of humane reason* (London, 1675). Inv.2.68; 2.2.8.52; C93 <6410.., h> *EC65.C6125.674tb

[Another edition] (London, 1736). Inv.3.62; 2.4.5.4; C233 <641208, h> *EC75.H7267.Zz725m

CLIPSHAM, ROBERT. *The grand expedient for suppressing popery examined* (London, 1685). 4.3.8.4; C221 <680711, r> *EC65.Cl187.685g

CLUNY, ALEXANDER. *The American traveller* (London, 1769). Inv.13.20; 6.1.3.10-11; B9 & C73 <700926> Original Hollis gift not located.

CLUVER, PHILIPP, 1580-1622.
Introductio in universam geographicam (London, 1711). 4.2.5.34; C48 (under Cluverius) <nd, h> *GC6.C6275I.1711

†[Another edition] (Amsterdam, 1729). 4.2.4.25; C48 (under Cluverius) <nd, h> *GC6.C6275I.1729

COADE, GEORGE. ‡*A letter to a clergyman* (London, 1746). 2.2.8.8; C109 <671209?, h> On title page: "by Mr. Code of Exeter." Br 1815.210*

COCCHI, ANTONIO, 1695-1758.
‡*Del vitto Pitagorico per uso medicina* (Florence, 1743). Inv.4.37; 2.3.5.25; C97 <641212?, h> On flyleaf: "Antonio Cocchi, a very accomplished and excellent Gentleman." *IC7.C6403.743d

Graecorum chirurgici (Florence, 1754). Inv.12.2; 6.1.1.8; C97 <690818, r> *IC7.C6403.754g

COCKBURN, CATHERINE (TROTTER), 1679-1749. *The works … theological, moral, dramatic, and poetical,* ed. Thomas Birch (London, 1751). Inv.4.64; 2.1.5.32-33; B9, C109 <641212?, h> Phil 8877.13* 2 v.

COCKBURN, JOHN, 1652-1729.
Defence of Dr. Cockburn against the calumnies and libels (London, [17—?]). Inv.4.138 (part); 2.2.5.23; C213 (under Burnet, Gilbert) <641212?, h> *EC65.B9343.S736t

A specimen of some free and impartial remarks (London, [1724]). Inv.4.138 (part); 2.2.5.23; C213 & C214 <641212?, h> *EC65.B9343.S736t

Codex apocryphus Novi Testamenti, ed. Johann Albert Fabricius (Hamburg, 1719). 4.1.8.20-21; C111 <nd, h> C 594.5.2*

Codex pseudepigraphus Veteris Testamenti, ed. Johann Albert Fabricius (Hamburg, 1722-1723). 4.1.8.24-25; C111 <nd, h> C 588.5* (A)

Codex Theodosianus, ed. Jacques Godefroy (Leiden, 1665). 4.3.2.21-26; C77 <nd, h> AH 7202.5 F* 6 v.

COKE, SIR EDWARD, 1552-1634. *The first part of the Institutes of the laws of England* ([London], 1738). 4.4.3.14; not in C <nd, r> Br 166.28.25 F*

Collectio Pisaurensis omnium poematum, & carminum (Pisauri, 1766). Inv.10.11; 4.4.4.4-9; C18 <680712, h> Harvard Depository KG 10299 6 v.

A collection of cases, and other discourses (London, 1694). 6.4.2.14; C160   Original Hollis gift not located.

A collection of state tracts (London, 1705). C77 & C148 <64....?, h> *EC7.A100.B705c 3 v.

A collection of state-trials and proceedings (London, 1766). 2.3.2.22-25; not in C <nd, r> Harvard Depository Br 89.5.5 v. 7-10 only

See also Emlyn, Sollom

COLLINS, ANTHONY, 1676-1729.

‡*Bibliotheca Antonii Collins, Arm.* (London, 1730/1). C32 <700926, r> A sale catalogue. On back flyleaf: "This catalogue of the learned Anthony Collins is particularly valuable on account of the great number of Titles of tracts relating to Britan [*sic*] and Ireland which it containeth; together with the names of the Authors of those Tracts." *EC75.H7267.Zz725c

‡*A discourse of free-thinking* (London, 1713). Inv.5.32 (part); 2.1.8.1; not in C <6506.., h> TH lists contents of tract volume on a flyleaf. *EC65.B4465.B715f

A discourse of the grounds and reasons (London, 1737). Inv.16.96; 2.2.6.2; C163 <670511, h> Phil 1930.5.37*

A dissertation on liberty and necessity (London, 1729). 4.4.7.25; C233 <nd, h> *EC7.C6922.B729v

An historical and critical essay, on the thirty-nine articles (London, 1724). Inv.16.98; 2.2.6.4; C163 & C168 (under Essay) <670511, h> *EC7.C6922.724h

A letter to the Reverend Dr. Rogers (London, 1727). 4.4.7.25; C273 <nd, h> *EC7.C6922.B729v

‡*A philosophical inquiry concerning human liberty* (London, 1717). 4.1.8.11; C233 <nd, r> On title page: "By Ant. Collins Esq." Interleaved; with annotation facing p.86, a passage speaking of "asserters of liberty": "Sikes – Hobbes – & I myself." *EC7.C6922.717p

The scheme of literal prophecy considered (London, 1727). Inv.8.49; 2.2.6.3; C163 <661001, r> Phil 1930.5.50*   TH gave a second copy, Inv.16.97 <670511>, not located.

A vindication of the divine attributes (London, 1710). 4.4.7.25; C273 <nd, h> *EC7.C6922.B729v

See also Bridges, John

COLLINS, ARTHUR, 1682-1760, ed. *Letters of state in the reigns of Queen Mary, Queen Elizabeth* ... (London, 1746). Inv.2.8; C146 <6410.., r> Br 73.41 F* 2 v. in 1

COMMELINUS, HIERONYMUS, see *Rerum britannicarum ... scriptores vetustiores*

COMMISSION FOR THE REVIEW AND ALTERATION OF THE BOOK OF COMMON PRAYER. *To the Kings most excellent majesty. The due account* (London, 1661). Inv.14.11; 6.1.7.35; C308 <700926, r> *EC65.B3365.661ab

Committee Appointed to Manage the Contributions for Clothing
French Prisoners of War. *Proceedings* (London, 1760). 2.2.3.20; C223 <61...., h>
Typography designed by TH, preface written by Samuel Johnson at TH's request. Kept
in President Holyoke's house, thus survived the fire of January 1764.
f*EC75.H7267.Zz759b (A)

Common sense: or, The Englishman's journal (London, 1738). 4.2.8.11-12; C109 <nd, h>
Br 2025.38.324* 2 v.

A compleat history of French invasions (London, 1744). C246 <6712.., xt> *EC7.A100.744c

A complete collection of the genuine papers ... in the case of John Wilkes (Berlin [i.e.,
London?], 1769). Inv.12.38; 6.2.8.22; C148 <690818, mottled calf> *EC75.W6524.767cb

‡*A complete history of England*, ed. White Kennett (London, 1706). 4.4.1.1-3; C58 <nd, h> In
v.1, sig.a1ʳ of the preface: "Mark this Character of the matchless John Milton."
*EC75.H7167.Zz706c 3 v.

Conn, George, d. 1640. ‡*De duplici statu religionis apud Scotos* (Rome, 1628). Inv.2.60;
2.4.7.14; C65 (under Conaeus) <6410.., 17th c. calf> On front flyleaf, bibliographical
notes by Robert Grey (a 17th c. physician), J. Creyk, and: "Mr. Creyk was Librarian to the
Earl of Wimbledon. TH." *EC.C7621.628da

The connexion (London, 1681). 2.2.7.30; C146 <670815?, h> *EC65.A100.681cll

Consideratio causarum hujus belli ... in Bohemia (Libertate [*sic*], 1647). Inv.3.104; 4.1.7.12;
C106 (under Bohemia) <641208, h> Ger 1865.3*

†*Considerations on behalf of the colonists* (London, 1765). 4.1.7.22; C241 <nd, h>
*AC7.Ot464.765ab (B)

Constantin, Robert, d. 1605. ‡*Lexicon graecolatinum* ([Geneva], 1592). Inv.12.50;
6.1.1.18-19; C202 <690818, h> On flyleaf of v. 1: "A fine copy of a rare work. It was
purchased, on behalf of those first rate scholars, often the most ingenuous of men, which
he hopes and believes are at this time forming in Harvard College, at Cambridge in New
England, out of the library of the late Duke of Newcastle, and cost four guineas. Palmal,
ap. 14, 1769." 4211.26 F* 2 v.

†*Constitutional considerations on the power of Parliament to levy taxes on the North American
colonies* (London, 1766). 4.1.4.7; C241 (under Considerations rel. to the N. Amer.
colonies) <nd, h> *AC7.B6382.B766t

The constitutional right of the legislature of Great Britain to tax the British colonies (London,
1768). 6.1.6.30; C242 <nd, h> US 2812.10*

Contarini, Gasparo, 1484-1542. *Della republica et magistrati di Venetia* (Venice, 1591).
Inv.3.150; 2.2.8.4; C55 <641208, h> *IC5.C7672.Ei544df

The contrast, or The Rev. Dr. Thomas Nowell ... against Dr. Nowell (London, 1769). 6.1.4.30;
C320 (under Nowell) <nd, xt> *EC75.A100.769c3

La conversione dell'Inghilterra al cristianesimo (Lucca, 1748). Inv.3.140; not in C <641208, v>
Br 1700.38*

Cooke, Edward, captain. *A voyage to the south sea, and around the world* (London,
1712). 6.3.4.34; C74 Original Hollis gift not located.

COOPER, JOHN GILBERT, 1723-1769,

‡*Letters concerning taste* (London, 1757). Inv.12.77; 6.1.6.15; C109 <690818, h> On back flyleaf: "Mr. Cooper likewise wrote, 'The Life of Socrates.' London, printed for R. Dodsley, 1750, in oct. — 'Poems on several subjects.' London printed for R. & J. Dodsley, 1764, in duod. Mr. Cooper died sometime this spring 1769. He was a worthy, accomplished Gentleman, a good friend to Liberty, and the Writer had the honor to rank among his friends. June 24, 1769. T·H." Phil 8403.6*

‡*The life of Socrates* (London, 1750). Inv.7.16; 2.4.5.9; C26 <651010, r> On flyleaf: "Thomas Hollis is desirous of having the honor to present this book, written by an accomplished Gentleman, an Assertor of Liberty civil & religious, to the public Library of Harvard College, at Cambridge in N. England. Pall Mall, june 24, 1765." *EC75.H7267.Zz750c

Poems on several subjects (London, 1764). Inv.12.89; 6.1.8.19; C141 <690818, r> *EC75.C7865.B764p

CORBET, JOHN, 1620-1680. *An historicall relation of the military government* (London, 1645). Inv.10.48; 4.4.7.28; C56 <680712, h> *EC65.C8102.645h (B)

CORBETT, THOMAS, ca. 1687-1751. *An account of the expedition of the British fleet to Sicily* (London, 1739). 2.1.6.18; B8 (under Byng), C231 (under Sicily) <nd, r> *EC7.C8107.739a

CORNARO, LUIGI, 1475-1566. *Discourses on a sober and temperate life* (London, 1768). Inv.11.8; 4.4.6.45; B10, C109 <6809.., r> *IC5.C8145.558tℓ

Corpus juris civilis (Amsterdam, 1663). 4.3.2.5-6; not in C <nd, h> AH 7203.29 F* 2 v.

Corpus juris civilis. Institutiones, tr. George Harris (London, 1761). 4.2.4.1; C77 <nd, r> AH 7203.31*

CORRY, WILLIAM.

‡*Reflections upon liberty and necessity* (London, 1759). Inv.2.99 (part); 4.1.7.15; C93 <6410.., h> On second flyleaf: "The tracts in this volume were written by the late William Corry, Esq, & sent by him, anonymously [*sic*], to T·H." Phil 5752.3.2*

[Another edition] (London, 1761). Inv.2.99 (part); 4.1.7.15; C93 <6410.., h> Phil 5732.3.2*

Remarks upon a pamphlet intitled, Reflections upon liberty and necessity (London, 1763). Inv.2.99 (part); 4.1.7.15; not in C <6410.., h> Phil 5752.3.2*

CORYATE, GEORGE. *Descriptio Angliae, et descriptio Londini* (London, 1763). 4.1.4.18; not in C <nd, h> *EC75.H7145.761o

COSRI, *see* Buxtorf, Johann

COSTA, EMANUEL MENDES DA, 1717-1791, *see* Cronstedt, Axel

COSTANTINI, GIUSEPPE ANTONIO, ca. 1692-1722. *Lettere critiche* (Venice, 1751). Inv.3.132; 2.3.8.19-25; not in C <641208, v> *IC7.C8237.744ℓi 7 v.

COSTARD, GEORGE, 1710-1782. *Dissertationes II critico-sacrae* (Oxford, 1752). 4.3.7.21; C277 <nd, h> *EC75.H7267.Zz746o

COSTEKER, JOHN LITTLETON. †*The fine gentleman* (London, 1732). 2.4.2.2; C221 <6410.., h> *EC75.H7267.Zz734e

COTTON, SIR ROBERT, 1571-1631. *The histories of the lives and raignes of Henry the Third, and Henry the Fourth* (London, 1642). C56 <nd, r> *EC.C8293.627sd

COUNCIL OF TRENT (1545-1563).
Sacrosancti et œcumenici concilii Tridentini (Leiden, 1734). Inv.4.149; C65 (under Canones) <641212?, h> C 172.3*

Le saint concile de Trent (Paris, 1680). Inv.5.49; not in C <6506.., black morocco> C 172.9.3*

COURTILZ DE SANDRAS, GATIEN, 1644-1712. *La vie de Gaspard de Coligny* (Cologne, 1686). Inv.12.72; 6.4.8.31; C26 (under Colinius) <690818, marbled boards> *FC7.C8357.686v

COWARD, WILLIAM, 1657?-1725.
The grand essay (London, 1704). Inv.4.32 (part); 2.2.5.35; C277 <641212?, h> Phil 477.4*

Farther thoughts concerning human soul (London, 1703). Inv.4.32 (part); 2.2.5.35; C277 <641212?, h> Phil 477.4*

The just scrutiny (London, [1705]). Inv.4.88; 2.1.7.36; C164 <641212?, h> *EC7.C8389.705j

Second thoughts concerning the human soul (London, 1704). Inv.4.178; 2.2.5.34; C164 <641212?, h> *EC7.C8389.702sb

CRASSO, LORENZO, b. 1623. *Elogii d'huomini letterati* (Venice, 1666). Inv.3.34; 2.4.4.4-5; C26 <641208, r> Ital 6135.3* 2 v.

CRISPINUS, JOANNES, *see Actiones et monumenta martyrum*

CROCE, GIULIO CESARE, 1550-1609.
Cosmographia poetica (Verona, 1538). Inv.3.107 (part); 2.3.5.20; not in C <641208, v> *IC5.C8717.608dha

Descrizione della vita di Giulio Cesare Croce (Verona, 1738). Inv.3.107 (part); 2.3.5.20; C141 <641208, v> *IC5.C8717.608dha

Palazzo fantastico e bizarro (Verona, 1738). Inv.3.107 (part); 2.3.5.20; not in C <641208, v> *IC5.C8717.608dha

Processo ovvero esame di carnevale (Verona, 1738). Inv.3.107 (part); 2.3.5.20; not in C <641208, v> *IC5.C8717.608dha

Ricercata gentilissima delle bellezze del Furioso (Verona, 1738). Inv.3.107 (part); 2.3.5.20; not in C <641208, v> *IC5.C8717.608dha

Sogni fantastichi della notte (Verona, 1738). Inv.3.107 (part); 2.3.5.20; not in C <641208, v> *IC5.C8717.608dha

CROFT, HERBERT, 1603-1691.

‡*The naked truth, or, The true state of the primitive church* ([London], 1675). C211 (under Church. Complaints) <nd, xt> On title page: "By — Crofts [*sic*], Bishop of Hereford." On verso of title page: "For the character of this work see page 3ᵈ of Andrew Marvell's defence." *EC65.C8747.675n

A short discourse concerning the reading His Majesties late declaration (London, 1688). 2.1.6.14; C222 <671209?, h> *EC65.C5614.681c

CRONSTEDT, AXEL. *An essay towards a system of mineralogy*, tr. Gustav von Engelström, rev. Emanuel Mendes da Costa (London, 1770). Inv.13.52; 6.1.4.9; C36 <700926, h> KE 31965*

CRULL, JODOCUS, d. 1713? ‡*Denmark vindicated* (London, 1694). Inv.12.88; 6.1.7.44; C59 (under Molesworth) <690818, h> On flyleaf: "A poor answer to an excellent work. Scarce however." Scan 565.6*

CRUSIUS, LEWIS, 1701-1775. *The lives of the Roman poets* (London, 1753). Inv.8.53; B10, C27 <661001> Original Hollis gift not located.

CUDWORTH, RALPH, 1617-1688. †*The true intellectual system of the universe* (London, 1678). Inv.2.15; 2.3.3.8; C93 <6410.., h> f*EC65.C8938.678t (A)

See also Halliwell, Henry

CUFFE, HENRY, 1563-1601. *The differences of the ages of mans life* (London, 1607). Inv.4.173; 2.2.8.30; C109 <641212?, h> Bears the autograph signature of John Donne. STC 6103

CUMBERLAND, RICHARD, 1631-1718.
De legibus naturae (London, 1672). Inv.16.2; 2.2.5.20; C83 <670511, h> *EC65.C9102.672d

An essay towards the recovery of Jewish measures and weights (London, 1686). C129 <nd, r> *EC65.C9102.686e

‡*A letter to the Right Reverend the Bishop of O—d* (London, 1767). 4.4.6.27; C228 (under Oxford, Bishop of) <nd, marbled boards> On flyleaf: "Written, it is said, by the v[ery] ingenious Mr. Bentley, Son of the late Dr. Bentley." *EC75.B5628.752s

Origines gentium antiquissime (London, 1724). Inv.2.95; 2.1.6.27; C4 <6410.., h> *EC65.C9102.724o

CUPERUS, GISBERTUS, 1644-1716.
Apotheosis vel Consecratio Homeri (Amsterdam, 1683). 4.3.6.19; C4 <nd, h> *MC6.C9202.683a

Harpocrates, sive Explicatio imagunculae argenteae perantiquae (Utrecht, 1687). 4.3.6.25; C4 <nd, r> AH 866.9*

D

DALE, ANTONIUS VAN, 1638-1708.
De oraculis veterum ethnicorum (Amsterdam, 1700). 4.4.5.17; C8 (under Vandale) <nd, h> *NC6.D1523.683db

‡*Dissertatio super Aristea* (Amsterdam, 1705). 4.4.6.36; not in C <nd, h> Offset on verso of title page: TH's instructions to the binder. Ga 102.110.2*

Dissertationes de origine ac progressu idolatriae et superstitionum (Amsterdam, 1696). 4.4.5.29; C39 <nd, h> 24215.10*

Dissertationes IX (Amsterdam, 1702). 4.4.5.11; C8 (under Vandale) <nd, h> *NC6.D1523.702d

DALRYMPLE, ALEXANDER, 1737-1808.
An account of the discoveries made in the South Pacific Ocean (London, 1767 [i.e., 1769]). Inv.14.54; 6.5.1.24; C74 <700926, h> *EC75.D1694.769a

‡*An historical collection of the several voyages and discoveries in the South Pacific Ocean* (London, 1770). Inv.14.20; 6.1.2.29; C74 <700926, h> On flyleaf: "Mr. Dalrymple, is, himself, an eminent Explorer, in East Indies, and an ingenious, worthy, active, public-hearted Gentleman. He is likewise A Fellow of the Society of Antiquaries of London. T·H." Oc 124.3.8*

DALRYMPLE, SIR DAVID, 1726-1792.
A catalogue of the Lords of session (Edinburgh, 1767). 6.1.3.18; not in C <700926, h> *EC75.H7267.Zz769d

An examination of some of the arguments for the high antiquity of Regiam Majestatem (Edinburgh, 1769). 6.1.3.18; not in C <700926, h> *EC75.H7267.Zz769d

Historical memorials concerning the provincial council of Scottish clergy (Edinburgh, 1769). Inv.13.8; 6.1.3.18; C66 <700926, h> *EC75.H7267.Zz769d

Memorials and letters relating to the history of Britain [in the reign of James I] (Glasgow, 1766). 4.3.8.1 & 4.1.8.7; C58 (under James I) <nd, r> Br 1810.9* (A)

Memorials and letters [in the reign of Charles I] (Glasgow, 1766). 4.1.8.7; C55 (under Charles I) <nd, h> Br 1815.9*

See also Salisbury, Robert Cecil

DALRYMPLE, SIR JOHN, 1726-1810. *An essay towards a general history of feudal property* (London, 1759). 4.1.8.42; C83 <nd, r> H 7037.59*

DANTZ, JOHANN ANDREAS, 1654-1727.
Manductio viam ostendens compendiosam ad Ebrææ linguæ analysin (Jena, 1732). 4.1.8.23; C235 (wrongly dated 1632) <nd, r> 2263.3*

Literator Ebraeo-Chaldaeus (Jena, 1745). 4.1.8.22; C235 <nd, r> 2263.10*

DAVANZATI, BERNARDO, 1529-1606. ‡*Scisma d'Inghilterra* (Padua, 1727). Inv.3.130; 2.3.8.17; C110 <641208, v> On flyleaf: "T·H: bought at Naples in August 1751." *IC5.D2714.B727s

D'AVENANT, SIR WILLIAM, 1606-1668.
The first days entertainment (London, 1651). Inv.4.103; 2.2.8.44; C110 <641212?, h> *EC.D2727.656f

The preface to Gondibert ... with an answer ... by [Thomas] Hobbes (Paris, 1650). Inv.3.66; 2.2.8.61; C222 (under Discourse upon Gondibert) <641208, r> *EC.D2727.650pb

DAVIES, JOHN, 1570-1644. ‡*Antiquæ linguæ britannicæ ... dictionarium duplex* (London, 1631). Inv.13.17; 6.1.2.28; C203 <700926, h> On flyleaf: "A fine copy of a rare work. It cost a guinea. T·H is fond of sending Lexicons and Grammars to Harvard College, in aid of those first-rate Scholars, possibly half a dozen, the noblest of all men, who, he trusts, are now forming there." TH goes on to quote Milton's *The reason of church government*: "—These thoughts possest me, and these other, that if I were certain to write as men buy leases for three Lives and downward, there ought no regard be sooner had than to God's glory, by the honour and instruction of my Country." STC 6347

DAVIES, MYLES, 1662-1720. ‡*Athenæ Britannicæ* (London, 1716). 2.3.8.40-41; not in C <nd, h> On title page: "A singular, & rare Book. T·H." 10467.54* 2 v.

DAWSON, BENJAMIN, 1729-1814.
An address to the writer of A second letter to the author of The confessional (London, 1768). 6.1.4.26; C279 <nd, h> *EC75.R7445.767eb

An answer to Letters concerning established confessions of faith (London, 1769). Inv.12.85; 6.1.4.26; C279 (under Utility of establishing – Part 3 of An examination) <690818, h> *EC75.R7445.767eb

An examination of An essay on establishments in religion (London, 1767). 6.1.4.26; C279 <nd, h> *EC75.R7445.767eb

An examination of Dr. Rutherforth's argument (London, 1766). 6.1.4.27; C279 <nd, h> *EC75.H7267.Zz767pc

A letter to the Rev. Dr. Rutherforth (London, 1767). 6.1.4.27; C279 <nd, h> *EC75.H7267.Zz767pc

DEAN, RICHARD, ca. 1727-1778. *An essay on the future life of brute creatures* (London, 1768). Inv.10.38; 4.4.8.24; C165 <680712, h> Phil 5813.1* 2 v.

DECKER, SIR MATTHEW, 1679-1749. *Serious considerations on the several high duties* (London, 1744). 4.2.7.17; C210 (under Duties) <nd, h> *EC75.H7267.Zz737t

Defence of Dr. Cockburn (London, [1724]). 2.2.5.23; C213 (under Burnet) <670815, h> *EC65.B9343.S736t

A defence of the Dissertation or inquiry concerning the Gospel according to Matthew (London, 1732). 6.1.5.40; C314 (under Matthew) <700926, h> *EC75.H7267.Zz731t

A defence of the old-stile (London, 1751). 2.4.5.28; C216 (under Stile old) <670815, h> *EC7.M1327.751sb

DEFOE, DANIEL, 1661-1731.
An argument proving that the design of employing and ennobling foreigners, is a treasonable conspiracy (London, 1717). 2.1.7.4; C223 (under Foreigners) <671209?, r> *EC7.D3623.717a

The case of dissenters as affected by the late bill (London, 1703). 2.1.6.14; not in C <671209?, h> *EC65.C5614.681c

An essay upon literature (London, 1726). 4.4.7.11; not in C <nd, r> *EC7.M2927.739c

The original power of the collective body of the people of England (London, 1769). Inv.15.34; C246 <691129, r> *EC7.D3632.B769o

‡*Peace without union* (London, 1704). 2.1.7.4; not in C <nd, r> On title page: "By Mr.Shoote [sic] afterwards L. Barrington." *EC7.D3623.703pd

A plan of the English commerce (London, 1727). Inv.13.18; 6.1.7.25; C38 (under Plan) <700926, h> *EC7.D3623.728p (B)

The political history of the Devil (London, 1754). Inv.15.19; 6.1.8.47; C112 <691129, r> 16428.12*

Reflections on the prohibition act (London, 1708). 2.1.7.4; not in C <671209?, r> *EC7.D3263.708r

Religious courtship (London, 1762). Inv.15.20; 6.1.8.46; C112 <691129, r> Phil 9163.1*

See also The judgment of whole kingdoms

DELAMER, BARON, *see* Warrington, Henry Booth, earl of

De morbo gallico omnia quae extant, ed. Luigi Luigini (Venice, 1566-1567). Inv.8.23; 6.3.4.10; C100 <661001, r> Med 262.50 F*

DEMPSTER, THOMAS, 1579?-1625. *De Etruriæ regali* (Florence, [1726]). Inv.3.11; 2.1.3.5; C4 <641208, r> Typ 725.26.320 F (A) 2 v.

DESCARTES, RENÉ, 1596-1650. *A discourse of a method* (London, 1649). Inv.4.193; 2.2.8.31; C93 <641212?, r> *FC6.D4537.Eg649d

DESGODETS, ANTOINE BABUTY, 1653-1728. ‡*Les édifices de Rome* (Paris, 1682). 4.1.1.1; not in C <nd, h> On flyleaf: "This is a fine copy of a very curious, scarce work. The preface shows its value. T·H has been content to send this Book to Harvard College, that, when, by Commerce, riches shall have flowen [sic] in upon the Good People of New England, then, it may serve as a faithful standard to them, of several of the most perfect, finest Edifices which were erected in the most polished Ages of Antiquity. Men of New England, beware however, again beware, of Refinements & Luxurys, the certain attendants upon Riches, and contend them to the Uttermost, with Tyranny their Offspring, by sumptuary Laws, by a quick rotation of offices and Power, and — by every means!" f*EC75.H7267.Zz682d

DESLANDES, ANDRÉ FRANÇOIS, 1690-1757. ‡*Histoire critique de la philosophie* (London, 1742). Inv.12.35; 6.1.8.50-52; C110 <690818, h> TH completes author's name on title page. Phil 803.1* 3 v.

DEVARIUS, MATTHAEUS, b. 1505? *De græcæ linguæ particulis liber* (Nuremberg, 1718). 4.2.8.41; C135 <nd, r> *IC5.D4915.588ℓe

D'EWES, SIR SIMONDS, 1602-1650. *The journals of all the parliaments* (London, 1682). Inv.10.3; 4.4.2.1; C146 <680712, h> Br 1735.15 F*

DEYRON, JACQUES, d. 1677. *Des antiquitez de la ville de Nismes* (Nimes, 1663). Inv.4.13; 2.1.3.5; C4 <641212?, r> Arc 825.1*

DÉZALLIER D'ARGENVILLE, ANTOINE-JOSEPH, 1680-1765. *L'histoire naturelle, éclaircie dans un de ses parties principales, la conchiliologie* (Paris, 1757). Inv.5.9; C71 <6506.., h> MCZ Special Collections

A dialogue agaynst the tyrannye of the papistes (London, 1652). 2.2.8.28; not in C <nd, h> STC 4407.5

A dialogue betwene a knight and a clerke (London, [1533?]). Inv.4.159 (under Oackham); C85 (misdated 1559, under Oakham) <641212?, early calf> STC 12511

Dialogus contra papistarum tyrannidem (London, 1652). 2.2.8.28; not in C <nd, h> STC 4407.5

DICTYS, CRETENSIS. *Ditte Candiotto e Darete Frigio Della guerra troiana* (Verona, 1734). Inv.4.29; C14 <641212?, v> Harvard Depository KF 24889

DIDEROT, DENIS, 1713-1784. ‡*Lettre sur les aveugles* (London [i.e., Paris], 1749). Inv.11.13; 6.2.8.14; B6 (under Aveugles), C123 (under Rond) <6809.., h> On title page: "Par Mons. D'Alembert." *FC7.D5618.749ℓ

DIGBY, SIR KENELM, 1603-1665.
A late discourse … touching the cure of wounds (London, 1664). 4.4.8.46; C110 <nd, h> *EC65.D5693.Eg658wd

Two treatises (Paris, 1644). Inv.3.70, Inv.4.183; 2.3.2.11; C93 <641208, 641212?, h> f*EC65.D5693.644t (B) Second copy not located.

DILLENIUS, JOHANN JAKOB, 1684-1747. *Hortus Elthamensis* (London, 1732). Inv.2.3; C31 <6410.., h> Bot 248.3*

DIMSDALE, THOMAS, 1712-1800. *The present method of inoculating for the small-pox* (London, 1769). Inv.13.74; 6.1.4.35; C98 <700926, h> Countway Rare Books RC 183.A2 D59 1769 c.1

DINGLEY, ROBERT, d. 1752? *A catalogue of the genuine and entire collection* ([London, 1753]). Not in C <nd, boards> A sale catalogue. B 1827.401*

DIODORUS, SICULUS. †*Bibliothecæ historicæ libri qui supersunt* (Amsterdam, 1746). 4.2.1.15-16; C14 <nd, h> Gd 27.18 F* 2 v.

DIONISIUS, OF HALICARNASSUS.
†*Antiquitatum romanorum libri X* (Oxford, 1704). Inv.4.16; 4.2.2.16-17; C14 <641212?, h> Gd 39.15 F* 2 v.

Delle cose antiche della citta' di Roma (Verona, 1738). C14 <670815?, v> KF 23269* 2 v.

A discourse concerning virtue and religion (London, 1732). 2.1.5.17; C346 <nd, h> *EC7.G5185.732d

A discourse on government and religion (London, [1749?]). 2.1.7.20; not in C <671209?, h> *EC65.W4574.653cb (B)

Dissertationum ludicrarum et amoenitatum, scriptores varii (Leiden, 1638). 4.4.8.50; C110 (misdated? 1644) Original Hollis gift not located.

DOBBS, ARTHUR, 1689-1765. *An account of the countries adjoining Hudson's Bay* (London, 1744). Inv.2.30; 2.3.4.9; B10, C74 <6410.., h> *EC7.D6516.744a

Dr. Sherlock's Two kings of Brainford brought upon the stage (London, 1691). 2.2.5.16; C251 <671209?, h> *EC75.H7267.Zz691t

DODWELL, HENRY, 1641-1711.
Christianity not founded on argument (London, 1743). 4.2.7.18; not in C <nd, h> *EC75.H7267.Zz730t

De parma equestri Woodwardiana dissertatio (Oxford, 1713). Inv.17.35; 4.4.5.2; C4 (misdated 1731) <68…., h> *EC65.D6647.713d

An epistolary discourse (London, 1706). Inv.14.25; 6.1.7.48; C93 & C166 <700926, h> *EC65.D6697.706e

Exercitationes duæ: prima, de ætate Phalaridis (London, 1704). 6.2.8.1; C110 <nd, h> Gp 26.53*

DOLCE, LODOVICO, 1508-1569, *see* Choniates, Nicetas

DOMAT, JEAN, 1625-1696. *The civil law in its natural order* (London, 1737). C77 <nd, h> f*FC6.D7112.Eg722sb 2 v.

DOMESDAY BOOK. ‡[*Domesday-book, seu liber censualis Willemi Primi regis Angliæ*, ed. Abraham Farley]. Not in C <nd, r> Single leaf of projected facsimile, ca. 1764-1770; full facsimile published 1783. On verso: "A specimen of Domesday Book, as it is now copying by order of the Commons House of Parlament [*sic*]." f MS Eng 1452

DOMENICHI, LODOVICO, 1515-1564. *La nobilta delle donne* (Venice, 1551). Inv.3.148; 2.4.8.16; C110 <641208, v> *IC5.D7125.549nb

DONI, ANTONIO FRANCESCO, 1513-1574. *I marmi* (Venice, 1552 [i.e., 1553]). Inv.3.47; 2.1.5.36; C118 (under Marmi) <641208, h> *IC5.D7178.552m

DONI, GIOVANNI BATTISTA, 1593 or 4-1647. *De restituenda salubritate agri romani* (Florence, 1667). Inv.3.27; 4.1.5.1; C110 (under Donius) <641208, v> *IC6.D7175.667da

DONNE, JOHN, 1573-1631, *see* Cuffe, Henry

DORSET, CHARLES SACKVILLE, DUKE OF, 1711-1769. *A treatise concerning the militia* (London, 1753). 2.2.5.7; C230 (under Sackville) <671209?, h> *EC75.H7267.Zz753t

DOSIO, GIOVANNI ANTONIO. *Urbis Romae ædificiorum illustrium quae supersunt reliquiae* ([n.p., 15—]). 4.2.3.29; C33 <nd, early calf gilt, not TH> Arc 758.2*

DOSSIE, ROBERT, d. 1777. ‡*Memoirs of agriculture* (London, 1768). Inv.14.3; 6.1.5.12; C1 <700926, h> On title page: "Ut spargam T·H." Agr 303.10*

DOUAZAC, MONSIEUR. *Dissertation sur la subordination* (Avignon, 1752). Inv.4.118 (part); 2.1.8.20; C231 (under Subordination) <641212?, h> Tr 511*

DOUGLAS, JAMES, 1675-1742. *Catalogus editionum Quinti Horatii Flacci* (London, 1739). Not in C <nd, r> B 1619.334*

DRYDEN, JOHN, 1631-1700, *see Examen poeticum; Miscellany poems*; Plutarch, *Lives*; *Sylvae*

DU CANGE, CHARLES DU FRESNE, SIEUR, 1610-1688.
Glossarium ad scriptores mediæ & infimæ græcitatis (Leiden, 1688). 4.3.3.16-17; C203 (under Fresne) <nd, r> 4281.8 F* 2 v.

[Another edition] (Paris, 1733-1736). 4.1.2.5-10; C203 (under Fresne) <nd, r>
Harvard Depository KJ 1051 6 v.

DUFF, WILLIAM, 1732-1815. *An essay on original genius* (London, 1767). 4.3.6.1; B12, C113
(under Genius)   Original Hollis gift not located.

DU FRESNOY, CHARLES ALPHONSE, 1611-1665. *The art of painting* (London, 1716).
Inv.4.180; C9 <641212?, r> *EC65.D8474.695db

DUGDALE, SIR WILLIAM, 1605-1686.
Monasticon anglicanum (London, 1718). 4.1.3.2; C66 <nd, r> Br 74.17.5 F* (A)

[Another copy] C66 <nd, r> Br 74.17.5 F* (B)

DU HALDE, JEAN-BAPTISTE, 1674-1743. *The general history of China* (London, 1736).
4.3.1.19-20; not in C Original Hollis gift not located.

DU MOULIN, LEWIS, 1606-1680.
An appeal of all the non-conformists (London, 1681). Inv.4.51 (part); 2.2.6.7; not in C
<651212?, h> *EC65.D8992.B681t

The conformity of the discipline and government (London, 1680). Inv.4.51 (part); 2.2.6.7;
not in C <641212?, h> *EC65.D8992.B681t

Moral reflections upon the number of the elect (London, 1680). Inv.4.51 (part); 2.2.6.7;
not in C <641212?, h> *EC65.D8992.B681t

Proposals, and reasons whereon some of them are grounded (London, 1659). Inv.4.12;
2.3.5.31; C119 <641212?, h> *EC65.D8992.659p

A short and true account of all the non-conformists (London, 1680). Inv.4.51 (part);
2.2.6.7; not in C <641212?, h> *EC65.D8992.B681t

DU MOULIN, PETER, 1601-1684. *Regii sanguinis clamor ad cælum* (The Hague, 1652).
2.3.8.2; C148 & C265 <nd, v> *EC65.M6427.R652d

DUNI, EMMANUELE, 1716-1781. *Origine, e progressi del cittadino ... di Roma* (Rome, 1763-
1764). 4.1.8.3-4; C83 <nd, h> *IC7.D9211.7630 2 v.

DUNTON, JOHN, 1659-1733, *see The judgment of whole kingdoms*

DU PÉRAC, ÉTIENNE, d. 1604. *I vestigi dell'antichità di Roma* (Rome, 1575 [i.e., 1600]).
2.2.1.21; not in C <nd, russia> Typ 625.00.342 F

DUPLEIX, JOSEPH FRANÇOIS, MARQUIS. *Memoire pour le sieur Dupleix contre la
Compagnie des Indes* (Paris, 1759). Inv.1.17; 2.2.4.22; C110 <631024, r> Ind 627.1*

DUPRÉ DE SAINT-MAUR, NICOLAS FRANÇOIS, 1695-1774, *see* Milton, John, *Le Paradis
perdu*

DURAND, DAVID, 1680-1763. ‡*La vie et les sentimens de Lucilio Vanini* (Rotterdam, 1717).
Inv.7.11; 2.2.7.29; C30 <651010, h> On title page: "Tres rare." *EC7.D9316.717v

DURY, JOHN, 1596-1680. *The reformed librarie keeper* (London, 1650). Inv.3.67; 2.2.8.63;
C110 <641208, h> B 7764.342*

Dutens, Louis, 1730-1812. ‡*Recherches sur l'origine des découvertes attribuées aux modernes* (Paris, 1766). 4.2.7.14; C110 <nd, h> On flyleaf: "Mr. Dutens is said to be a Divine of the Church of England & the Son of a French Refugee. He was at the Court of Turin with Mr. Stuart Mackensie, I believe as Chaplain & Secretary; and afterward there, in the same Capacity, to Mr. George Pitt." Phil 178.9* 2 v. in 1

E

Eachard, John, 1636?-1730. *Works* (London, 1705). Inv.16.101; C167 <670511> Original Hollis gift not located.

Earbery, Matthias. *Impartial reflections on Dr. Burnet's posthumous history* (London, 1724). Inv.4.138 (part); 2.2.5.23; C213 (under Burnet) <641212?, h> *EC65.B9343.S736t

Earle, Jabez, 1676?-1768. *The popish doctrine of purgatory* (London, 1735). Not in C <6506.., h> *EC75.H7267.Zz735s

Echard, Laurence, 1670?-1730. *An answer to Dr. Edmund Calamy's letter* (London, [1718?]). 6.1.6.42; C213 (under Calamy, Answer to his letter) <690818, r> *EC7.C1253.718ℓ

Eden, Robert, 1701-1759. *Jurisprudentia philologica* (Oxford, 1744). 4.2.5.15; C77 <nd, r> AH 7203.26*

Edmundson, Henry, 1607?-1659. ‡*Lingua linguarum, the naturall language of languages* (London, 1655). Inv.10.45; 4.4.8.44; C135 <680712, h> On back flyleaf: "No other copy of this work ever seen by T. Hollis. He is fond of sending these kind of Books, in furtherance to those <u>first-rate</u> Scholars that He hopes are now forming in Harvard College." EducT 20916.55*

Edwards, John, 1637-1716. *Some new discourses of the uncertainty ... of human knowledge* (London, 1714). Inv.14.17; 6.1.7.28; C110 <700926, r> *EC65.Ed967.714s

Edwards, Thomas, 1699-1757.
The doctrine of irresistible grace (Cambridge, 1759). Inv.13.10; 6.1.5.19; C168 <700926, h> C 1190.12.30*

Epistola ad doctissimum virum Robertum Lowthium (Cambridge, 1765). Inv.13.33 (part); not in C <700926, h> Andover-Harvard S.C.R. 366.4 Edwards

Prolegomena in libros Veteri Testamenti poeticos (Cambridge and London, 1762). Inv.13.33 (part); C40 <700926, h> Andover-Harvard S.C.R. 366.4 Edwards

Two dissertations (London, 1766). Inv.13.11; 6.1.5.20; C282 <700926, h> C 1190.13.06*

See also Bible. O.T. Psalms. English

Egan, Anthony, B.D. *The Romanists designs detected* (London, 1674). 2.4.5.19; C222 Original Hollis gift discarded as a duplicate.

Eggeling, Johann Heinrich, 1639-1713. *Mysteria Cereris et Bacchi* (Bremen, 1682). 4.3.7.6; C4 <nd, h> *GC6.Eg334.682m

See also Feller, Joachim

EISENSCHMIDT, JOHANN CASPAR, 1656-1712. *De ponderibus et mensuris veterum Romanorum* (Strasburg, 1737). 4.4.8.7; C129 <nd, h> *GC7.Ei846.708db

ELIOT, ANDREW, 1718-1778. †*A sermon* [an election sermon on the Stamp Act] (London, 1765). 4.2.7.1; C283 (under Election sermon) <nd, h: bound with Jonathan Mayhew, *The snare broken*, (Boston, 1766)> *AC7.Eℓ441.765sba

See also The American gazette

ELLIOTT, ROBERT, fl. 1715. ‡*A specimen of the Bishop of Sarum's posthumous History* (London, 1735). Inv.4.138 (part); 2.2.5.23; C213 (under Burnet) <641212?, h> On title page: "A curious Volume." On flyleaf, TH completes its table of contents. *EC65.B9343.S736t

ELLYS, ANTHONY, 1690-1761. ‡*The spiritual and temporal liberty of subjects in England* (London, 1765). 4.1.4.16; C83 <nd, r> On flyleaf: "—As for Divines medling with Politics, he has in the former part of his Preliminaries to Oceana delivered his opinion; 'That there is Something in the making of a Commonwealth; then in the governing of it; and last of all in the leading of its Armies; which, though there be great Divines, great Lawyers, great Men in all Professions seems to be peculiar only to the the Genius of a Gentleman: For, it is plain in the universal series of Story, that if any one founded a Commonwealth He was first a Gentleman,' the truth of which assertion he proves from Moses downward. The Life of James Harrington." Laid down is a cutting from the *St. James's chronicle* attacking rotten boroughs. Br 167.65*

ELLYS, SIR RICHARD, ca. 1674-1742. ‡*Fortuita sacra* (Utrecht, 1744). 2.1.6.25; C40 <sent by TH 650919 via Jonathan Mayhew, h> On endleaves: "The Author Sir Richard Ellys Kt. See the Dedication to the Britannia Romana of the learned, excellent John Horsley, who was a Dissenting Minister at Morpeth in Northumberland. Sir Richard left a very choice Library to Hobart, Earl of Buckinghamshire, who was, it is apprehended a Relation, of his. But so independent were his connections & noble his Dispositions, that it is not impossible, had he lived to have seen the British Musæum, or to have heard of the calamitous fire at Harvard College, at Cambridge, in New England, for he affectionated the Colonists, those of N. E. especially, a manly, good People, he would have bestowed it, a common benefit, on one of those Institutions." C 1195.1.5*

ELSTOB, ELIZABETH, 1683-1756. *The rudiments of grammar in the English-Saxon tongue* (London, 1715). 4.3.7.42; C51 <nd, h> 9286.21*

ELSYNGE, HENRY, 1598-1654. *The manner of holding parliaments in England* (London, 1768). Inv.12.32; 6.1.8.16; C80 <690818, r> Br 132*

EMLYN, SOLLOM, 1697-1754, ed. ‡*A complete collection of state-trials* (London, 1742). Inv.5.1; 2.3.2.16-21; C148 <6506.., h> On leaf inserted before title page, v. 6: "Two additional volumes of 'State Trials' are expected to be published the ensuing summer. If T·H should then be living, and well; he will cause them to be added to these volumes." Harvard Depository Br 89.5.5 6 v.

See also A collection of state-trials

EMPEREUR VAN OPPIJCK, CONSTANTIJN L'. *Oratio inauguralis de linguæ Hebrææ dignitate ac utilitate* (Leiden, 1627). 4.4.7.12; C236 (under L'Empereur) <nd, h> 2255.13*

ENGLAND, GEORGE, fl. 1735. *An enquiry into the morals of the ancients* (London, 1735). Inv.13.57; 6.1.3.19; C46 <700926, r> Phil 8829.1*

An enquiry into the causes of the late rebellion (London, 1746). Inv.2.96; 2.1.6.12; C245 (under Britain) <6410.., h> *EC75.H7267.Zz751t

An enquiry into the origin of human appetites and affections (Lincoln, 1747). Inv.13.19; 6.1.7.16; C46 <700926, r> Phil 9420.3*

Enqviry into the condvct of a late Right Honovrable commoner (London, [1766]). 4.1.7.11; not in C <nd, r> Br 2060.369*

ENTY, JOHN, 1675?-1743.
  A defence of the proceedings of the late assembly at Exon (London, 1719). Inv.5.30; 2.3.7.7; C283 <6506.., xt> *EC7.En875.719d

  ‡*Truth and liberty consistent and maintain'd* (London, 1720). 2.3.7.5; C283 <6506.., marbled boards> On flyleaf: "The three volumes, relating to this Controversy, were collected by the late Rev. Joseph Burroughs, Dissenting Minister at Barbican, London." *EC7.P3551.720p This is the first of the three volumes. Volume 2 has been assigned the call number *EC7.B3551.720p; v. 3, formerly Tr 206, was broken up and the tracts catalogued individually.

ÉON DE BEAUMONT, CHARLES D', 1728-1810. *Considerations historiques & politiques sur les impots des Égyptiens* (London, 1764). 4.2.6.25-26; C110 (under D'Eon) <nd, h> Harvard Business School, Kress Library 2 v.

EPICTETUS. *Enchiridion*, Greek and Latin (Cambridge, 1655). Inv.17.36; 4.3.8.40; C14 <68...., h> *OGC.Ep42.655 (B)

Epigrammata et poematia vetera (Paris, 1590 [colophon 1589]). Inv.2.106; C141 <6410.., v> L 145*

ERASMUS, DESIDERIUS, d. 1536.
  De utrius[que] verborum ac rerum copia (Amsterdam, 1645). 4.4.8.49; C111 <nd, v> *NC5.Er153D.1645

  Moriæ encomium (Leiden, 1648). 4.2.8.49; C111 Original Hollis gift not located.

ERIZZO, SEBASTIANO, 1525-1585. *Discorso ... sopra le medaglie de gli antichi* (Venice, 1568). Inv.3.48; 2.1.6.7; C129 <641208, early diced russia> *IC5.Er478.559dc

ERPENIUS, THOMAS, 1584-1624.
  Arabicæ linguæ tyrocinium (Leiden, 1656). 4.3.7.22; C51 (misdated 1756) <nd, h> 3234.27*

  Grammatica Arabica (Leiden, 1748). 4.2.7.4; C51 <nd, r> 3234.29*

  ‡*Rudimenta linguæ arabicæ* (Leiden, 1733). 4.2.7.31; C51 <nd, h> On flyleaf: "When occasion has offered, & the Cost not been great, T·H has at times, not refused a Duplicate for Harvard College. Colleges, American Colleges cannot be too well stocked in this Way." 3234.21* No second copy located.

An essay on liberty and independency (London, 1747). 2.3.7.38; C249 (under Liberty) <641208, h> *EC75.H7267.Zz735t

An essay on modern education (London, 1747). 4.2.7.16; C222 (under Education) <nd, h> *EC75.H7267.Zz740m

An essay on polite behaviour (London, 1740). 4.2.7.16; C229 (under Polite behaviour) <nd, h> *EC75.H7267.Zz740m

An essay on the trade of the northern colonies … in North America (London, 1764). 4.1.7.19; C209 Original Hollis gift not located.

ESSEX, ARTHUR CAPEL, EARL OF, 1631-1683. *Letters* (London, 1770). Inv.14.19; 6.3.2.15; C145 (under Capel) <700926, h> *EC65.Es751.770ℓ

ESTIENNE, HENRI, 1531-1598.
Annotationes in Sophoclem & Euripidem ([Geneva], 1568). 4.4.8.11; not in C <nd, r> *FC5.Es864.568a (B)

‡*Thesaurus graecæ linguæ* ([Geneva] 1572). 4.3.2.14-18; C205 <nd, v> On flyleaf: "T·H has been looking out, above two Years, for a fine copy of Harry Stephens Greek Thesaurus for Harvard College. At length he purchased one out of the Library of the late learned Dr. Samuel Chandler. It is hardly to be imagined, what difficulty there is, even when money & industry are not wanting, to secure good Copies of the Old & best Editions of Classical & prime Authors. Time has consumed many of them. And many others, by common agreement of all our principal Booksellers, have been returning back for Years past, as they came on sale, to the European Continent from our Island. So much for the Dissipation, Ignorance of the times!" 4213.3* 5 v.

ESTIENNE, ROBERT, 1503-1559.
Thesaurus linguæ latinæ (London, 1734). Inv.8.17; 4.1.1.4-7; C205 <661001, h> 5211.8 F* 4 v.

†[Another copy] 4.2.1.5-8; C205 <nd, h> 5211.9 F* 4 v.

See also Cicero, *Opera*

EURIPIDES. *Supplices mulieres*, Greek and Latin (London, 1763). 4.4.4.3; C14 <nd, h> *OGC.Eu73T.763

EUSTACHI, BARTOLOMEO, d. 1574. *Tabulae anatomicae* (Rome, 1728). 4.3.2.8; C2 <nd, v> Countway Rare Books ff QM 25.E79 1728 c.1

EVELEIGH, JOSIAH, d. 1736.
An account of why many citizens of Exon have withdrawn from the ministry of Mr. Joseph Hallet and Mr. James Peirce (London, 1719). Inv.5.30 (part); 2.3.7.7; not in C <6506.., xt> *EC7.Ev225.719d

A defence of the account, &c. (London, 1719). Inv.5.30 (part); 2.3.7.7; not in C <6506.., xt> *EC7.Ev225.719d

EVELYN, JOHN, 1620-1706.
Fumifugium (London, 1661). Inv.5.35 (under Inconveniency); 2.3.8.7; C111 <6506.., h> *EC65.Ev226.661f

Numismata: A discourse of medals (London, 1697). C129 <nd, r> f*EC65.Ev226.697n (A)

EWER, JOHN, d. 1774. ‡*A sermon* [on Rom.x.14] (London, 1767). Inv.9.50; C284 <680711, calf (bound in Cambridge, Mass., in 1768 by J. Smith, Jr.)> On p.23, TH underlined this passage: "Even the Romish superstition, within a province lately added to British dominions, is completely allowed in all points; it hath Bishops and seminaries." In the margin TH writes: "'Completely allowed in all points'! Weep ye Protestants! Ye North Americans, the whole Continent through, Weep bitterly!" *EC75.Ew367.767s

Examen poeticum, the third part of Miscellany poems (London, 1706). Inv.3.125 (under Dryden; part); B11, C141 (under Dryden) <641208, r> *EC65.D8474.B709m v. 3

EXETER, ENGLAND. Assembly of united ministers of Devon and Cornwall, 1719. *A true account of what was transacted at the assembly, met May 5 and 6, 1719* (London, 1719). Inv.5.30 (part); 2.3.7.7; not in C <6506.., xt> Tr 206*

F

FABER, BASILIUS, d. 1575 or 1576. *Thesaurus eruditionis scholasticae* (Frankfurt & Leipzig, 1749). 4.1.1.18-19; C203 <nd, h> 5222.7* 2 v.

FABRETTI, RAFFAELE, 1618-1700.
De aquis et aqueductibus veteris Romæ (Rome, 1680). Inv.3.87; 2.4.4.9; C4 <641208, r> *IC6.F1145.680d (A)

Inscriptionum antiquarum … explicatio (Rome, 1702). 4.3.4.3; C4 <nd, h> Class 6481.2 F*

FABRI, DOMENICO, 1711-1761, ed. ‡*Delle lettere familiari d'alcuni Bolognesi* (Venice, 1745). Inv.3.127; 2.3.8.35-36; C116 (under Lettere) <641208, v> On flyleaf: "T.H. bought at Naples July 1751." *IC7.F1145.744db 2 v.

FABRICIUS, GEORG, 1516-1571. *Antiquitatis monumentum insignia* (Basel, [1549]). Inv.2.124; 2.1.7.38; C4 <6410.., red morocco with arms of Louis XIV> Class 6005.49*

FABRICIUS, JOHANN ALBERT, 1668-1736.
Bibliographia antiquaria, sive Introductio in notitiam scrioptorum (Hamburg & Leipzig, 1716). 4.2.6.23; C111 <nd, h> Harvard Depository AH 7.16 (B)

Bibliotheca græca (Hamburg, 1708-1728). 4.2.6.9-22; C111 <nd, h> Class 1207.05.6* 14 v.

Bibliotheca latina (Venice, 1728). 4.2.5.20-21; C111 <nd, h> Class 2006.96.10* 2 v.

Codex pseudepigraphus veteris testamenti (Hamburg, 1722). 4.1.8.248; C111 <nd, h> C 588.5* (A) 2 v.

Codicis Apocryphi novi testamenti (Hamburg, 1719). 4.1.8.20; C111 <nd, h> C 594.5.2* 2 v.

FACULTÉ DE MÉDICINE DE PARIS. ‡*Traduction des statuts*, tr. Michel Bermingham (Paris, 1754). Inv.4.194; 2.2.7.17; not in C <641212?, h> On flyleaf: "A Present from the Translator to TH." *FC7.B4565.754t

FAIRFAX, BRYAN, 1676-1749. *A catalogue of the genuine and valuable collection* ([London, 1751]). 2.1.6.7; not in C <nd, h (boards)> A sale catalogue. B 1827.401*

FALCONER, WILLIAM, 1732-1769. *An universal dictionary of the marine* (London, 1769). Inv.13.73; 6.1.3.5; C203 <700926, h> 9251.37*

FALDA, GIOVANNI BATTISTA, ca. 1640-1678. *Le fontane di Roma* ([Rome, 1691]). 6.3.1.35; C33 <nd, h> FA 2185.32 PF*

FALKLAND, HENRY CARY, VISCOUNT, d. 1633, attributed author. *The history of the life, reign, and death of Edward III* (London, 1680). Inv.2.115; 4.4.3.13; C27 (under Edward II [*sic*]) <6410.., h> f*EC.F1875.680h

FALSTER, CHRISTIAN, 1690-1752. *Amœnitates philologicæ* (Amsterdam, 1729). 4.4.7.23; C112 <nd, h> MLf 256.30*

FAUNO, LUCIO, 16th cent. *Delle antichita della citta di Roma* ([Venice, 1548]). Inv.4.106 & Inv.4.126; 2.4.8.15; C4 (lists only one copy) <641212?, v> Second copy not located; a duplicate entry? *IC5.F2745.548d

FAZELLO, TOMMASO, 1498-1570.
De rebus Siculis decades duæ ([Palermo, 1558]). Inv.3.24; 4.4.3.24; C4 <641208, h> Ital 5010.1 F*

[Another edition] (Catania, 1749-1753). 4.2.3.15-17; C52 <nd, v> Ital 5010.1.3* 2 v.

FELINI, PIETRO MARTIRE. *Trattati nuovo delle cose maravigliose dell'alma città di Roma* (Rome, 1610). Inv.4.89; 2.4.8.9; C6 (under Martire) <641212?, v> Typ 625.10.387

FELL, PHILIP, 1632 or 3-1682. *Lex talionis, or, The author of Naked Truth stript naked* (London, 1676). 2.4.5.19; C211 (under title) <nd, xt> *EC65.F3358.676ℓ

FELLER, JOACHIM, 1628-1691. *Vindiciæadversus Johann Henrici Eggelingii* (Leipzig, 1685). 4.1.7.6; not in C <nd, h> Class 9246.82*

FELTON, HENRY, 1679-1740. *A dissertation on reading the classics* (London, 1753). Inv.4.189; 4.2.8.31; B11, C112 <641212?, r> 9278.111* (A)

[Another copy] B11, C112 <670815?, r> 9278.111* (B)

FENDT, TOBIAS, 16th cent. ‡*Monvmenta sepvlcrorvm* (Breslau, 1574). 4.3.4.16; C4 <nd, h> On flyleaf: "Sum ex libris Thomae Hollis"; on title page: "+Ex Liberalitate. [quoted from the engraved title] Rariss. T·H." *EC75.H7267.Zz574f

FERGUSON, ADAM, 1723-1816. *An essay on the history of civil society* (London, 1768). 4.3.4.22; B12, C83 Original Hollis gift not located.

FERRETI, GIOVANNI BATTISTA, 1640?-1682. *Musae lapidariae* (Verona, 1672). Inv.2.19; 2.2.3.3; C6 <6410.., v> AH 816.72 F*

FESTUS, SEXTUS POMPEIUS, 2nd cent. *De verborum significatione lib. xx* (Venice, 1560). 4.4.8.35; C15 (under Flaccus) <nd, h> *SC5.Ag970.560fa

FEUILLÉE, LOUIS, 1660-1732. *Journal des observations physiques, mathematiques et botaniques* (Paris, 1714-1725). 4.1.5.26-28; C112 Declared lost, June 1999.

FIELDING, SIR JOHN, 1721-1780. *An account of the receipts and disbursements relating to Sir John Fielding's plan* ([London, 1779]). C223 (dated 1770) <nd, r> Soc 2270.52*

FILMER, SIR ROBERT, d. 1653.

‡*The free-holders grand inquest* (London, 1680). Inv.15.10; 6.1.7.42; C80 (misdated 1679) <691129, h> On flyleaf: "As the Patriarcha gave occasion to two of the noblest works which were ever executed by man, the 'Discourses of Government' by Algernon Sydney, and 'The Treatises of Government' by John Locke; I have been willing to send all the Publications of Sir Robert Filmer, to Harvard College, that so the whole of those Works by the curious may be compared. Aug. 12. 69. T·H Floreat Libertas!" *EC65.F4874.B679fc

Patriarcha, or The natural power of kings (London, 1680). 6.1.7.42; C83 <691129, h> *EC65.F4874.B679fc

‡[Another edition] (London, 1685). 4.1.8.19; C83 <nd, h> On flyleaf: "This Scrub Book, gave occasion to two of the noblest Works, that ever the Mind of Man hath produced: Algernon Sydney's 'Discourses concerning Government;' and, John Locke's 'Two Treatises of Government.'" *EC65.F4874.680pc

FINCH, RICHARD, fl. 1725-1755. *The nature and duty of self-defence* (London, 1746). Inv.2.96 (part); 2.1.6.12; C231 (under Self-defence) <6410.., h> *EC75.H7267.Zz751t

FINO, ALEMANIO, d. ca. 1586. *La historia di Crema* (Venice, [1566]). Inv.3.43; 2.3.5.24; C56 <641208, calf> *IC5.F4982.566h

FITZSTEPHEN, WILLIAM, d. 1191. *Vitae sancti Thomæ Cantuariensis archiepiscopi* (London, 1723). 4.4.2.25; not in C <nd, h> f*EC7.Sp264.723ha

FLEETWOOD, WILLIAM, 1656-1723.

Chronicon preciosum, or An account of English gold and silver money (London, 1745). Inv.5.23; 2.1.6.2; C129 <6506.., h> Econ 216.1*

The life and miracles of St. Wenefrede (London, 1713). 2.2.5.8; C207 (under Winnifrede) <nd, h> *EC75.H7267.Zz745t

FLEMING, CALEB, 1698-1779.

An antidote for the rising age (London, 1765). 2.1.8.12; C153 <65...., h> A note in Thomas Hollis Papers, Massachusetts Historical Society, states that this title was forwarded via Rev. Jonathan Mayhew on July 3, 1765. C 1205.36.2*

‡*An apology for a protestant dissent* (London, 1755). 2.1.6.1; C287 <6410.., h> TH replaces missing title page in manuscript and identifies author on the first page of the printed text. *EC75.H7267.Zz743m

Civil establishments in religion (London, 1767). 6.1.4.28; C287 <nd, h> *EC75.H2448.767o (A)

The claims of the Church of England seriously examined (London, 1764). 2.4.6.2; not in C <nd, h> *AC7.M4537.B766m v. 2

‡*A comment on the Rev'd Mr. Warburton's Alliance between church and state* (London, 1748). 2.4.5.4; C287 <nd, h> TH identifies author. *EC75.H7267.Zz725m

The devout laugh, or Half an hour's amusement (London, 1750). 2.2.5.22; C287 <nd, h> *EC75.H7267.Zz737h

The Jesuit unmask'd (London, 1737). 2.2.5.22; C287 <nd, h> *EC75.H7267.Zz737h

A letter from a Protestant-dissenting-minister (London, 1768). Inv.10.31; 4.3.6.26; not in C <680712, h> C 5001.9*

The root of Protestant errors examined (London, 1767). 6.3.2.14; C287 <69....?, xt> C 1205.38*

A scale of first principles (London, 1755). Inv.2.116; 2.1.8.6; C169 <6410.., h> Phil 8880.7*

Some thoughts upon the grounds of man's expectation of a future state (London, 1739). 4.2.7.18; C286 (under Thoughts) <nd, h> *EC75.H7267.Zz730t

‡[Another copy] 2.1.6.11; C286 (under Thoughts) <6410.., h> TH identifies author. *EC75.H7267.Zz743m

‡*St. Paul's heretic* (London, 1735). 2.1.6.11; C286 <6410.., h> TH identifies author. *EC75.H7267.Zz743m

‡*Theophilus to Gaius* (London, 1753). 2.1.6.11; C287 (under Letter on the inexpediency) <6410.., h> TH identifies author. *EC75.H7267.Zz743m

‡*Three letters concerning systematic taste* (London, 1755). Inv.4.84; 2.1.6.16; C169 <641212?, h> TH identifies author. *EC75.H7267.Zz755f

See also Chauncy, Charles

Fleta seu commentarius juris anglicani (London, 1647) Inv.16.90; 2.3.5.14; C80 <670511> Original Hollis gift not located.

‡[Another edition] (London, 1685). Inv.10.20; 4.4.5.6; C80 <680712, calf and marbled boards> On flyleaf: "Mr Selden, the first edition, was printed London, 1647, in quarto." Br 1455.5.2*

FLEURY, CLAUDE, 1640-1723. *Les moeurs des Israelites* (Paris, 1712). Inv.12.67; B12, C69 <690818, h> Andover-Harvard S.C.R. 342 Fleury

FOGLIETTA, UBERTO, 1518-1581. *Opera subsciva opuscula varia* ([Rome, 1571]). 4.3.7.14; C112 (under Folieta) <nd, calf> *IC5.F6894.B579o

FOLKES, MARTIN, 1690-1754.
A catalogue of the ... collection of coins ([London, 1756]). Not in C <nd, h (boards)> A sale catalogue. B 1827.401*

A catalogue of the ... collection of mathematical instruments ([London, 1755]). Not in C <nd, h (boards)> A sale catalogue. B 1827.401*

‡*A catalogue of the ... library* ([London, 1756]). Not in C <nd, h (boards)> A sale catalogue; TH marked desiderata. B 1827.401*

Tables of English silver and gold coins (London, 1763). Inv.2.28; 2.1.4.18; C129 <6410.., h> f*EC75.H7267.Zz763f 2 v.

FONTANA, CARLO, 1634-1714. *Discorso sopra l'antico Monte Citatorio* (Rome, 1708). Inv.16.2; 2.3.3.15; C4 <670511, v> Typ 725.08.402 F

FONTANINI, GIUSTO, 1666-1736. ‡*Della eloquenza italiana* (Venice, 1737). Inv.3.88; 2.4.4.6; B12, C149 <641208, v> On flyleaf: "T.H. bought at Naples in June 1751. Ts." *IC7.F7358.706dg

FORBES, DUNCAN, 1685-1747. *Reflexions on the sources of incredulity* (Edinburgh, 1750). 6.2.8.20; C169 <nd, h> *EC7.F7424.750rb

FORBES, PATRICK, ed. *A full view of the public transactions in the reign of Q. Elizabeth* (London, 1740). Inv.16.6; 2.3.2.3-4; C58 <670511, h> Br 1735.8 F* 2 v.

FORCADEL, ESTIENNE. *Valesiorum Franciæ regum origo* (Paris, 1579). Inv.4.168 (under Ferentulus); 2.1.8.4; C4 (under Forcatuli) <641212?, r> Tr 501*

FORDUN, JOHN DE. *Scotichronicon*, ed. Thomas Hearne (Oxford, 1722). 6.1.51-5; not in C <nd, h> Br 8240.15* 5 v.

FORSTER, JOHANN REINHOLD, 1729-1798.
‡ *An introduction to mineralogy* (London, 1768). 4.4.6.4; C36 <nd, h> On flyleaf: "A Professorship of Chemistry & Mineralogy, to be instituted in Harvard College, which, alone, would, it is apprehended, bestow wealth upon New England, with maintenance of its industry, cannot be too much recommended to the Gentlemen there, as Individuals & Legislators. T·H April 14, 68." *GC7.F7748.768i

[Another copy] Inv.13.53; 6.1.7.15; C36 <700926, h>
Kummel Library of the Geological Sciences

FORSTER, NATHANIEL, 1718-1757. *An answer to a pamphlet, entitled, "The question stated"* (London, 1769). Inv.15.25; 6.3.2.14; C251 (under Question stated. Answer) <691129, xt> Annotation by Amos Adams, Harvard librarian: "N:B: The Pamphlet to which this is an Answer is to be found in an Octavo Volume – Letter'd on the Back – Political Tracts 6.1.6.32." *EC75.F7753.769a

See also Meredith, Sir William

FORSTER, THOMAS, RECTOR OF HALESWORTH.
A brief defence of the divine institution of the episcopal order (London, 1768). 6.1.6.33; C301 (under Howe, Thomas) <nd, h> Tr 201*

Two letters ... with an answer (London, 1764). 6.1.6.33; C288 <nd, h (marbled boards)> Tr 201*

FORTESCUE, SIR JOHN, 1394?-1476? *De laudibus legum angliæ* ([London], 1741). Inv.16.57; 2.3.3.4; not in C <670511, h> Br 166.16.6 F*

FOSCARINI, MARCO, 1695-1763. ‡*Della letteratura veneziana libri otto* (Padua, 1752). Inv.4.1; 2.4.1.12; C56 <641212?, v> On half-title: "July 3, 1758. The gift of John Marsili, Doctor of Philosophy and Physic in the University of Padova; Member of divers learned Academies in Italy; and F.R.S. and F.S.A; to Thomas Hollis of Lincolns Inne." On flyleaf: "Marco Foscarini, Cavaliere della Stela doro, e Procuratore di San Marco, Istoriografo della Republica, Uno di Riformatori dell'Università di Padova, Ambasciatore extraordinario alla Corte di Roma. This accomplished, excellent Gentleman Mark Foscarini, succeeded Francis Loredano in the Dogale, but died not long after his election." On second flyleaf, TH quotes six lines of poetry by Gabriello Chiabrera. Typ 725.52.403 F (B)

FOSTER, JOHN, 1731-1774. *An essay on the different nature of accent and quantity* (Eton, 1763). 2.3.6.37; not in C <nd, h> 5215.54*

FOSTER, SIR MICHAEL. *A report of some proceedings on the commission* [trial of the rebels of 1745] (Oxford, 1762). Inv.1.6; 4.4.3.12; not in C <630924, r> Br 2050.180.41 F*

Four dissertations (Philadelphia, 1766). 4.4.6.1; B25, C146 (under Dissertations four) <nd, h> *AC7.A100.766fb

FOWLER, EDWARD, 1632-1714.
Certain propositions by which the doctrine of the H. Trinity is so explain'd (London, 1694). Inv.2.55; C343 <6410..> Original Hollis gift not located.

A vindication of the divines of the Church of England (London, 1689). 2.2.5.16; C252 (under title) <671209?, h> *EC75.H7267.Zz691t

FOXE, JOHN, 1516-1587. *Ad inclytos ac præpotentes Angliæ proceres* (Basel, [1557]). 2.2.8.28; C223 <nd, h> STC 4407.5

FOY-VAILLANT, JEAN, 1632-1706.
Numismata imperatorum (Amsterdam, 1700). Inv.5.6 (under Numismatum imperatorum); 2.2.3.13; C130 <6506.., h> Arc 1455.4 F*

Nummi antiqui familiarum Romanorum (Amsterdam, 1703). Inv.5.5; 2.2.3.16-17; C130 <6506.., r> Arc 1475.6 F* 2 v.

FRANCE. PARLEMENT (Paris). *Remonstrances du Parlement au roi, du 9 avril 1753* ([Paris?], 1753). 2.2.7.23; not in C <670815?, h> *FC7.C3974.753t

FRANCKLIN, RICHARD, d. 1765. *A short state of the case* [concerning publishing rights to Bolingbroke's works] ([London, 1754]). 2.1.4.21; not in C <670511, r> *EC7.B6385.C754w v. 1

FRANCKLIN, THOMAS. *A letter to a bishop, concerning lectureships* (London, 1768). 6.1.6.35; C226 (under Lectureships) <nd, h> Tr 405*

FRANKLAND, THOMAS, 1633-1690. *The annals of King James amd King Charles the First* (London, 1681). Inv.14.60; 6.1.1.13; C58 (under James I) <700926, r> f*EC65.F8541.681a (B)

FRANKLIN, BENJAMIN, 1706-1790. *Experiments and observations on electricity* (London, 1769). Inv.12.15; 6.1.3.27; C138 <690818, r> *AC7.F8545.751ed (B)

FREE, JOHN, 1711?-1791.
The analysis of man (London, [1764?]). Inv.12.29 (part); 6.1.6.18; C290 <690818, h> *EC75.H7267.Zz750f v. 2

The bloody methods of propagating the popish religion (London, 1746). Inv.12.29 (part); 6.1.6.18; not in C <690818, h> *EC75.H7267.Zz750f v. 2

Common safety the cause and foundation of human society (London, [1769?]). 6.1.6.16; not in C <690818, h> *EC75.F8754.768ec

A display of the bad principles of the Methodists (London, 1759). Inv.12.29 (part); 6.1.6.19; C290 <690818, h> *EC75.H7267.Zz750f v. 3

Dr. Free's proposals for opening two divinity schools ([London, 1767?]). Inv.12.29 (part); 6.1.6.17; not in C <690818, h> *EC75.H7267.Zz750f v. 1

Dr. Free's remarks upon Mr. Jones's letter (London, 1759). Inv.12.29 (part); 6.1.6.19; not in C <690818, h> *EC75.H7267.Zz750f v. 3

England's warning piece (London, [1768]). Inv.12.92; 6.1.6.16; C290 (under Sermon on the untimely death) <690818, h (a "mourning" binding)> *EC75.H7267.Zz750f v. 3

[Another edition] (London, [1768?]). Inv.12.29 (part); 6.1.6.18; C290 <690818, h> *EC75.H7267.Zz750f v. 2

‡*An essay towards an history of the English tongue* (London, 1749). Inv.12.29 (part); 6.1.6.17; B11 (under English tongue), C235 <690818, h> On flyleaf of tract volume: "The collection of Dr. Free's works, such of them as could be obtained, now sent to Harvard College, is very curious. T·H Palmal, ap. 14, 1769." *EC75.H7267.Zz750f v. 1

A genuine petition to the King (London, 1762). Inv.12.29 (part); 6.1.6.18; C233 (misdated 1763) <690818, h> *EC75.H7267.Zz750f v. 2

Matrimony made easy (London, 1764). Inv.12.29 (part); 6.1.6.18; C233 <690818, h> *EC75.H7267.Zz750f v. 2

The monthly reviewers reviewed by an antigallican (London, 1765). Inv.12.29 (part); 6.1.6.17; not in C <690818, h> *EC75.H7267.Zz750f v. 1

Of the reason and necessity for written laws (London, [1753]). 6.1.6.18; not in C <690818, h> *EC75.H7267.Zz750f v. 2

The operations of God and nature (London, [1764]). Inv.12.29 (part); 6.1.6.18; not in C <690818, h> *EC75.H7267.Zz750f v. 2

The petition of John Free (London, 1763). Inv.12.29 (part); 6.1.6.18; C223 <690818, h> *EC75.H7267.Zz750f v. 2

A plan for founding in England … a free university (London, 1766). 4.4.6.26; C223 <671209, xt> *EC75.F8754.766pb

[Another copy]. Inv.12.29 (part); 6.1.6.17; C223 <690818, h> *EC75.H7267.Zz750f v. 1

Poems and miscellaneous pieces (London, 1751). Inv.12.86 (part); 6.1.7.13; C141 <690818, r> *EC75.F8754.B751p

Poems on several occasions (London, 1757). Inv.12.95; 6.1.8.41; C141 <690818, h> *EC75.F8754.B751pb

Rules for the discovery of false prophets (London, 1759). Inv.12.29 (part); 6.1.6.19; not in C <690818, h> *EC75.H7267.Zz750f v. 3

‡*Seasonable reflections upon the importance of the name of England* (London, 1755). Inv.12.29 (part); 4.4.6.26 & 6.1.6.17; C246 <690818, h> TH supplies handwritten title page; on sig. B1: "Seasonable Reflections, etc." *EC75.H7267.Zz750f v. 1 Second copy not located.

A specimen of an universal liturgy (London, 1766). Inv.12.29 (part); 6.1.6.17; not in C <690818, h> *EC75.H7267.Zz750f v. 1

The speech of Dr. John Free (London, 1753). Inv.12.29 (part); 6.1.6.17; C246 (under Speech at the town hall) <690818, h> *EC75.H7267.Zz750f v. 1

Stadia physiologica duo; or, Two stages in physiology (London, 1762). Inv.12.93; C98 <690818, h> Countway Rare Books QP29.F87 c.1

‡*Terms, or conditions of national unanimity* (London, 1756). Inv.12.16 (part, under Sermon before the Antiquarian Society); 6.1.3.23; not in C <690818, h> TH annotates a genealogical table of the House of Brunswick. *EC7.F8754.756t

A volume of sermons preached before the University of Oxford (London, 1750). Inv.12.94; 6.1.7.38; not in C <690818, h> *EC75.F8754.B750v

‡*The voluntary exile* (London, 1765). Inv.12.16 (part); 6.1.3.23; not in C <690818, h> On title page: "By Dr Free" and subscription price corrected to "1 Shil." *EC75.F8754.756t

The whole speech which was delivered (London, [1759]). Inv.12.29 (part); 6.1.6.19; not in C <690818, h> *EC75.H7267.Zz750f v. 3

†*The free-thinker* (London, 1722-23 [i.e., 1739]). 2.4.5.5; C112 <660425, h> 16451.1.10*

FREY, ANDREAS. *A true and authentic account of Andrew Frey* (London, 1753). Inv.9.33; 4.4.6.17; C291 <680711, h> *EC75.H7267.Zz755f2

FROELICH, ERASMUS, 1700-1758. *Annales compendiarii regum, & rerum Syriæ* (Vienna, 1754). Inv.5.7; 4.4.3.3; C129 <6506.., h> Arc 14201 F* (A)

FRONTINUS, SEXTUS JULIUS. *De aquæductis urbis Romæ commentarius* (Padua, 1722). Inv.3.29; 2.3.4.1; C4 <641208, v> Typ 725.22.407

See also Cleonides

FULMAN, WILLIAM, 1632-1688. *Rerum anglicanarum scriptores veterum* (Oxford, 1687). Not in C <nd, r> Br 98.304 F* v. 1 only

FULVIO, ANDREA, fl. 1510-1543. *Antiquitates urbis* ([Rome, 1527?]). Inv.3.20; 2.3.3.23; C4 (under Fulvius) <641208, h> *IC5.F9598.527a

FUNCK, JOHANN NICOLAUS, 1693-1777.
De adolescentia latinæ linguæ (Marburg, 1723). 4.3.6.39; C135 <nd, h> Class 2007.23*

De imminenti latinæ linguæ senectute (Marburg, 1736). 4.3.6.38; C135 <nd, h> Class 2007.23.7*

De virili ætate latinæ linguæ (Marburg, 1727, 1730). 4.3.6.36-37; C135 <nd, h> Class 2007.23.4* 2 v.

FURNEAUX, PHILIP, 1726-1783. ‡*Letters to the honourable Mr. Justice Blackstone* (London, 1770). Inv.14.52; 6.1.5.35; B12, C83 <700926, h> On title page: "Ut spargam T·H." Br 327.70*

G

GAFFAREL, JACQUES, 1601-1681. *Curiositez inouyes de la sculpture talismanique* ([n.p.], 1637). Inv.4.114; C112 <641212?, 17th c. v> 24215.12*

GAGLIARDI, PAOLO, 1675-1742. *Parere intorno all'antico stato de' Canomani* (Padua, 1724). Inv.4.108; 2.3.8.37; C4 <641212?, v> *IC7.G1217.724p

GALE, THEOPHILUS, 1628-1678. †‡*The court of the Gentiles* (London, 1672-1677). Inv.4.9; C171 <641212?, h> Extensive notes and additions by TH. *EC65.G1319.669cb 4 v.

GALE, THOMAS, 1635?-1702, ed.
Historiæ britannicæ ... scriptores XV (Oxford, 1691-1687). 4.2.3.19-20; not in C <nd, h (v. 2 r)> Br 98.307 F* 2 v.

Opuscula mythologica physica et ethica (Amsterdam, 1688). Inv.2.39; C17, C128 <6410.., v> Sold as a duplicate by librarian J. G. Cogswell to Prof. John S. Popkin; to Conyers Francis, 1852; to Charles Eliot Norton, 1889; purchased with the Norton library, 1905. *EC65.G1320.671ob (A) Second copy not located.

GAMUCCI, BERNARDO. *Le antichita della citta di Roma* ([Venice, 1580]). Inv.4.127; 2.3.8.50; C4 <641212?, v> *IC5.G1498.565ℓc

GAND, LOUIS DE. *Parallelum olivæ* (London, 1656). 2.5.1.22; C26 (under Brachey) <nd, h> *EC75.H7267.Zz656g

GANDY, HENRY, 1649-1734. *Some remarks, or, short strictures* (London, 1704). Inv.4.38 (part); 2.3.5.33; not in C <641212?, xt> *EC7.G1538.704s

GAROFALO, BIAGIO, 1677-1762. *De antiquis ... fodinis* (Vienna, 1757). 4.2.5.13; C36 (under Carophylus) <nd, h> Class 3227.57*

GARTH, SIR SAMUEL, 1661-1719. *The dispensary* (London, 1726). 4.2.8.8; C141 <nd, r> 15462.40*

GAY, JOHN, 1685-1732.
The Mohocks (London, 1712). C227 <nd, r> *EC7.G2523.712m (A)

A panegyrical epistle to Mr. Thomas Snow (London, 1721). 4.2.3.22; C240 (under Snow) <nd, h> f*EC75.H7267.Zz740p

GEDDES, JAMES, d. 1748? *An essay on the composition of the ancients* (Glasgow, 1748). 4.3.7.1; C112 <nd, r> Gp 83.355*

GEDDES, MICHAEL, 1650?-1713.
Miscellaneous tracts (London, 1702, 1705, 1706). Inv.1.28 (part); 2.2.6.8-10; C112 <631024, r> *EC7.G2672.702m 3 v.

Several tracts against popery (London, 1715). Inv.1.28 (part); 2.2.6.11; C112 (= v.4 of *Miscellaneous tracts*) <631024, h> *EC7.G2672.715sa

GEE, JOSHUA, WRITER ON COMMERCE.
The trade and navigation of Great Britain considered (London, 1729). 4.2.7.17; C210 <nd, h> *EC75.H7267.Zz737t

[Another edition] (London, 1767). 4.1.8.43; C37 <nd, h> Econ 217.1.3*

GELLI, GIOVANNI BATTISTA, 1498-1563.
La Circe ([Florence?, ca. 1550?]). Inv.3.146; 2.4.8.22; C113 <641208, v> *IC5.G2829.544ce (B)

A general history of all the rebellions, insurrections and conspiracies in England (London, 1717). 2.1.6.19; C245 (under Britain) <6712.., xt> Br 307.17*

GENNES, PIERRE DE, 1701-1759. †*Memoire pour le sieur de la Bourdonnais* (Paris, 1751).
Inv.1.31; 2.2.6.42-44; C106 <631024, h> Fr 1321.2.16* 3 v.

GENTLEMAN OF IRELAND, PSEUD. *The present settlement vindicated* (London, 1690).
2.2.5.16; not in C <671209, h> *EC75.H7267.Zz691t

GEORGE II, KING OF ENGLAND. *Letters, in the original, with translations, that passed
between the King, Queen, Prince, and Princess of Wales* (London, 1737). 4.2.7.11; C249
(under title) <nd, r>
*EC75.C1527.747ℓ

GIANNONE, PIETRO, 1676-1748.
Anecdotes ecclésiastiques (Amsterdam, 1738). Inv.5.47; 2.4.8.8; C64 (under title)
<6506.., v> *IC7.G3488.Eh738e

‡*Dell'istoria civile del regno di Napoli* (Naples, 1723). Inv.4.6; 2.3.4.21-24; C57
<641212?, v> On flyleaf: "This Work Book was purchased by Me at Naples in February
1752, & it being both prohibited & very scarce I paid for it (that is for the 4 Vols) £[coded
price]. TH." *IC7.G3488.723d 4 v.

Opere posthume (Venice, 1768). Not in C The Widener Official Catalogue recorded this
title as a Hollis gift; the original gift copy was rejected as a duplicate, September 1920.

Professione di fede ([Venice?, 1735?]). Inv.3.131; 2.3.8.9; C171 <641208, v>
*IC7.G3488.735p

GIBBON, EDWARD, 1737-1794. ‡*Critical observations on the sixth book of the Æneid*
(London, 1770). C235 (under Æneid) <nd, xt> TH identifies the author on the title
page. *EC75.G3525.770c

GIBSON, EDMUND, 1669-1748, *see* Anglo-Saxon Chronicle; Camden, William; Church of
England

GIGGEO, ANTONIO. ‡*Thesaurus linguæ arabicæ* (Milan, 1632). 4.1.3.7-10; C203 <nd, h>
Note inserted in v. 1: "This is a fine Copy of a very scarce ~~Book~~ Work. T·H has been
particularly industrious in collecting Grammars & Lexicons of the Oriental, Root
Languages, to send to Harvard College, in hope of forming by that Means, assisted by
the Energy of the Leaders, always beneficent, a few PRIME Scholars, Honors to their
Country & Lights to Mankind. Two other works He wishes to have been able to send
to that College. 'Gazophylacium Linguae Persarum', Amst. 1684, in folio. 'Meninski,
Thesaurus Linguarum Orientalium' [containing the Arabic, Persic & Turkish Languages]
Viennae, 1687. Tom. 4, in folio. The first used to appear in Catalogues, at a Guinea,
25s. price. The last, even within these four Years, at about four Guineas. Now, when
they appear, but that most rarely, ten, twenty Guineas is given for the former & fifty for
the latter. This Change has proceeded from the Gentlemen of our East India Factorys
buying up all the Copies thay can meet with of these Books; the more ingenious for
themselves, artful, to make presents to the Great Men & Literati of the East, to many of
whom it seems, Books of this Kind, and the Gentlemen of Harvard will still rejoice at
it as it may lead further, are particularly acceptable. Lord Clive paid, it is said Twenty
Guineas for the 'Gazophylacium' just before he sailed from England. And Governor
Van Sittart lately for his Brother, Fifty for the 'Meninski'. There is no contending with
Asiatics, Nabobbers!" 3231.4 F* 4 v.

GILBERT, SIR GEOFFREY, 1674-1726, *see* Locke, John, *An abstract*

GILDON, CHARLES, 1665-1724. *The deist's manual* (London, 1705). Inv.4.177; 2.2.5.38; C171 <641212?, h> Phil 8661.13*

GILL, ALEXANDER, 1565-1635. ‡*Logonomia anglica* (London, 1621). Inv.4.54 *or* Inv.15.17; 6.1.8.3; C135 <641212? *or* 691129, r> On colophon: "Note. The great Milton had his Instructions from this Author, whose praise he celebrates in a Latin poem." On title page, Thomas Hearne records its purchase, 7 May 1733, from Mr. Broughton of Oxford, bookseller, who had bought it "with many others" from the Christ Church library. STC 11874 Second copy not located.

GILLIES, JOHN, 1712-1796. *An inquiry, whether the study of the ancient languages be a necessary branch of modern education* (Edinburgh, 1769). Inv.11.15 (part); 6.1.6.34; C236 <6809.., sheep & marbled boards> *EC75.Us344.766f A second copy, Inv.15.30 <691129>, not located.

GINGLE, JACOB, PSEUD. *The Oxford sermon versified* (London, 1729). Inv.14.23; 6.1.7.17; C239 (under title) <700926, h> *EC7.M6942.727t

GIOVANE, GIOVANNI, 16th cent. *De antiquitate, et varia Tarentinorum fortuna* (Naples, 1589). Inv.3.18; 2.3.3.22; not in C <641208, h?> *IC5.G4391.589d

GIOVIO, PAOLO, 1483-1552.
‡*Le iscrittioni poste sotto le vere imagini de gli huomini famose* (Florence, 1552 [i.e., 1551]). 4.3.6.30; C27 <nd, h> On flyleaf: "Che tra l'uom del sepolcro, ed in vita il serba. Petrarca." *IC5.G4395.Ei551o

Le vite di dicenove huomini (Venice, 1561). Inv.3.106; 2.3.5.38; C27 <641208, v> *IC5.G4395.Ei561d (A)

GIRAUDEAU, BONAVENTURE, 1697-1774. *Praxis linguæ sacræ* (La Rochelle, 1757). 4.1.5.13; C203 <nd, h> 2272.6*

GLANVILL, JOSEPH, 1636-1680.
A blow at modern sadducism (London, 1668). Inv.14.30; 2.2.7.19; not in C <700926, h> *EC65.G4593.557bd

Essays on several important subjects (London, 1676). Inv.13.55; 6.1.7.32; not in C <700926, r> *EC65.G4593.B672e (B)

Plus ultra, or, The progress and advancement of knowledge (London, 1668). Inv.4.119; 2.2.7.19; not in C <641212?, h> *EC65.G4593.668p A second copy, Inv.14.31; <700926>, not located.

‡*Sadducismus triumphatus* (London, 1726). Inv.8.50; 2.3.7.39; not in C <661001, r> On flyleaf: "A curious, strange Book." 24244.16.2*

GLOVER, A NON-CONFORMIST. *The argument a priori concerning the existence … of God* (London, 1737). 2.2.5.17; C293 (under GOD) <nd, h> *EC7.G5185.732d

GLOVER, PHILIP, 1732-1751. *An inquiry concerning virtue and happiness* (London, 1751). 2.2.5.17; not in C <nd, h> *EC7.G5185.732d

See also A discourse concerning virtue and religion

GLOVER, RICHARD, 1712-1785. *Leonidas, a poem* (London, 1737). 4.1.5.7; C141 <nd, h> *EC75.H7267.Zz737g

‡[Another edition] (London, 1738). 4.2.8.6; C141 <nd, h> On title page: "The author's age, when the first edition was published, was only 25 years." *EC75.G5187.737ℓd

GLOVER, ROBERT, 1544-1588. *Nobilitas politica vel civilis* (London, 1608). Inv.8.22; 4.3.1.11; C118 (under Milles, Thomas) <661001, r> STC 11922 F

GODWIN, FRANCIS, 1562-1633. †*De præsulibus angliæ commentarius* (Cambridge, 1743). Inv.1.3; 2.2.1.9; C66 <631024, h> Br 192.10 F*

GOLDSMITH, OLIVER, 1730?-1774. *An enquiry into the present state of polite learning in Europe* (London, 1759). Inv.2.73; 2.3.8.42; B12, not in C <6410..> Original Hollis gift not located.

GOLIUS, JACOBUS, 1596-1667. *Lexicon arabico latinum* (Leiden, 1653). 4.2.2.20; C203 <nd, r> 3231.7 F*

GOLTZIUS, HUBERTUS, 1526-1583. *De re nummaria antiqua* (Antwerp, 1708). Inv.5.54; 2.4.1.16; C129 <6506.., h> Typ 730.08.432 F

GOODWIN, THOMAS, 1586 or 7-1642. *Moses and Aaron* (London, 1685). Inv.4.30; C4 (1685) <641212?, r.> *EC.G5497.625mn

GOODWIN, THOMAS, 1600-1680. *A discourse of the punishment of hell* (London, 1680). Inv.4.151; 2.1.7.14; C171 <641212?, h> *EC.G6375.680d

GORDON, GEORGE, HISTORIAN. *The history of our national debts and taxes* (London, 1753). Inv.2.58 & Inv.2.59; 2.1.5.1-2; C146 <6410..> Original Hollis gift not located.

GORDON, JOHN. ‡*A new method of demonstrating from reason and philosophy the four fundamental points of religion* (London, 1756). Inv.4.129; 4.4.6.26; C233 <641212?, r> On flyleaf: "Said to have been written ~~written~~ [*sic*] by a Young Gentleman Son of <u>Tacitus</u> Gordon." On title page: "By Mr. Gordon of the Temple." Phil 8586.2*

GORDON, THOMAS, d. 1750.
A cordial for low spirits (London, 1763). Inv.16.102; 2.1.7.44; C171 <670511, h> Br 2095.55* 3 v.

‡*An essay on government* (London, 1747). 2.3.7.38; C247 (under Government) <641208, h> On title page: "The author, Mr. Gordon's son –." *EC75.H7267.Zz735t

A political dissertation on bull-baiting (London, 1718). 2.2.5.32; C224 <nd, h> *EC75.H7267.Zz737h

See also The independent Whig; Tacitus; Trenchard

GORI, ANTONIO FRANCESCO, 1691-1757. *Storia antiquaria Etrusca* (Florence, 1749). 4.4.7.31; C235 <nd, r> *IC7.G6754.749s

GOUGH, RICHARD, 1735-1809. ‡*Anecdotes of British topography* (London, 1768). Inv.12.8; 6.1.3.4; C3 (under title) <690818, h> On flyleaf: "The ingenious Author of this much wanted work is said to be Richard Gough Esq., an English Gentleman, Fellow of the Society of Antiquaries of London. A second edition of this work, from the nature of it, will much improve it. Jan. 1, 69." Br 3637.68*

GOUSSET, JACQUES, 1635-1704. *Commentariæ linguæ ebraicae* (Amsterdam, 1702). 4.3.3.15; C135 <nd, h> 2271.20 F*

GRAEVIUS, JOANNES GEORGIUS, 1632-1703. *Syntagma variarum dissertationum* (Utrecht, 1702). Inv.13.54; 6.1.7.13; C113 <700926, r> ML 27.02*

GRAHAM, WILLIAM, 1720-1796. *A letter to the Right Reverend the Lord Bishop of Bangor* (London, 1750). 2.1.7.20; not in C <671209?, h> *EC65.W4574.653cb (B)

Grammatici illustres XII, ed. Jean Thierry (Paris, [1516]). Inv.10.16; 4.4.4.12; C135 <680712, h> L 505*

GRANT, SIR FRANCIS, BART., 1658-1726. *Sadducismus debellatus* (London, 1698). 4.4.6.18; not in C <680930, h> *EC75.H7267.Zz698r

GRASCOME, SAMUEL, 1641-1708? *Remarks on a sermon preach'd January the 31ˢᵗ, 1703/4* (London, [1704]). Inv.4.38 (part); 2.3.5.33; not in C <641212?, xt> *EC65.G7686.704r

GRAUNT, JOHN, 1620-1674. *Natural and political observations* (London, 1662). 2.3.8.7; not in C <6506.., h> *EC65.Ev226.661f

GRAVIER, JEAN, OF GENOA? *Recueil de toutes les uniformes qui se sont signalé durant le siege de la ville de Genes* (Genoa, 1752). Inv.3.31; 2.3.4.2; not in C <641208, v> Typ 725.52.435

GREAT BRITAIN.
An act for the security of his highnes [sic] (London, 1657). Inv.2.20; 4.1.5.4; not in C <6410.., h> Bound with 25 more printed acts and declarations, all dated 1657. *EC65.G798L.B657a

A collection of acts and ordinances (London, 1658). Inv.2.23; 2.3.3.6; C148 <6410.., h> Often referred to as Scobell. Br 67.33 F*

‡*A collection of all the publicke orders, ordinances and declarations* (London, 1646). Inv.2.21; 2.2.3.26; C147 <6410.., r> On flyleaf, a long quotation from Milton, Of reformation; on title page: "Out of the library of the excellent Dr. John Wallis. Ut spargam." Br 67.39 F*

A collection of several acts of Parliament … for providing maintenance for ministers (London, 1657). Inv.4.63; 2.1.7.21; C79 (under Acts of parliament) <641212?, h> Br 1800.3*

Debates in the House of commons [1667-1694], ed. Anchitell Grey (London, 1763). 2.3.6.27; C146 <nd, h> Br 1880.15* 10 v.

Ephemeris parliamentaria (London, 1654). Inv.3.28; 2.2.4.10; C146 <641208, h> *EC65.F9594.654g

‡*An exact collection of all remonstrances* [1641-1643] (London, 1643). Inv.2.38 (under Husband; dates misread as 1741, 1743); C115 (under Husband, Edward) <6410.., h> On flyleaf, Hollis has transcribed twelve lines from a text he identifies as: "A short treatise of Politike Pouuer [sic], and of the true obedience which subjects owe to Kings & other civil Gorvernors with an exhortation to all true English-men, compyled by D. J. P. B. R. W. and printed at Geneva in small octavo 1556." In the excerpt itself he has emphasized "or those that have appointed office upon trust, have not autoritie [sic] upon just occasion,

AS THE ABUSE OF IT, to take away what they gave?" On verso: "Note. The before cited tract was written with extraordinary spirit & beauty of stile by Dr John Poynet, or Ponnet first Bishop of Rochester, & then of Winchester; a prelate of distinguish'd learning & Character. He died, a voluntary exile, at Strasburg in Germany. — In the year 1642 this tract was republished to serve the Parliament cause, then daringly attacked and trampled on." On title page: "Out of Dr John Wallis's collection." Br 1800.32* (B)

The history and proceedings of the House of Commons (London, 1742-1744). 2.4.6.19-32; C146 <nd, r> Lamont Documents, Brit Doc 9000.65 14 v.

The history and proceedings of the House of Lords (London, 1742). 2.4.6.9-16; C146 <nd, r> Lamont Documents, Brit Doc 9000.50 8 v.

Proceedings and debates of the House of commons, in 1620 and 1621 (Oxford, 1766). 2.4.6.17; C146 <nd, h> Br 1810.32* 2 v.

Protest [in the House of Lords] *against the bill to repeal the American stamp act* (Paris, 1766). 4.1.7.20; C241 <nd, h> *EC75.G798P.766p

Second protest [in the House of Lords] *with a list of the voters against the bill to repeal the American stamp act* (Paris, 1766). 4.1.7.20; C241 <nd, h> *EC75.G798P.766s

‡*Speeches and prayers of this great and happy parliament* (London, 1641). Inv.2.42 (misdated 1740-1741); 2.1.7.9; C147 <6410.., h> TH quotes *Areopagitica* on flyleaf, beginning "For when God shakes a Kingdom …" to "… some new enlighten'd steps in the discovery of truth." On title page: "Ut spargam" and "Once belonging to the very eminent Dr. John Wallis." On p. 7, caption-title corrected to read "Feby" for "November." *EC65.G788P.B641sb

The statutes at large, ed. Owen Ruffhead (London, 1763-1765). Inv.5.2; C81 (under Ruffhead) <6506.., v. 1, 3-4 h, v. 2, 5-9 r> TH subscribed to it in person, see *Diary*, November 1-2, 1764, having loaned his copies of the Decree of Star Chamber and Milton's *Areopagitica* to the editor. Br 67.46* 9 v.

See also D'Ewes, Sir Simonds

GREAVES, JOHN, 1602-1652. *Miscellaneous works* (London, 1737). C113 <nd, r> 14465.59* 2 v.

GREEN, MATTHEW, 1696-1737. *The spleen* (London, 1738). 4.2.7.16; C238 <nd, h> *EC75.H7267.Zz740m

GREGORY, OF NYSSA, SAINT, ca. 335-ca. 394. *De S. D. N. resurrectione concio* (Paris, 1597). 4.3.8.29; C15 (under Hierocles) <nd, h> *OGC.H532.597

GREGORY, JOHN, 1724-1773. ‡*Observations on the duties and offices of a physician* (London, 1770). Inv.13.27; 6.1.4.14; C99 <700926, h> On flyleaf: "The author, Dr. Gregory, medical professor at Edinburgh, in Scotland." On title page: "By Dr. Gregory." *EC75.G8625.770o

GREVILLE, FULKE, BARON BROOKE, 1554-1628.
Certain learned and elegant workes (London, 1633). 6.1.3.20; C141 (under Brooke) <nd, h> STC 12361 (A)

†[Another copy] Inv.3.92; 2.4.4.13; C141 (under Brooke) <641208, h> STC 12361 (B)

GREY, ANCHITELL, d. 1702, *see* Great Britain. *Debates in the House of commons*

GRONOVIUS, JOANNES FREDERICUS, 1611-1671.
Observationum liber novus (Deventer, 1652). 4.4.8.48; not in C <nd, v>
*NC6.G9985.651o

Observationum libri tres (Leiden, 1662). 4.4.8.20; not in C <nd, 17th c. v>
Class 9716.5.5* (A)

GROSVENOR, BENJAMIN, 1676-1744. *Persecution and cruelty in the principles ... of the Romish Church* (London, 1735). Not in C <6506.., h> *EC75.H7267.Zz735s

GROTIUS, HUGO, 1583-1645. †*Le droit de la guerre et de la paix* (Leiden, 1759). 4.2.4.12-13; C83 <nd, h> Int 940.30* 2 v.

GROVE, HENRY. *A system of moral philosophy* (London, 1749). 2.4.6.33; C47 <nd, h> *EC7.G9195.749s 2 v.

GRUTERUS, JANUS, 1560-1627. *Inscriptiones antiquæ totius orbis romani* (Amsterdam, 1707). 4.4.1.5-6; C5 <nd, h> Class 6007.07 F* 2 v.

GUADAGNOLI, FILIPPO. *Breves arabicæ linguæ institutiones* (Rome, 1642). 4.3.4.16; C51 <nd, v> 3231.24*

GUARIN, PIERRE. *Grammatica hebraica et chaldaica* (Paris, 1724). 4.2.5.5-6; C57 <nd, h> 2261.21* 2 v.

GUARINO, OF FAVERA, BISHOP OF NOCERA, d. 1537. *Magnum dictionarium* (Venice, 1712). 4.2.1.22; C204 <nd, h> 4221.25 F*

GUAZZO, STEFANO, 1530-1593. *Dialoghi piaceuoli* (Piacenza, 1587). Inv.3.144; 2.4.8.14; C113 <641208, v> *IC5.G9327.586db

GUDE, MARQUARD, 1635-1689.
Antiquæ inscriptiones (Leeuwarden, 1731). 4.4.1.14; C5 <nd, h>
*EC75.H7267.Zz731g (A)

Epistolæ (The Hague, 1714). 4.3.5.21; not in C <nd, h> ML 157.14*

GUICCIARDINI, LODOVICO, 1521-1589. *Descrittione ... di tutti i Paese Bassi* (Antwerp, 1581). Inv.2.11; C48 <6410.., v>
Map Collection, Pusey Library MAP-LC DH33.G9 1581 F*

GUILLIMAN, FRANÇOIS, d. 1612. *Helvetia* (San Vittorino, 1623). Inv.3.110; 2.4.7.18; C57 <641208, 17th c. calf> Swi 131.1*

GURDON, THORNHAGH, 1663-1733. ‡*The history of the High court of Parliament* (London, 1731). Inv.10.25; 4.7.1.2; C80 <680712, r> In v.2, on p.8: "Floreat Libertas, Pereat Tyrannis! xxx d. Jan. MDCCLXVIII T·H." Br 134.13* 2 v.

GWATKIN, THOMAS, b. 1742? *Remarks upon the first of three letters against The confessional* (London, 1768). 6.1.4.28; C276 (under Confessional) <nd, h> *EC75.H2448.767o (A)

GYLLENBORG, CARL, GREVE, 1679-1746. *Letters which passed between Count Gyllenborg, the Barons Gortz, Sparre, and others* (London, 1717). 2.1.7.4; C204 (under title) <nd, xt> *QSC7.G9975.Eg717lb

H

HABERLIN, FRANZ DOMINICUS, 1720-1787. *Familiæ Augustæ Wilhelmi Conquestoris Regis Angliæ* (Göttingen, 1745). 6.1.3.29; C224 <nd, h> *EC75.H7267.Zz769t

HACKET, JOHN, 1592-1670. *Scrinia reserata* ([London], 1693). Inv.12.48; 6.3.2.11; C27 (under Life of Archbishop Williams) <690818, h> *EC65.H1158.693s (B)

HAILES, SIR DAVID DALRYMPLE, LORD, *see* Dalrymple, Sir David

HAKEWILL, WILLIAM, 1574-1655. ‡*The libertie of the subject, against impositions* (London, 1641). Inv.10.50 (part); 4.4.7.42; C247 <680712, h> On flyleaf of tract volume: "A volume of scarce tracts relating to the important subjects of Impositions & Ship-money." *EC65.G798P.B641t

HALE, SIR MATTHEW, 1609-1676. ‡*The history of the common law of England* ([London], 1739). 4.2.7.12; C80 <nd, r> On title page: "very scarce." Law School UK 903 HAL

HALIFAX, GEORGE SAVILE, MARQUIS OF, 1633-1695. *Miscellanies* (London, 1704). Inv.13.5; 6.1.7.36; B13, C113 <700926, h> 15493.16.100*

HALL, JOSEPH, 1574-1656. *Virgidemiarum. Satires in six books* (Oxford, 1753). Inv.4.187; C142 <641212?, r> 14454.23*

HALLET, JOSEPH, 1692-1744.

> *A free and impartial study of the holy scriptures recommended* (London, 1729-1732-1736). Inv.4.71; 2.2.5.13-15; B13, not in C <641212?, h> C 1224.72.30* 3 v.

> *Reflections on some passages in Mr. Peirce's answer to Mr. Enty's Truth and liberty* (London, 1721). 2.3.7.5; not in C <6506.., marbled boards> *EC7.P3551.720p

HALLIWELL, HENRY, d. 1703? *Deus justificatus, or, The divine goodness vindicated* (London, 1668). Inv.3.138 (under Cudworth); 2.2.7.18; C164 (ascribed to Ralph Cudworth) <641208, h> *EC65.H1599.668d (A)

HAMMOND, ROBERT, 1621-1654.

> ‡*Letters* (London, 1764). 4.4.6.9; C147 <nd, h> On front flyleaf, a note about General Ireton; back flyleaf, about Dr. Joseph Letherland. *EC75.H7267.Zz764h

> *Reflections on some passages in Mr. Peirce's answer* (London, 1721). Not in C <6506.., marbled boards> *EC7.P3551.720p

HAMPDEN, JOHN, 1594-1643. *The tryal of John Hambden* [*sic*] (London, 1719). Inv.3.73; 4.3.3.12; B13, C146 <641208, r> Br 1820.10 F*

HARDOUIN, JEAN, 1646-1729.

> †*Ad censuram Scriptorum Veterum prolegomena* (London, 1766). 2.4.6.8; not in C <nd, h> *EC75.H7267.Zz766h

> *Opera selecta* (Amsterdam, 1709). C5 <nd, r> Tipped in, MS. declaration by the author defending his work, December 27, 1708 (contemporary copy). C 1224.2 F*

HARE, FRANCIS, 1671-1740. ‡*The difficulties and discouragements which attend the study of the scriptures* (London, 1729). 4.2.7.8; C173 <nd, h> Facing title page: "+ Afterward Bishop Hare." *EC7.H2225.714di

Harington, Sir John, 1560-1612. *Nugæ antiquæ* (London, 1769). Inv.14.32; not in C <700926, r> *EC.H2254.769n

Hariri, 1054-1152. *Concessus Haririi quartus, quintus & sextus*, ed. Albert Schultens (Leiden, 1740). 4.2.7.24; not in C <nd, h> OL 22200.91*

The Harleian miscellany (London, 1744-1746). 4.1.5.17-24; C113 <nd, v.2-5, 7-8 h, other volumes r> Br 260.85* 8 v.

Harmony without uniformity (London, 1740). 4.2.7.11; C224 <nd, r> *EC75.C1527.747ℓ

Harrington, James, 1611-1677.

†‡*The common-wealth of Oceana* (London, 1656). 4.2.4.2; C84 <nd, h> On flyleaf: "Concerning James Harrington, the ingenuous James Harrington; and Henry Neville, the ingenuous Henry Neville, his Friend: See 'A. Sydney on Gov.' the last edit. in the notes, and 'Plato Redivivus' edit 4." On title page: "Rare." On dedication page (to Oliver Cromwell): "The whole Dedication. He could address, with honest art, but not flatter, a Tyrant." *EC65.H2381.656c

†‡*The Oceana ... and his other works* (London, 1700). 4.4.3.1; C84 <67...., h> On flyleaf: "This Toland's own edit. of the <u>Oceana</u>, is the correctest of that most noble work. Praise him, Reader. Palmal, aug. 12, 67." At foot of frontispiece: "Felicity is Freedom and Freedom is Magnanimity. Thucyd." At foot of title page: "Ut spargam T·H." The verso of the title page and the recto of the dedication bear offsets of TH's instructions to the binder. Soc 730.1 F*

The Oceana and other works (London, 1747). Inv.1.7; 2.3.3.7; C84 <631024, r> Soc 730.1.2 F*

Harris, James, 1709-1780.

Hermes (London, 1751). Inv.1.21; 2.4.5.31; C135 <631024, h> *EC75.H2421.751h (B)

†‡ [Another edition] (London, 1765). 2.1.5.20; C135 <nd, h> On flyleaf: "For the character of this MASTER work See Lowth's English Grammar." On the closing paragraphs on p. 426: "Mark, Youth, mark well, the justness, beauty of this closing Passage!" Designed and sponsored by TH. *EC75.H7267.Zz765h (A)

Three treatises (London, 1744). Inv.1.23; 2.4.5.32; C113 <631024> Phil 9245.12*

[Another edition] ([London, 1765]). 2.1.5.21; C113 <nd, r> Designed and sponsored by TH. This copy lacks its title page. *EC75.H2421.744tb

Harris, Thomas. *Popery and slavery displayed* (London, 1745). 2.2.5.8; C224 <671209?, h> *EC75.H7267.Zz745t

Harris, Walter, 1686-1761. *The history of the life and reign of William-Henry* (Dublin, 1749). Inv.16.8; 2.2.2.22; C27 <670511, r> Br 1960.47 F*

Harris, William, 1675?-1740.

A discourse concerning transubstantiation (London, 1735). C297 <6506.., h> *EC75.H7267.Zz715s2

A second discourse concerning transubstantiation (London, 1735). Not in C <6506.., h> *EC75.H7267.Zz715s2

HARRIS, WILLIAM, 1720-1770. ‡*An historical and critical account of the life of Oliver Cromwell* (London, 1762). 2.3.5.7; C27 <611014, r (in May, 1848)> On flyleaf: "Thomas Hollis of Lincoln's Inne, is desirous of having the honor to present this book, written by the Rev. & learned William Harris, Dissenting Minister of Honeyton in Dorsetshire, to the public library of Harvard College in New England – oct. 14, 1761." On pp. 372-3: "The scheme related in this master letter was eminently accomplishing, without the Quixotism or Ambition of it, under the late Pittonian, & most noble Administration." John Langdon Sibley thought (wrongly) that this was Thomas Hollis V's earliest surviving gift to the Harvard College Library. *EC75.H7267.Zz762h2

HARRISON, AMOS.
The duties and dignities of gospel ministers (London, 1742). Inv.12.60 (part); 6.1.7.24; C297 <690818, h> Tr 433*

The New Year's gift defended (London, 1743). Inv.12.60 (part); 6.1.7.14; C297 <690818, h> Tr 433*

A *New Year's gift humbly offered* (London, 1742). Inv.12.60 (part); 6.1.7.14; B13, C297 <690818, h> Tr 433*

Remarks on the vicar's complaint (London, 1742). Inv.12.60 (part); 6.1.7.14; C297 <690818, h> Tr 433*

The uncertainty of life (London, 1724). Inv.12.60 (part); 6.1.7.14; C297 <690818, h> Tr 433*

HARTE, WALTER, 1709-1774.
An essay on reason (London, 1736). 4..2.3.22; C238 <nd, h> f*EC75.H7267.Zz740p

‡*Essays on husbandry* (London, 1764). Inv.5.20; 2.4.5.22; C1 <6506.., h> On flyleaf: "The Author, The Rev. Walter Hart, Prebendary of Windsor. Written like a Good man, a Scholar, and a Gentleman. T·H." Agr 444.10*

[Another copy.] 2.1.4.22; C1 <nd, h> Agr 444.10.2* (A)

‡[Another copy.] Inv.14.28; 6.1.4.3; C1 <700926, h> On title page: "Ut spargam. T·H." Agr 444.10.2* (B)

HARTLEY, DAVID, 1705-1757. *Observations on man* (London, 1749). Inv.12.23; 6.1.6.28-29; C94 <690818, h> TP 2038.30* 2 v.

HARVEY, WILLIAM, 1578-1657. *Opera omnia* (London, 1766). C99 <nd, h> Printed by William Bowyer; title page follows a design favored by TH. Wrongly plated as ex dono "Societatis de Prom: Evang. Nov.-Angl. Et Partibus Adjacentibus." Med 258.15.2 F*

HAURIS, BENNO KASPAR, ed. *Scriptores historiæ romanæ latini veteres* (Heidelberg, 1743-1748). 4.3.1.11-13; C19 (under title) <nd, h> L 565.2 F* 3 v.

HAVERKAMP, SIWART, 1684-1742. *Nummophylacium reginæ Christianæ* (The Hague, 1742). Inv.5.60; C129 <6506.., h> Arc 1455.2 F*

HAWKINS, RICHARD. *A discourse of the natural excellencies of England* (London, 1658). Inv.3.136; C139 (under England, a discourse) <641208, r> Br 1820.133*

HAWKINS, WILLIAM. *The pretences of enthusiasts considered and confuted* (Oxford, 1769). Inv.15.31; C298 <691129, h> *EC75.H3148.769p

HAYM, NICOLA FRANCESCO. *Biblioteca italiana* (Venice and Milan, 1741). Inv.3.95; 2.3.5.5; C32 <641208, v> Ital 6030.5.5*

HAYNE, THOMAS, 1582-1645. *Linguarum cognatio* (London, 1648). Inv.13.47; 6.2.8.15; C135 <700926, r> *EC65.H3327.639ℓb

HAYTER, THOMAS, 1702-1762, attributed author. ‡*An essay on the liberty of the press* (London, 1755). 2.4.5.4; C229 (under Press) <nd, h> On first page: "chiefly as it respects personal slander. By John Asgill." *EC75.H7267.Zz725m

HEARNE, THOMAS, 1678-1735, ed.
‡*A collection of curious discourses* (Oxford, 1720). Inv.10.22; 4.4.5.7; B14, C25 <680712, h> On flyleaf: "Way, considerable, has been made with <u>Hearne's pieces</u>. The rest shall be sent as they can be obtained; toward which attainment, neither money nor industry is wanting. Of some Copies, only a hundred were printed; and almost all of them are scarce, the large Paper copies especially. — T·H For one book only, I know I am to pay three guineas whenever I get it; with thanks." On verso of title page, offset of TH's instructions to the binder. Br 260.76*

Hemingi chartularium ecclesiæ Wigornensis (Oxford, 1723). 4.1.6.15-16; C25 <nd, r> Br 1035.22* 2 v.

Historia vitæ et regni Ricardi II (Oxford, 1729). 4.1.6.14; C5 <nd, h> Br 1530.4*

Liber niger scacarii (Oxford, 1728). 4.1.6.17-18; C5 <nd, r> Br 82.5* 2 v.

See also Adam, of Domerham; Bible. N.T. Acts; Bible. N.T. Gospels. Gothic; Caius, Thomas; Gill, Alexander; Hemingford, Walter de; Joannes, Glastoniensis; Morins, Richard de; Peter, of Langtoft; Rous, John; Sprott, Thomas; Thomas, of Elmham; William, of Newburgh

HEATH, BENJAMIN, 1704-1766. *Notæ sive lectiones* [on Greek dramatists] (Oxford, 1762). Inv.12.6; 6.1.2.26; not in C <690818, h> Class 9722.4*

HEINECCIUS, JOHANN GOTTLIEB, 1681-1741. *Operum ad universam iuris prudentiam* (Geneva, 1744-1749). 4.1.6.19-26; C114 <nd, h> Gov 6563.6* 8 v.

HEISTER, LORENZ, 1683-1758. *A general system of surgery* (Amsterdam, 1750). Inv.7.4; 2.2.4.29; C99 <651010, h> Countway Library 1.Mv.21

HEMINGFORD, WALTER DE, fl. 1300. *Historia de rebus gestis Edvardi I*, ed. Thomas Hearne (Oxford, 1731). Inv.17.12; 4.4.5.22-23; C5 <68…., r> Br 1460.7* 2 v.

HEPHAESTION. *Enchiridion de metris et poemate* (Utrecht, 1726). 4.4.6.16; C15 Original Hollis gift not located.

HERBELOT, BARTHELEMY D', 1625-1695. *Bibliotheque orientale* (Paris, 1697). 2.3.2.5; C133 <nd, r> Asia 36.97 F*

HERBERT OF CHERBURY, EDWARD HERBERT, BARON, 1583-1648.
De religione gentilium (Amsterdam, 1663). Inv.7.5; 2.1.6.46; not in C <651010, h> Her 6.14*

[Another edition] (Amsterdam, 1700). Inv.1.29; 2.1.7.15; not in C <631024, h> Phil 2040.35.2*

A dialogue between a tutor and his pupil (London, 1768). 6.1.3.12; C114 <651010, h> Her 6.14*

HERNE, THOMAS, d. 1722.

An account of all the considerable books [in the Trinitarian controversy] (London, 1720). 6.1.7.9; not in C <700926, h> *EC7.H4317.B719h

An account of all the considerable pamphlets (London, 1719). 6.1.7.9; C224 <700926, h> *EC7.H4317.B719h

A continuation of the account of all the considerable pamphlets (London, 1720). 6.1.7.9; C224 <700926, h> *EC7.H4317.B719h

The false notion of a Christian priesthood (London, 1718). Inv.13.4; 6.1.7.9; C324 (under Priesthood) <700926, h> *EC7.H4317.B719h

HERODOTUS. *Dell' imprese de' greci e de' barbari* (Verona, 1733). Inv.4.17; C15 <641212?, v> Gh 44.345.2* 2 v.

HERPORT, BUAT.

†*An essay on truths of importance* (London, 1767). Inv.10.23; 4.4.5.30; C114 <680712, h> *EC75.H7267.Zz768h (B)

†‡[Another copy] Inv.11.7; 6.1.6.14; C114 <6809.., h> On flyleaf: "Extract of a Letter from a Friend to T·H. 'I have read over Mr. Herport's excellent tract, and cannot but think, the Translator in some passages has missed of the sense of the Original. It will be a seasonable present for the Times; though surely the Document in Section cxxiiii will not well square with some of his Principles laid down, & seems to grant, all that our present Advocates for subscription contend for, and certainly more than the civil Magistrate ought to claim: But, upon the whole, He is an extraordinary man, and his memory much to be honored.'" *EC75.H7267.Zz768h (A)

HERVEY, JAMES, 1714-1758. *Many made righteous … two sermons* (London, 1769). Inv.15.32; C298 (under Two sermons) <691129, r> *EC7.H4458.769m

HESIOD. *The works of Hesiod*, tr. Thomas Cooke (London, 1728). 4.4.5.5; C15 <nd, r> Gh 46.260* (A)

HESYCHIUS, OF ALEXANDRIA. *Lexicon: cum notis* (Leiden, 1746-1766). 4.2.1.3-4; C203 <nd, h> Gh 47.15 F* 2 v.

HEYLYN, PETER, 1600-1662.

Augustus: or, An essay of those means and councils (London, [1710?]). 2.3.7.38; C244 (under Augustus) <641208, h> *EC75.H7267.Zz735t

Cosmography (London, 1670). 6.4.1.14; C48 Original Hollis gift not located.

HICKERINGILL, EDMUND, 1631-1708. *The works* (London, 1716). Inv.4.75; 2.3.7.30; C114 <641212?, calf> *EC65.H5255.C716w

HICKES, GEORGE, 1642-1715.

Antiquæ literaturæ septentrionalis libri duo (Oxford, 1705). Inv.16.30; 2.2.2.14-15; not in C <670511, h> f*EC65.H5256.705a (A) 2 v.

†‡*Institutiones grammaticæ Anglo-Saxonicæ* (Oxford, 1689). Inv.8.9; 4.2.5.26; C51 <661001, h> On title page: "Semper aut discere, aut docere, aut scribere dulce habui T·H." *EC65.H5256.689i (B)

HIEROCLES, OF ALEXANDRIA, fl. 430. *De providentia et fato* (Paris, 1597). 4.3.8.29; C15 <nd, h> *OGC.H532.597

HILL, JOSEPH, 1625-1707. *The interest of these United Provinces* (Middleburg, 1673). 2.4.5.19; C232 <nd, xt> *EC65.H5534.Eg673ib

HILL, SIR RICHARD, BART., 1733-1808.
Goliath slain (London, 1768). 6.1.4.29; C299 <nd, xt> *EC75.H5553.768g

A letter to the Reverend Dr. Nowell (London, 1769). 6.1.4.30; C299 <nd, xt> *EC75.H5553.769ℓ

Pietas oxoniensis (London, 1768). 6.1.4.30; C299 <nd, xt> *EC75.H5553.768pb

HIPPOCRATES. *Opera omnia ... quæ extant* (Geneva, 1657). Inv.8.5; 4.4.1.7-8; C99 <661001, russia (not TH)> Gh 58.10 F* 2 v.

HIRSCH, JOHANN CHRISTOPH, 1698-1780. *Bibliotheca numismatica* (Nuremberg, 1760). Inv.17.6; 4.4.3.11; C129 <68...., r> Arc 1329.1 F*

The history of non-conformity (London, 1708). Inv.12.84; 6.1.7.27; C68 <690818, h> *EC7.A100.704h2a

HOADLY, BENJAMIN, 1676-1761.
†‡*The common rights of subjects, defended* (London, 1719). Inv.8.48; 2.3.7.20; not in C <661001, h> On title page: "Ut Spargam T·H." *EC7.H6502.719c

The measures of submission to civil magistrates consider'd (London, 1710). Inv.1.25; 2.7.7.35; C84 <631024, h> *EC7.H6502.706md

The original and institution of civil government (London, 1710). Inv.1.24; 2.1.6.33; C84 <631024, h> *EC7.H6502.710o

See also Cerri, Urbano

HOBBES, THOMAS, 1588-1679.
Leviathan (London, 1651). Inv.2.34; C84 <6410.., h> f*EC65.H6525.651ℓ (B)

Philosophical rudiments concerning government and society (London, 1651). 4.4.8.39; C84 <nd, r> *EC65.H6525.Eg651p

Tracts of Mr. Thomas. Hobbs [sic] (London, 1682). Inv.1.30; 2.2.6.32; C114 <631024, r> *EC65.H6525.B682c

See also D'Avenant, Sir William, *Preface*

HODGES, NATHANIEL, 1629-1688. *Loimologia, or, An historical account of the plague in London* (London, 1721). 4.2.7.13; C99 <nd, 18th c. calf> Br 4690.20.3*

HOFMANN, JOHANN JAKOB, 1635-1706. *Lexicon universale, historiam sacram et profanam ... explanans* (Leiden, 1698). 4.4.1.9-12; C114 Original Hollis gift not located.

HOLBACH, PAUL HENRI THIRI, BARON D', 1723-1789. *Le christianisme dévoilé* (London [i.e., Amsterdam], 1767). Inv.17.37; 4.4.8.15; C162 <68...., h> *FC7.H6903.766cc (B)

HOLDSWORTH, EDWARD, 1684-1746. †*Remarks and dissertations on Virgil* (London, 1768). Inv.10.12; 4.4.4.13; B14, not in C <680712, h> Lv 19.225*

HOLE, WILLIAM, 1710-1791. ‡*The ornaments of churches considered* (Oxford, 1761). 4.1.4.18; C127 (under Wilson) <nd, h> On flyleaf: "There is much ingenuity in this Book. Of however different opinion T·H is in some points, he still exceedingly respects the Author of it, the learned, excellent Dr. Thomas Wilson, Prebendary of Westminster." *EC75.H7145.761o

HOLLAND (PROVINCE) STATEN. *Deductio, sive declaratio ord. Hollandiæ West-Frisiæque ex ipsis fundamentis regiminis Belgici desumpta* (Leiden, 1654). 2.2.8.60; C146 (under Deductio) <6410.., h> Neth 2351.3*

HOLLAND, GUY, 1587?-1660. ‡*The prerogative of man* ([Oxford], 1645). 2.2.5.2; C335 (under Soul) <671209?, h> At front of first volume, TH's acquisition note. *EC75.H7267.Zz706ℓ 3 v.

HOLLAND, HENRY, 1583-1650? *Heroologia anglica* (Arnhem, [1620]). Inv.3.82; 2.3.3.33; C28 (under Holland, Hugh) <641208, h> STC 13682a

HOLLIS, THOMAS, 1720-1774, comp. ‡*The true sentiments of America* (London, 1768). 6.1.6.13; C185 & C242 <nd, sheep and marbled boards> On p. 111, at the beginning of John Adams, *Dissertation on the canon and the feudal law*, passage marked and at foot of page: "A beauty." Wrongly attributed as the gift of Joseph J. Cooke, December 22, 1783. *AC7.M382G.768t

See also Bell, John

HOLWELL, JOHN ZEPHANIAH, 1711-1798. *Interesting historical tracts* [concerning Bengal and Indostan] (London, 1766). 4.3.6.32-33; B14, C114 <nd, h> Ind 7135.5* 2 v.

HOME, FRANCIS, 1719-1813. ‡*The principles of agriculture* (London, 1762). Inv.9.32; 4.3.6.7; C1 <680711, h> On flyleaf: "It is apprehended, the institution of a Professorship of Chemistry and Mineralogy at Cambridge in N.E. on the plan of those instituted in Sueden and some parts of Germany, which plan might easily be procured, would prove of more real, lasting benefit to North America, than all the vast wealth of a Nabob. T·H." *EC75.H7267.Zz762h

HOMER. *Odyssea Graece et Latine*, ed. Samuel Clarke (London, 1758). 6.3.7.4; C15 <nd, contemporary calf> Harvard Depository KE 30455 v. 2 only.

HOOKE, ROBERT, 1635-1703.
A description of helioscopes (London, 1606). 2.4.4.17; C215 <nd, r> *EC65.St935.B681t

Lampas, or, Descriptions of some mechanical improvements of lamps (London, 1677). 2.4.4.17; C215 <nd, r> *EC65.St935.B681t

Lectures and collections (London, 1678). 2.4.4.17; C215 <nd, r> *EC65.St935.B681t

Lectures de potentia restitutiva (London, 1670). 2.4.4.17; C215 <nd, r> *EC65.St935.B681t

HOOKER, RICHARD, 1553 or 4-1600. *The works of that learned and judicious divine* (London, 1723). Inv.16.31; 2.2.2.17; C78 (under Laws of ecclesiastical polity) <670511, r> C 1238.3 F*

HOPKINS, WILLIAM, 1706-1776.

‡*An appeal to the common sense* (London, 1754). Inv.12.24; 6.1.8.40; C174 <690818, h>
On flyleaf: "The Author, The Rev. William Hopkins, of Cuckfield, in Sussex, an excellent
Gentleman." C 1236.27.35*

‡*The trinitarian controversy reviewed* (London, 1760). Inv.12.25; 6.1.7.11; C174
<690818, h> TH identifies author. C 1236.27.30*

HORACE. *Epistolæ ad Pisones, et Augustum*, ed. & tr. Richard Hurd (London, 1766).
4.1.8.16-18; not in C <nd, h> Lh 8.567* 3 v.

HORNE, ANDREW, d. 1328. *La somme appelle Miroir des iustices* (London, 1642). Inv.1.40 *or*
Inv.2.121; 2.2.8.27 *or* 2.2.8.37; C80 <631024 *or* 6410..> Original Hollis gifts not located.

HOROLOGGI, GIUSEPPE, *see* Choniates, Nicetas

HORSLEY, JOHN, 1685-1737. *Britannia romana* (London, 1732). Inv.16.61; 2.4.2.9; B15, C5
<670511, r> Arc 855.200 F*

HORSLEY, WILLIAM, 1701?-1776? *Serious considerations on the high duties examin'd*
(London, 1744). 4.2.7.17; C210 <nd, h> *EC75.H7267.Zz737t

HOTMAN, FRANÇOIS, 1524-1590.

†‡ *Francogallia* ([Geneva], 1573). Inv.8.13; 2.4.8.6; C57 & C84 <661001, h> On flyleaf: "Ut
spargam T·H." *FC5.H7981.573f

‡*Franco-Gallia,* tr. Robert Molesworth (London, 1721). Inv.1.20; 2.4.5.25; C57 & C84
<631024, h> On flyleaf: "The Translator's preface to the Franco-gallia, and the preface
to the Acc. of Denmark are two of the noblest prefaces in the English language. Thomas
Hollis." On title page: "The Translator Ld. Molesworth." On p. vij, where Molesworth
makes "a publick Confession of my Political Faith," TH notes "and mine."
*EC75.H7267.Zz721h (A)

HOTTINGER, JOHANN HEINRICH, 1620-1667.

Elementale quadrilingue (Zurich, 1654). 4.4.7.12 (part); not in C <nd, r> Broadside
specimen of Semitic types: Hebrew, Chaldaic, Samaritan, Syriac, Arabic; punchcutter
and typecaster, Balthasar Koeblin. pp *GB6.A100.654e

Historia orientalis (Zürich, 1651). 4.1.7.35; C133 <nd, v> Sem 254*

Promtuarium, sive Bibliotheca orientalis (Heidelberg, 1658). 4.1.7.35; C133 (misdated
1758) <nd, v> Sem 254*

Smegma orientale (Heidelberg, 1658). 4.1.6.29; C133 <nd, v> Sem 254*

HOUGHTON, JOHN, MASTER OF A SCHOOL AT NAMPTWICH IN CHESHIRE. *A new
introduction to English grammar* (Salop, 1766). Inv.8.12; C51 <661001, h>
EducT 20757.66.10*

HOWARD, SIR ROBERT, 1626-1698. ‡*The history of religion* (London, 1694). Inv.16.44;
2.1.8.10; C114 <670511, h> On flyleaf: "By Sir Robert Howard, a friend and Protector of
John Milton." *EC65.H8364.694h

See also Person of honour, pseud.

HOWE, THOMAS, fl. 1765-1805. *Episcopacy, a letter to the Rev. Mr. Forster* (London, 1765). 6.1.6.3; C301 <nd, h> Tr 201*

HOWSON, ROBERT. *The second part of The boy of Bilson* (London, 1698). 4.4.6.18; C260 <680930, h> *EC75.H7267.Zz698r

HUBER, MARIE, 1695-1753. *The world unmask'd* (London, 1736). 6.1.6.27; C127 <nd, r> Phil 182.24*

HUET, PIERRE-DANIEL, 1630-1721. *The history of romances* (London, 1715). Inv.4.158; 2.1.8.51; C114 <641212?, early calf> Lit 946.70.7*

HUGHES, OBADIAH, 1695-1751. ‡*The veneration of saints* (London, 1735). C301 <6506.., h> On title page: "Ut spargam. T·H." *EC75.H7267.Zz735s

HUNT, JEREMIAH, 1678-1744. *The sources of corrupting both natural and revealed religion* (London, 1735). Not in C <6506.., h> *EC75.H7267.Zz735s

HUNT, THOMAS, 1696-1774.

‡*De antiquitate, elegantia, utilitate linguæ arabicæ* (Oxford, 1739). 4.2.5.3; C236 <nd, h> On flyleaf of tract volume: "This is a rare & choice volume. Much difficulty there has been to render it complete." *EC75.H7267.Zz748h

De usu dialectorum orientalium (Oxford, 1748). 4.2.5.3; C236 <nd, h> *EC75.H7267.Zz748h

A dissertation on Proverbs (Oxford, 1743). 4.2.5.3; C236 <nd, h> *EC75.H7267.Zz748h

HUNTER, ALEXANDER, 1729-1809. *Georgical essays* (London, 1764). Inv.12.69; 6.1.8.53; C1 <690818, h> Agr 479.10*

HURD, RICHARD, 1720-1808.

‡*Moral and political dialogues* (London, 1759). 2.3.7.29; C225 <6410.., h> TH identifies author. *EC75.H7267.Zz759m

[Another edition] (London, 1765). 4.1.8.13-15; C115 <nd, h> Designed by TH. *EC75.H7267.Zz759md (A) 3 v.

See also Horace

HUS, JAN, 1369?-1415. *A seasonable vindication* (London, 1660). 2.1.5.3; not in C <671209, h> *EC65.P9567.B660t

HUSBAND, EDWARD, *see* Great Britain. *Collection of remonstrances*

HUTCHESON, FRANCIS, 1694-1747.

‡*De naturali hominum socialitate oratio inauguralis* (Glasgow, 1730). Inv.4.57; 2.1.6.15; C84 <641212?, h> TH notes one erratum at the end. Soc 532.21*

An essay on the nature and conduct of the passions and affections (London, 1728). 2.1.8.35; C47 <641024, h> Phil 2053.60.2*

Philosophiæ moralis institutio compendiaria (Glasgow, 1742). Inv.16.105; 2.2.7.24; C47 <670511, h> Phil 2053.40*

Reflections upon laughter (Glasgow, 1750). 2.1.8.35; not in C <641024, h> Phil 2053.60.2*

A short introduction to moral philosophy (Glasgow, 1753). Inv.2.102; 2.1.8.46; C47 <6410.., h> Phil 2053.41*

[Another edition] (Glasgow, 1764). 4.2.8.26-27; C47 <nd, r> XP 3276* 2 v.

A system of moral philosophy (Glasgow, 1755). Inv.16.69; 2.2.4.7-8; C47 <670511, r> *EC7.H9706.755s (B) 2 v.

HYDE, THOMAS, 1636-1703.
Mandragorias, seu Historia shahiludii (Oxford, 1694). Inv.6.10; 2.1.7.34-35; C133 <650817, h> SG 3619.94 F* 2 v.

Syntagma dissertationum quas olim auctor … Thomas Hyde … edidit (Oxford, 1767). 4.4.4.18-19; C133 <68....?, h> Declared lost, 2002.

Veterum Persarum et Parthorum et Medorum religionis historia (Oxford, 1760). Inv.16.91; 4.4.4.20; C133 <670511, r> R 1520.3.2*

[Another copy] Inv.9.15; C133 <680711> Original Hollis gift not located.

I

IBBETSON, JAMES, 1717-1781. *A plea for the subscription of the clergy* (London, 1768). 6.1.4.27; C303 <nd, h> *EC75.Ib230.767pc

IHRE, JOHAN, 1707-1780.
Analecta Ulphilana (Uppsala, 1769). 6.1.3.34; C41 <700926, h> 8267.82.6*

Glossarium suidogothicum (Uppsala, 1769). Inv.13.64; 6.1.1.9-10; C204 <700926, h> f*QSC7.Ih710.769g 2 v.

See also Bible. N.T. Gospels. Gothic

IMBONATI, CARLO GIUSEPPE, d. 1697. *Bibliotheca latino-hebraica* (Rome, 1694). 4.2.3.13; C133 (under Imbonatus) <67....?, calf> Part of Bartolucci, *Bibliotheca magna rabbinica*, q.v. f*IC6.B28574.675b (B) v. 5

‡*The immortality of mans soule* (London, 1645). 2.2.5.2; C335 (under Soul) <671209, h> On front flyleaf of tract volume: "This collection was formed by T·H, with pains & expence, not long after he returned from his Travells." *EC75.H7267.Zz706ℓ 3 v.

An impartial history of Michael Servetus (London, 1724). Inv.4.77; 2.1.6.26; B22, C29 (under Servetus) & C207 (under title) <641212?, r> *EC7.A100.724i

[Another copy] 2.4.6.37; B22, C29 & C207 (under title) <671209?, h> *EC75.H7267.Zz718s

INCHOFER, MELCHIOR, 1585-1648, *see* Scotti, Giulio Clemente

‡*The independent Whig* (London, 1752-1753). Inv.16.47; 2.1.7.9; C113 (under Gordon) & C116 (under title) <670511, h> On flyleaf: "Long live the Memories of John Trenchard, and Thomas Gordon! T·H." *EC75.H7267.Zz752g 4 v.

INETT, JOHN, 1647-1717. *Origines anglicanæ: or, A history of the English church* (London, 1704). 4.2.3.25; C66 <nd, h> Br 326.85.5 F*

An inquiry into the miracle (London, 1730). Inv.2.92; 2.3.7.4; C345 (under Trinity)
<6410.., h> *EC7.Sy442.715ic

[Another copy] 6.1.5.40; C345 (under Trinity) <700926, h> *EC75.H7267.Zz731t

INTERIANO, PAOLO, 16ᵗʰ cent. *Ristretto delle historie genovesi* ([Lucca, 1551]). Inv.3.46;
2.3.5.29; C58 (under Interianus) <641208, calf> *IC5.In837.551r

An introduction of the ancient Greek and Latin measures into British poetry (London, 1737).
4.2.7.16; C239 (under Poetry) <nd, h> *EC75.H7267.Zz740m

IRELAND. LAWS, STATUTES, ETC. *A list of such of the names of the nobility, gentry and
commonalty … attainted of high treason* (London, 1690). 2.2.5.16; C247 (under James II)
<671209?, h> *EC75.H7267.Zz691t

J

JACKSON, JOHN BAPTIST, 1701-1780?
    ‡*An enquiry into the origin of printing in Europe* (London, 1752). Inv.7.3 (part); 2.2.4.32;
    C9 <651010, h> On flyleaf: "John Baptist Jackson, Artist. an ingenious irregular."
    B 4507.52*

    An essay on the invention of engraving and printing in chiaro oscuro (London, 1754).
    Inv.7.3 (part); 2.2.4.32; C9 <651010, h> B 4507.52*

    See also Sidney, Algernon, *Discourses concerning government* (1751)

JACKSON, RICHARD, M.A. *Literatura græca* (London, 1769). Inv.15.16; 6.1.8.15; B15, C115
<691129, r> AH 4817.69*

JACOB, GILES, 1686-1744. *A new law-dictionary* ([London], 1762). Inv.6.2; 4.2.2.22; C80
<650817, h> Gov 5077.62 F*

JACOMB, GEORGE, fl. 1719. *A particular account of the proceedings of the assembly at Exeter*
(London, 1719). Inv.5.30 (part); 2.3.7.7; C303 <6506.., xt> *EC7.J1595.719p

JENKIN, ROBERT, 1656-1727. ‡*A brief confutation of the pretences against natural & revealed
religion* (London, 1702). 2.2.7.1; not in C <670815?, r> TH identifies the author.
Ga 84.145*

JENNINGS, DAVID, 1691-1762. *An introduction to the knowledge of medals* (London, 1764).
Inv.16.1; 2.2.6.21; C129 <670511, h> Typ 705B2.64.466

JENYNS, SOAME, 1704-1787. †*The objections to the taxation of our American colonies*
(London, 1765). Inv.16.38 (part); 4.1.7.22; C241 (under title) <670511, h>
*AC7.Ot464.765ab (B)

JOANNES, GLASTONIENSIS. *Chronica, sive historia de rebus Glastoniensibus*, ed. Thomas
Hearne (Oxford, 1726). Inv.12.55; 6.1.4.1-2; C5 <690818, r> Br 5187.92.2* 2 v. A second
copy, Inv.17.31 <68….>, not located.

JOBERT, LOUIS, 1637-1719. ‡*The knowledge of medals* (London, 1699). Inv.16.104; 2.2.5.37;
C130 (under Medals) <670511, h> On back flyleaf: "The Author Pere Joubert The
Translator Roger Gale." *EC75.H7267.Zz697j

JOHNSON, SAMUEL, 1649-1703.
Reflections on the history of passive obedience ([London, 1689]). 2.2.5.16; not in C
<671209?, h> *EC75.H7267.Zz691t

‡*The works* (London, 1713). Inv.2.25; 2.3.3.1; C116 <6410.., r> At foot of title page: "Ut
spargam." f*EC65.J6371.C710wb

JOHNSON, SAMUEL, 1709-1784, *see* Committee Appointed to Manage the Contributions
for Clothing French Prisoners of War; Baretti, Giuseppe; Browne, Sir Thomas; Ascham,
Roger

JOLLIE, THOMAS, 1629-1703.
The Surey demoniack ([London, 1689]). 4.4.6.18; C339 (under Surrey) <680930, h>
*EC75.H7267.Zz698r

A vindication of the Surey demoniack (London, 1698). 4.4.6.18; C339 (under Surrey)
<680930, h> *EC75.H7267.Zz698r

JONES, BASSETT. ‡*Hermælogium, or, An essay on the rationality of the art of speaking*
(London, 1659). Inv.10.47; 4.4.8.42; C136 <680712, marbled boards> From the estate of
Anthony a Wood; evidently given to TH V by his great-uncle, TH III (1659-1731), who
inscribed it in 1709. *EC75.H7267.Zz659j

JONES, DAVID, fl. 1676-1720. *The life of James II. late king of England* (London, 1705).
2.3.5.33; not in C <64...., xt> *EC7.J7134.702ℓba

JONES, JOHN, 1700-1770.
A farther appeal to the unprejudiced judgment of mankind (London, 1766). 4.4.6.27;
C320 (under North American Indians) <nd, h (marbled boards)> *EC75.B5628.752s

[Another copy] 2.4.6.2; C320 (under North American Indians) <nd, h>
*AC7.M4537.B766m v.2

A short and safe expedient (London, 1769). 6.1.5.6; C165 (under Dawson, Benjamin)
<690818, h> C 1259.20.31*

JONES, ROWLAND, 1722-1774. *The origin of language and nations* (London, 1764). Inv.17.33;
4.3.6.8; C116 <68....> Original Hollis gift not located.

JONES, WILLIAM, 1726-1800.
The Catholic doctrine of a Trinity (London, 1767). 6.1.5.14; C176 <700926, h>
*EC75.J7285.753fb

An essay on the first principles of natural philosophy (Oxford, 1762). Inv.14.18; 6.1.3.9;
C138 <700926, h> *EC75.J7285.762e (B)

‡*A full answer to the Essay on spirit* (London, 1753). Inv.2.84; 6.1.5.15; C304 <6410.., h>
TH identifies the author. *EC75.J7285.753f

[Another edition] (London, 1770). Inv.14.33; 6.1.5.14; C304 <700926, h>
*EC75.J7285.753fb

A letter to a young gentleman at Oxford (London, 1769). Inv.14.53; 6.1.5.15; C304
<700926, h> C 1259.5.45*

Remarks on the principles and spirit of a work, entitled The confessional (London, 1770). 6.1.5.5; C304 <700926, h> C 1259.5.45*

JORTIN, JOHN, 1698-1770. *The life of Erasmus* (London, 1758-1760). 4.4.4.15-16; C28 <nd, r> Harvard Depository KG 6775

‡*Journal de ce qui s'est passé à Genes* ([Genoa?], 1749). 2.3.4.2; C116 <641208?, v> On flyleaf: "Bought at Genoa, in Nov. 1752, by T·H then upon his Travells." Typ 725.52.435

‡*The judgment of whole kingdoms and nations, concerning the rights, power, and prerogative of kings, and the rights, privileges, and properties of the people* (London, 1713). Inv.8.11; C84 <661001, h> On flyleaf: "VT SPARGAM T·H." First published as *Vox populi, vox dei* (1709) and variously attributed to Daniel Defoe; John Somers, baron Somers; and John Dunton. *EC7.D6323.A709vi

JULIAN, EMPEROR OF ROME, 331-363.
   Opera (Paris, 1583). 4.1.8.35; C16 <nd, h> Gi 29.12*

   ‡*Les Césars* (Paris, 1683). Inv.5.13; 2.3.4.12; not in C <6506.., h> On title page: [translated] "By the very learned excellent Spanheim." KG 10283*

JUNIUS, FRANCISCUS, 1589-1677.
   De pictura veterum libri tres (Rotterdam, 1694). 4.3.2.11; C5 <nd, r> Fine Arts X Cage XFA3236.1 Folio

   Etymologicum anglicarum (Oxford, 1743). 4.2.2.1; C204 <nd, h> f*NC6.J9592.743e

   †*The justice and necessity of taxing the American colonies* (London, 1766). Inv.16.38 (part); 4.1.7.22; C267 <670511, h> *AC7.Ot464.765ab (B)

JUSTICE OF PEACE. *A letter from a justice of peace to a counsellor at law* ([London, 1670?]). 2.4.5.19; not in C <nd, xt> *EC65.A100.670ℓ

K

KALS, JOHANNES GUILJELMUS, b. 1702. *Grammatica hebræo-harmonica* (Amsterdam, 1758). 4.1.6.27; C52 <nd, h> 2265.8*

KEITH, SIR WILLIAM, 1680-1749. ‡*The history of the British plantations in America* (London, 1738). Inv.17.8; 4.3.5.13; C58 <68...., h> On title page: "Rare; no other part was published. T·H." P. 172-3, passage on education and conversion of Indians underlined; at foot of p. 173: "An ingenious, beneficent, active North American, might enquire out, what that 'then only practicable Scheme for instructing the <u>Indians</u>, which <u>succeeded wonderfully</u>,' was. T·H." On back flyleaf: "<u>The Society</u>, the glorious Society, <u>instituted in London, for promoting Learning</u>, having existed but a little while, through scrubness of the times; no other than PART I of this History was published: and it is very scarce." US 18391.50*

KEMP, JOHN, 1665-1717. ‡*Monumenta vetustatis Kempiana*, ed. Robert Ainsworth and John Ward (London, 1720). Inv.16.40; C5 (under Kempiana) <670511> On p. 8, item 16: "†penes T·H"; p.126, on items 3 & 4: "T·H."

KENNETT, BASIL, 1674-1715.

‡*The lives and characters of the ancient Greek poets* (London, 1735). Inv.12.27; 6.1.6.39; B16, C28 <690818, r> On p. 65, under a picture of a headless statue of Pindar: "And there a Pindar stood without a Head." Class 1446.97.4* 2 v. in 1

Romæ antiquæ notitia: or, The antiquities of Rome (London, 1746). Inv.4.131; 2.1.5.36; C5 <641212?, h> Harvard Depository KE 39715

KENNETT, WHITE, 1660-1728.

‡*Bibliothecæ americanæ primordia ... an American library* (London, 1713). C32 & C116 <67...., h> On flyleaf: "A curious & rare Book, and particularly proper for the Library of Harvard College, at Cambridge in N.E. Palmal. aug. 12. 67." On title page: "White Kennet. Bishop Kennet. [sic]" Numerous passages emphasized passim. P. ix, ref. to John Eliot with note: "Singularly expressed; the late excellent Dr would have been pleased to have seen this passage." P. xiv: "Man Of New England, Owe much good will to Mr Hutchinson, for his curious, valuable 'History of the Colony of Massachusets' [sic] bay. T·H." The additional annotations hereafter are perhaps not by TH. P. xv: "TROVBLE and expence." P. 82, correction of typographic errors. P. 89, 157 & 498, identifies author of *A short story of the rise ...* as "By Tho. Welde." P. 93, identifies Thomas Lamb as "an independent of New England." P. 95 & 495, identifies author of *The simple cobbler of Agawam* as "by Nathaniel Ward." P. 215, under *A specimen of Papal and French persecution*: "This work was republished by Dr Priestley 1788." US 57.11*

A compassionate enquiry into the causes of civil war (London, 1704). 2.3.5.33; C304 <671209, r> *EC7.K3948.704cb

‡*An historical register* (London, 1744). Inv.16.70; 2.2.2.13; C58 <670511, h> On preface leaf: "A biassed but useful author." Br 1890.72 F*

Moderation maintain'd (London, 1704). Inv.4.38; 2.3.5.33; C304 <641212?, xt> *EC7.D3623.704m2

A sermon preach'd before the Honourable House of Commons ... January xxx, 1705/6 (London, 1706). Inv.4.38 (part); 2.3.5.33; C304 <641212?, xt> *EC7.K3948.706s

See also A complete history of England

KENNICOTT, BENJAMIN, 1718-1783. *The state of the collation of the Hebrew manuscripts* (Oxford, 1761). Inv.14.51; 6.1.4.4; C41 <700926, r> *EC75.K3972.761s

KENRICK, WILLIAM, 1725?-1779.

The grand question debated (Dublin, 1751). Inv.4.134 (part); 2.2.5.1; C335 (under Soul) <641212?, r> Phil 8635.1*

A reply to The grand question debated (London, 1751). Inv.4.134 (part); 2.2.5.1; C335 (under Soul) <641212?, r> Phil 8635.1*

KEYSSLER, JOHANN GEORG, 1693-1743. ‡*Antiquitates selectæ septentrionales* (Hanover, 1720). Inv.10.42; 4.3.8.43; C6 <680712, gilt paper and v> On title page: "rariss." Typ 720.20.480

KING, EDWARD, 1735?-1807. *An essay on the English constitution* (London, 1767). 4.3.8.15; B16, C84 <nd, h> Br 167.67*

King, Peter King, Lord, 1669-1734. *An enquiry into the constitution, discipline, unity and worship of the primitive church* (London, [1719]). 6.3.4.20; C177 <nd, h> C 2057.20*

King, William, 1685-1763.
Miltonis epistola ad Pollionem (London, 1738). 4.2.3.22; C239 (under Milton) <nd, h> f*EC75.H7267.Zz740p

Milton's Epistle to Pollio, translated (London, 1740). 4.2.3.23; not in C <nd, h> f*EC75.H7267.Zz740p

Kirby, John Joshua, 1716-1774. ‡*Dr. Brook Taylor's method of perspective made easy* (London, 1765). Inv.7.1; 2.1.1.18, 2.2.4.31; C140 <651010, r> V. 2 has title supplied by TH in imitation of typography: "PLATES | TO | TAYLOR'S PERSPECTIVE | BY KIRBY | LONDON 1765". Fine Arts X Cage XFA5643.3.2 & XFA 5643.3.2 Folio

Kircher, Athanasias, 1602-1680. *Prodromus coptus sive ægyptiacus* (Rome, 1636). 4.3.5.25; C133 <nd, v> Andover-Harvard 606.2 K58.4p 1636a

Kirchmann, Johann, 1575-1643. *De annulis liber singularis* (Leiden, 1672). Inv.3.63; 2.2.8.56; C6 <641208> Declared lost, 1986.

Kirsten, Peter, 1577-1640.
‡*Grammatices arabicæ* (Breslau, 1609). 4.2.3.24; C51 <nd, h> On flyleaf: "This is a curious Book, & came out of a valuable Library. T·H would have been glad to have sent a better Copy of it, as of many other Books. He has been particularly fond of sending Grammars & Lexicons; in hope, to assist mainly thereby the formation of first-rate, master Men of Learning and Science." 3231.22 F*

Notæ in Evangelium S. Mathei (Breslau, 1611). 4.2.3.4; not in C <nd, h> 3131.22 F*

Tria specimina characterum Arabicorum (Breslau, 1608). 4.2.3.23; not in C <nd, h> 3231.22 F*

Knowles, Thomas, 1723-1802. *An answer to An essay on spirit* [by Robert Clayton] (London, 1753). 2.2.5.6; not in C <6410.., h> *EC7.C5797.751ec

Knox, John, ca. 1514-1572. *The historie of the reformation of the Church of Scotland* (London, 1644). 4.4.3.22; B16, C67 <nd, contemporary calf> Br 8215.72.5*

Knox, William, 1732-1810.
The controversy between Great Britain and her colonies reviewed (London, 1769). Inv.12.26; C146 <690818, h (rebacked)> *EC75.K7795.769ca

A letter to a member of Parliament (London, 1765). C241 (under America) <66...., r, xt> *EC75.K7795.765ℓ

Koran. English. *The Koran*, tr. George Sale (London, 1734 [i.e., 1733]). Inv.2.35; 2.3.4.32; C123 <6410.., r> OL 24303.11*

Krafft, Georg Wolfgang, 1701-1754. *Description et representation exacte de la maison de glace* (St. Petersburg, 1741). 6.1.3.29; C225 <nd, h> *EC75.H7267.Zz759t

Krebs, Johann Tobias, 1718-1782. *Decreta romanorum pro ludæis* (Leipzig, 1769). Not in C <nd, r> Gi 10.95*

L

LA BAUME-DESDOSSAT, JACQUES-FRANÇOIS DE, 1705-1756. *La Christiade ... par souscrition* (Paris, 1752). Inv.4.66 (part) <641212?, r> 14487.22* v. 3

LA BOÉTIE, ÉTIENNE DE, 1530-1563. †‡*A discourse of voluntary servitude* (London, 1735). Inv.12.70; 6.1.8.45; C82 <690818, h> Title page supplied in MS. by TH, with note "rariss." On second flyleaf: "T·H is desirous of having the honor to lodge this small but excellent work, in the public library of Harvard College, at Cambridge, in New England. Palmal, jan. 1, 1769." *EC75.H7267.Zz735ℓ

LA BRUYÈRE, JEAN DE, 1645-1696. *Les caractères* (Amsterdam, 1743). 4.2.8.4-5; C107 (under Bruyere) <nd, h> *FC6.L1157.688ct (B) 2 v.

LACOMBE, FRANÇOIS, 1733-1795. *Dictionnaire du vieux langage François* (Paris, 1766). 4.2.7.22; C204 <nd, h> *FC7.L1189.766d (B)

LA FONTAINE, JEAN DE, 1621-1695. *The loves of Cupid and Psyche,* tr. John Lockman (London, 1744). 4.1.7.33; C112 <nd, r> 39527.34*

LAKEMACHER, JOHANN GOTTFRIED. *Elementa linguæ arabicæ* (Helmstadt, 1718). 4.4.7.13; C52 <nd, h> 3234.41*

LA METTRIE, JULIEN OFFRAY DE, 1709-1751. *L'homme machine* (Leiden, 1748). Inv.5.74 (part); 2.2.8.48; C94 <6506..> Original Hollis gift not located.

LAMI, GIOVANNI, 1697-1770. *De eruditione Apostolorum liber singularis* (Florence, 1738). 4.3.8.38; not in C <nd, h> Andover-Harvard OLD DIV 514 Lami

LA MOTHE LE VAYER, FRANÇOIS, 1583-1672. †‡*Cincq dialogues* (Frankfurt, 1716). Inv.4.92 (under Tubero); 2.1.8.55; C125 (under Tubero) <641212?, h> TH identifies author. *FC6.L1937.630de 2 v.

LAMPE, FRIEDRICH ADOLPH, 1683-1729. *De cymbalis veterum libri tres* (Utrecht, 1703). Inv.3.57; 4.8.35; C6 <641208, v> *GC7.L1962.703d

LANCELOT, CLAUDE, 1615?-1695.
Grammaire générale et raisonnée (Paris, 1660). Inv.2.108; not in C <6410..> Original Hollis gift not located.

New method of learning with facility the Greek tongue, tr. Thomas Nugent (London, 1759). Inv.13.9; 6.1.4.8; C52 (under Port-Royal) <700926, later russia> Gutman Library EducT 21117.59

Nouvelle methode pour apprendre facilement la langue grecque (Paris, 1754). Inv.13.50; 6.1.6.38; C52 (under Port-Royal) <700926, h> 4251.25*

Nouvelle methode pour apprendre facilement la langue latine (Paris, 1736). Inv.13.51; 6.1.6.37; C52 (under Port-Royal) <700926, h> Gutman Library EducT 40917.36

LANGFORD, ABRAHAM, 1711-1774. *A catalogue of the ... collection of ... coins and medals* ([London, 1751]). Not in C <nd, h (boards)> A sale catalogue. B 1827.401*

LANGHORNE, DANIEL, d. 1681. *Elenchus antiquitatum albionensium* (London, 1675). 4.3.8.20; C6 <nd, r> *EC65.L2652.673eb

LANGUET, HUBERT, 1518-1581. ‡*Vindiciæ contra tyrannos* ([Montbéliard], 1580 [i.e., 1599]). Inv.5.48; 2.4.8.7; C84 (under Iunius) <6506.., v> On flyleaf: "Hujus libri, nonnulli quidem Theodorem Bezam, alii vero Hubertum Languetum auctorem fuisse censuerunt." On title page: "Ut spargam. T·H." *FC5.L2697.579vg.

LANGWITH, BENJAMIN, 1684?-1743. *Observations on Doctor Arbuthnot's dissertation on coins* (London, 1754). Inv.16.80; C130 <670511, r> Arc 1350.4.2*

LA PEYRÈRE, ISAAC DE, 1594-1676. ‡*Men before Adam* (London, 1656). Inv.4.116; C182 <641212?, contemporary calf> On flyleaf: "A singular & very scarce book. T·H." An 2056.56*

LAPORTE, JOSEPH DE, 1713-1779. *Observations sur l'esprit des loix* (Amsterdam, 1751). 4.2.8.7; C85 (under title) <nd, r> 39594.3.25*

LARDNER, NATHANIEL, 1684-1768. *Memoirs of the life and writings* (London, 1769). Inv.13.60; 6.1.7.4; C28 <700926, h> C 1271.18*

LA ROCHE, JEAN BAPTISTE LOUIS DE, ABBÉ. *Critique de l'esprit des loix* (Geneva, 1750). 4.2.7.38; C83 <nd, r> 39594.3.20*

LA ROCHEFOUCAULD, FRANÇOIS, DUC DE, 1613-1680. *Reflexions* (Paris, [1736?]). 4.1.8.32; C122 (under Rochefoucault) <nd, h, title page lacking> *FC6.L3273M.736

LASENA, PIETRO, 1590-1636. *Dell' antico ginnasio napoletano* (Rome, 1641). Inv.5.16; C6 <6506..> Arc 726.2 Declared lost, 2002.

[Another edition] (Naples, [1688]). Inv.3.45; 2.3.5.24; C6 <641208, r> Arc 726.2.2*

LASSELS, RICHARD, 1603?-1668. *The voyage of Italy* (Paris, 1670). Inv.4.150; 2.1.8.50; C75 <641212?, h> *EC65.L3374.670v

LAUDER, WILLIAM, d. 1771. *A letter to the Reverend Mr. Douglas* (London, 1751). Inv.14.15; 6.1.3.17; C238 <700926, h> *EC7.M4617.732c

LAVAL, ANTOINE FRANÇOIS, 1664-1728. *Voyage de Louisiane* (Paris, 1728). Inv.8.29; 4.2.4.8; C75 <661001, h> Sci 2707.28*

LAVINGTON, GEORGE, 1684?-1762. *The enthusiasm of Methodists and Papists compared* (London, 1754). Inv.4.176; 2.1.7.34-35; C178 <641212?, contemporary calf> C 8067.49.25* 2 v.

LAW, EDMUND, 1703-1787. ‡*Observations occasioned by the contest about literary property* (Cambridge, 1770). C226 <nd, xt> On half-title: "Said, by Dr. Law, Bishop of Carlisle." *EC75.L4107.770o

LAW, JOHN, 1671-1729. *Money and trade considered* (Glasgow, 1750). Inv.4.157; C37 <641212?, r> Econ 222.1*

See also Paterson, William

LAWRENCE, THOMAS, A.M. *Mercurius centralis, or, A discourse of subterranean cockle, muscle and oyster-shels* [*sic*] (London, 1664). Inv.3.64; 2.2.8.59; C71 <641208> Original Hollis gift not located.

LAYARD, DANIEL PETER, 1721-1802. *An essay on the bite of a mad dog* (London, 1763). 4.1.7.34; C100 <nd, h> Countway Rare Books RC148.L45 1763 c.1

LAYTON, HENRY, 1622-1705.

‡*An argument concerning the human souls seperate [sic] subsistance* ([London?], 1699). 2.2.5.2; C335 (under Soul) <671209, h> On flyleaf of tract volume: "This Collection was formed by T·H, with pains & expence, not long after he returned from his Travells." *EC75.H7267.Zz706ℓ v. 1

Arguments and replies (London, 1703). 2.2.5.3; not in C <671209, h> *EC75.H7267.Zz706ℓ v. 2

Observations upon Mr. Wadsworth's book ([London, ca. 1690]). 2.2.5.2; not in C <671209, h> *EC75.H7267.Zz706ℓ v. 1

‡*Observations upon a sermon entituled, A confutation of atheism* (London, [1696?]). 2.2.5.2; not in C <671209, h> On caption-title: "By Dr Bentley in Boyle Lectures." *EC75.H7267.Zz706ℓ v. 1

‡*Observations upon a short treatise written by Mr. Timothy Manlove* ([London, 1697?]). 2.2.5.2; C311 (under Manlove) <671209, h> On caption-title: "By Mr Layton. Henry Layton Esqr" *EC75.H7267.Zz706ℓ v. 1

Observations upon a treatise intitled A discourse concerning the happiness (London, 1704). 2.2.5.3; not in C <671209, h> *EC75.H7267.Zz706ℓ v. 2

Observations upon a treatise intitled Psychologia ([London, 1704?]). 2.2.5.3; not in C <671209, h> *EC75.H7267.Zz706ℓ v. 2

Observations upon a treatise intituled, A vindication of the separate existence of the soul ([London, 1703?]). 2.2.5.3; not in C <671209, h> *EC75.H7267.Zz706ℓ v. 2

Observations upon a treatise intituled Vindiciae mentis ([London, 1703?]). 2.2.5.3; not in C <671209, h> *EC75.H7267.Zz706ℓ v. 2

Observations upon Mr. Wadsworth's book of the souls immortality ([London, ca. 1690]). 2.2.5.2; not in C <671209, h> *EC75.H7267.Zz706ℓ v. 1

Observations upon Dr. Nicholls's book, intituled, A conference with a theist ([London, 1703]). 2.2.5.3; not in C <671209, h> *EC75.H7267.Zz706ℓ v. 2

A search after souls ([London], 1706). 2.2.5.4; not in C <671209, h> *EC75.H7267.Zz706ℓ v. 3

LAZERI, PIETRO, 1710-1789. *Della consecrazione del Panteon* (Rome, 1749). Inv.3.120 (under Palermo; part); 2.4.7.12; C226 <641208, h> *IC7.A100.B752h

LEAKE, STEPHEN MARTIN, 1702-1773. *An historical account of English money* (London, 1745). Inv.4.136; 2.7.6.23; C130 <641212?, r> Arc 1538.5*

LEAVESLY, THOMAS, fl. 1727-1735. *The reasons and necessity of the reformation* (London, 1735). Not in C <6506.., h> *EC75.H7267.Zz735s

LE CLERC, JEAN, 1657-1736.
  ‡*Five letters concerning the inspiration of the Holy Scriptures* (London, 1690). Inv.4.160;
  2.2.8.18; not in C <641212?, h> On title page, in unidentified hand: "Mons. LeClerc."
  Added by TH: ", being the author." C 1273.30.46*

  [Another copy] Inv.10.37; 4.4.8.36; not in C <680712, r> C 1279.30.40*

  Harmonia evangelica (Amsterdam, 1700). Inv.10.7; 4.3.4.8; C41 <680712, h>
  Bi 1357.00 F*

  Historia ecclesiastica (Amsterdam, 1716). Inv.10.13; 4.3.5.9; C65 <680712, h> C 1967.16*

  Opera philosophica (Amsterdam, 1722). Inv.10.30; 4.4.8.28-31; C109 <680712, v. 2,4 h,
  v. 1,3 r> Phil 186.5.2* 4 v.

  Parrhasiana, or, Thoughts upon several subjects (London, 1700). Inv.10.32; 4.4.7.10; C109
  <680712, r> 38563.55*

  See also Bible. N.T. Latin

LEECHMAN, WILLIAM, 1706-1785.
  The nature, reasonableness, and advantages of prayer (Glasgow, 1755). Inv.3.61; 2.2.8.46;
  B16, C178 <641208, h> C 1273.16.35*

  The temper, character, and duty of a minister (Glasgow, 1755). Inv.3.61; 2.2.8.46; not in C
  <641208, h> C 1273.16.35*

LEFORT DE LA MORINIÈRE, ADRIEN CLAUDE.
  Les vapeurs, comédie (Paris, 1753). Inv.4.118 (part); 2.1.8.20; C221 <641212?, h> Tr 511*

  Le temple de la paresse … comédie (Paris, 1753). Inv.4.118 (part); 2.1.8.20; C221
  <641212?, h> Tr 511*

LEFROY, ANTHONY. *Catalogus numismaticus* (Leghorn, 1763). 2.3.5.28; C130 <64...., h>
  Lefroy sent TH 25 copies in sheets to be bound in London and distributed (Diary,
  January 24 & 31, 1764); the binder was John Shove. Harvard is on TH's list of 25
  recipients. As Harvard Hall was in the process of rebuilding, President Holyoke retained
  it in his house. Arc 1335.10 F*

  See also Venuti, Filippo

LEHMANN, JOHANN GOTTLOB, d. 1747. *Traités de physique, d'histoire naturelle, de
  mineralogie et de metallurgie* (Paris, 1759). Inv.5.41; 2.2.6.34-36; C71 <6506.., h>
  MCZ 476 3 v.

LEICESTER, ROBERT DUDLEY, EARL OF, 1532?-1588, *see* Sansovino, Francesco

LEIGH, RICHARD, 1561?-1588, *see The state of England in 1588*

LEIGHTON, ROBERT, 1611-1684. *Prælectiones theologicæ* (London, 1693). Inv.3.105; 2.1.6.3;
  C178 <641208, h> C 274.30*

LELAND, JOHN, 1506?-1552.
  Commentarii de scriptoribus Britannicis (Oxford, 1709). Inv.17.23; 4.4.5.19; C116
  <68...., r> 10443.5* 2 v.

  The itinerary (Oxford, 1744-1745). 4.2.5.28-32; C6 <nd, h> Br 3617.10.5* 9 v. in 5

Leland, John, 1691-1766. *A view of the principal deistical writers* (London, 1754-55). Inv.4.186; 2.1.5.29-31; C178 <641212?, h> Inventory calls for v.1 only, but all 3 v. are in Hollis bindings. Phil 8520.5.2* 3 v.

Le Long, Jacques, 1665-1721. *Bibliotheca sacra* (Paris, 1723). 4.2.2.4; C42 <nd, h> Bi 3.25.5 F* 2 v.

Lemery, Nicolas, 1645-1715. *Pharmacopée universelle* (Paris, 1763-1764). 4.2.5.1-2; C90 <nd, h> Countway Rare Books RS78.L54 1763 2 v.

Lenfant, Jacques, 1661-1728.
‡*Histoire du Concile de Constance* (Amsterdam, 1714). Inv.16.82; 2.3.4.12-13; C67 <670511, h> Passages on xlvii and xlviii marked for attention. C 168.10* 2 v.

Histoire du concile de Pise (Amsterdam, 1724). Inv.2.31 *or* Inv.6.7; 2.3.4.15-16 *or* 2.3.4.19-20; C67 <6410.. *or* 650817, r> C 167.10* 2 v. Second copy not located.

Lenthal, William, 1591-1662. *Mr. Speakers speech, with His Majesties speech* ([London], 1641). 2.1.7.9; not in C <6410.., h> *EC65.G798P.B641sb

Leonhard, Johann.
An account of the Grisons (London, 1711). Inv.4.45 (part); 2.2.6.16; not in C <641212?, h> Swi 1230.11*

Brevis descriptio democratici liberæ (London, 1704). Inv.4.45 (part); 2.2.6.16; not in C <641212?, h> Swi 1230.11*

Le Page du Pratz, d. 1775. *Histoire de la Louisiane* (Paris, 1758). 4.1.8.29-31; C75 Declared lost, May 2002.

Le Paulmier, Jacques, 1587-1670. *Exercitationes in optimos fere auctores græcos* (Leiden, 1668). 4.4.7.14; not in C <nd, h> Class 9778.3*

Leslie, Charles, 1650-1722. *The finishing stroke* (London, 1711). Inv.12.62; 6.1.7.14; C83 (under title) <690818, h> *EC65.L5656.711f

Letherland, Joseph, 1699-1764, ‡*A catalogue of the ... library* ([London], 1765). Not in C <nd, r> An auction catalogue, marked and used by TH during the sale; he bought lot 2861, "One Hundred and Forty-five Volumes and single Tracts relating to the History of England, but chiefly during the Civil Wars," as a gift to Catherine Macaulay, for use in her history of England. On flyleaf of catalogue: "The late Dr. Leatherland [*sic*] was an eminently learned man, as appears by this Catalogue, and a thorough Friend to Liberty and the Principles of the Revolution. T·H." B 1827.185*

Leti, Gregorio, 1630-1701.
Conclavi de' pontifici romani ([Geneva], 1667). Inv.3.38; 2.3.5.9; C65 (under title) <641208, h> *IC6.L5685.667c

Il nipotismo di Roma ([Amsterdam], 1667). Inv.4.112; 2.5.8.39; C60 (under title), C123 (under Rome) <641212?, v> *IC6.L5685.667nb (B)

A letter from a gentleman in Edinburgh ([London], 1769). C226 (under Literary property) <nd, xt> *EC75.A100.769ℓ3

A letter from Amsterdam to a friend in England (London, 1678). 2.4.5.19; C244 <nd, xt> *EC65.A100.678ℓ

A letter to Dr. Calamy (London, [1718?]) 6.1.6.42; C213 (under Calamy, Letter to him)
<690818, r> *EC7.C1253.718ℓ

A letter to the author of the Discourse of the grounds and reasons of the Christian religion
(London, 1726). 2.2.6.2; not in C <nd, h> Phil 1930.5.37*

A letter to the Rev. Mr. George Whitefield (London, 1769). 6.1.4.30; C350 (under Whitefield)
<nd, xt> *EC75.A100.760ℓr

Letters to the right honourable the Earl of Hillsborough (London, [1769?]). Inv.13.6; 6.1.6.3;
C147 <700926, h> *AC7.M382C4.769ℓb (A)

LEVESQUE DE POUILLY, LOUIS-JEAN, 1691-1750. *Théorie des sentimens agréables*
(Paris, 1748). Inv.4.95; C95 & C354 <641212?, r> Phil 5402.4*

LEWIS, EDWARD, 1701-1784. *The patriot king displayed* (London, 1769). Inv.12.31; 6.1.8.9;
B16, C28 <690818, h> Br 1655.44*

LEWIS, WILLIAM, 1708-1763.
‡*Commercium philosophico-technicum* (London, 1763). 2.4.3.26-27; C9 <nd, h>
Bound in at the end, an advertisement for publishing by subscription *A compleat
course of chemistry* (1744); on back flyleaf: "The 'compleat Course of Chemistry'
was not published, but the Manuscript now lyes, with valuable additions to it, in the
possession of Mʳ Ambrose Godfrey, Nephew of the late Mʳ A. Godfrey, at his House in
Southampton Street, Covent Garden London. Pall Mall, aug. 14, 1766. T·H."
Chem 7107.63* 2 v.

An experimental history of the materia medica (London, 1761). 6.3.2.5; C90 <nd, h>
Countway Rare Books 22.X.31

Leycesters commonwealth ([London],1641). Inv.4.50; 2.2.6.20; not in C <641212?, h>
*EC.A100.584cb (B)

L'HOSPITAL, MICHEL HURAULT DE. *Discours sur l'état de France* ([n.p.], 1588). Inv.4.169;
2.1.8.26; C246 (under France) <641212?, h> Fr 1232.3.10*

LHUYD, EDWARD, 1660-1709. ‡*Archaeologica Britannica* (Oxford, 1707). 4.4.3.7; C6
<nd, h> On flyleaf: "At Sir Charles John Sebright's, at Beachwood, near Market-street,
in Hertfordshire, there is said to be a large collection of Manuscripts of the late Mr.
Lhuyd's; with many other valuable papers. T·H." 3271.4 F*

†‡[Liberty prints commissioned by TH] ([London, 1755-1764]). Inv.2.4; 2.4.1.2; C33 (under
Hollis) <6410.., h> On flyleaf: "Che trae l'huom del sepolcro, ed in vita il serba.
Petrarca. Thomas Hollis, an Englishman, a Lover of Liberty, Citizen of the World, is
desirous of having the honor to present this set of prints to Harvard College at Cambridge
in New England. Pall Mall, Sept. 14, 1764." Thirteen prints, the majority by Giovanni
Battista Cipriani. f*EC75.H7267.Zz760h

LICETI, FORTUNIO, 1577-1657. *De lucernis antiquorum reconditis* (Utini, 1653). 4.2.3.5; C6
(under Licetus) <nd, r> f*IC6.L6168.621dba

LIGHTFOOT, JOHN, 1602-1675. ‡*The works* (London, 1684). Inv.13.63; 6.1.1.6-7; C179
<700926, h> On recto of frontispiece of v. I: "There are many curious, valuable
remarks, concerning the <u>Heptaglott Lexicon,</u> and the <u>English Polyglott Bible,</u> in 'The
preface to the Reader,' 'The author's life,' and 'The Appendix to the author's life.' See

likewise, under many prejudices concerning them, A. Wood, in his Athenae Oxoniensis vol. 2, in his accounts of Brian Walton, Samuel Clarke, John Owen, & others. T·H" f*EC75.H7267.Zz684ℓ 2 v.

LILY, WILLIAM, 1468?-1522. *A short introduction of grammar* (London, 1662). Inv.12.65; 6.1.8.17; not in C <690818, sheep and marbled boards> *EC.L6289G.1662

LIMBORCH, PHILIPPUS VAN, 1623-1712.
‡*Historia Inquisitionis* (Amsterdam, 1692). Inv.6.5; 2.3.3.12; C67 <650817, contemporary calf> On title page: "Ut spargam. T·H." C 5466.92 F*

†*The history of the inquisition* (London, 1731). 4.1.4.22; C67 <nd, h> C 5466.92.5* 2 v. in 1

LIMOJON DE ST. DIDIER, ALEXANDRE TOUSSAINT, d. 1689. *La ville et la république de Venise* (Paris, 1680). Inv.3.60; 2.2.8.41; C49 <641208> Original Hollis gift not located.

LINDENBROG, FRIEDRICH, 1573-1648, ed. ‡*Codex legum antiquarum* (Frankfurt, 1617). Inv.12.51; 6.1.2.13; C81 <690818, h> On flyleaf: "The old books are become very scarce. Three years have passed, before this copy, a fine one, could be obtained. And when the old Books do appear, they are usually purchased for abroad, the times, at home, leading rather to Pleasure and Ambition, than to Literary and Ingenuous Pursuits. Ap. 14, 1769." On title page: "rar." Gov 5218.5 F*

LINDSAY, JOHN. *The Scripture doctrine, history and laws, relating to oaths and vows* (London, 1761). 6.1.6.35; C320 (under Oathes and vows) <nd, h> Tr 405*

LINGUET, SIMON NICOLAS HENRI, 1736-1794. *Histoire impartial des Jésuites* ([Paris], 1768). Inv.15.14; 6.1.8.43-44; C58 (under Jesuites) <691129, h> C 427.68* 2 v.

LIVINGSTON, WILLIAM, 1723-1790. *A letter to the Right Reverend Father in God, John, Lord Bishop of Llandaff* (London, 1768). 6.1.6.35; C308 <nd, xt> Formerly bound with Tr 405*. *AC7.L7269.768ℓc

LIVY. ‡*Historiarum ab urbe condita* (Amsterdam, 1738-1744). 4.2.4.15-21; C16 <64…., h> On flyleaf of v. 7: "Be it remembered, o yet ingenuous Youth, that the Writers, Prose and Poetical, of the Augustan Age and Court, were all Commonwealth Scholars, nor can such Writers be produced under Tyranny when fixed, however mild & polished at fits. T·H." *EC75.H7267.Zz738ℓ 7 v.

LLOYD, CHARLES, 1735-1773. *The conduct of the late administration examined* (London, 1767). 4.1.7.21; C242 (under America. Conduct) <67…., r> *EC75.Al582.766c v. 3

LLOYD, PHILIP, 1729-1790. *The new style the true style* (London, 1753). 2.4.5.28; not in C <670815?, h> *EC7.M1327.751sb

LOCKE, JOHN, 1632-1704.
An abstract of Mr. Locke's Essay on human understanding [by Sir Geoffrey Gilbert] (London, 1752). 2.4.5.4; C233 (under Gilbert) <nd, h> *EC75.H7267.Zz725m

Familiar letters (London, 1742). Inv.2.100; 2.4.7.13; C117 <6410.., r> Sold as a duplicate by Joseph Cogswell; repurchased, April 30, 1838. Phil 2115.75*

[Another copy] Inv.5.22; 2.3.7.42; C117 <6506.., h> Phil 2115.75.2*

‡*A letter concerning toleration* (London, 1689). Inv.15.5; 6.1.6.24; C117 <691129, h>
Includes *Second letter*, 1690, and two tracts by Jonas Proast, *q.v.* On flyleaf: "A curious,
valuable Volume. Mr. Archdeacon Proast's tracts are exceeding scarce. See further
concerning them, 'Letters concerning Toleration. By John Locke. London, printed,
1765,' in quarto — in the Preface." On title page: "By John Locke. ... Translated from the
Latin by M͏ʳ Popple." P. 1: "Translated by M͏ʳ Popple." *EC65.L7934.B691t

‡[Another edition] (London, 1690). Inv.2.37; 2.1.7.1; C117 <6410.., h> First flyleaf: "The
first edition of M͏ʳ Lock's most excellent Letter on Toleration, was printed in Latin at
Gouda, in the year 1689 in 12°. and it is now in my possession. This book was collected
by the learned D͏ʳ Conyers Middleton. Considering the pains he took with it, it is
strange he did not add the first edition. April 14, 1756 TH. See a curious account
concerning M͏ʳ Locke & the first writers on Toleration, in Sykes's Dissertation intitled
'The nature of Jewish Theocracy consider'd' beginning at p. 156." Second flyleaf: "For the
Latin edition it is said in the title ad clarissimum virum T.A.R.P.T.O.L.A. id est Theologiae
apud remonstrantes professorem, tyrannidis osorem, Limburgium, Amsterlodamensen
And scripta a P.A.P.O.I.L.A. id est Pacis amico, persecutionis osore, Johanne Lockio,
Anglo. See his life, p. 13. M͏ʳ Popple, author of the rational Catechism, is said to have
translated M͏ʳ Locke's first letter on Toleration into English." Back flyleaf; "Epistola de
Tolerantia | ad clarissimumn virum | T·A·R·P·T·O·L·A | scripta a | P·A·P·O·I·L·A | Goudae |
apud Justum ab Hoeve | MDCLXXXVIIII." *EC65.L7934.B692t

‡*A second letter concerning toleration* (London, 1690). 2.1.7.1; C117 <6410.., h> On title
page: "By M͏ʳ Locke." *EC65.L7934.B692t

A third letter for toleration (London, 1692). Inv.15.6; 6.1.6.25; not in C <691129, h>
*EC65.L7934.692t

†‡*Letters concerning toleration* (London, 1765). Inv.5.67; 2.3.3.32; C117 <6506.., h> On
flyleaf: "Thomas Hollis, an Englishman, Citizen of the World, is desirous of having
the honor to present this Book to the Library of Harvard College, at Cambridge in N.
England. Pall Mall, jan. 1, 1765." f*EC75.H7267.Zz765ℓ

Observations on the growth and culture of vines and olives (London, 1766). Inv.8.14; not
in C <661001> Original Hollis gift not located.

Two treatises of government (London, 1698). Inv.1.26; 2.2.6.1; C84 <631024> Declared
lost, 1931.

‡*Two treatises of government* (London, 1764). 4.4.6.29; C84 <640604, h> On flyleaf:
"Thomas Hollis, an Englishman, a Lover of Liberty, The principles of the Revolution, &
the Protestant Succession in the House of Hanover, Citizen of the World, is desirous of
having the honor to present this book to the public Library of the College at Cambridge,
in New England. London june 4, 1764." Designed and sponsored by TH.
*EC75.H7267.Zz764ℓ

See also Barrow, Isaac, and Bell, John

LOCKMAN, JOHN, 1698-1771. *The entertaining instructor: in French and English* (London,
1765). Inv.5.45; 2.2.6.40; C117 <6506.., r> 37578.29.5*

LODGE, JOHN, 1692-1774. *The usage of holding parliaments ... in Ireland* (London, 1770).
6.1.7.20; not in C <nd, xt> *EC75.L8215.770uc

LOMBARD, DANIEL, 1678-1746. *Succinct history of ancient and modern persecutions* (London, 1747). 2.1.6.19; C214 <nd, xt> *EC7.L8382.747s (A)

LONGINUS, 1ˢᵗ cent. *Peri hypsous, kai talla heuriskomena* (Utrecht, 1694). Inv.8.30; 4.2.5.4; B17, C16 <661001, r> Gl 21.15* A second copy, Inv.9.17; C16 <680711>, not located.

LOUIS XIV, KING OF FRANCE, *see* Fabricius, Georg

LOVE, JOHN. *Geodaesia, or the art of surveying* (London, 1760). 6.3.4.32; C91 <nd, r> Cabot Science Library Eng 487.60

LOWER, RICHARD, 1631-1691. *Tractatus de corde* (London, 1680). Inv.16.103; C167 <670511> Original Hollis gift not located.

LOWMAN, MOSES, 1680-1752.
A dissertation on the civil government of the Hebrews (London, 1745). Inv.8.37; 2.4.5.11; C70 <661001, r> Jud 1915.50.2*

The principles of popery schismatical (London, 1735). Not in C <6506.., h> *EC75.H7267.Zz715s

LOWTH, ROBERT, 1710-1787.
De sacra poesi Hebrӕorum (Oxford, 1763). Inv.16.15; 2.1.5.8; C42 <670511, h> Sold as a duplicate in 1823 to Prof. J. S. Popkin; returned December 7, 1854 by Mrs. Sarah Campbell after Popkin's death. Jud 4400.30.2*

A letter to the right reverend author [William Warburton] (London, 1766). 2.4.5.10; C179 <nd, h> *EC75.L9558.765ℓb

A short introduction to English grammar (London, 1763). Inv.1.33; C52 <631024, h> EducT 20757.63.12*

[Another edition] (London, 1764). Inv.4.167; 2.2.7.36; C52 <641212?, h> EducT 20757.64.12*

[Another edition] (London, 1767). Inv.16.16; not in C <670511> Original Hollis gift not located.

LUCAN.
†‡*Pharsalia* (Leiden, 1728). 4.2.4.24; B17, C16 <nd, h> On front flyleaf: "Felicity is Freedom and Freedom is Magnanimity Thucyd." At l. 123 of the text: "Floreat Libertas!" On back flyleaf: "... Manus haec inimica Tyrannis Ense petit placidam sub Libertate quietem. A. Sydney." Ll 17.136*

Pharsalia, tr. Nicholas Rowe (London, 1718). Inv.2.5; 2.4.1.9; B17, C17 <6410.., r> Ll 17.205 F*

Pharsalia, tr. Thomas May (London, 1631). Inv.2.119; 2.2.8.32; C16 (misdated 1633) <6410.., h> STC 16888

LUCAS, CHARLES, 1713-1771. *The political constitutions of Great-Britain and Ireland* (London, 1751). 4.4.6.31-32; B17, not in C <nd, h> *EC7.L9625.B751p 2 v.

LUCRETIUS. †*De rerum natura* (Leiden, 1725). 4.2.4.22-23; C17 <nd, h> Typ 732.25.534 2 v.

Ludlow, Edmund, 1617?-1692. *Memoirs* (London, 1751). Inv.1.9; 2.2.3.18; C28 <631024, h> *EC65.L9663.698mc

Ludolph, Hiob, 1624-1704.

Historia Æthiopica (Frankfurt, 1681). 4.2.3.4; C59 <nd, h> Afr 4556.81 F*

Lexicon ætheiopico-latinum (London, 1661). C204 Declared lost, June 2002.

Luigini, Luigi, b. 1526, *see De morbo gallico*

Luther, Martin, 1483-1546. *Dris Martini Lutheri colloquia mensalia, or, Dr. Martin Luther's divine discourses at his table* (London, 1652). Inv.12.49; not in C <690818> Original Hollis gift not located.

Luzac, Elie, 1723-1796. *L'homme plus que machine* (London, 1748). Inv.5.74 (part); 2.2.8.48; C94 <6506..> Original Hollis gift not located.

Lye, Edward, 1694-1767, *see* Bible. N.T. Gospels. Gothic

Lyons. *The infallibility of human judgment* (London, 1724). Inv.14.72; 6.1.8.48; C94 <700926, h> Phil 8591.11*

Lyttelton, George Lyttelton, baron, 1709-1773. ‡*Observations on the life of Cicero* (London, 1733). 4.2.7.16; C207 <nd, h> On flyleaf: "This ingenious Pamphlet was written by Mr. Lyttelton, afterwards Sir George, now Lord Lyttelton. Having read it, See the Life of Cicero by Dr. Middleton." Also annotations on pp. 49-50. *EC75.H7267.Zz740m

M

Mabbut, George. †*Sir Isaac Newton's tables* (London, 1758). 4.4.4.43; not in C <680611, h> *EC65.M1136.686tga

Macaulay, Catherine, 1731-1791.

‡*The history of England* (London, 1763-1765). Inv.5.68; 2.3.4.5-6; C59 <6506.., h> On flyleaf: "Thomas Hollis, an Englishman, Citizen of the World, is proud of the honor of presenting this Work, written by an accomplished, magnanimous English Lady, Catherine [Sawbridge] Macaulay, to the Library of Harvard College at Cambridge in N. England. Pall Mall, mar 25, 1765." Br 1805.13* 2 v.

[Second edition] (London, 1766). 4.1.4.1; <nd, h> Edition designed by TH and with engraved portrait (Basire after Cipriani) of Mrs. Macaulay as frontispiece in v. 1. *EC75.H7267.Zz766m

†‡*The history of England* (London, 1767). 6.1.4.3; C59 <nd, h> Designed by TH. Laid down is a proof of a newspaper advertisement for this volume. On flyleaf: "vt spargam t·h For the Public Library at Harvard College, in Cambridge, in New England. Felicity is Freedom, and Freedom is Magnanimity! Thucyd." *EC75.H7267.Zz766m v. 3

†*The history of England* (London, 1768). Inv.12.4; 6.1.4.4; C59 <690818, h> Designed by TH. *EC75.H7267.Zz768m v. 4

Loose remarks on certain positions to be found in Mr. Hobbes's Philosophical rudiments (London, 1767). 4.4.6.27; C249 <nd, h (marbled boards)> Probably a Hollis design, with a typographical liberty cap on the title page. *EC75.B5628.752s

[Another edition] (London, 1769). C249 <nd, xt> Designed and sponsored by TH. *EC75.G7601.767ℓb

MacBride, David, 1726-1778. ‡*Experimental essays on medical and philosophical subjects* (London, 1767). 6.3.4.10; C100 <67…., h> On flyleaf: "If this book should be the means of preserving one life only of that most useful, gallant Body of men, the Sailors, it will be most happily bestowed. T·H Palmal, aug. 12, 1767." Countway Rare Books 1.Ha.108

Macclesfield, George Parker, earl of, 1697-1764.
The Earl of Macclesfield's speech in the House of Peers [on New Style dating] (London, 1751). 2.4.5.28; C215 <670815?, h> *EC7.M1327.751sb

Remarks on the solar and lunar years (London, 1751). 2.4.5.28; C215 <670815?, h> *EC7.M1327.751sb

MacDonald. *Al signor D. Domenico Vernier* [concerning eruption of Vesuvius] ([Naples, 1755]). 6.1.3.29; not in C <nd, h> *EC75.H7267.Zz769t

Machiavelli, Niccolò, 1469-1527.
‡*Opere inedite* (London [i.e., Lucca], 1760). 4.2.5.24; C117 <nd, red morocco> On pastedown (unidentified hand): "Al Sigre. Tommaso Hollis Gentil: Inglese saggio Forta Benefico in signo di Amicizia e di Gratitudine." On flyleaf (by TH): "Felicity is Freedom and Freedom is Magnanimity. Thucyd." *IC5.M1843.760o

Tvtte le opere ([Geneva], 1550 [i.e., ca. 1620 or ca. 1645]). Inv.8.33; 2.3.5.16; C117 <661001> Original Hollis gift not located.

‡*The works*, tr. Henry Neville (London, 1675). Inv.5.69; 2.2.3.23; C117 <6506.., calf> On flyleaf: "Translated by Henry Neville, author of Plato Redivivus." On verso of title page: "These works were reprinted 1680, in the same size and under the same Licence, by John Starkey, Charles Harper and John Amory, at the Mitre, the Flower de Luce, and the Peacock in Fleetstreet." *IC5.M1843.Eg675n

The works (London, 1680). Inv.2.16; 2.2.3.10; C117 <6410.., calf> *IC5.M1843.Eg675nb (B)

Macintyre, Duncan Ban, 1724-1812. ‡*Orain ghaidhealach* (Edinburgh, 1768). Inv.14.46; 6.3.8.40; C142 <700926, r> On flyleraf: "This collection of Erse or Galic Songs, was printed at Edinburgh, by Alexander Donaldson, for the author of it, Donald Macintire." *EC75.M1898.768o

Maclaine, Archibald, *see* Mosheim, Johann Lorenz

Macpherson, James, 1736-1796.
Temora (London, 1763). Not in C <nd, xt> *EC75.M2414.763t

The works of Ossian, the son of Fingal (London, 1765). Inv.13.34 (misdated 1762); 6.1.4.22-23; C145 <700926> Original Hollis gift not located.

Macpherson, John, 1710-1765. ‡*Critical dissertations on the origin … of the ancient Caledonians* (London, 1768). Inv.17.9; 4.3.5.1; C117 <68…., h> On p. 150, TH marked the sentence "The same ingenious arts which improve the taste, and polish the manners, have a tendency to effeminate the soul, so as to prepare it for slavery." At foot of page he writes: "and so the World goes round! T·H." On bookplate: "Duplicate for sale. C. Folsom, Libn." Br 8310.15*

MAFFEI, SCIPIONE, MARCHESE, 1675-1755.
La religion de gentili (Parigi, 1736). Inv.2.52; 6.1.3.29; C208 (under title) <6410.., h> *EC75.H7267.Zz769t

‡Verona illustrata (Verona, [1731-1732]). 4.3.1.15; C8 (under title) <nd, v> On title page: "Bought at Verona, in the Autumn of 1752, by T·H then upon his Travells." Typ 725.31.548 F

MAIMONIDES, MOSES, 1135-1204. Constitutiones de fundamentis legis (Franeker, 1684). 4.4.6.24; not in C <nd, v> *GC6.W1235.B692d

MAITTAIRE, MICHEL, 1667-1747.
Marmora Arundelliorum, Seldeniorum (London, 1732). Inv.16.54; 2.4.2.12 or 4.3.2.19; C6 <670511, h> AH 4807.32 F* Second copy not located.

‡Opera et fragmenta veterum poetarum latinorum (London, 1713). Inv.15.2; 6.1.1.11-12; C17 (under title) <691129, h> On title page: "Rar." L 73 F* 2 v.

The majesty and singular copiousness of the Hebrew language (London, 1744). 4.3.7.11; C236 (under Hebrew) <nd, h> *EC75.H7267.Zz746o

MAJOR, JOHN, 1469-1550. Historia Maioris Britanniæ ([Basel, 1521]). Inv.2.93; 2.3.7.17; C59 <6410.., h> *EC.M2885.521h (B)

MAJOR, THOMAS, 1720-1799. The ruins of Pæstum (London, 1768). Inv.11.1; 6.3.1.10; C33 <6809..> Original Hollis gift not located.

MALAVOLTI, ORLANDO, 1515-1596. Dell' historia di Siena (Venice, 1599). Inv.3.50; 2.4.5.33; C59 <641208, calf> *IC5.M2918.574hb (B)

MALCOLME, DAVID, d. 1748.
A collection of letters (Edinburgh, 1739). 4.4.7.11; not in C <nd, r> *EC7.M2927.739c

‡An essay on the antiquities of Great Britain (Edinburgh, 1738). 4.4.7.11; C236 (under Great-Britain) <nd, r> On flyleaf, the contents of the tract volume in TH's hand, and a note on one of the authors. *EC7.M2927.739c

MALVASIA, CARLO CESARE, CONTE, 1616-1693. Marmora felsinea (Bologna, 1690). Inv.3.84; 4.3.4.28; C6 <641208, v> *IC6.M2995.690m

MANDEVILLE, BERNARD, 1670-1733.
An enquiry into the causes of frequent executions at Tyburn (London, 1725). 4.3.7.18; not in C <680711, h> *EC7.M3125.732e

An enquiry into the origin of honour (London, 1732). Inv.9.22; 4.3.7.18; C117 <680711, h> *EC7.M3125.732e

MANNI, DOMENICO MARIA, 1690-1788, ed. Chronichette antiche di varii scrittori (Florence, 1733). Inv.3.96; 2.3.5.4; C34 (under title) <641208, v> *IC7.M3164.733c

MANSTEIN, CRISTOF HERMANN, 1711-1757. *Memoirs of Russia, from the year 1727, to the year 1744* (London, 1773). 6.3.2.21; C59 <nd, contemporary calf> Slav 950.6*

MANUZIO, PAOLO, 1512-1574.
Commentarius ... in epistolas Ciceronis ad Atticum (Venice, 1572). 4.2.8.44; not in C <nd, v> *IC5.M3196.547ig

In epistolas ... ad M. Iunium Brutum ... commentarius (Venice, 1562). 4.2.8.42; not in C Declared lost.

MANWARING, EDWARD. *An historical and critical account of the most eminent classic authors* (London, 1737). 4.2.7.27; B17, C118 <nd, r> *EC75.M3194.737h

MARCHMONT, HUGH HUME, EARL OF, 1708-1794. *A state of the rise and progress of our disputes with Spain* (London, 1739). 4.2.7.17; C252 (under Vox coeli) <nd, h> *EC75.H7267.Zz737t

MARCUS AURELIUS, EMPEROR OF ROME. *Meditations* (Glasgow, 1749). Inv.4.68; 2.2.8.20-21; B6, C12 (under Antoninus) <641212?, r> KC 15615* 2 v.

MARGARIT I PAU, JOAN, CARDINAL, 1421-1484. *Episcopi Gerundensis paralipomenon Hispaniæ* ([n.p.], 1545). Inv.3.12; 2.3.3.2; C56 (under Gerund) <641208, 16th c. boards rebacked> Span 190.1 F*

MARINO, GIAMBATTISTA, 1569-1625. *Lettere gravi, argute, e familiari facete* (Venice, 1673). Inv.3.164; 2.2.8.50; C118 <641208, r> Ital 7920.70*

MARKHAM, WILLIAM, 1719-1807. *Concio ad clerum in synodo provinciali Cantuariensis* (London, 1769). 6.1.3.29; C311 <nd, h> *EC75.H7267.Zz759t

MARKLAND, JEREMIAH, 1693-1776. *Remarks on the epistles of Cicero to Brutus* (London, 1745). 4.4.6.7; B17, C118 <nd, h> Lc 40.465*

MARLIANI, BARTOLOMMEO, d. 1560.
Le antichita di Roma (Rome, 1622). 2.4.8.41; C6 <nd, v> *IC5.M3438.Ei548bb

Urbis Romae topographia (Rome, 1544 [i.e., 1549?]). Inv.3.16; 2.3.3.18; C6 <641208, h> Typ 525.49.558 F

MAROZZO, ACHILLE, 16th cent. ‡*Opera nova chiamata duello* (Modena, 1540?). Inv.3.154; C118 <641208, v> Signed in Naples in 1752 by TH's Italian fencing masters. H 5695.50*

MARRIOTT, SIR JAMES, 1730?-1803. *The rights and privileges of both the universities* (Cambridge, 1769). C227 <nd, xt> *EC75.M3496.769r

MARTI, MANUEL, 1663-1737. *Epistolarum libri duodecim* (Amsterdam, 1738). Inv.10.14; C118 <680712, h> Andover-Harvard S.C.R. 627.83 N378cp 1738

MARTIN, BENJAMIN, 1705-1782.
Biographica philosophica (London, 1764). Inv.9.14; 4.3.6.6; C28 <680711, h> *EC75.M3632.755ga

Institutions of language (London, 1748). C136 <nd, h> *EC75.M3632.749ℓ (B)

An introduction to the English language and learning (London, 1766). 2.3.8.38 *or* 39; C52 <670406, contemporary calf> Gift of the author, probably transmitted by Hollis. Gutman Library EducT 20757.66.14

Lingua britannica reformata [preface and introduction only] (London, 1749). Inv.16.18; 2.3.5.21; not in C <670511, h> *EC75.M3632.749ℓ (B)

The philosophical grammar (London, 1762). 4.3.6.13; C139 <nd, r> *EC75.M3632.735pf (A)

Martini, Giuseppe.
Theatrum basilicæ Pisanæ (Rome, 1727). Inv.3.5 (part); 2.3.1.5; C6 <641208, v> Typ 725.28.560 F (B)

Appendix ad Theatrum basilicæ Pisanæ (Rome, 1723 [i.e., 1728?]). Inv.3.5 (part); 2.3.1.5; not in C <641208, v> Typ 725.28.560 F (B)

Mareuil, Pierre de, *see* Milton, John, *Le Paradis reconquis*

Marvell, Andrew, 1621-1678.
‡*Mr. Smirke* ([London], 1676). 2.4.5.19; C118 <nd, xt> Verso of title page: "By Andrew Marvell, the incorruptible." *EC65.M3685.676mab

‡[Another copy] Inv.4.43; C227 <641212?, h> On title page (perhaps not TH's hand): "The author Mr. Andrew Marvell." *EC65.M3685.676mb

†‡*The rehearsal transpos'd: the second part* (London, 1673). Inv.6.9 (part); 2.2.7.46; C122 (under Rehearsal) <650817, h> In margin of p. 1: "Dʳ Sermon, a Quack of those days?" *EC65.M3685.673r

†*The rehearsal transpros'd* [*sic*] (London, 1672). Inv.6.9 (part); 2.2.7.45; C122 <650817, h> *EC65.M3685.672rb (A)

†*The works* (London, 1726). Inv.5.50; 2.2.7.48-50; C142 <6506.., h> *EC75.H7267.Zz726m 3 v.

See also Parker, Samuel

Masclef, François, 1622 or 3-1728. *Grammatica hebraica* (Paris, 1731). Inv.14.29; 6.1.8.21-22; C52 <700926; h> 2263.21* 2 v.

Mason, John, 1706-1763.
Essay on elocution (London, 1748). Inv.3.122 (part); 2.1.6.5; C149 <641208, r> 9280.748.20*

Essay on the power of numbers … in poetical composition (London, 1749). Inv.3.122 (part); 2.1.6.5; C149 <641208, r> 9280.748.20*

Essay on the power and harmony of prosaic numbers (London, 1749). Inv.3.122 (part); 2.1.6.5; C149 <641208, r> 9280.748.20*

Self-knowledge (London, 1753). Inv.4.113; 2.1.7.39; B17, C47 <641212?, h> *EC75.M3811S.1753

Mason, William, 1725-1797.
Ode to the legislator elect of Russia (London, 1766). 6.1.3.29; not in C <nd, h> *EC75.H7267.Zz759t

‡*Poems* (London, 1764). Inv.9.13; 4.3.5.22; B18, C142 <680711, h> On flyleaf: "Ex dono authoris T·H." On thick paper. *EC75.M3816.B764pa

MASSACHUSETTS. COUNCIL. *Letters to the Right Honourable the Earl of Hillsborough* (Boston, printed, London, reprinted, [1769]). 6.1.6.3; C147 <700926, h> *AC7.M382C4.769ℓb (A)

MASSAZZA, PAOLO ANTONIO. *L'arco antico di Susa descritto* (Torino, 1750). Inv.16.10; 4.3.1.23; C6 <670511, r> Arc 720.207 F*

MASSEY, WILLIAM, 1691-1764? *The origin and progress of letters* (London, 1763). Inv.2.54; 2.1.5.25; C9 <6410.., r> B 4157.63*

MASSIE, JOSEPH, d. 1784. †*An historical account of the naval power of France* (London, 1762). 4.1.4.7; not in C <nd, h> *AC7.B6382.B766t

MATHER, COTTON, 1663-1728. *The wonders of the invisible world* (Boston, 1693). Inv.9.9 (part); C311 <680711> Orignal Hollis gift not located, probably rejected as a duplicate. The tract volume that contained it was disbound.

MATY, MATTHEW, 1718-1776. *Authentic memoirs of the life of Richard Mead* (London, 1755). 4.4.7.11; C207 (under Mead) <nd, r> *EC7.M4615.Zc755a

MAUDUIT, ISRAEL, 1708-1787. *A short view of the history of the colony of Massachusetts Bay* (London, 1769). C243 <70…, xt> *EC75.M4427.769s (B)

MAUNDRELL, HENRY, 1665-1701. *A journey from Aleppo to Jerusalem* (Oxford, 1740). Inv.2.70; 2.4.5.20; C75 <6410.., h> *EC75.H7267.Zz740m2

MAY, THOMAS, 1595-1650.
‡*A breviary of the history of parliament* (London, 1650). Inv.4.100; 2.2.8.54; C59 <641212?, h> TH identifies the author. Br 1820.110.3*

‡*The history of the parliament* (London, 1647). Inv.2.22 (wrongly dated 1740); 2.3.3.34; C59 <6410.., h> On flyleaf, a long quotation from *Areopagitica*. On title page: "This book belonged to the excellent Dr. John Wallis." On back flyleaves, long quotations from Neville's *Plato redivivus* and Trenchard's *Standing armies*. Br 1820.110*

Supplementum Lucani libri VII (London, 1646). Inv.2.112; 2.2.8.62; C17 <6410.., h> ML 176.30*

The tragedie of Julia Agrippina ([London, 1654]). 2.2.8.54; C131 <670815?, h> Br 1820.110.3*

The victorious reigne of King Edward the third (London, 1635). 2.2.8.16; C59 <6410.., h> STC 17719

See also Lucan

MAYHEW, JONATHAN, 1720-1766.
A defence of the observations (London, 1764). 2.4.6.2; C315 <nd, h> *AC7.M4537.B766m v. 1

Observations on the charter and conduct (London, 1763). 2.4.6.2; C315 <nd, h> *AC7.M4537.B766m v. 1

Remarks on an anonymous tract (London, 1764). 2.4.6.2; not in C <nd, h>
*AC7.M4537.B766m v.2

†*The snare broken* (Boston, 1766). 4.2.7.1; C315 (under Sermon on the repeal of the stamp
act) <nd, h: bound with Andrew Eliot, *A sermon* (Boston, 1765)> *EC7.Eℓ441.765sba

MAZZOCCHI, GIACOMO, 16ᵗʰ cent. *Epigrammata antiquæ urbis* ([Rome, 1521]). Inv.8.28;
2.4.3.28; C4 (under title) <661001, calf> *IC5.M4596.521e

MEAD, RICHARD, 1673-1754.
Bibliotheca Meadiana ([London, 1754]). 4.4.7.1; C130 <nd, r> A sale catalogue.
*EC7.M4615.Zc755a

A catalogue of pictures ([London, 1755]). 4.4.7.1; not in C <nd, r> A sale catalogue.
*EC7.M4615.Zc755a

A catalogue of the genuine and entire collection of valuable gems ([London, 1755]).
4.4.7.11; not in C <nd, r> A sale catalogue. *EC7.M4615.Zc755a

A catalogue of the genuine, entire and curious collection of prints and drawings ([London,
1755]). 4.4.7.11; not in C <nd, r> A sale catalogue. *EC7.M4615.Zc755a

Museum Meadianum (London, [1755]). C130 <nd, h (boards)> B 1827.564*

[Another copy] C130 <nd, h (boards)> B 1827.401*

[Another copy] 4.4.7.11; C130 <nd, r> *EC7.M4615.Zc755m (A)

[Another copy] Inv.2.69; 2.3.5.36; C130 <6410.., h> *EC7.M4615.Zc755m (B)

‡*Oratio anniversaria Harveiana* (London, 1724). Inv.12.3; 6.1.3.1; C118 <690818, h> On
flyleaf: "This Oration, gave rise to many learned & curious Controversy relating to the
importance and dignity of Physicians among the Ancients.   Dr. Conyers Middleton, of
Cambridge, attacked the Oration and Dr. John Ward, Rhetoric Professor at Gresham
College defended it.   Several tracts were written on both sides.   These tracts are now
very scarce, and very little known.   T·H." On the bookplate in another hand: "Duplicate
for sale. C. Folsom, Librarian." *EC7.M4615.724o

‡[Another copy] Inv.13.67; 6.1.3.3; C118 <700926, h> On front flyleaf: "Liber Thomae
Hollis, Hospitii Lincolniensis, Regalis et Antiquariorum Societatum Londini Sodalis,
Libertatis Patriae, praestantisque ejus Constitutionis laudatissime anno MDCLXXXVIII
recuperatae, amatoris studiosissimi." Two pages listing Harveian orations, dated
"Palmal, Jan 23, 1770. T·H." Back flyleaf: "'—I shall distinguish such as I esteeme to
have been hinderers of Reformation into three sorts, Antiquarians, for so I had rather
call them than Antiquaries, whose labors are useful and valuable. 2. Libertines. 3.
Politicians.' etc. Of Reformation touching Church-Discipline in England, and the causes
which hitherto have hindered it. Two books, written to a friend. Printed 1641, in quarto.
The author, John Milton." *EC75.H7267.Zz724m

MEADOWCOURT, RICHARD, 1695-1760. *A critique on Milton's Paradise regain'd* (London,
1732). Inv.14.12; 6.1.3.17; C143 (under Milton) <700926, h> *EC7.M4617.732c

MECATTI, GIUSEPPE MARIA. *Discorso I, dell'origine, e antichita, e situazione del Vesuvio*
([Naples, 1752]). Inv.3.120 (under Palermo; part); 2.4.7.12; C232 (under Vernon, Giov.)
<641208, h> *IC7.A100.B752h

MEERMAN, GERARD, 1722-1771.
Novus thesaurus juris civilis et canonici (The Hague, 1751-1753). 4.1.1.20-26; C77 <nd, h> Gov 5218.8 F* 7 v.

‡*Origines typographiae* (The Hague, 1765). Inv.8.26; 2.4.3.25; C9 <661001, h> On flyleaf: "A Gift from an accomplished, excellent Gentleman, the Author, who masters a noble Library, formed by himself!" With a quotation from *Areopagitica* beginning "The free and ingenuous sort of men evidently were born to study & love Learning for itself ..." B 4507.765*

MEGISERUS, HIERONYMUS, ca. 1553-1618. *Institutionum linguæ Turcicæ* ([Leipzig], 1612). 4.2.8.38-40; C52 <nd, h> *GC5.M4736.612i 3 v.

MEIJER, CORNELIS, b. ca. 1640. *L'arte de restituere à Roma la tralasciata navigatione del suo Tevere* (Rome, 1685). Inv.3.2; 2.3.1.10; C118 <641208, r> Typ 625.85.565 (B)

MELANI, ENEA GAETANO. *La peste di Messina* (Venice, 1747). C141 (under Gaetanus) <641208?, v> *IC7.M4805.747p

MELMOTH, WILLIAM, 1710?-1799. *The letters of Sir Thomas Fitzosborne* (London, 1763). Inv.13.45; 6.1.4.15; C118 <700926, r> 15493.57*

See also Cicero; Pliny, the Younger

MELVILLE, SIR JAMES, 1535-1617.
The memoires of Sir James Melvil (London, 1683). Inv.5.12 (under Sir James Melvin [*sic*]); C59 <6506.., r> Br 1783.7.2*

The memorials of the English and French commissioners concerning the limits of Nova Scotia or Acadia (London, 1755). 4.1.4.23-24; C147 <nd, h> Can 310.4* 2 v.

MENELAUS, OF ALEXANDRIA. *Menelai sphæricorum libri III* (Oxford, 1758). Inv.12.59; 6.1.6.41; C50 <690818, h> *EC7.H1552.758m

MENESTRIER, CLAUDE FRANÇOIS, 1631-1705. *Histoire du roy Louis le Grand* (Paris [i.e., Amsterdam?], 1691). 4.4.3.25; C130 <nd, r> f*FC6.M5245.689hb

MERCATI, GIUSEPPE MARIA. *Descrizione della lava scorsa nel mese di luglio dell'anno 1754* (Naples, 1754). 6.1.3.29; C254 <nd, h> *EC75.H7267.Zz769t

MERCURIALE, GIROLAMO, 1530-1606. *De arte gymnastica libri sex* (Amsterdam, 1672). 4.4.5.4; C118 <nd, v> *IC5.M5395.569af

MEREDITH, SIR WILLIAM, BART., 1725?-1790. *The question stated* [concerning John Wilkes] ([London, 1769]). Inv.15.26; 6.1.6.32; C251 <691129, xt> *EC75.M5415.769qb

MERRICK, JAMES, 1720-1769, *see* Bible. O.T. Psalms. English

MEURS, JOHANNES VAN, 1579-1639. *Athenæ Batavæ* (Leiden, 1625). Inv.3.109; C28 (under Meursius) <641208, h> Neth 3483.3*

MICHAELIS, JOHANN DAVID, 1711-1791.
‡*A dissertation on the influence of opinions on language* (London, 1769). Inv.12.76; 6.1.3.2; C136 <690818; h> TH transcribes a long quotation from Joseph Priestley in the introduction. 1231.9*

In Roberti Lowth prælectiones De sacra poesi Hebræorum (Oxford, 1763). Inv.16.23; 2.1.5.9; C42 <670511> Original Hollis gift not located.

MIDDLETON, CONYERS, 1683-1750.
Epistles of M. T. Cicero to M. Brutus (London, 1743). 4.4.6.5; C13 (under Cicero) <nd, h> *EC75.H7267.Zz742m v. 1

History of the life of Cicero (London, 1757). Inv.1.16; 2.2.4.17-18; C28 <631024, r> KG 10842* 2 v.

The miscellaneous works (London, 1752). Inv.2.27; 2.4.1.14-17; C118 <6410.., v. 1-2 r, 3-4 h> C 1290.1* 4 v.

MILDMAY, SIR WILLIAM, BART., 1705-1771. *The laws and policy of England, relating to trade* (London, 1765). Inv.8.10; 4.2.6.3; C37 <661001, h> *EC75.H7267.Zz765m

MILLER, EDMOND. *Some remarks upon a letter entituled, The present state of Trinity College* (London, 1710). Inv.9.23 (part); 6.1.8.14; C227 <680711, h> *EC65.B4465.B710b

MILLER, JAMES, 1706-1744. *Are these things so?* (London, 1740). 4.2.3.22; C237 (under title) <nd, xt> f*EC75.H7267.Zz740p

MILLS, JOHN, d. 1784? ‡*An essay on the management of bees* (London, 1766). 2.4.6.4; C71 <nd, h> On title page: "An important Subject to Colonists." *EC75.H7267.Zz766m

MILNER, JOHN, 1628-1702. ‡*A view of the dissertation upon the epistles of Phalaris* (London, 1698). 4.3.8.14; not in C <nd, r> On title page: "rare." *EC7.Or755.698d (B)

MILTON, JOHN, 1608-1674.
A brief history of Moscovia (London, 1682). Inv.2.110; 2.1.8.4; C49 <6410.., h> *EC65.M6427.682b (A)

A complete collection of the historical, political, and miscellaneous works (Amsterdam, 1698). 4.1.8.16; C119 <nd, h> Original v. 1-2 not located; present v. 1-2 bequeathed by William S. Thayer, 1933. 14491.5.5 F* v. 3 only

‡*Eikonoklastes*, ed. Richard Baron (London, 1756). Inv.2.7; 2.1.4.1; B11 (under title), C119 <6410.., r> On flyleaf, a long quotation in French from a 1652 French edition; underdotting for emphasis on title page and pp. ii, iv-vii; annotations on pp. iv-vii. f*EC75.H7267.Zz756m3

Literæ pseudo-senatus anglicani ([London?], 1676). Inv.14.2; 6.2.8.36; C147 <700926, v> B 1835.92*

‡*Paradise lost* (London, 1674). 4.2.8.16; C142 <nd, h> On flyleaf: "The first edit. of Paradise Lost in twelve Books. Very scarce." *EC75.H7267.Zz674m

[Another edition] (London, 1688). 2.4.2.2; C142 <nd, h> 14486.3.6 F*

[Another edition] ed. Richard Bentley (London, 1732). Inv.3.79; C142 <641208> Original Hollis gift not located.

‡[Another edition], ed. Thomas Newton (London, 1754). Inv.3.72; 2.1.4.6; C143 <641208, r> On frontispiece portrait, v. 1: "Fumbled after the painting in the collection of the R. H. Arthur Onslow." V. 1, p. lvi-lvii: "The two pictures in the Possession of Milton's Widow were, That afterward purchased by Charles Stanhope; bought at the sale

of his effects by T·H And that in the Collection of Mr. Onslow. The Picture in crayons was drawn by Faithorne, to ingrave after it that plate which served for the print, that was prefixed to Milton's 'History of Britain,' the print here noticed by the very eminent, excellent Prelate Dr. Newton. The Crayons [sic] never was in her possession. T·H The Plate for the Print for the folio edition of Milton's Prose works in three volumes, published 1698, was ingraven by White, after the Print of Faithorne's." V. 1, p. lx: "It is apprehended, that Milton had no other attachment to Cromwell, the Tyrant yet specious Cromwell, than that of simply writing his Latin Letters. See more concerning this matter, in the Tryal of A. Sydney, the new edit. in the notes. T·H." V. 2, under the frontispiece (Milton aet. 62, engraved by George Vertue): "Manner'd after the Crayons, and Faithorne's print." 14486.7.3* 2 v.

‡*Le Paradis perdu,* tr. Nicolas-François Dupré de Saint-Maur; *Le Paradis reconquis,* tr. Pierre de Mareuil (Paris, 1743). Inv.4.66; C143 <641212?, r> On title pages of v. 1-2 & half title of v. 3: script "TH." Also contains (v.3) a prospectus for *La Christiade* by Jacques-François de La Baume-Desdossat, *q.v.* 14487.22* 3 v.

‡*Paradise regain'd,* ed. Thomas Newton (London, 1757). 2.1.4.8; C143 <64...., r> On the frontispiece portrait: "Spurious beyond a doubt." In the preface, sig.A3r, opposite the words *a very fine head:* "spvriovs." On the words *the chaff of Mr. Peck's remarks:* "Mr. Peck having consulted Mr. George Vertue, that eminent and faithful English Antiquarian, concerning the originality of the Painting after which the print prefixed to his work in 2v. qo. was taken, and Mr. Vertue having declared to him, as he afterward assured me in conversation jan. 1, 1755, that he believed it to be spurious for many reasons; Mr. Peck replied, 'I'll have a Scraping from it however, and let Posterity settle the Matter.' T·H, Pall Mall, oct. 24, 1764." 14486.7.3.5*

‡*Il paradiso perduto* ([Verona], 1742). Inv.3.9; 2.4.1.13; C142 <641208, v> On blue paper; on flyleaf: "This Edition of Paradise Lost was really printed by Tumermani in Verona, & there this Copy was bought in October 1752 by TH, then upon his Travells." Typ 725.42.573 F

Paradisus amissa (London, 1686). Inv.4.41; 2.4.7.8; C143 <641212?, h> *EC75.H7267.Zz686m

The poetical works of Mr. John Milton (London, 1695). Inv.3.77; 2.2.3.21; C143 <641208, h> 14482.5 F*

Pro populo anglicano defensio (London, 1651). Inv.3.76; 2.3.3.3; C147 (misdated 1652) <641208, h> f*EC65.M6427.651pb (C)

†‡*The works* [in prose], ed. Richard Baron (London, 1753 [i.e., 1756]) 2.1.4.2; C119 <590111, h> On flyleaf of v. 1: "Thomas Hollis, an Englishman, a Lover of Liberty, his Country & its excellent constitution as most nobly restored at the happy Revolution, is desirous of having the honor to present Milton's prose works, and Toland's life of Milton, to the public library of Harvard College in New England. Jan. 1, 1759." Numerous annotations in v. 1, only five annotations in v. 2. An extraordinary binding by Richard Montagu. Extra-illustrated with 4 portraits of Milton by Cipriani and two facsimiles of the death warrant of Charles I. Survived the library fire of 1764 because it was kept in President Edward Holyoke's house; an accompanying copy of Toland's life of Milton was destroyed, and replaced by Hollis in October, 1764. f*EC75.H7267.Zz756m2 2 v.

Figure 5. John Milton, *The Works* [in prose] (London, 1753 [i.e., 1756]).
Bound in brown diced calf. Hollis's printed bookplate was altered and
annotated to reflect the sale of this duplicate set. See Checklist, p. 136.
f*EC65.M6427.B753wa 2 v. 30 cm.

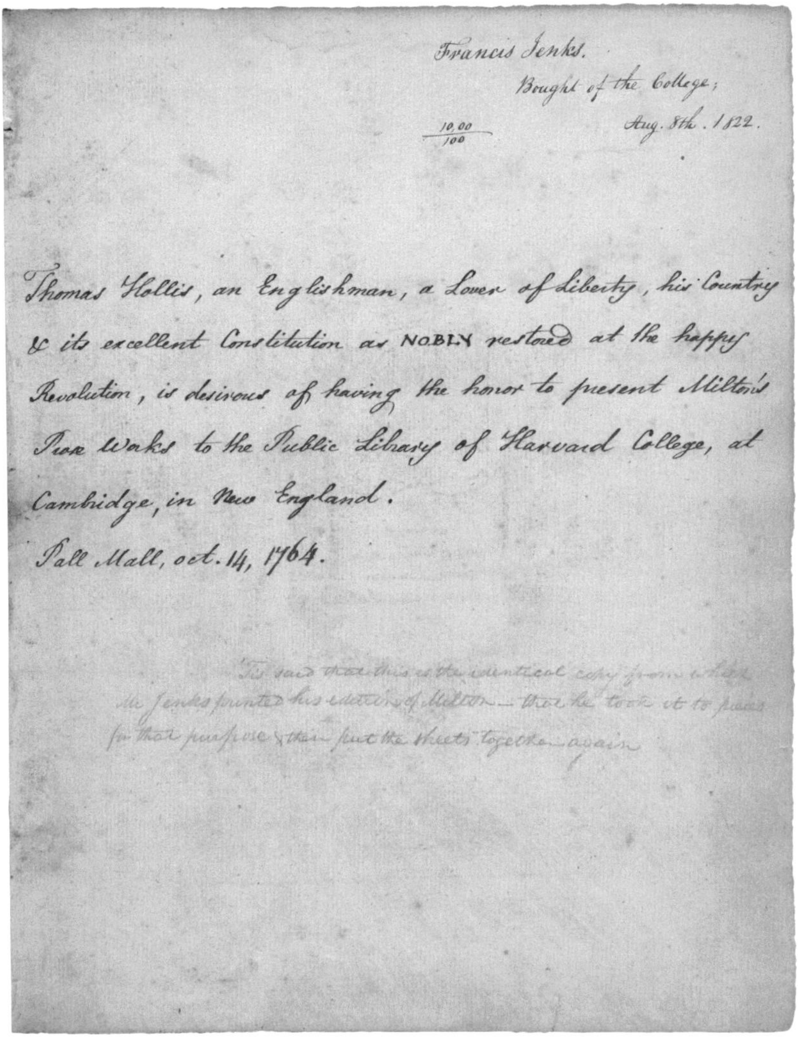

Francis Jenks.

Bought of the College;

$\frac{10.00}{100}$ Aug. 8th. 1822.

Thomas Hollis, an Englishman, a Lover of Liberty, his Country & its excellent Constitution as NOBLY restored at the happy Revolution, is desirous of having the honor to present Milton's Prose Works to the Public Library of Harvard College, at Cambridge, in New England.

Pall Mall, oct. 14, 1764.

It is said that this is the identical copy from which Mr. Jenks printed his edition of Milton — that he took it to pieces for that purpose & then put the sheets together again

Figure 6. On the flyleaf, opposite the altered bookplate shown in Figure 5, TH notes the function of the Harvard library within the larger community. Other annotations track the release of the two-volume set, its ownership by the Rev. Francis Jenks, and its return to Harvard in 1831.

‡[Another copy] Inv.16.78; 2.1.4.4; C119 <670511, h> On flyleaf of v. 1: "Thomas Hollis, an Englishman, a Lover of Liberty, his Country & its excellent Constitution as NOBLY restored at the happy Revolution, is desirous of having the honor to present Milton's Prose Works to the Public Library of Harvard College, at Cambridge, in New England. Pall Mall, oct. 14, 1764." Many other annotations in v. 1; none in v. 2. Extra-illustrated like the preceding copy. Sold as a duplicate to the Rev. Francis Jenks by Joseph Cogswell, 1822, returned by Jenks as a gift, 1831. f*EC65.M6427.B753wa 2 v.

See also King, William

The ministry of the letter vindicated from the Charge of anti-Christianism (London, 1724). Inv.10.28 (part); 4.3.7.29 <680712, h> C 1397.19.08*

MINTERT, PETER. *Lexicon græco-latinum* (Frankfurt, 1728). 4.1.7.39; C204 <nd, h> Andover-Harvard S.C.R. 508.2 Mintert

MIRABEAU, VICTOR DE RIQUETTI, MARQUIS DE, 1715-1589. *The œconomical table* (London, 1766). 4.3.6.23; C119 <nd, r> Econ 253.2.6*

Miscellany poems, the first part (London, 1707-1708). Inv.3.125 (under Dryden; part); B11, C141 (under Dryden) <641208, r> *EC65.D8474.B709m 2 v.

MITCHELL, JOHN, 1711-1768. *The present state of Great Britain and North America* (London, 1767). 4.4.6.10; not in C <69…., h> Econ 6067.67* 2 v.

MITCHELL, JOSEPH, 1684-1738. ‡*A tale and two fables in verse* (London, 1727). Inv.14.21 (under Poltis king of Thrace); 6.1.7.17; C240 (under title) <700926, h> TH identifies author. *EC7.M6942.727t

MOLESWORTH, ROBERT MOLESWORTH, VISCOUNT, 1656-1725. ‡*An account of Denmark* (London, 1737 [i.e., 1738]). Inv.1.22; 2.4.7.4; B18, C59, C61 (under Robinson) <631024, r> On flyleaf: "The preface to the Acc. of Denmark, & the Translator's preface to Hottoman's Franco-gallia are two of the noblest in the English Language." Includes Robinson, John, *Account of Sueden*. *EC75.H7267.Zz738m

See also Hotman, François

MONCK, MARY MOLESWORTH, ca. 1677-1715. ‡*Marinda: Poems and translations* (London, 1716). 4.4.7.17; C143 (under Molesworth , Rob.) <nd, h (rebacked)> On front flyleaf: "R. Molesworth Afterward created Lord Molesworth of Ireland, Author of divers Excellent Works, & two golden Prefaces, the Preface to his 'Account of Denamrk' and the Preface to his translation of 'Franco Gallia,' one of the last of the English!" On back flyleaf: "R. Molesworth was, several years, British Minister at Florence." *EC75.H7267.Zz716m

MONCLAR, *see* Ripert de Monclar, Jean Pierre François de

MONTAGU, EDWARD WORTLEY, 1713-1776. *Reflections on the rise and fall of ancient republics* (London, 1760). 4.2.6.11; B18, C119 <nd, r> John Langdon Sibley, Harvard librarian, doubted that this was a Hollis gift. AH 307.60*

MONTAGU, ELIZABETH ROBINSON, 1720-1800. ‡*An essay on the writings and genius of Shakespear* (London, 1769). Inv.14.50; 6.1.4.2; C119 (under Montague) <700926, h> On back flyleaf: "The Author is said to be the Hon. Mrs. Montagu." 12462.9*

Montaigne, Michel de, 1533-1592. *The essays of Michael seigneur de Montaigne*, tr. Peter Coste (London, 1759). Inv.12.56; 6.1.5.2-4; C119 <690818, r> Mon 31.7* 3 v.

Montesquieu, Charles de Secondat, baron de, 1689-1755. *Oeuvres* (Amsterdam, 1758). 4.2.4.3-5; C124 (under Secondat) <nd> Orignal Hollis gift not located.

Monumenta Patavina (Padua, 1652). 2.2.3.25; C8 <670815?, h> Arc 726.6 F*

A moral discourse on the attributes of God (London, 1754). 2.1.6.9; not in C <6410.., h> *EC7.C5797.B755t

More, Alexander, 1616-1670. *Causa Dei* (Middleburgh, 1653). 2.4.5.19; C182 <nd, xt> *FC6.M8131.653c

More, Henry, 1614-1687. ‡*An antidote against atheisme* (London, 1653). Inv.12.34; 6.1.8.38; C182 <690818; 17th c. calf> On title page: "A curious & rare book." *EC65.M8135.653a

More, Sir Thomas, 1478-1535.
†*A fruitful, pleasant, & wittie work … Utopia* (London, [1556]). Inv.5.52; 2.2.8.47; C84 <6506.., h> STC 18095.5

De optimo republica statu … Utopia (Glasgow, 1750). Inv.16.22; 2.2.8.15; C84 <670511, r> 12437.32*

Morel, Andreas, 1646-1703. *Thesaurus Morellianus* (Amsterdam, 1734). Inv.5.53; 2.4.1.7-8; C130 <6506.., h> Arc 1475.3 F* 2 v.

Morell, Thomas, 1703-1784. *Thesaurus græcæ poeseos* (Eton, 1762). 4.1.5.31-32; C204 <nd, h> Typ 705.62.580 2 v.

Morins, Richard de, d. 1242. *Chronicon, sive Annales prioratus de Dunstaple*, ed. Thomas Hearne (Oxford, 1733). Inv.17.32; 4.4.5.8-9; C5 <68...., h> Br 5176.132* 2 v.

Morland, Sir Samuel, 1625-1695. ‡*The history of the evangelical churches of the valleys of Piemont* (London, 1658). Inv.5.70; 2.3.3.29; C67 <6506.., h> On title page: "Ut spargam T·H." On rear endpaper, TH writes out Milton's sonnet on the massacre in Piedmont. Much additional annotation: a note stating that the dedication to Cromwell is scarce, having been withdrawn; etc. "Reader, Whomsoever thou mayest be that shalt peruse these lines, whether Pagan or Jew, Christian or Mohammedan or Sceptic, consider well the Doctrines, Practices, Massacres of Papists; and, so long as the arm of Popery is uplifted against thee, so long be thine uplifted against Popery, in justice to thyself and to Mankind." C 7866.58*

Morris, Robert, 1701-1754.
Have at you all (London, 1740). 4.2.3.22; C237 <nd, h> f*EC75.H7267.Zz740m

Yes they are (London, 1740). 4.2.3.22; C237 (under title) <nd, h> f*EC75.H7267.Zz740p

Mortimer, Thomas, 1730-1819.
‡*The national debt no national grievance* (London, 1768). 6.1.6.32; C249 <nd, xt> On title page: "By Mr. Mortimer, lately Vice Consul at Ostend & dismiss'd from that office not long since T:H." *EC75.M8447.768n

‡*The remarkable case of Thomas Mortimer* (London, 1770). Inv.14.58; 6.1.7.7; C119 <700926, h> On flyleaf: "Truely [*sic*] a 'remarkable case'!" *EC75.M8447.770rb

MORTON, THOMAS, 1564-1659. *An exact account of Romish doctrine ... reprinted and published by Ezerel Tonge* (London, 1679). 2.4.5.19; C232 (under Tonge) Original Hollis copy discarded as a duplicate.

MOSCARDO, LODOVICO, CONTE, 17th cent.
Historia di Verona (Verona, 1668). Inv.3.49; not in C <641208> Original Hollis gift not located.

Note overo memorie del museo di Lodovico Moscardo (Padua, 1656). Inv.4.3; 2.3.3.19; C6 <641212?, v> f*IC6.M8507.656n (B)

MOSELY, RICHARD, d. 1754. *A letter to the Right Reverent [sic] the Bishop of Clogher* (London, 1752). 2.2.5.6; not in C <6410.., h> *EC7.C5797.751c

MOSHEIM, JOHANN LORENZ, 1694?-1755. ‡*An ecclesiastical history*, tr. Archibald Maclaine (London, 1765). Inv.6.8; 2.3.4.7-8; C67 <650817, r> Said to replace the copy given by TH, but preserving a leaf with his comments: "I have sometimes thought when Ecclesiastics were endowed the worldly preferments Hodie venenum infunditur in Ecclesiam, For, to use the speech of Genesis IV. Ult. according to the sense which it hath in the Hebrew, Then began men to corrvpt the worship of God etc. etc. etc. A Letter [a fine one] from John Wall to John Milton. See the Iconoklastes of John Milton edit. 2, in the Preface to that edition." C 1833.25.10* 2 v.

Motuum britannicorum (Rotterdam, 1647). Inv.2.113; 2.2.8.26; C55 (under Britannici motus) <6410.., h> Br 1815.95*

MOYLE, WALTER, 1672-1721.
The works (London, 1726). Inv.16.14 (part); 2.2.5.28-29; C119 <670511, r> *EC7.M8752.726w 2 v.

The whole works (London, 1727). Inv.16.14 (part); 2.2.5.30; C119 <670511, r> Constitutes v. 3 of *Works* (1726). *EC7.M8752.B727wa

MUELHAUSEN, YOM TOV LIPMANN, 14th/15th cent. *Nitsahon* (Nuremberg, 1644). 4.2.7.36; C133 <nd> Original Hollis gift not located.

MÜNSTER, SEBASTIAN, 1489-1552. *Dictionarium chaldaicum* (Basel, 1527). 4.4.5.28; C204 <nd, 16th c. pigskin> *GC5.M8895.527a

MURATORI, LODOVICO ANTONIO, 1672-1750.
‡*Annali d'Italia* (Milan, 1753-1756). Inv.4.87; 2.4.7.30-46; C59 <641212?, boards with v spine> On flyleaf of v. 1: "The best edition." *IC7.M9335.744ad 17 v.

Della pubblica felicita (Lucca, 1749). Inv.3.128; 2.3.8.10; C119 <641208, v> *IC7.M9335.749d

See also Catalani, Giuseppe

MURET, MARC ANTOINE, 1526-1585.
Variarum lectionem libri VIII (Venice, 1559). 4.4.6.42; C236 <nd, h> *FC5.M9425.559v

Variarum lectiones libri XV (Paris, 1586). 4.4.6.42; not in C <nd, h> *FC5.M9425.559v

Musei capitolini (Rome, Italy). *Museo capitolino* (Rome, 1750). 4.3.5.18; C6 <nd, r> Fine Arts Arc 362.1.8

The muses fountain clear: or, The dutiful Oxonian's defence of his mother's loyalty (London, 1717). 2.1.7.4; not in C <nd, xt> *EC7.A100.717m

Mussard, Pierre, 1627-ca. 1680. *Les conformitez des ceremonies modernes avec les anciennes* ([Leiden], 1667). Inv.3.39 *or* Inv.4.97; 2.2.6.41; C161 (under title; lists only one copy) <641208 *or* 641212?, h> *FC6.M9757.667c (A) Second copy not located.

Muzio, Girolamo, 1496-1576. *La polvere* ([Venice, ca. 1555]). Inv.3.149; 4.2.8.30; not in C <641208, v> *IC5.M9885.545pb

N

N., N. *see America, or an exact description of the West-Indies*

Nalson, Valentine. *Twenty sermons* (London, 1737). Not in C <nd, h> C 1296.11.15*

Nanni, Giovanni, 1432?-1502. *I cinque libri di le antichita de Beroso* (Venice, 1550). Inv.3.155; C3 <641208, v> AH 405.50*

The narrative history of King James (London, 1657). Inv.2.53; 2.3.8.18; C58 (under James I) <6410.., r> *EC65.Sp266.651n (C)

Nathan ben Jehiel, of Rome, 1035-ca. 1110. *Sefer ha Aruch* (Venice, 1531). 4.2.5.7; C132 (under Aruck liber) <nd, h> Andover-Harvard safe 362 Nathan

Neal, Daniel, 1678-1743.
   The history of the Puritans (London, 1754). Inv.16.84; 2.2.4.24-25; C67 <670511, r> Br 1805.9.14* 2 v.

   The supremacy of St. Peter (London, 1735). Not in C <6506.., h> *EC75.H7267.Zz735s2

Neander, Michael, b. 1529. *Synopsis mensurarum et pondarum* (Basel, [1555]). Inv.3.124; 2.4.7.10; C6 <641208, h> AH 925.55*

Nedham, Marchamont, 1620-1678.
   †‡*The excellencie of a free state* (London, 1767). 4.1.7.6; B24, C84 <nd, h> On front flyleaf: "Liber Thomae Hollis, Angli, Hospitii Lincolniensis, Regalis et Antiquariorum Societatum Londini Sodalis; Libertatis, Patriae, praestantisque ejus Constitutionis laudatissime anno mdclxxxviii recuperatae, amatoris studiosissimi." On back flyleaf: "For the Public Library of Harvard College, at Cambridge, in New England." *EC65.N2845.656eb (A)

   [Another copy] 4.1.7.8; B24, C84 <nd, r> *EC65.N2845.656eb (B)

   Honesty's best policy ([London, 1678]). 2.4.5.19; C251 <nd, xt> *EC65.N2845.678h

   The pacquet-boat advice (London, 1678). 2.4.5.19; not in C <nd, xt> *EC65.N2845.A678p

   A pacquet of advices and animadversions (London, 1676). 2.4.5.19; not in C <nd, xt> *EC65.N2845.676p

A second pacquet of advices and animadversions (London, 1677). 2.4.5.19; not in
C <nd, xt> *EC65.N2845.677s

NEEDHAM, JOHN TURBERVILLE, 1713-1781. ‡*De inscriptione quadam Aegyptiaca* (Rome,
1761). 6.2.8.21; C208 <nd, h> TH identifies author. *EC75.Sh487.759rb

The negotiators, or Don Diego brought to reason (London, 1738). 4.2.3.22; C239 <nd, h>
f *EC75.H7267.Zz740p

NEPOS, CORNELIUS. *Vitæ excellentium imperatorum* (Leiden, 1734). 4.2.7.26; not in C
<nd, h> KD 53753*

NERI, ANTONIO, d. 1614. *L'arte vetraria* (Florence, 1612). 4.1.7.7; C9 <nd, h>
Chem 7556.12*

NEUMANN, CASPAR, 1683-1737.
  The chemical works (London, 1759). 4.1.4.8; C36 <nd, h> Chem 368.1.5*

  [Another edition] (London, 1773). 6.3.4.7-8; C36 <nd, h> Restored 9 June 1851 by
  Samuel A. Green "after an absence from the library of more than 30 years."
  Chem 368.1.6* 2 v.

NEVILLE, HENRY, 1620-1694.
  ‡*Discourses concerning government* [i.e., *Plato redivivus*] (London, 1698). Inv.1.39;
  2.4.8.13; C84 <631024, r> On title page: "A curious book." *EC65.N4165.680pc

  ‡*Plato redivivus* (London, 1681). Inv.4.196; 2.1.8.39; C84 <641212?, r> On title page: "A
  curious book T·H." *EC65.N4165.680p

 †‡[Another edition] (London, 1763). Inv.5.42; 2.2.7.13; B19, C84 <6506.., h> On flyleaf:
  "Thomas Hollis, an Englishman, a Lover of Liberty, the Principles of the Revolution &
  of the Protestant Succession in the House of Hanover, is desirous of having the honor to
  present this Book to the Public Library of Harvard College at Cambridge in N. England.
  London, march 13, 1765." *EC65.N4165.680pda

  See also Machiavelli

NEWMAN, JOHN, ca. 1677-1741. *The popish doctrine of merit and justification* (London,
1735). Not in C <6506.., h> *EC75.H7267.Zz715s

NEWTON, SIR ISAAC, 1642-1727.
  †*Arithmetica universalis* (London, 1722). Inv.9.21; 4.4.6.35; C91 <680711, h>
  *EC65.N4844.707ab

  †*The chronology of ancient kingdoms amended* (London, 1728). Inv.9.5; 4.4.4.31; C35
  <680711, h> *EC65.N4844.728cb

  †*De mundi systemate liber* (London, 1731). Inv.9.8; 4.3.5.12; C139 <680711, h>
  *EC65.N4844.728db

  †*Lectiones opticae* (London, 1729). Inv.9.7; 4.4.4.33; C138 <680711, h>
  *EC65.N4844.729ℓ

  The mathematical principles, tr. Andrew Motte (London, 1729). C139 <680711?, r> No
  trace remains of provenance. *EC65.N4844.Eg729m 2 v.

†*Observations upon the prophecies of Daniel* (London, 1733). Inv.9.6; 4.4.4.32; C283
<680711, h> Sold as a duplicate by Joseph Cogswell, Harvard librarian; given back by
Kenneth B. Murdock, November 28, 1922. *EC65.N4844.733o (B)

[Another copy] Not in C <nd, h (grey boards)> Sent by TH to the Hollis Professor of
Divinity. f*AC7.H2618H.160

†*Optice* (London, 1719). Inv.9.18; 4.4.6.28; C139 <680711, h> *EC65.N4844.Ef706ob

†*Opuscula* (Lausanne, 1744). Inv.9.4; 4.4.4.24-26; C139 <680711, h>
*EC65.N4844.Ef706ob 3 v.

†*Philosophiae naturalis principia mathematica* (London, 1726). Inv.9.2; 4.4.4.30; C139
<680711, h> *EC65.N4844.687pe (B)

†[Another edition] (Geneva, 1739). Inv.9.3; 4.4.4.27-29; C39 (misdated 1729) <680711, h>
*EC65.N4844.687pf (B) 3 v.

† *Tables for renewing and purchasing the leases* (London, 1758). Inv.9.29; 4.4.8.43; C226
<680711, h> *EC65.M1136.686tga

See also Mabbut, George

NEWTON, RICHARD, 1676-1753.
†*The expence of a university education reduced* (London, 1733). 2.4.7.2; C222 (under
Education) <6410.., h> *EC75.H7267.Zz734e

‡*Pluralities indefensible* (London, 1743). Inv.4.80; C183 <641212?, h> On title page:
"By Dr Richard Newton, Principal of Hertford College; and Canon of Christ Church."
C 10410.5*

NICETAS CHONIATES, *see* Choniates, Nicetas

NICHOLS, WILLIAM, 1664-1712. *Defensio Ecclesiæ Anglicanæ* (London, 1707). Inv.2.118;
2.2.8.1; B19, not in C <6410.., h> *EC7.N5194.707d

NICKOLLS, SIR JOHN, b. 1722. *Remarks on the advantages and disadvantages of France and
Great Britain* (London, 1754). Inv.5.44; 2.2.7.14; C38 <6506..> Original Hollis gift not
located.

NICOLAI, JOHANN, 1665-1708. *Tractatus de siglis veterum* (Leiden, 1703). 4.3.6.3; C6
<nd, v> *GC6.N5425.703t

NICOLAI, JOHANN FRIEDRICH, 1639-1683. *Hodogeticum orientale harmonicum* (Jena,
1670). 4.4.6.19; C133 (misdated 1672) <nd, h> 2253.6*

NICOLSON, WILLIAM, 1655-1727. *The English, Scotch and Irish historical libraries* (London,
1736). Inv.16.55; 2.1.3.11; B19, C60 <670511, h> Br 55.85 F*

NORFOLK, CHARLES HOWARD, DUKE OF, 1720-1786. *Thoughts, essays and maxims*
(London, 1768). 6.2.8.21; C225 (under Howard) <nd, h> *EC75.Sh487.759rb

NORIS, ENRICO, 1631-1704. *Cenotaphia Pisana* (Venice, 1681). 4.3.2.13; C6 <nd, v>
AH 8936.2 F*

NORTH, ROGER, 1653-1734. *Examen; or, An inquiry into the credit* (London, 1740). Inv.9.10;
4.3.4.24; C60 <680711, r> Br 307.06.7*

The North Briton (London, 1763). 4.2.8.23-24; C147 <nd, h> Br 14.2* 2 v.

Notitia dignitatum, see Pancirolo, Guido

NOWELL, THOMAS, 1730-1801. *An answer to a pamphlet* [by Sir Richard Hill] (Oxford, 1769). 6.1.4.29; C320 <nd, xt> *EC75.N8667.768ab

NYE, STEPHEN, 1648?-1719.
The doctrine of the Holy Trinity (London, 1701). 4.3.8.4; C320 <680711, xt> *EC65.N9855.701d

The explication of the articles of the divine unity (London, 1715). 2.4.6.37; not in C <671209?, h> *EC75.H7267.Zz718s

Observations on national establishments (London, 1767). 6.1.4.28; C297 <nd, h> *EC75.H2448.767o (A)

O

†*Observations on a new plan for the education of a young prince* (London, 1732). 2.4.7.2; not in C <6410.., h> *EC75.H7267.Zz734e

Observations on public liberty (London, 1769). Inv.15.33; C250 <691129, r> *EC75.A100.769o2

‡*Observations on the present state of the English universities* (London, 1759). C232 (under Universities) <nd, xt> On title page: "This endeavor is incomplete, and partial." *EC75.A100.759o

The occasional paper (London, 1697-1698). 4.3.6.31; C87 <nd, smooth calf> *EP65.Oc131

OCCO, ADOLF, 1524-1606.
Imperatorum romanorum numismata (Milan, 1730). Inv.5.57; 2.3.1.24; C130 (under Mediobarbus) <6506.., h> f*GC5.Oc130.579ie

Inscriptiones veteræ in Hispania repertæ ([Heidelberg], 1596). Inv.2.10; 2.4.1.25; C6 <6410.., h> f*GC5.Oc130.596i

OCHINO, BERNARDINO, 1487-1564.
De corporis Christi præsentia in cœnæ sacramento (Basel, [1561]). Inv.1.37; 2.2.8.22; C184 (under Ochinus) <631024, r> *IC5.Oc350.561ℓ

Dialogi xxx (Basel, 1563). Inv.1.36; 2.1.8.48; C184 (under Ochinus) <631024, calf> *IC5.Oc350.Ef563c 2 v.

Expositio epistolæ divi Pauli ad Romanos (Augsburg, [ca. 1550]). Inv.1.38; 2.2.8.23; C184 <631024, h> Andover-Harvard Safe Z243 Ochino

OCKLEY, SIMON, 1678-1720.
An account of south-west Barbary (London, 1713). Inv.2.62; 2.1.7.23; C49 <6410.., h> Afr 1607.13*

The history of the Saracens (London, 1718). Inv.16.94; 2.2.5.9-10; B19, not in C <670511, r> Asia 125.5.4* 2 v.

Introductio ad linguas orientale (Cambridge, 1706). 4.1.8.36; C136 <nd, h> 2255.18*

Ökonomische Gesellschaft des Kantons Bern. ‡*Recueil de memoires concernants l'oeconomie rurale* (Zürich, 1760-1761). Inv.2.66; 2.3.7.23-26; C1 (under Memoires) <6410.., h> On flyleaf of v. 1, part 1: "But the liberal deviseth liberal things, and by liberal things shall he stand." On the next flyleaf: "Go little Books, may you excite the worthy, ingenious, wealthy, numerous Inhabitants of Boston in N. England, to institute a Society like that of the small but respectable City of Berne, to the great emolument of their City, Province, & Mother Country, and satisfaction and elegance of their private lives!" Sci 1615.5* 4 v.

Oesel, Philippus.
Introductio in accentionum Hebræorum metricam (Leiden, 1714). 4.1.7.31; C136 (under Ousel) <nd, h> 2286.33*

Introductio in accentionum Hebraeorum prosaicum (Leiden, 1715). 4.1.7.31; C136 (under Ousel) <nd, h> 2286.33*

†*Of education* (London, 1734). 2.4.7.2; C222 (under Education) <6410.., h> *EC75.H7267.Zz734e

‡*The oglio of traytors* (London, [1660]). 4.2.8.48; C147 <nd, h> On front flyleaf: "Floreat Libertas! Pereat Tyrannis! T·H." *EC.C3804.Z660o

Oldmixon, John, 1673-1742.
The history of England (London, 1739-1736-1735). Inv.16.63; 2.4.2.3-5; C60 <670511, h> f*EC7.Oℓ175.B739h 3 v.

Memoirs of the life of John Lord Somers (London, 1716). Inv.4.175; 2.4.7.27, 6.5.3.15; B23 (under Somer), C60 (under Somer) <641212?, calf> *EC7.Oℓ175.716m2 Second copy not located.

Remarks on a false, scandalous, and seditious libel (London, 1711). Not in C <670815, xt> *EC7.Oℓ175.711r

The old whig, see Avery, Benjamin

Oliva, Giovanni, 1689-1750. *In marmor Isaicum Romæ nuper effossum exercitationes* (Rome, 1719). 4.2.7.34; C6 <nd, h> Arc 785.10*

Ollyffe, George, 1710-1782. ‡*Vocabula hebraica* (London, 1750). 4.3.7.21; C236 <nd, h> TH identifies author. *EC75.H7267.Zz746o

Ollyffe, John, 1647-1717. *A defence of ministerial conformity* (London, 1702). Inv.12.83; 6.1.8.2; C184 <690818, h> *EC65.Oℓ985.702d

Original pieces concerning the present situation of the Protestants and Greeks in Poland (London, 1767). 4.4.6.27; C229 (under Poland) <nd, h (marbled boards)> *EC75.B5628.752s

Orpheus, *see Argonautica*

Orrery, Charles Boyle, earl of, 1676-1731. ‡*Dr. Bentley's dissertations* (London, 1698). Inv.17.19; 4.3.8.14; C106 (under Boyle) <68...., r> On title page: "rare." *EC7.Or755.698d (B)

ORSATO, SERTORIO, CONTE, 1617-1678.

Explanatio notarum et litterarum, quae frequentius in antiquis lapidibus ... occurrunt (Paris, 1723). Inv.1.34; 4.4.8.4; C8 (under Ursatus) <631024, h> Class 6107.23*

Historia di Padova (Padua, 1678). Inv.3.13; 2.3.3.9; C60 <641208, v> f*IC6.Or804.678h

Monumenta Patavina (Padua, 1652). Inv.4.5; 2.2.3.25; C8 (under Ursatus) <641212?, h> Arc 726.6*

ORSINI, FULVIO, 1529-1600. *Familiae romanæ ... in antiquis numismatibus* (Rome, [1577]). Inv.5.58; 4.1.3.23; C130 (under Ursinus) <6506.., h> Typ 525.77.657 F (B)

[Another edition], ed. Charles Patin (Paris, 1663). Inv.5.59; 2.4.1.11; C130 <6506.., h> Arc 1475.4 F*

OSBORNE, FRANCIS, *see* Sprigg, William

OSTERMANN, JOHANN ERICH. *De mutatione punctorem Ebræorum* (Wittenberg, 1633). 4.4.7.12; C236 <nd, h> 2255.13*

OTHO, JOHANN HEINRICH, 1651-1719. *Lexicon rabbinico-philologicum* (Geneva, 1675). 4.3.8.39; C134 <nd, v> Andover-Harvard S.C.R. 211.1 Otho

OVERTON, RICHARD, fl. 1646. ‡*Mans mortalitie* (Amsterdam, 1644). 2.2.5.2; C311 (under title) <671209, h> On flyleaf of v. 1: "This collection was formed by T·H, with pains & expence, not long after he returned from his Travells." *EC75.H7267.Zz706ℓ v. 1

OWEN, JOHN, 1560?-1622. *Epigrammatum* (London, 1676). Inv.6.12; C143 <650817, r> *EC.Ow267.B676e

OWEN, JOHN, 1616-1683. *Of the divine ... original of the scriptures* (Oxford, 1659). Inv.14.73; C184 <700926> Original Hollis gift not located.

OWTRAM, WILLIAM, 1626-1679. *De sacrificiis libri duo* (Amsterdam, 1678). 4.4.8.21; C184 <nd, v> R 250.11*

The Oxford expulsion condemned (London, 1769). 6.1.4.29; not in C <nd, xt> *EC75.A100.769o3

OXFORD UNIVERSITY, *see* University of Oxford

P

PACIAUDI, PAOLO, 1710-1785.

Ad nummos consulares IIIviri Marci Antonii (Rome, 1757). Inv.3.25 (part); 4.1.5.8; C130 <641208, marbled boards> Typ 725.57.670

De athletarum kubisteisi in palæstra gracorum commentariolum (Rome, 1756). Inv.3.25 (part); 2.2.4.1; C6 <641208, h> AH 4837.56*

De Beneventarum Cereris Augustæ mensore exegesis (Rome, 1753). Inv.3.25 (part); 2.2.4.1; not in C <641208, h> AH 4837.56*

De sacris christianorum balneis (Rome, 1758). Inv.3.25 (part); 4.1.5.9; not in C <641208, h> Typ 725.57.670

Diatribe qua Graeci anaglyphi interpretatio traditur (Rome, 1751). Inv.3.25 (part); 2.2.4.1; not in C <641208, h> AH 4837.56*

Skadiophorema, sive De umbrellæ gestatione commentarius (Rome, 1752). Inv.3.25 (part); 2.2.4.1; not in C <641208, h> AH 4837.56*

A packet from Rome (London, 1745). 2.2.5.8; C23 (under Rome) <nd> Declared lost, June 2002.

PAETUS, LUCAS, 1512 or 13-1581. *De mensuris et ponderibus romanis et græcis* (Venice, 1573). 2.3.3.13; not in C <641208, r> f*IC5.P1926.593n

PAGETT, THOMAS CATESBY PAGET, 1689-1742.
   An essay on human life ([London? 17..?]) Inv.8.16 <661001> Original Hollis gift not located.

   ‡*Some reflections upon the administration of government* (London, 1740). 4.2.7.11; C250 <nd, r> On title page: "By Lord Paget. very rare." *EC75.C1527.747ℓ

   ‡[Another copy] 2.3.7.38; C250 <641208, h> On title page: "By Lord Paget. There is another very scarce pamphlet by Lord Paget entituled [*sic*] || Reflections on human Nature." *EC75.H7267.Zz735t

PALERMO, EVANGELISTA. *A grammar of the Italian language* (London, 1755). 2.2.5.12; B19, C52 <641208, h> Gutman Library EducT 21917.55

PALLADIO, ANDREA, 1508-1580.
   ‡*I qvattro libri dell'architettvra* (Venice, 1581). Inv.3.21; 2.3.3.21; C8 <641208, v> On front flyeaf: "Bought of Tumesmanni at Verona in October 1752 by TH, then upon his Travells, for 50 Lisi Veneti, or about £1,5,, Sterling. Mem: The best Editions of Palladio are the three first; These were published as follows, In 1570, by Fransceschi, in Venezia. 1581, by Carampello in Venezia. 1642, by Borgillo in Venezia. These are all said to have been from the same Wooden plates, and consequently the first Edition is the most desirable; But all three Editions have long been very scarce, and there has been frequently paid for each of them Four, Five, Six, or Ten Zecchins. This copy is of the second Edition, & wants the Title page only." FA 1545.203.2 F*

   ‡[*Another edition*] (Venice, 1570 [i.e., 1767]). Inv.10.4; 4.4.3.2; C8 <680712, red morocco with arms of Consul Smith> On flyleaf: "A pompous edition of a most elegant Author, printed at Venice by Joseph Smith Esq. 1767; the prints in which are said to be stricken off from the Plates made use of for the first edition. T·H." Typ 725.67.671 F

   See also Caesar, Julius

PALLAVICINO, FERRANTE, 1615-1644.
   L'ambasciatore invidiato (Venice, 1654). Inv.3.165 (part); C120 (under Le opera) <641208, contemporary calf> Tr 1348*

   Le bellezze dell'anima (Venice, 1654). Inv.3.165 (part); C120 (under Le opera) <641208, contemporary calf> Tr 1348*

   Le dve Agrippine (Venice, 1654). Inv.3.165 (part); C120 (under Le opera) <641208, contemporary calf> Tr 1348*

Opere scelte (Villafranca, 1666). Inv.3.163; 2.4.8.38; C120 <641208, r>
*IC6.P1785.B6660 (B)

Il principe hermafrodito (Venice, 1656). Inv.3.165 (part); C120 (under Le opera)
<641208, contemporary calf) Tr 1348*

Scena retorica (Venice, 1654). Inv.3.165 (part); C120 (under Le opera)
<641208, contemporary calf) Tr 1348*

PANCIROLO, GUIDO, 1523-1599. *Notitia utraque dignitatum* (Venice, 1593). Inv.3.14;
2.3.3.13; C6 <641208, r> f*IC5.P1926.593n

PANCRAZI, GIUSEPPE MARIA, d. 1764. ‡*Antichita Siciliane* (Naples, 1751). 4.1.1.2-3; C6
<67....?, h> On a 4° leaf inserted in v. 1: "The Fate of Father Joseph Mary Pancrazi was
singular, and afflicts me even now! In the Autumn of 1752 he lodged in the Theatin
Convent, the Convent of his order, at Naples. There he was attacked by a violent Fever,
which impaired & broke his Constitution. In that feeble state, he applied however to his
Work; &, in order, the more speedily to publish the third Volume of it, found means, in
the Year 1753, to sell a few rare medals which he had collected to the King, by whom he
had the honor to be personally known, & respected. The Superior of the Convent, some
how got intelligence of that Transaction; claimed the money arising from the Sale of the
Medals for the Uses of the Convent; And obtained it. When Father Pancrazi became
apprized of that Event, he went distracted directly; and after languishing, with intervals,
miserably some Years; at length ended his wretched Life! T·H." On flyleaf of v. 1:
"Thomas Hollis, an Englishman, an Assertor of Liberty, a Well-wisher to all ingenuous
Pursuits, devotes this Work to the Library of Harvard College, at Cambridge in New
England, in remembrance of Joseph Maria Pancrazi, the author of it, a good Man! Who
rendered him Hospitality, & by whose Letters, particularly, he travelled throughout
Sicily & Malta. Pall Mall, jan. 1, 1767. Che tra l'uom del Sepolcro, ed in Vita il serba.
Petrarca." On the map facing p.1, dedicated to the Prince of Torremuzza: "The Prince
of Torremuzza, now living, is a learned accomplished, excellent Nobleman, Author of
several valuable Works, and a great Patron to all ingenious Travellers. He is collecting
the antient Inscriptions found in Sicily, for Publication." On plate xx, by M. Tuscher: "a
Beautiful Plate of Medals! Tuscher died a few years after the engraving of it in Denmark,
in the Service of that King!" Two plates are dedicated to TH, one to Thomas Brand
Hollis. Arc 730.200 F* 2 v.

PANVINIO, ONOFRIO, 1529-1568.
‡*Antiquitatum Veronensium libri VIII* ([Padua], 1648). 4.3.2.7; C6 <nd, v> On title page:
"Bought at Verona in October 1752 by T·H then upon his Travels. This is a very scarce
book." Arc 720.204 F*

‡*De ludibus circensibus libri II* (Venice, 1600). 4.4.1.13; C6 <nd, v> On title page:
"Bought at Verona in October 1752 by TH upon his Travells. This is a very scarce book
& very valuable. It cost 4 Zecchins unbound." AH 7836.00 F*

The papists bloody oath (Salisbury, [1745?]). 2.2.5.8; C228 <nd, h> *EC75.H7267.Zz745t

PARIS, MATTHEW, 1200-1259. *Historia major* (London, 1640-1639). Inv.3.75; 4.1.3.16-17;
C60 <641208, h> STC 19210 F 2 v. TH gave a second set, not located.

PARKER, MATTHEW, 1504-1575. †*De antiquitate britannicæ ecclesiæ* (London, 1729).
Inv.1.5; 2.2.1.19; C68 <631024, h)> Br 201 F*

PARKER, RICHARD, ca. 1712-1742. *An essay on the usefulness of Oriental learning* (London,
1739). 4.3.7.21; C236 (under Oriental literature) <nd, h> *EC75.H7267.Zz746o

PARKER, SAMUEL, 1640-1688. *Disputationes de Deo* (London, 1679). Inv.3.93; 2.3.5.3; C185
<641208, h> *EC65.P2284.678d

The parliamentary or constitutional history of England (London, 1762-1763). 2.3.6.3-26; not in
C <nd, h (some volumes rebound> Lamont Brit Doc 9000.25 24 v.

PARSONS, JAMES, 1705-1770. †‡*Remains of Japhet* (London, 1767). Inv.17.7; 4.3.4.27; not
in C <68…., h> On flyleaf: "This learned, ingenious work, will probably occasion the
sending to Harvard College, as they can be gotten, for they are scarce, of some Irish,
Welch, Scotish [*sic*] Grammars and Dictionaries; the writer being very desirous to
contribute his whole Mite toward the forming of some first rate Scholars, the noblest of
all Men, in that College. Palmal, dec. 21, 67." TH subscribed for 6 copies. 1261.8*

PARSONS, JOSEPH, d. 1774. *An apology for the Church of England* (London, 1767). 6.1.3.29;
C321 <nd, h> *EC75.H7267.Zz769t

PASCAL, BLAISE, 1623-1662. *Pensées* (Paris, 1734). Inv.4.122; 4.2.8.5; B20, C185
<641212?, r> Phil 2805.40.11*

PASSERANI, ALBERTO RADICATI, CONTE DI, *see* Radicati, Alberto

PATERSON, WILLIAM, 1658-1719. *Proposals and reasons for constituting a council of trade
in Scotland* (Glasgow, 1751). Inv.4.155 (under Law); 2.4.8.10; C37 (under Law, John)
<641212?, r> Econ 222.1.5*

PATIN, CHARLES, 1633-1693.
Familiæ romanæ in antiquis numismatibus (Paris, 1663). 2.4.1.11; C130 <nd> Original
Hollis gift not located.

Thesaurus numismatum ex eijus museo (Amsterdam, 1672). Inv.11.5 (part); 6.1.3.22; C130
<6809.., h> Arc 1370.2*

Thesaurus numismatum, antiquorum & recentiorum, ab Petro Mavroceno (Venice,
[1683]). Inv.11.5 (part); 6.1.3.22; not in C <6809.., h> Arc 1370.2*

See also Orsini, Fulvio

PATSALL, MRS. ‡*An apology for the Catholics of Great Britain and Ireland* (London, 1768).
Inv.10.44; 4.3.8.32; C153 (under title) & C267 (under Catholics) <680712, h> On flyleaf:
"A very confident Book." *EC75.P2764.768aa

[Another copy] 6.2.8.21; C153 & C267 <nd, h> *EC75.Sh487.759rb

PAUSANIUS. *Græciæ descriptio accurata* (Leipzig, 1696). 4.2.3.1; C18 <nd, h> Gp 20.120 F*

PAUTEREN, JOHAN VAN, d. 1520. *Commentarii grammatici* (Paris, 1537 [1538]). Inv.10.8;
4.3.4.12; C135 (under Despauterius) <680712, h> f*NC5.P2878C.1538

PAUW, JAN CORNELIS VAN, d. 1749. *Notæ in Pindari Olympia* (Utrecht, 1748 [i.e., 1747]).
4.2.7.5; C18 <nd, r> Gp 75.410*

Paxton, Peter, d. 1711. ‡*Civil polity* (London, 1703). Inv.17.20; 4.4.7.18; C85 (under title) <68...., h> On flyleaf: "Said to have been written by Peter Paxton, a Physician." On title page: "Curious, Rare." Gov 526.4*

Pearce, Zachary, 1690-1774.

‡*A review of the text of Milton's Paradise lost* (London, 1733). 2.2.5.26; not in C <65...., h> On flyleaf: "The Author, at this time, the very eminent Prelate, Dʳ Zachary Pearce, Bishop of Rochester. Mar. 25, 1765. T·H." On title page: "very scarce." 14487.5* (A)

‡[Another copy] Not in C <nd, h (rebacked)> On first flyleaf: "The Author, at this time, a very eminent Prelate, Dʳ Zachary Pearce, Bishop of Rochester." On second flyleaf, a quotation from Akenside: "——Morpheus, on thy dewy wing | Such fair auspicious visions bring | As sooth'd great Milton's injur'd age, | When in prophetic dreams he saw, | The tribes unborn, with pious awe | Imbibe each Virtue from his heav'nly page." On title page: "exceeding scarce." Bookplate of George Ticknor, who wrote: "Bo't as a duplicate from Harv. College Library." Returned by Ticknor's heirs, May 29, 1885. 14487.5* (B)

Pearson, John, 1613-1686. *Opera posthuma chronologica* (London, 1688). 4.2.6.4; C35 <nd, h> C 1317.15*

Peckard, Peter, 1718?-1797.

Farther observations on the doctrine of an intermediate state (London, 1757). Inv.2.96 (part); 2.1.6.12; C322 <6410.., h> *EC75.H7267.Zz751t

Observations on the doctrine of an intermediate state (London, 1756). Inv.2.96 (part); 2.1.6.12; C322 <6410.., h> *EC75.H7267.Zz751t

Peirce, James, 1673-1726.

An answer to Mr. Enty's Defence of the proceedings of the assembly at Exon (London, 1719). Inv.5.30 (part); 2.3.7.7; C322 <6506.., xt> *EC7.P3551.719a

The case of the ministers ejected at Exon (London, 1719). Inv.5.28 (part); 2.3.7.7; C322 <6506.., xt> *EC7.P3551.719c

A defence of the case of the ministers ejected at Exon (London, 1719). Inv.5.30 (part); 2.3.7.7; not in C <6506.., xt> *EC7.P3551.719d

Inquisition- honesty display'd: or, The Western inquisition defended (London, 1722). Inv.5.29 (part); 2.3.7.6; C323 <6506.., h (marbled boards)> *EC7.P3551.720w

A justification of the case of the ministers ejected at Exon (London, 1719). Inv.5.30 (part); 2.3.7.7; C322 <6506.., xt> *EC7.P3551.719j

Propositions relating to the controversy (London, 1720). Inv.5.30 (part); 2.3.7.5; not in C <6506.., h (marbled boards)> *EC7.P3551.720p

Remarks upon the account of what was transacted in the assembly at Exon (London, 1719). Inv.5.30 (part); 2.3.7.7; C322 <6506.., xt> *EC7.P3551.719r

A reply to Mr. Enty's late piece (London, 1721). Inv.5.28 (part); 2.3.7.5; C283 (under Enty … Reply) <6506.., h (marbled boards)> *EC7.P3551.720p

The security of truth without the assistance of persecution (London, 1721). Inv.5.30 (part); 2.3.7.5; not in C <6506.., h (marbled boards)> *EC7.P3551.720p

Two sermons: the one on John 1.46 ... the other on 1 Cor.iii.11 (London, 1720). B20, C323 <6.....?, r> *EC7.P3551.720t

A vindication of the dissenters (London, 1718). Inv.16.20; 2.2.5.27; B20, C186 <670511, h> C 6417.10.7*

Vindiciæ fratrum dissentientium in Anglia (London, 1710). Inv.16.19; 2.2.5.26; C186 <670511, h> *EC7.P3551.710v

The western inquisition (London, 1720). Inv.5.29 (part); 2.3.7.6; C323 <6506.., h (marbled boards)> *EC7.P3551.720w

PELLEGRINO, CAMILLO, 1598-1663. *Apparato alle antichita di Capua* (Naples, 1651). Inv.3.44; 2.3.5.27; C6 <641208, calf> *IC6.P3644.651a

PEMBERTON, HENRY, 1694-1771. *Observations on poetry* (London, 1738). 4.2.8.13; not in C <nd, h> *EC75.H7267.Zz738p

PENN, WILLIAM, 1644-1718.
England's present interest discover'd ([London], 1675). 2.4.5.19; not in C   Original Hollis gift discarded as a duplicate.

The peoples ancient and just liberties asssrted [*sic*] ([London], 1670). 2.4.5.19; C229 <nd, xt> *AC6.P3808.670pb

Three letters tending to demonstrate how the security against al [*sic*] *future persecution* (London, 1688). 2.1.6.14; C274 (under Conscience) <671209, h> *EC65.C5614.681c

See also The second part of the peoples antient and just liberties asserted

PERCY, THOMAS, 1729-1811. *Reliques of ancient English poetry* [2nd edition] (London, 1767). Inv.9.40; 4.4.7.43-45; C143 <680711, h> *EC75.H7267.Zz767p 3 v. A second copy, Inv.17.14 <68....>, not located.

PERIZONIUS, JACOBUS, 1651-1715.
Animadversiones historicæ (Amsterdam, 1685). 4.4.8.13; not in C <nd, h> AH 307.69*

Origines babylonicæ et ægypticæ (Leiden, 1711). 4.2.8.32-33; C35 <nd, h> *NC7.P4197.711o 2 v.

[Another copy] 4.4.6.40-41; C35 <nd, v> *NC7.P4197.711oa 2 v.

PERRAULT, NICOLAS, ca. 1611-1661. *La morale des Jésuites* (Mons, 1667). Inv.3.35; 2.3.4.33; C115 <641208, h (rebacked)> *FC6.P4265.667m

PERRIN, JEAN BAPTISTE, fl. 1786. *Essai sur l'origine et l'antiquité des langues* (London, 1767). 4.2.8.20; not in C <nd, h> 1237.10*

See also Brevis ad artem cogitandi introductio

PERRY, FRANCIS, d. 1765. ‡*A series of English medals* (London, 1762). 6.3.2.14; C234 <69....?, xt> Designed and sponsored by TH; see Diary, January 7, 9, 13, 16, 1761. Numerous annotations throughout concerning specimens in TH's cabinet and other collections. Arc 1540.13*

Persepolis illustrata (London, 1739). Inv.3.10; 2.3.2.1; not in C <641208, r> Arc 485.202 F*

PERSON OF HONOUR, PSEUD. *A free discourse wherein the doctrines which make for tyranny are display'd* (London, 1697). 4.4.7.33; C146 (under Sir Robert Howard) Original Hollis gift not located.

PETER, OF LANGTOFT, d. 1307? *Chronicle*, ed. Thomas Hearne (Oxford, 1725). Inv.12.54; 6.1.3.32-33; C5 <690818, h> Br 1465.8* 2 v.

PETIT, PETER. *The Hebrew guide* (London, 1752). 4.3.5.19; <nd, h> Contains instructions to the binder in an unidentified hand. 2261.29*

PETIT, PIERRE, 1617-1687. *Miscellanearum observationum libri quatuor* (Utrecht, 1682). 4.4.7.19; not in C <nd, h> Class 9828.4* (A)

PETIT, SAMUEL, 1594-1643. *Leges atticæ* (Paris, 1635). 4.2.2.15; C77 <nd, h> AH 4136.35 F*

PETRARCA, FRANCESCO, 1304-1374. ‡*Il Petrarca, con l'espositione d'Alessandro Vellutello* (Venice, 1560). Inv.4.22; 2.4.4.35; C143 <641212?, v> On flyleaf: "Bought at Genoa in December 1752 by TH then upon his Travells, & gave a Zecchin for it." Ital 7105.60*

PETRELLI, GIACOMO, b. 1683. *Nuova, e esatta descrizione del celeberrimo fonte* (Palermo, 1737). Inv.3.120 (under Palermo; part); 2.4.7.12; C227 (under Presti) <641208, h> *IC7.A100.B752h

PETRIE, ALEXANDER, 1594?-1662. *A compendious history of the Catholick church* (The Hague, 1662). Inv.3.80; 2.3.3.20; C68 <641208, early calf> With bookplate: "Sir Thos. Brand Knt. Gentleman Usher of the Green Rod and Gentleman Usher Daily Waitr. to His Majesty Anno 1735." f*EC65.P4482.662c

PETTER, NICOLAES. ‡*Klare onderrichtinge der voortreffelijcke worstel-kunst* (Amsterdam, 1674). 4.4.5.3; C33 <nd, r> On flyleaf: "Manly Exercises cannot be too much encouraged by ingenuous, that is free, Nations. T·H." A treatise on wrestling, illustrated by Romeyn de Hooghe. Typ 632.74.683

PETTINGAL, JOHN, 1708-1781.
A dissertation upon the Tascia (London, 1763). 2.1.8.20; C234 <6410.., h> *EC75.H7267.Zz763p

†‡*An enquiry into the use amd practice of juries among the Greeks and Romans* (London, 1769). Inv.12.11; 6.1.2.2; B20, C85 <690818, h> On front flyleaf: "Felicity is Freedom & Freedom is Magnanimity. Thucyd." On back flyleaf: "It is apprehended, this work, and the 'Observations on the more ancient Statutes,' by the Hon. Daines Barrington, are two of the noblest productions which have appeared for some time past. T·H ap. 14, 1769." AH 137.69*

The Latin inscription, on the copper table (London, 1763). 2.1.8.20; C208 <6410.., h> *EC75.H7267.Zz763p

PETTY, SIR WILLIAM, 1623-1687. *A treatise of taxes and contributions* (London, 1662). 2.3.8.7; not in C <6506.., h> *EC65.Ev226.661f

PETYT, WILLIAM, 1676-1707.
‡*The antient right of the Commons of England* (London, 1680). Inv.2.74; C85 <6410..,
h (rebacked)> On front flyleaf, a long quotation from Henry Neville, *Discourses concerning government*; on title page: "ut spargam"; on back flyleaf: "See 'Miscellanea Parliamentaria' printed in the same year, by the same Gentleman, in octavo." Br 143.2*

Miscellanea parliamentaria (London, 1680). 2.1.8.45; C85 <nd, h> Br 143.4*

PEYTON, SIR EDWARD, BART., 1588?-1657. *The divine catastrophe of the kingly family* (London, 1731). 2.2.5.22; C214 <nd, h> *EC75.H7267.Zz737h

PEZRON, PAUL, 1639-1706. *The antiquities of nations* (London, 1706). Inv.17.25; 4.4.7.5; B20, C6 <68...., h> AH 8548.2.5*

PHALARIS, *see* Pseudo-Phalaris

The Phenix, or, A revival of scarce and valuable pieces (London, 1707-1708). 4.2.7.41-42; C120 <nd, r> *EC7.D9235.707p2 2 v.

PHILALETHES, PSEUD.
Pandaemonium, or, A new infernal expedition (London, 1750). Inv.14.13; 6.1.3.7; C238 (under Lauder) <700926, h> *EC7.M4617.732c

A philosophical dissertation upon the inlets to human knowledge (London, 1739). 4.2.7.15; not in C <nd, h> *EC75.H7267.Zz746t

PHILANAX, PSEUD. *A letter to a member of the House of Commons* ([London, 1674?]). 2.4.5.19; C226 <nd, xt> *EC65.A100.674ℓ

PHILELEUTHEROS, TYRO, PSEUD. *An address to the rational advocates* (London, 1769). 6.1.4.28; not in C <nd, h> *EC75.H2448.767o (A)

PHILIPPS, JENKIN THOMAS, d. 1755.
†‡*A compendious way of teaching ancient and modern languages* (London, 1758). 2.4.7.22; C120 & C229 <6412.., h> On flyleaf: "There is a curious treatise of education by Obadiah Walker; and yet the cunning of the World & Popery lurks under it." Text includes a reprint of Milton, *Of education*; in the margin of pp.126-127: "Outlined, in one single sheet in quarto, with MATCHLESS Understanding." *EC7.P5392.B750t

Dissertatio ... de atheismo (London, 1716). 4.4.7.32; not in C <nd, h> *EC7.P5492.716d

PHILIPS, JOHN, 1676-1709. *The whole works of Mr. John Philips* (London, 1720). Inv.8.51; 2.3.7.41; B20, C143 <661001, h> 15464.32*

PHILLIPS, EDWARD, 1630-1696? *The new world of words* (London, 1720). 4.4.3.8; C204 <nd, h> *EC65.P5425.658nga

PHILLIPS, JOHN, *see* Casas, Bartolome de las

PHILONOMOS, PSEUD. ‡*The right method of maintaining security* (London, 1751). Inv.11.10; 6.1.6.21; C85 <6809.., h> On flyleaf: "Written under the influence of Mr. Sherive Janssen; now Sir Stephen Theodore Janssen Bar. The worthy Chamberlain of London. July 1, 68. T·H." *EC75.A100.751r

PHILOSTRATUS. [*Opera*] *omnia* (Leipzig, 1709). Inv.10.2; 4.2.2.1 *or* 4.4.1.4; C18 <680712, r> Gp 59.15 F* Second copy not located.

PIANURA, N., CONTE DI. *Lettera al reverendissimo padre d. Gian Francesco Baldini* ([Naples?, 1751?]). Inv.3.120 (under Palermo; part); 2.4.7.12; C219 (under Baldini) <641208, h> *IC7.A100.B752h

PICCOLOMINI, ALESSANDRO, 1508-1578. *Della institutione morale* (Venice, 1575). Inv.3.111; 2.4.5.21; C47 <641208, v> *IC5.P5823.560de

PIERRE, DE MARICOURT, 13th cent. *Opusculum perpetua memoria dignissimum, de natura magnetis* (Cologne, 1562). 4.4.6.2; not in C <nd, h> *FC5.M9425.559v

PIERSON, JAN, 1731-1759. *Verisimilium libri duo* (Leiden, 1752). 4.3.6.14; not in C <nd, h> Class 9831.3*

PIGANIOL DE LA FORCE, JEAN-AIMAR, 1673-1753. ‡*Description de Paris* (Paris, 1742). Inv.4.65; 2.2.7.5-12; C49 <641212?, r> TH's initials on title page of v. 8. Fr 7457.42* 8 v.

PIGNA, GIOVAN BATTISTA, 1529-1575. *Historia de principi di Este* (Ferrara, 1570). Inv.2.14; 2.4.1.21; C61 <6410.., v> *IC5.P6262.570h

PIGNORIA, LORENZO, 1571-1631.

> *Characteres Ægyptii* (Frankfurt, 1608). Inv.2.51 (part); 4.3.6.2; not in C <6410.., h> *IC6.P6275.605v

> *De servis … commentarius* (Padua, 1656). Inv.2.51 (part); 4.3.6.2; C208 <6410.., h> *IC6.P6275.605v

> *Magnæ deum matris Idææ & Attidis* (Venice, 1624). Inv.2.51; 4.3.6.2; C208 <6410.., h> *IC6.P6275.605v

> ‡*Mensa Isiaca* (Amsterdam, 1669). 4.3.5.15; C6 <nd, v> On plate facing p.2 of second treatise: "Penes T·H, 1767." *IC6.P6275.605vc

> [Another copy] Inv.2.51 (part); 4.3.6.2; C208 <6410.., h> *IC6.P6275.605v

> *Vetustissim tabulæ Æneæ … accurata explicatio* (Venice, 1605). Inv.2.51 (part); 4.3.6.2; C208 <6410.., h> *IC6.P6275.605v

PILES, ROGER DE.

> *Abregé de la vie des peintres* (Paris, 1715). Inv.4.156; 2.1.8.11; B20, C29 <641212?, h> *FC6.P6425.699ac (A)

> [Another copy] 4.2.8.2; B20, C29 <nd, r> *FC6.P6425.699ac (B)

> *Cours de peinture* (Paris, 1708). Inv.4.96; 2.1.7.50; C9 <641212?, h> Typ 715.08.693

PINCOT, DANIEL. ‡*An essay on the origin, uses and properties, of artificial stone* (London, 1770). Inv.14.64; 6.1.5.16; C9 <700926, h> On flyleaf: "An ingenious tract." Eng 637.70*

PIRANESI, GIOVANNI BATTISTA, 1720-1778.

> *Antichita d'Albano e di Castel Gandalfo* (Rome, 1764). 6.3.1.4; C7 & C33 <nd, r> Fine Arts X Cage XFA 6227.970.62 PF

> *Le antichita romane* (Rome, 1756). 6.3.1.11-14; C33 <nd, r> Fine Arts X Cage XFA 6227.970.54 PF

> *De Romanorum magnificentia et architectura* (Rome, 1761). 6.3.1.5; C7 & C33 <nd, r> Fine Arts X Cage XFA 6227.970.64 PF

Lapides capitolini ([Rome, 1762]). 6.3.1.6; C7 <nd, r>
Fine Arts X Cage XFA 6227.970.52 PF

Le rouine del castello dell'Acqua Giulia ([Rome, 1761]). 6.3.1.3; C7 & C33 <nd, r>
Fine Arts X Cage XFA 6227.970.58 PF

Trofei di Ottavio Augusto (Rome, 1753). C33 <nd, r>
Fine Arts X Cage XFA 6227.970.56 PF

Note: The preceding six titles of Piranesi are rebound similarly, without marks of provenance, and are presumably (not positively) the gift of TH, who knew Piranesi in Italy and later sent him a set of drawing instruments in a shagreen case.

PITISCUS, SAMUEL, 1637-1727. *Lexicon antiquitatum romanorum* (Leeuwarden, 1713). 4.3.1.17-18; C6 (under Petiscus) <nd, h> f*NC7.P6826.713ℓ 2 v.

PITT, WILLIAM, EARL OF CHATHAM, 1708-1778. *The celebrated speech of a celebrated commoner* (London, 1766). 4.1.7.20; C242 <67…., r> *EC75.Aℓ862.766c v.2

PITTIS, WILLIAM, 1674-1724. *Memoirs of the life of Charles Montague, late earl of Halifax* (London, 1715). 6.1.7.37; C113 (under Halifax) <nd, h> 15463.65*

PLACCIUS, VINCENT. ‡*Theatrum anonymorum et pseudonymorum* (Hamburg, 1708). 4.3.3.9-10; C120 <nd, h> On a slip inserted before the first flyleaf: "A curious work, & rare, and a fine copy of it. It is sent with an Eye toward those FIRST RATE Scholars, which it is hoped will be produced by Harvard College." B 550.3 F* 2 v.

†*A plain and seasonable address to the freeholders of Great Britain* (London, 1766). Inv.16.38 (part); 4.1.7.22; C267 <670511, h> *AC7.Ot464.765ab (B)

Plain-dealing, or a particular examination of a late treatise, entituled, Humane reason (London, 1675). 2.2.8.52; not in C <641208, h> *EC65.C6125.674tb

Plain English humbly offered to the consideration of His Majesty (London, 1690). 2.2.5.16; C250 <671209?, h> *EC75.H7267.Zz691t

PLANK, STEPHEN. *An introduction to the only method for discovering longitude* (London, 1714). 2.1.7.4; C216 <nd, r> *EC7.P6937.714i

PLATO.
The Republic of Plato, tr. H. Spens (Glasgow, 1763). Inv.9.16; 4.3.5.11; B23, C18 <680711, r> Harvard Depository KPF 2346

Opera omnia, ed. Marsilio Ficino (Frankfurt, 1602). 4.2.1.21; C18 <nd, r> GP 82.120 F* (A)

PLINY, THE ELDER. *Historia naturale*, tr. Cristoforo Landino (Venice, 1543). Inv.3.41; 2.3.5.37-8; not in C <641208, v> Lp 27.205* 2 v.

PLINY, THE YOUNGER.
The letters of Pliny, tr. William Melmoth (London, 1757). Inv.13.35; 6.1.4.19-20; C18 <700926, r> *EC75.H7267.Zz757p

Panegyrick upon the emperor Trajan, tr. George Smith (London, 1702). Inv.9.27; not in C <680711> Original Hollis gift not located.

PLINY, THE YOUNGER, PSEUD. *Letters to the Earl of Hillsborough* (London, 1770). 6.1.4.5; not in C <700926, h> *EC75.A100.770ℓ

PLUTARCH.

†‡*Plutarch's Lives* [with a Life of Plutarch by John Dryden] (London, 1758). 2.1.5.14-19; B20, C19 <65...., h> On flyleaf: "Thomas Hollis, an Englishman, Assertor of Liberty, Citizen of the World, is desirous of having the honor to present to the Public Library of Harvard College at Cambridge, in New England, 'Plutarch's Lives'; a work, which at School he read avidly at times he might have slept, and to which he afterward became indebted for the honestest and finest dispositions of his Mind. Pall Mall, nov. 1, 1765." Gp 86.365* 6 v.

Omnia quae extant operum (Paris, 1624). Inv.8.18 (under Moralia); 4.1.2.2-4; C18 <661001, r> f*OGC.P746.624 (B) v. 2 only, bound in 3 parts

†‡*Vitæ parallelæ*, ed. Augustine Bryant (London, 1723-1729). 2.1.4.9-13; C19 <nd, h> In v. 1: "Ut spargam T·H." Gp 86.150 F* 5 v.

See also Quevedo, Francisco de

POCOCKE, EDWARD, 1604-1691, *see* Bar Hebraeus

A poem on the glorious atchievements of Admiral Vernon (London, 1740). 4.2.3.22; C240 (under Vernon) <nd, h> f*EC75.H7267.Zz740p

Poetical miscellanies, the fifth part (London, 1704). C141 (under Dryden) <nd, r> *EC65.D8474.B709m v.5

Poetical miscellanies, the sixth part (London, 1709). C141 (under Dryden) <nd, r> *EC65.D8474.B709m v.6

POIVRE, PIERRE, 1719-1786. *Voyages d'un philosophe* (Yverdon, 1768). Inv.15.21; 6.2.8.17; C126 <691129> Declared lost, 2002.

Political aphorisms or, The true maxims of government (London, 1690). 2.2.5.16; C250 <671209, h> *EC75.H7267.Zz691t

The political conduct of the Earl of Chatham (London, 1769). Inv.15.27; 6.1.6.32; C245 (under Chatham) <691129, xt> *EC75.A100.769p (A)

The political register and impartial review [for 1769] (London, 1769). Inv.15.8; C87 (issues for May, July, August, September only, present but not identified as TH gifts). <691129, r> Br 2062.16*

POLIZIANO, ANGELO, 1454-1494, *see* Cleonides

POLLUX, JULIUS, OF NAUCRATIS. *Onomasticum græce & latine* (Amsterdam, 1706). 4.2.3.17-18; C19 <nd, h> Gp 91.15 F* 2 v.

POLYBIUS.

De' fatti de'Romani, tr. Lodovico Domenichi (Verona, 1741). Inv.4.21; 2.4.4.25-26; C19 <641212?, v> KE 30442*

The general history, tr. James Hampton (London, 1756). Inv.12.74; C19 <690818, h> Gp 95.185 F*

Historiarum libri qui supersunt, ed. Isaac Casaubon (Paris, 1609). 4.1.3.11; C19 <nd, r> Gp 95.120 F*

†[Another edition] (Amsterdam, 1670). 4.1.8.8-10; B20, C19 <nd, h> Gp 95.126* 3 v.

Historico greco, tr. Lodovico Domenichi (Venice, 1546). Inv.3.143; 2.1.8.42; C19 <641208, h> Gp 95.220*

POMPONAZZI, PIETRO, 1462-1524.
‡*Opera* (Basel, [1567]). Inv.12.39; 6.3.8.43; not in C <690818, h> TH adds date of publication to title page. Phil 4200.1.10*

‡*Tractatus de immortalitate animæ* ([France?], 1634 [i.e., ca. 1660?]). Inv.7.22 *or* Inv.12.71; 2.2.8.45; C94 & C187 <651010 *or* 690818, contemporary red morocco> On title page: "Rariss." *IC5.P7729.516tc Second copy not located.

PONTOPPIDAN, ERICH, 1698-1764. *The natural history of Norway* (London, 1755). Inv.16.53; 2.3.2.10; C72 <670511, r> f*QDC7.P7795.Eg755b (B)

POPPLE, WILLIAM, d. 1708. ‡*A rational catechism* (Amsterdam, 1712). Inv.14.47; 6.2.8.28; not in C <700926, h> TH identifies the author on the title page. On flyleaf (unidentified hand): "note. Mr. Popple, the author of this Catechism, translated into English Mr Locke's first letter on Toleration." Andover-Harvard 824 Safe

PORPHYRY, ca. 234-ca. 305. *De abstinentia ab animalibus necandis libri quatuor* (Cambridge, 1655). 4.3.8.40; C19 <nd, h> *OGC.Ep42.655 (B)

PORRÉE, JONAS. *Traité des anciennes cérémonies* (Charenton, 1662). Inv.4.121; 2.2.7.20; not in C <641212?, h> *FC6.P8283.662t

PORTA, ENRICO DI. *De linguarum orientalium praestantia* (Milan, 1758). Inv.10.15; 4.1.5.8; B14, C134 <680712, h> 2255.23*

PORTA, GIOVANNI BATTISTA DELLA, 1540-1615.
‡*De humana physiognomia libri iiii* (Vico Equense, 1586). Inv.17.4; 4.3.4.13; C141 <68...., h> On title page: "Liber rar. et sing. T·H." f*IC5.P8304.586d (B)

Coelestis physiognomiæ libri sex (Naples, 1603). Inv.9.31; 4.3.5.16; C121 <680711, 17th c. dark brown morocco> *IC5.P8304.601cb (B)

POSTEL, GUILLAUME, 1510-1581.
Absconditorum a constitutione mundi clavis (Amsterdam, 1646). Inv.3.65; 2.2.8.53; C121 <641208> Original Hollis gift not located.

Cosmographicæ disciplinæ compendium (Basel, 1561). Inv.3.103 (part); 2.1.5.4; C121 <641208, h> *FC5.P8458.B561c

De cosmographia disciplina (Leiden, 1636). Inv.3.167; 2.4.8.44; C121 <641208, r> Geog 756.36*

De Etruriæ regionis (Florence, 1551). Inv.3.108; 2.1.5.12; C7 <641208, h> AH 8907.7*

De Foenicum literis ... commentatiuncula (Paris, 1552). Inv.3.160; 2.2.8.38; C136 <641208, h> 1247.5*

De la republique des Turcs (Poitiers, 1560). Inv.3.100; 2.3.5.32; C121 <641208, h> Ott 3005.60*

De nativitate mediatoris ... opus ([Basle, ca. 1547?]). Inv.3.118; 2.2.6.17; C121 <641208, h>
C 1325.7.30*

De originibus seu de Hebraicæ linguæ & gentis antiquitate (Paris, 1588). Inv.3.103 (part);
2.1.4.4; C136 <641208, h> *FC5.P8458.B561c

De republica ... Atheniensium (Leiden, 1635). Inv.16.24; 2.4.8.46; C7 <670511, v>
AH 5305.5*

Grammatica Arabica (Paris, [1538?]). Inv.3.103 (part); 2.1.5.4; C52 <641208, h>
*FC5.P8458.B561c

Linguarum duodecim characteribus differentium alphabetum, introductio (Paris, [1538]).
Inv.3.103 (part); 2.1.5.4, 4.1.7.1; C52 <641208, h> *FC5.P8458.B561c Second copy not
located.

Syriæ descriptio ([Paris], 1540). Inv.3.142; 2.1.8.31; C49 <641208, h> Ott 3615.3*

POTTER, JOHN, 1673 or 4-1747. *Archæologia Græca* (London, 1764). Inv.16.93; 2.1.5.22; C7
(under Antiq. of Greece) <670511, h> *EC7.P8533.699ab 2 v.

POWNALL, THOMAS, 1722-1805. †*The administration of the colonies* (London, 1766).
4.1.7.18; C85 <66....?, h> *EC75.P8758.764ac

The present state of the revenues and forces ... of France and Spain (London, 1740). 4.2.7.17;
not in C <nd, h> *EC75.H7267.Zz737t

PRICE, RICHARD, 1723-1791. *A review of the principal questions and difficulties in morals*
(London, 1769). Inv.13.46; 6.1.4.36; C47 <700926, h> Phil 2215.30.2*

Priest-craft exposed (London, 1691). 2.1.6.14; C229 <671209?, h> *EC65.C5614.681c

PRIESTLEY, JOSEPH, 1733-1804.
Considerations on church-authority (London, 1769). Inv.15.29; 6.1.4.24; C212 <691129, h
(marbled boards)> *EC75.P9338.B769r

A description of a chart of biography (Warrington, 1765). Inv.8.15 & Inv.8.1; 6.3.1.1; C34
<661001, r> C 1329.42*

An essay on a course of liberal education ([London], 1765). Inv.8.44; 2.3.7.21; C121
<661001, r> *EC75.P9338.765e

An essay upon the first principles of government (London, 1768). 6.1.4.24; C250 <nd, h
(marbled boards)> *EC75.P9338.B769r

‡*A free address to protestant dissenters* (London, 1769). 6.1.6.35; C325 <nd, xt> TH
identifies author. Formerly bound in Tr 405*. *EC75.P9338.769f

[Another edition] 6.1.4.24; C325 <nd, h (marbled boards)> *EC75.P9338.B769r

The present state of liberty in Great Britain and her colonies (London, 1769). Inv.15.35
(?*see next entry*); C243 (under America), C245 (under Britain) <691129, xt>
*EC75.P9338.769p

[Another edition] (London, 1769). Inv.15.35?; C243 (under America), C245 (under
Britain) <691129, xt> *EC75.P9338.769pc

Remarks on some paragraphs in the fourth volume of Dr. Blackstone's Commentaries (London, 1769). Inv.15.28; 6.1.4.24; C250 <691129, h (marbled boards)> *EC75.P9338.B769r

A view of the principles and conduct of the protestant dissenters (London, [1769]). 6.1.4.24; C325 <nd, h (marbled boards)> *EC75.P9338.B769r

PRIMATT, WILLIAM, 1701 or 2-1770. *Accentus redivivi* (Cambridge, 1764). 6.3.4.22; C136 <nd, h> 4257.21*

PROAST, JONAS.

‡*The argument of the Letter concerning toleration, briefly consider'd* (Oxford, 1690). Inv.15.5 (part); 6.1.6.24; not in C <691129, h> On title page: "By Mʳ Archdeacon Proast." *EC65.L7934.B691t

‡*A third letter concerning toleration* (Oxford, 1691). Inv.15.5 (part); 6.1.6.24; not in C <691129, h> On title page: "By Mʳ Proast." *EC65.L7934.B691t

The progress of envy: a poem (London, 1751). Inv.14.14; 6.1.3.17; C238 (under Lauder) <700926, h> *EC7.M4617.732c

PRUDENTIA CHRISTIANIA, PSEUD. *A letter from a lady to the bishop of London* (London, [n.d.]). 6.1.6.35; C308 (under Letter) <nd, h (sheep and marbled boards)> Tr 405*

PRYNNE, WILLIAM, 1600-1669.

†*The antipathie of the English lordly prelacie* (London, 1641). Inv.2.46; 2.1.7.11; C85 <6410.., h> *EC65.P9567.641a (A)

‡*A breviate of the life of William Laud* (London, 1646). Inv.8.8; 4.4.4.11; C29 <661001, h> On front flyleaf: "The friendly loadstone has not more combin'd | Than Bishops cramp'd the Commerce of Mankind. State Poems by A. Marvell." *EC65.P9567.644bb (A)

‡*An exact chronological vindication* (London, 1666). Inv.13.2 (part); 6.1.1.20-21; not in C <700926, h> On first flyleaf of v. 1: "It has been thought proper, to bind this copy of a very curious and scarce work, in <u>six</u> volumes, for the conveniency of the ingenuous Students of Harvard College, at Cambridge, in New England, who shall consult it. The copy was complete, in three tomes, when purchased a few years ago; but was mutilated afterward, shamefully, in a manner not so proper to relate, and the scarcer part of the scarcer tome, from p. 848 to p. 993, stolen! Palmal, oct. 1, 69 See the address 'to the Reader,' at the end of Tome 2, or Vol. 3." On second flyleaf of v. 1: "It is supposed, that there are not six copies of this valuable work, at this time, in Britain!" On flyleaf of v. 2, essentially the same statement about mutilation. At foot of p.848: "From page 848 to page 993, stolen, in a manner singularly shameful!" See Diary, September 20 and November 13, 1766; TH believed that the mutilation took place in his binder's shop, the work of a papist. f*EC65.P9567.666f 2 v.

†*The first and second part of a seasonable, legal, and historicall vindication* (London, 1655). Inv.2.48; 2.1.7.5; C85 (under Vindication) <6410.., h> *EC65.P9567.B655s

The history of King John (London, 1670). Inv.13.2 (part); 6.1.1.24-25; C61 <700926, h> *EC65.P9567.668ta (B) 2 v.

Histrio-mastix (London, 1633). Inv.2.45; 2.4.7.23; C122 <6410.., r> STC 20464a (A)

An humble remonstrance against the tax of ship money (London, 1643). Inv.4.35; 2.1.5.3; C229 & C251 <641212?, h> *EC65.P9567.B660t

Minors no senators (London, 1643). 2.1.5.3; not in C <671209?, h> *EC65.P9567.B660t

†*A new discovery of the prelates tyranny* (London, 1641). Inv.2.47; 2.1.7.25; C12 (under Prelates) <6410.., h> *EC65.P9567.641n (A)

The opening of the great seale (London, 1643). 2.1.5.3; C251 <671209, h> *EC65.P9567.B660t

‡*A seasonable, legall, and historicall vindication* (London, 1654-1657). Inv.10.49; 4.4.7.2; C85 <680712, h> On flyleaf: "Floreat Libertas, T·H." *EC65.P9567.654s

The second tome of an exact chronological vindication (London, 1665). Inv.13.2 (part); 6.1.1.22-23; not in C <700926, calf> *EC65.P9567.665s 2 v.

The soveraigne power of parliaments (London, 1643). Inv.1.18; 2.3.5.15; C229 <631024, h> Andover Harvard Safe K33 Prynne

[Another copy] Inv.4.10 <641212?> Original Hollis gift not located.

†*The third part of a seasonable, legal, and historical vindication* (London, 1657). Inv.2.49; 2.1.7.10; C85 (under Vindication) <6410.., h> *EC65.P9567.657t

‡*The treachery and disloyalty of papists* (London, 1643). 2.4.4.20; C229 <670815?, calf (with the arms of John Conybeare)> "This book is of inestimable value to all lovers of Liberty, being a Magazine or Storehouse of learning on the subject; containing citations innumerable of all Nations & Countrys, in defence of the Rights of Mankind in general, & of the People of England in particular. This copy was rebound by the very learned & excellent Bishop Conibeare, and his arms were impressed on it. T·H." *EC65.P9567.B643t3

[Another copy] C229 <nd, h> *EC75.H7267.Zz643pb

The unbishoping of Timothy and Titus (London, 1636). Inv.4.58; 2.1.7.24; C188 <641212?, h> STC 20476 (B)

See also Christi servus

PSEUDO-PHALARIS. *Epistolæ* (Oxford, 1695). Inv.17.38; 4.3.7.20, 4.4.7.22; C18 <68...., h> *EC75.H7267.Zz695p Second copy not located.

PTOLEMY, 2ⁿᵈ cent., *see* Bertius, Petrus

PUFENDORF, SAMUEL, FREIHERR VON, 1632-1694.
   †*Le droit de la nature & des gens*, tr. Jean Barbeyrac (Leiden, 1759). 4.1.4.28-29; C85 <nd, h> Int 1710.15* 2 v.

   An introduction to the history of Europe (London, 1764). Inv.8.45; 2.4.5.29-30; C61 <661001, r> H 237.64.2* 2 v.

PUJATI, GIUSEPPE ANTONIO. ‡*Della preservazione della salute de' letterati* (Venice, 1762). 4.1.8.27; B21, C122 <66....?, h> On first flyleaf: "To the Learned, at Harvard College, in Cambridge, in New England, T·H, benevolently. Pall Mall, aug. 12, 1766." On second flyleaf: "Mark Foscarini was a very accomplished, excellent Gentleman, and died soon after having been elected Doge of Venice." (The book is dedicated to Foscarini.) Lit 70.9*

PURVER, ANTHONY, 1702-1777, *see* Bible. English

PUTSCHE, ELIAS. ‡*Grammaticæ Latinæ auctores antiqui* (Hanover, 1605). Inv.12.14; 6.1.3.21; not in C <690818, early calf> On flyleaf: "A valuable & very rare book, which was purchased by T·H, in benefit to the ingenuous Youth now studying hard at Harvard College, in Cambridge, in New England, out of the Library of the late Duke of Newcastle, for £ 1,,1,,6. April 14, 1769." L 510*

PUTEO, PARIS DE. *Duello libro de re* (Venice, 1540). 2.4.8.21; C110 (under title) <641208, 16th c. v> *IC.P8799.Ei518dh

PYE, BENJAMIN, 1726?-1808.
Five letters on several subjects, religious and historical (London, 1767). 4.4.6.27; C327 <nd, h (marbled boards)> *EC75.B5628.752s

[Another edition] (London, 1769). 6.1.6.34; C327 <nd, h> *EC75.Us344.766f

Q

QUEVEDO, FRANCISCO DE, 1580-1645. *In Plutarchum Marcum Brutum excursus politici* (The Hague, 1660). Inv.3.114; C19 (under Plutarchus) <641208, h (rebacked)> Gp 86.615*

R

R. H., *Motives to holy living, or, Heads for meditation* (Oxford, 1688). Inv.12.18 (under Walker, Obadiah); 6.1.7.12; C198 <690818, h> Sometimes ascribed to Abraham Woodhead, 1609-1678. *EC65.W8570.688m

RADICATI, ALBERTO, CONTE DI PASSERANI, 1698-1737.
‡*Recueil de pièces curieuses* (Rotterdam, 1736). Inv.2.101; 2.2.5.32; C122 <6410.., h> Bibliographical notes on verso of title page and recto of back flyleaf. C 1866.1.2*

A succinct history of priesthood (London, 1737). 2.2.5.33; C122 (under Radicati) <6506.., h> *IC7.P2666.Eg737tb

Twelve discourses concerning religion and government (London, 1734 [i.e., 1737]). Inv.5.33; 2.2.5.33; C122 (under Radicati) <6506.., h> *IC7.P2666.Eg737cb

RALEIGH, SIR WALTER, 1552?-1618.
The history of the world (London, 1736). Inv.16.9; 2.3.2.8; C61 <670511, r> AH 276.14.3 F* 2 v.

The perogative [*sic*] *of parliaments* ([London], 1640). Inv.4.56; 2.2.6.23; C250 <641212?, h> STC 20650

The works of Sir Walter Raleigh (London, 1751). Inv.2.80; 2.3.7.1-2; C122 <6410.., r> *EC.R1384.B751w (B) 2 v.

RALPH, JAMES, d. 1762.

‡*The history of England* [reigns of William II, Anne, George I] (London, 1744). Inv.13.22; C61 <700926, h> On flyleaf: "This History is said to have been written, as a continuation to 'A general History of England, by William Guthrie,' printed, London, 1744, in three volumes in folio — though in a different spirit. The author of it was the late ingenious, indigent Mr. James Ralph, a Lover of Liberty at all times, and, for the most part, an Assertor of it. Beside this work, he wrote, The Axe laid to the root, etc. in four or five parts, in octavo. The other side of the question, Or an attempt to rescue the characters of the Royal Sisters Q. Mary and Q. Anne out of the hands of the Duchess Dowager of Marlborough, etc. By a Woman of Quality. 1742, in oct. The Use and abuse of Parliaments. 1744, 2 vol. In octavo. 'The Groans of Germany,' in oct. price 1s. — a political pamphlet, unseen of T·H, fifteen thousand copies of which are said to have been sold! 'The case of authors by profession stated.' — a very curious tract, in oct. p. 1/6. And many other political with some poetical pieces, unkown of T·H Palmal, mar. 3, 1770." Br 1955.7 F* 2 v.

[Another copy] Inv.13.66; C61 <700926, h> Br 1955.6 F* 2 v.

‡*The other side of the question* (London, 1742). 6.1.7.8; not in C <700921, h> On flyleaf: "Written, it is said by the late Mr. James Ralph. March 9, 1770. T·H." *AC7.R1397.742o

Zeuma: or, The love of liberty (London, 1729). Inv.8.42; 2.3.7.37; C143 <661001, r> *AC7.R1397.729z

RAMESEY, WILLIAM, 1627-1675 or 6. *Ho anthropos kat'exochel, or Mans dignity and perfection vindicated* (London, 1661). Inv.4.105; 2.2.8.39; C95 <641212?, h> Phil 665.4*

RAMSAY, ALLEN, 1713-1784. *Thoughts on the origin and nature of government* (London, 1769). 6.1.6.30; C247 <nd, xt> *EC75.R1486.769t

RAMSAY, ANDRÉ MICHEL DE, 1686-1743.
The life of François de Salignac de la Motte Fenelon (London, 1723). Inv.4.170; 2.1.8.17; C27 <641212?, r> 38551.104.20*

Poemata. Inv.2.40; not in C <6410..> Not identified or located.

RAVIGLIO ROSSO, GIULIO, fl. 1560. *Historia d'Inghilterra* (Ferrara, 1591). Inv.3.52; 2.4.7.6; C61 <641208, h> *IC5.R1976.560sa

RAWLINSON, RICHARD, 1690-1755. ‡*The life of Mr. Anthony a Wood* (London, 1711). Inv.7.18; 4.2.5.9; C29 <651010, calf> On flyleaf: "Thomas Hollis, Fellow of the Society of Antiquaries of London, is glad to be able to preserve this the only copy of an exceeding rare book that he hath ever seen*, in remembrance of A·WOOD; to whose Industry the public owe great obligation. Pall Mall, june 24, 1765. *this work was never made public. See life of Leland &c. p. 2 preface." (The annotation has a footnote, as indicated.) *EC7.R1997.711ℓ

RAY, JOHN, 1627-1705.
‡*Select remains* (London, 1760). Inv.7.15; 2.3.5.30; B10 (under Derham), C122 <651010, h (rebacked)> On front flyleaf, a quotation from *Rasselas,* followed by TH: "written by Mr. Johnson. The above is the hand-writing of the learned, excellent editor, George Scot Esq. etc." Also corrections and revisions in the text passim by TH, and a long quotation from *Leviathan* on the last flyleaf. *EC65.R2122.760s

Travels through the Low-countries (London, 1738). Inv.8.40; 2.4.5.23-24; C76 <661001> Original Hollis gift not located.

RAY, NICHOLAS. †*The importance of the colonies of North America* (London printed, New-York reprinted, 1766). 4.1.4.7; C251 <nd, h> *EC7.B6382.B766t

RAYNAUD, THÉOPHILE, 1583-1663. *Tractatus de pileo* ([Leiden, 1655]). Inv.15.3; C118 (under Maridot) <691129, r> Fine Arts X Cage XFA 1450.5

REAL ACADEMIA ESPAÑOLA. ‡*Diccionario de la lingua castellana* (Madrid, 1726-1739). 4.3.3.18-23; C203 <67...., r> Inserted note: "This Dictionary is much esteemed. There are good Books in Spanish and I was willing to send it; that, as the N. Americans, many of them, are likely, more than ever, to partake of Spanish Wealth, some of them may also partake in Spanish Wisdom & Literature. T·H Pall Mall, jan 21, 1767." f*SC7.Ac121.726d 6 v.

The real antiquity and authority of the church of Rome vindicated (London, 1768). Inv.11.15 (part); C324 <6809.., h> *EC75.Us344.766f

‡*The real seeker* (London, 1769). Inv.13.14; 6.1.4.12; C189 <700926, h> On flyleaf: "A dark, Popish Publication." TH bought 7 copies in sheets, October 26, 1769 (Diary). C 1332.38*

Reasons against a standing army (London, 1717). 2.2.5.7; C219 (under Army) <671209?, h> *EC75.H7267.Zz753t

RECKENBERGER, JOHANN LEONHARD. *Liber radisum, sive Lexicon Hebraicum* (Jena, 1749). 4.3.6.2; C204 (misdated 1748) <nd, v> 2273.32*

Recueil de memoires concernants l'œconomie rurale, *see* Ökonomische Gesellschaft des Kantons Bern

REELAND, ADRIANUS, 1676-1718. *Four treatises concerning the divine discipline and worship of the Mahometans* (London, 1712). 2.4.6.37; not in C <671209?, h> *EC75.H7267.Zz718s

REINESIUS, THOMAS, 1587-1667.
Epistolæ (Jena, 1670). 4.3.7.23; not in C <nd, h> Class 9843.2*

Epistolarum ad Nesteros, patrem et filium (Leipzig, 1670). 4.4.7.4; C7 (wrongly dated 1660) <nd> Original Hollis gift not located.

Syntagma inscriptionum antiquarum (Leipzig & Frankfurt, 1682). 4.3.2.20; C7 <nd, r> Class 6006.82 F*

A relation of the diabolical practices of above twenty wizards and witches (London, [1698]). 4.4.6.18; not in C <680930, h> *EC75.H7267.Zz698r

Remarks on Bishop Burnet's History of his own times (London, [1724?]). Inv.4.138 (part); 2.2.5.23; C213 (under Burnet) <641212?, h> *EC65.B9343.S736t

Remarks on some passages in a sermon, preached before the Lord-mayor (London, 1753). 2.1.7.20; not in C <671209, h> *EC65.W4574.653cb (B)

Remarks on some strictures (Oxford, 1770). Not in C <nd, xt> *EC75.A100.770r

Remarks on the Appendix to The present state of the nation (London, 1769). 6.1.6.30; C250 (under Nation) <nd, h> US 2812.10*

&ed otherwife, while we live in this world?) and fome good
men haply, did fuffer fome hard ufage at the hands of evill; but
did the King ever *ftop* His eares at any Petition? Did He ever
deny Juftice to any that did require it? Or did He ever *harden* His
Heart from fhewing mercy,where ere it was needful? There was
perhaps much whifpering abroad, and murmuring in Corners, but
was there alwayes a caufe? Mans Nature is apt fome time to
complaine for nothing, even when there is more reafon to be
thankfull. I will name the main particulars of offence, and let the
world judge, what matter of blame,did truly arife from them unto the King.

1. The *Bifhops* were cryed out upon to be too *Rigorous* : but
hath not the carriages of that faction, (which the *Bifhops* did op-
pofe) fince they have gotten Head, largely acquitted them of
that imputation, in the judgement of all wife men? furely they
forefaw the mifchief which we all now feel, and did labour (as
became them in their places) to prevent the fame : Perhaps every of them did not go the beft way to work, nor did ufe fuch *apt
Inftruments* as the cafe and time required, I juftifie no man in all
particulars ; and perhaps too, fome of us, (who are now impri-
foned, banifhed, and divefted of all we have, by this *Reforming*
Parliament)did in thofe dayes fuffer more moleftation from fome
of their unworthy Officers, then many of thofe did, who fince
that time have been moft revengefull. Three factious fellows had
their ears clipt, by the fentence of the Lords in the *Star-Chamber*,
and were fet in the *Pillory*; and this was exclaimed upon for great
cruelty in the *Bifhops*,(becaufe they (having been abufed by them)
did not beg their pardon ;) but how truly their necks alfo defer-
ved the *Halter*, hath well appeared by the late temper of their
fpirits ; and the little good ufe they have made of that their too
fmall, and gentle chaftifement.

2. The *Star-Chamber* and high *Commiffion* were two great
Eye-fores : for many great and heavy fines, were layd on men,
(for their fins fake) in thofe Courts, by the Kings *Nobles*, and
Judges ; (fome of whom are now great men with His greateft
Enemies :) But how many of thofe fines did His Majefty in His
tenderneffe and goodneffe afterwards remit, or caufe to be mi-
tigated? and fince the people would fo have it, He hath now
                      given

§.3.

[marginalia, left margin, handwritten:] intentions; Abide thou & they descendants Stedfast in the principles of liberty and the Revolution. T.H.

Figure 7v. Edward Symmons, *A Vindication of King Charles* (London, 1748). TH adds some emphatic marginal notes directed to the beneficiaries of his gifts. See Checklist, p. 185. *EC65.Sy653.647vb 19 cm.

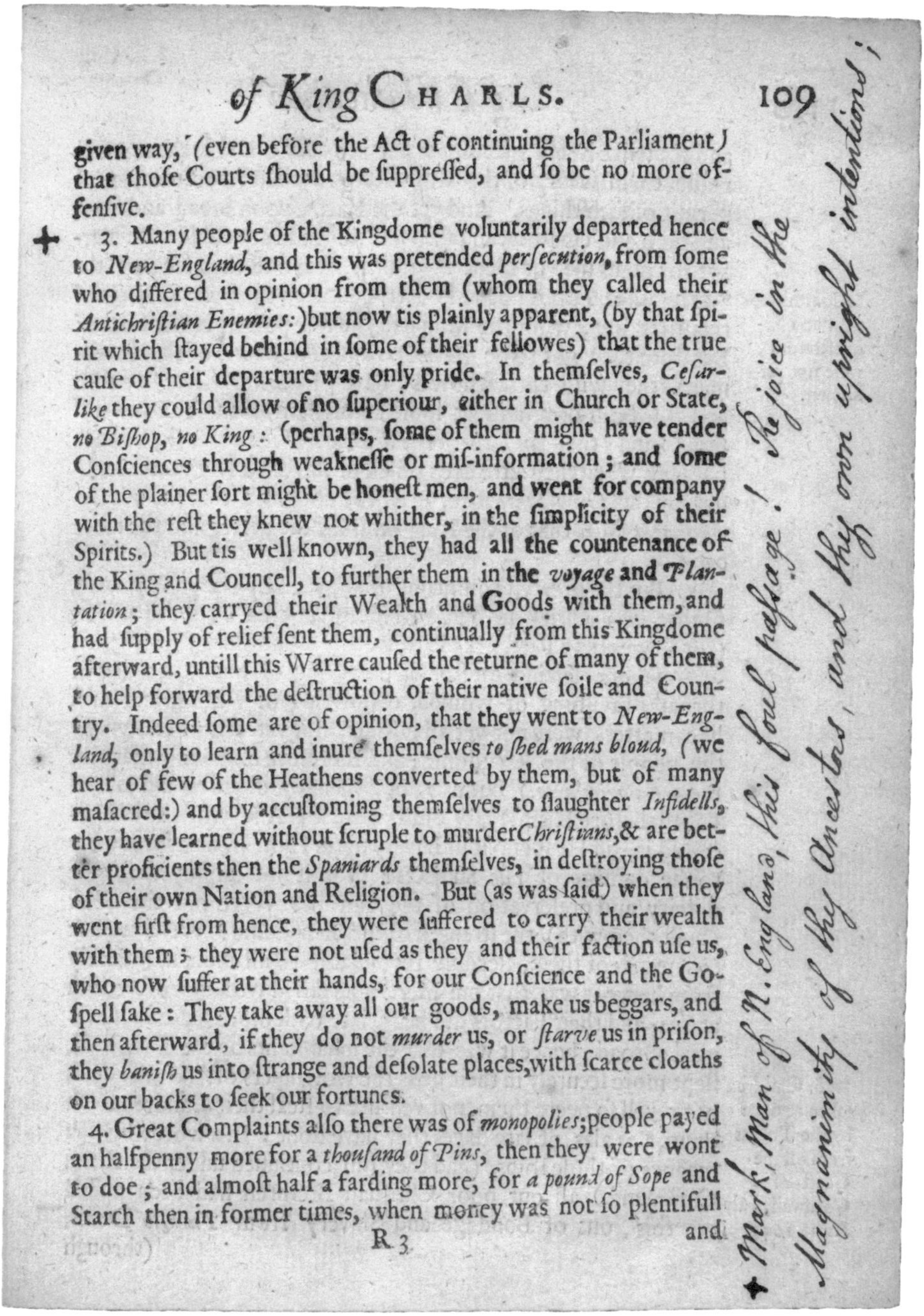

given way, (even before the Act of continuing the Parliament) that thofe Courts fhould be fuppreffed, and fo be no more of-fenfive.

3. Many people of the Kingdome voluntarily departed hence to *New-England,* and this was pretended *perfecution,* from fome who differed in opinion from them (whom they called their *Antichriftian Enemies:*)but now tis plainly apparent, (by that fpi-rit which ftayed behind in fome of their fellowes) that the true caufe of their departure was only pride. In themfelves, *Cefar-like* they could allow of no fuperiour, either in Church or State, *no Biſhop, no King :* (perhaps, fome of them might have tender Confciences through weakneffe or mif-information ; and fome of the plainer fort might be honeft men, and went for company with the reft they knew not whither, in the fimplicity of their Spirits.) But tis well known, they had all the countenance of the King and Councell, to further them in the *voyage* and *Plan-tation;* they carryed their Wealth and Goods with them, and had fupply of relief fent them, continually from this Kingdome afterward, untill this Warre caufed the returne of many of them, to help forward the deftruction of their native foile and Coun-try. Indeed fome are of opinion, that they went to *New-Eng-land,* only to learn and inure themfelves *to ſhed mans bloud,* (we hear of few of the Heathens converted by them, but of many mafacred:) and by accuftoming themfelves to flaughter *Infidells,* they have learned without fcruple to murder*Chriſtians,*& are bet-ter proficients then the *Spaniards* themfelves, in deftroying thofe of their own Nation and Religion. But (as was faid) when they went firft from hence, they were fuffered to carry their wealth with them ; they were not ufed as they and their faction ufe us, who now fuffer at their hands, for our Confcience and the Go-fpell fake : They take away all our goods, make us beggars, and then afterward, if they do not *murder* us, or *ſtarve* us in prifon, they *baniſh* us into ftrange and defolate places,with fcarce cloaths on our backs to feek our fortunes.

4. Great Complaints alfo there was of *monopolies;*people payed an halfpenny more for a *thouſand of Pins,* then they were wont to doe ; and almoft half a farding more, for *a pound of Sope* and Starch then in former times, when money was not fo plentifull R 3 and

Mark, Man of N. England, this foul paffage ! Rejoice in the Magnanimity of thy Anceftors, and thy own upright intentions ;

Figure 7R. Edward Symmons, *A Vindication of King Charles* (London, 1748).

RÉMY, NICOLAS, ca. 1525-1612. *Daemonolatreiæ libri tres* (Leiden, 1595). Inv.12.52; 6.1.3.24; C122 <690818, v> 24244.5*

RENAUDOT, EUSÈBE, 1646-1720. *Liturgiarum orientalium collectio* (Paris, 1716). 4.1.5.11-12; C134 <nd, v (v.2 r)> C 9010.13* 2 v.

A reply unto the letter … in defense of the Royal Society (London, 1671). 2.4.4.17; not in C <nd, r> *EC65.St935.B681t

Rerum Anglicarum scriptorum veterum (Oxford, 1684). 4.2.3.23; not in C <nd, r> Br 98.304 F*

Rerum Britannicarum … scriptores vetustiores, ed. Hieronymus Commelinus (Heidelberg, 1687). 4.2.3.8; not in C <nd, h> Professor J. M. French believed that the section devoted to Gildas was annotated by John Milton, but the ascription is dubious. Br 98.319 F*

Review of Bishop Burnet's History of his own times (London, 1724). Inv.4.138?; 2.2.5.23; C213 (under Burnet) <690815?, h> *EC65.B9343.S736t

REYNOLDS, GEORGE, 1699 or 1700-1769. ‡*A dissertation or inquiry* (London, 1732). 6.1.5.40; not in C <700926, h> TH identifies author. *EC75.H7267.Zz731t

REYNOLDS, JOHN, 1671-1758. *Historia græcarum et latinarum literarum* (Eton, 1752). 4.1.5.25; C122 <nd, h> 5315.53*

REYNOLDS, JOHN, MERCHANT OF EXETER. *Vox coeli, or Newes from heaven* (Elisium [i.e., London], 1624). 2.1.7.16; C252 <670815?, h> STC 22098 (B)

REYNOLDS, JOHN, 1669-1727. ‡*A view of death* (London, 1725). Inv.4.14; 2.4.4.33; C143 <641212?, h> On title page: "Written at the request of Mr. Locke:". *EC7.R3363.709dd (B)

RHYS, UDAL AP. *An account of the most remarkable places and curiosities in Spain and Portugal* (London, 1749). Inv.4.185; C76 <641212?> Original Hollis gift not located; title from British Library catalogue.

RICHARDS, TOM. *Antiquæ linguæ britannicæ thesaurus* (Bristol, 1759). Inv.9.19; 4.3.6.11; C205 <680711, h> 3276.26*

RICHARDSON, JONATHAN, 1665-1745.
Explanatory notes and remarks on Milton's Paradise lost (London,1734). Inv.16.99; 4.3.7.2; not in C <670511, h> *EC75.H7267.Zz734r

‡[Another copy] 2.2.5.25; not in C <nd, h> On title page: "very scarce." Note inside front cover (unidentified hand): "One of two copies Presented by Tho. Hollis; Sold as a duplicate to Prof. Geo. Ticknor, & generously restored by Him to the Public Library March 30. 1832." *EC65.M6427.T734r

RIDLEY, GLOCESTER, 1702-1774.
‡*The life of Dr. Nicholas Ridley* (London, 1763). 4.1.4.13; C29 <nd, h> Heavily annotated. *EC75.R4375.763ℓ

‡*Three letters* [concerning *The confessional*] (London, 1768). 6.1.4.25; C329 <nd, h> TH identifies author. *EC75.R4375.B768t

RIDPATH, GEORGE. *Parliamentary right maintain'd* ([London], 1714). Inv.2.91; 2.3.7.29; C250 (under Parliament) <6410.., h> *EC75.H7267.Zz759m

The rights of the British colonies considered (London, [1765?]). 4.1.7.23; C242 <66...., r> *EC75.A100.765r

The rights of the colonies (London, 1769). Inv.16.38?; 6.1.6.30; C243 <670511, h> US 2812.20*

‡*The rights of the people* (London, 1658). Inv.2.114; 2.2.8.33; not in C <6410.., h> On title page: "ut spargam." On flyleaf: "By Judge Yelverton Yelverton, Justice, said, when a new case comes, for which there is no positive law before; we do as the Sophonists and Civilians, resort to the law of nature, which is the reason and ground of all laws, and of that which is most beneficial for the Commonwealth make a law. Lawrence's Marriage by the moral law of God vindicated, London 1680 in p. 83. alike curious as scarce." *EC.W5883.641ℓc

RIMIUS, HENRY, d. 1759?
   A candid narrative of the rise and progress of the Herrenhutters (London, 1753). 4.4.6.17; C329 <6807.., h> *EC75.H7267.Zz755f2

   A supplement to the Candid narrative (London, 1755). 4.4.6.17; C329 <6807.., h> *EC75.H7267.Zz755f2

RIPERT DE MONCLAR, JEAN PIERRE FRANÇOIS DE, 1711-1773. *Compte rendu des constitutions des Jésuites* ([n.p.], 1763). Inv.15.15; 6.1.8.25; C122 <691129, h> C 427.63*

ROBE, THOMAS, d. 1746. *Ways and means to man the navy* (London, 1740). 4.2.7.17; not in C <nd, h> *EC75.H7267.Zz737t

ROBERT, OF GLOUCESTER, fl. 1260-1300. *Robert of Gloucester's Chronicle*, ed. Thomas Hearne (Oxford, 1724). Inv.17.11; 4.4.5.13-14; C5 <68...., r> Br 1345.60.4* v. 1 only Widener Br 1345.60.4 v. 2 Declared lost, September 2002.

ROBERTSON, JOHN, 1690-1761. *The true and antient manner of reading Hebrew* (London, 1747). 4.4.7.11; C236 (under Hebrew, true and antient) <nd, r> *EC7.M2927.739c

ROBERTSON, WILLIAM, d. 1686? *The first gate* (London, [1653?]). Inv.13.72; 6.3.8.42; C53 <700926, h> *EC65.R5496.653gb

ROBERTSON, WILLIAM, 1705-1783. *An attempt to explain the words* (London, 1768). 4.4.8.8; B11 (under Explanation), C189 <nd, h> C 1336.1.30*

ROBERTSON, WILLIAM, 1721-1793. *The history of the reign of the emperor Charles V* (London, 1769). Inv.12.7; C61 <690818, calf> Harvard Depository Ger 1635.6.2 3 v.

ROBINSON, JOHN, BISHOP OF LONDON, 1650-1723, *see* Molesworth, Robert Molesworth, viscount

ROBLES, M. *Bigotry, superstition and hypocrisy worse than atheism* (London, 1742). Inv.14.59; 6.1.8.39; C189 <700926, h> Phil 8597.10*

ROBORTELLO, FRANCESCO, 1516-1567. *Oratio Venetiis habita* (Venice, [1549]). 4.4.6.2; C230 <nd, h> *FC5.M9425.559v

ROGERS, THOMAS, *Leycesters ghost* ([London], 1641). 2.2.6.20; not in C <670815?, h> *EC.A100.584cb (B)

ROISECCO, GREGORIO. ‡*Roma antica e moderna* (Rome, 1750). Inv.17.13; 4.3.8.33-35; C7 (under title) <68...., v> Three flyleaves contain TH's lists of persons to consult and places to visit in Rome. Typ 725.50.750 (B) 3 v.

ROLLIN, CHARLES, 1661-1741. †*New thoughts concerning education* (London, 1735). 2.4.7.2; C230 <6410.., h> *EC75.H7267.Zz734e

ROME (ITALY). PALAZZO BARBERINI. *Dichiaratione delle pitture della sala de'signori Barberini* (Rome, 1640). Inv.3.120 (under Palermo; part); 2.4.7.12; C219 <641208, h> *IC7.A100.B752h

RORARIO, GIROLAMO, 1485-1556. *Quod animalia bruta ratione utantur melius homine* (Paris, 1648). Inv.14.45; 6.1.8.42; C95 <700926, h> Phil 5827.2*

ROSS, JOHN, 1411-1491, *see* Rous, John

ROSSI, OTTAVIO, 1570-1630. *Le memorie Bresciane* (Brescia, 1693). Inv.3.30; 2.3.4.10; C7 <641208, v> *IC6.R7358.616md

ROTHERAM, JOHN, 1725-1789. ‡*Essay on establishments in religion* (London, 1767). 6.1.4.26; C330 <nd, h> TH identifies author. *EC75.R7445.767eb

ROUS, JOHN, 1411-1491. *Historia regum Angliæ*, ed. Thomas Hearne (Oxford, 1745). 4.2.5.33; C5 <nd, h> Br 1605.9*

ROUSTAN, ANTOINE JACQUES, 1734-1808. *Lettres sur l'état présent du Christianisme* (London, 1768). Inv.10.46; 4.3.8.18; C190 <680712, h> C 1336.44.30*

ROWE, NICHOLAS, 1674-1718, *see* Lucan

ROWLAND, JOHN, 1606-1660. †*Pro rege et populo Anglicano apologia* (Antwerp, 1652). 4.4.8.47; not in C <nd, h> The tools are inverted on this binding, indicating disapproval. *EC65.M6427.Z651rb

ROWLANDS, HENRY, 1655-1723. *Mona antiqua restorata* (London, 1766). 2.4.3.23; C7 <nd, h> Arc 861.1.6*

ROWLANDS, RICHARD, ca. 1550-1640, *see* Verstegan, Richard

ROYAL SOCIETY (GREAT BRITAIN).
‡*Diplomata et statuta* (London, 1752). Inv.5.72; 2.4.4.16; C151 <6506.., r> On front flyleaf: "Liber Thomae Hollis, Angli, Hospitii Lincolniensis, Regalis et Antiquariorum Societatum Sodalis; libertatis, patriae, praestantisque ejus consitutionis laudatissime anno 1688 recuperatae amatoris studiosissimi." Cuttings from *St. James's chronicle* laid down on 3 back flyleaves: on George III's patronage of the Royal Society, and the proposal, funded by Frederick V of Denmark, to explore Arabia, after which TH writes: "A master-plan for a noble Enterprize!" LSoc 1816.15*

The list of the Royal society MDCCLXIX ([London, 1769]). 6.1.4.29; not in C <nd, h> *EC75.H7267.Zz769t

†‡*Philosophical transactions*, v. 49 part 2-v. 56 inclusive (London, 1757-1767). Inv.9.1; 4.3.5.26-36; C151 <680711, h> LSoc 1816.12* TH also gave v. 58 (1769), Inv.15.4; 6.1.3.31; C151 <691129, h> Same call number.

‡*Rules and orders* (London, 1760). Inv.2.64; 2.4.5.35; not in C <6410.., h> Note: The R.S.A. was known to TH (an active member) as the Society for the Promotion of Arts and Commerce (abbreviated by him as SPAC). The yearly leaflets of rules and prizes were printed according to his habitual designs, and bore engravings of the society's medal, designed by James Stuart and TH. The earliest bears a motto in TH's hand: "But the liberal deviseth liberal things, and by liberal things shall he stand." (Isaiah 32.8). All the rest have the motto, in TH's hand, "Do they not err that devise evil? But mercy & truth shall be to them that devise good. prov." (Proverbs 14.22), and in that for 1761 he adds, beneath the engraving of the medal, a favorite quotation from *Paradise Regained:* "By deeds of peace." *EC75.R8123Aℓ.1760a

‡[Another edition] (London, 1761). Not in C <nd, h (marbled wrappers)> *EC75.R8123Aℓ.1761a

‡[Another edition] (London, 1763). Not in C <nd, h (marbled wrappers)> *EC75.R8123Aℓ.1763a (B)

‡[Another copy] (London, 1763). Not in C <nd, h (marbled wrappers)> *EC75.R8123Aℓ.1763a (C)

‡[Another edition] (London, 1766). Not in C <nd, h (marbled wrappers)> *EC75.R8123Aℓ.1766a

‡[Another edition] (London, 1768). Inv.15.36; not in C <691129, h (marbled wrappers)> *EC75.R8123Aℓ.1768a

[Another edition] (London, 1769). Inv.15.37; not in C <691129, h (marbled wrappers)> *EC75.R8123Aℓ.1769a

Rubens, Albert, 1614-1657. *De re vestiaria veterum* (Antwerp, 1665). Inv.3.86; 2.2.4.10; C7 <641208, h> *NC6.R8230.665d

Ruffhead, Owen, 1723-1769, *see* Great Britain. *Statutes at large*

Ruggle, George, 1575-1622. *Ignoramus* (Westminster, 1737). 4.4.8.5; C7 <nd, r> MLr 592.36*

Rusconi, Giovanni Antonio, *see* Vitruvius Pollio

Rushworth, John, 1612?-1690. *Historical collections* (London, 1659-1701). Inv.16.34; 2.1.3.19-25; C62 <670511, h> Br 1800.53 F* 7 v.

See also Strafford, Thomas Wentworth

Rust, George, d. 1670. *A discourse of the use of reason in matters of religion* (London, 1683). Inv.4.47; 2.4.7.11; C190 <641212?, h> *EC65.R9242.683d

Rutherford, Samuel, 1600?-1661. ‡*The preeminence of the election of kings* (London, 1648). 4.2.7.43; C85 <nd, h> On flyleaf: "A curious & scarce Book. On my memory, the Author was troubled afterward on account of it in the reign of C.II, A. Wood and Crookshank, both of them take notice of him. T·H." *EC65.R9336.644ℓc

Rutherforth, Thomas, 1712-1771.
A defence of a charge concerning subscriptions (London, 1767). 6.1.4.27; C330 <nd, h> *EC75.H7267.Zz767pc

A vindication of the right of Christian churches (London, [1766]). 6.1.4.27; C330 <nd, h> *EC75.H7267.Zz767pc

A second vindication of the right of Christian churches (London, 1766 [i.e., 1767]). 6.1.4.27; not in C <nd, h> *EC75.H7267.Zz767pc

RYE, GEORGE. *A treatise against the nonconforming nonjurors* (London, 1719). Inv.12.87; 6.1.7.22-23; C190 <690818, contemporary calf> C 6427.6* 2 v.

RYMER, THOMAS, 1641-1713.
An essay, concerning critical and curious learning (London, 1698). Inv.13.70 (part); 2.2.7.32, C111 (under Essay) <700926, h> *EC75.H7267.Zz698e A second copy, Inv.4.165, 6.2.8.19 <641212?>, not located.

Fœdera (London, 1726-1735). 2.1.2.1-20; not in C <64…., mostly r> According to Diary, TH paid 20 guineas for this set. Br 70.3 F* 20 v.

A vindication of An essay concerning critical and curious learning (London, 1698). Inv.13.70 (part); 2.2.7.32; not in C <700926, h> *EC75.H7267.Zz698e

S

SACHEVERELL, HENRY, 1674?-1724, DEFENDANT. ‡*The tryal of Dr. Henry Sacheverell* (London, 1710). Inv.2.24; 2.3.3.5; C148 <6410.., contemporary calf (rebacked)> On title page: "Ut spargam." On title page following p. 327: "These are rare. T·H." f *EC7.Sa145.710t

SADLER, JOHN, 1615-1674.
‡*Rights of the kingdom* (London, 1649). Inv.4.101; 2.2.8.35; C85 (under title) <641212?, h> On title page: "Ut spargam T·H." *EC65.Sa154.649r

‡[Another edition] (London [i.e., Holland?], 1649). 4.3.7.9; C85 <670815?, h> On flyleaf: "I am th'ungenerous Gloss of slavish Minds | The Owl-ey'd Race, whom virtue's lustre blinds; | Spite of the learned in the Ways of Vice, | And all who prove, that each Man has his price. April 14, 1754. T.H." *EC65.Sa154.649rb

SAINT GERMAN, CHRISTOPHER, 1460?-1540. *Doctor and student* ([London], 1721). 4.4.8.9; not in C <nd, r> Law School storage UK 903 SAI

ST. JOHN, OLIVER, 1598?-1673.
An argument of law concerning the bill of attainder (London, 1641). 2.1.7.9; not in C <6410.., h> *EC65.G798P.B641sb

Mr. St.-John's speech … concerning ship-money ([London], 1641). Inv.10.50 (part); 4.4.7.42; not in C <680712, h> *EC65.G798P.B641t

ST. PAUL, P. *Methodus Hebræa* (London, 1741). Inv.9.12; 4.4.5.10; C52 <680711, h> 2261.26*

SALISBURY, ROBERT CECIL, 1ST EARL OF, 1563-1612. *The secret correspondence … with James VI*, ed. Sir David Dalrymple (Edinburgh, 1766). 4.1.8.33; C145 (under Burghley) <nd, r> Br 1810.18*

SALISBURY, WILLIAM, fl. 1768. *Two grammatical essays: first, On a barbarism* (London, 1768). Inv.11.15 (part); C235 <6809.., h> *EC75.Us344.766f

SALLENGRE, ALBERT-HENRI DE, 1694-1723. *Novus thesaurus antiquitatum romanorum* (The Hague, 1716-1724). Inv.3.7; 2.4.1.4-6; C7 <641208, calf> f*NC7.Sa343.716na 3 v.

SALLUST.
[*Opera*] *quæ exstant* (Amsterdam, 1742). Inv.8.7; 4.1.5.14-15; C19 <661001, contemporary calf> Harvard Depository KG 13357 v. 2 only; v. 1 declared lost.

Works, tr. William Crosse ([London], 1629). 6.3.8.46; C19 <nd, r> STC 21624

The works, tr. Thomas Gordon (London, 1744). Inv.5.11; 2.2.4.9; B12, C19 <6506.., r> *EC7.G6587.744s

SALOMONI, JACOPO. *Agri Patavini inscriptiones sacræ, et prophanæ* (Padua, 1696). Inv.4.20; 2.4.4.36; C7 <641212?, 17th c. v> AH 8986.5*

SANDYS, GEORGE, 1578-1644. *Travels into the Levant* (London, 1673). 4.2.3.14; C36 <nd, calf> Ott 3100.5.7 F*

SANNAZARO, JACOPO, 1458-1530.
De partu Virginis ([Venice], 1527). Inv.15.22; 6.3.8.41; C144 <691129, h> *IC5.Sa585.526dd (A)

Opera omnia (Venice, 1570). Inv.15.23; 6.3.8.44; C144 <691129, red straight grain morocco> *IC5.Sa585.B570o (B)

SANSOVINO, FRANCESCO, 1521-1586. *Dell'historia universale dell'origine et imperio de Turchi* (Venice, [1560]). Inv.3.42; 2.4.5.8; C62 <641208, 16th c. calf with arms of Robert Dudley, earl of Leicester> *IC5.Sa587.560d

SANTORIO, SANTORIO, 1561-1636. *Medicina statica: being the aphorisms of Sanctorius*, tr. John Quincy (London, 1737). 2.4.6.38; C102 <nd, h> Countway Rare Books R 128.7.S59 E3 1737 c.1

SARPI, PAOLO, 1552-1623.
Historia particolare delle cose passata tra'l sommo pontifice Paolo V e la serenissima republica di Venetia (Mirandola, 1624). Inv.3.97, Inv.3.129, & Inv.4.36; 2.4.4.21; not in C <641212?, v> Ital 4858.1* Two other copies not located.

A treatise of matters beneficiary (London, 1680). Inv.3.81; 2.3.3.25; C120 <641208, r> f*EC65.D4353.680t

See also St. Paul, P.

SAUMAISE, CLAUDE, 1588-1653.
Defensio regia ([Leiden], 1649). Inv.3.71; 2.3.2.15; C148 <641208, h> f*EC65.M6427.R649sa

[Another edition] ([Belgium?], 1649). Inv.12.73; 6.2.8.38; C148 <690818, v> *EC65.M6427.R649sf

De Hellenistica commentarius (Leiden, 1643). 4.4.8.37; C136 <nd, h> *FC6.Sa865.643d (B)

De modo usurarum liber (Leiden, 1639). 4.4.8.33-34; C123 <nd, h> *FC6.Sa865.639d 2 v.

De usuris liber (Leiden, 1638). 4.4.8.26; C123 <nd, h> The frontispiece is probably the source for the portrait of Saumaise in the Cipriani/Hollis print *Milton victorious over Salmasius.* *FC6.Sa865.638d

Epistolarum liber (Leiden, 1656). 4.4.5.24; C123 <nd, h> *FC6.Sa865.656e

Plinianæ exercitationes (Utrecht, 1689). 4.3.1.8; C7 <nd, stiff v> A prize book from the University of Amsterdam, awarded to Isaac ab Heule in 1699. Ls 37.22 F*

SAVOT, LOUIS, 1579-1640. ‡*Discours sur les medailles antiques* (Paris, 1627). Inv.5.15; 2.4.4.11; C130 <6506.., h> On title page: "a curious Book T·H." Arc 1373.2*

SCALIGERO, GIULIO CESARE, 1484-1558. *De causis linguæ latinæ* ([Geneva], 1580). 4.4.7.49; C136 <nd, 16ᵗʰ c. v> *FC5.Sca454.540db

SCAPULA, JOHANN, ca. 1540-ca. 1600. *Lexicon græco-latinum* (London, 1652). 2.4.2.7; C205 <nd, r> 4212.14 F*

SCARAMUCCIA, LUIGI PELLEGRINI, CALLED IL PERUGINO, 1616-1680. *Le finezze de Pennelli italiani* (Pavia, [1674]). 4.4.5.27; C9 <nd, v> Typ 625.74.774

SCHAAF, CAROLUS, 1646-1729.
· *Lexicon Syriacum, & Nov. Test. Syriacum* (Leiden, 1717). 4.2.4.6-7, C205 <nd, h> Typ 732.17.210 2 v.

Opus aramæum (Leiden, 1686). Inv.14.66; 4.3.8.19, 6.1.8.12; C134 <700926, h> 3222.12* Second copy not located.

SCHEUCHZER, JOHANN JAKOB, 1672-1733. *Physique sacrée, ou Histoire naturelle de la Bible* (Amsterdam, 1732). Not in C <nd, h> Bi 2507.31.59 F* 8 v.

SCHINDLER, VALENTIN, d. 1604. *Lexicon pentaglossum* (Hanover, 1612). 3.1.2.14; C205 <nd, h> 2252.5 F*

SCHINNER, MATHÄUS, CARDINAL, 1465-1522. *Oratio philippica,* ed. John Toland (London, 1707). Inv.9.36; 4.4.7.29; C125 <680711, 18ᵗʰ c. (not Hollis) binding> Br 1760.10*

SCHOPPE, KASPAR, 1576-1649.
Auctarium ad grammaticam philosophicam (Amsterdam, 1659). 4.4.8.23; not in C <nd, v> *GC6.Sch655.B660g (B)

‡*Consultationes* (Amsterdam, 1665). 4.4.8.40; C124 (under Scioppi) <nd, h> TH writes a long comment on the merits of this book. *EC75.H7267.Zz665s

Grammatica philosophica (Amsterdam, 1659). 4.4.8.23; C53 <nd, v> *GC6.Sch655.B660g (B)

Paradoxa literaria (Amsterdam, 1659). 4.4.8.23; C236 (under Grosippus) <nd, v> *GC6.Sch655.B660g (B)

Suspectarum lectionum libri quinque (Amsterdam, 1664). 4.4.8.42; C237 <nd, v> *GC6.Sch655.596vb

Symbola critica in L. Apuleij … opera (Amsterdam, 1664). 4.4.8.42; C237 <nd, v> *GC6.Sch655.596vb

Verisimilium libri quatuor (Amsterdam, 1662). 4.4.8.42; C237 <nd, v> *GC6.Sch655.596vb

SCHOTTUS, FRANCISCUS, 1548-1622. ‡*Itinerario d'Italia* (Rome, 1737). Inv.3.139; 2.4.8.5; C76 <641208, v> On flyleaf: "Bought in December 1750 at Venice by TH upon his Travells." *NC6.Sch678.600is

SCHRAMM, JOHANN MORITZ. ‡*De vita & scriptis … Vanini* (Küstrin, 1715). Inv.7.9; 2.2.7.28; C29 <651010, h> On title page: "Rariss." *GC7.Sch694.709db

SCHULTENS, ALBERT, 1686-1750.
De defectibus hodiernis linguæ Hebræe (Franeker, 1731). 4.1.7.14; not in C <nd, r> 2285.25*

Monumenta vetustiora Arabiæ (Leiden, 1740). Not in C <nd, h> OL 22200.91*

Institutiones ad fundamenta linguae hebraeae (Leiden, 1737). 4.1.7.37; C53 <nd, h> 2263.23*

Oratio inauguralis de fontibus ex quibus omnis linguæ Hebrææ notitia manavit ([Franeker?, 1724?]). 4.2.6.28; not in C <nd, h> 2285.24*

Origines hebrææ (Franeker, 1724-1738). 4.2.6.28; C134 <nd, h> 2285.24*

See also Hariri

SCHWARTZ, JOHANN CONRAD, 1677-1747. *Commentarii critici et philologici linguæ græcæ* (Leipzig, 1736). 4.3.6.10; C43 <nd, h> Andover-Harvard S.C.R. 517 Schwarz [*sic*]

SCHWENTER, DANIEL, 1585-1636. *Ventilatio grammatica gemina* (Nuremberg, [1627?]). 4.4.7.12; C235 (under Gchwenter) <nd, h> 2255.13*

SCOBELL, HENRY, d. 1680, *see* Great Britain. *Collection of acts*

SCOTT, DANIEL, 1694-1759. ‡*Appendix ad thesaurum græcæ linguæ* (London, 1746). 4.2.2.13-14; C205 <nd, h> TH identifies the dedicatee as [Archbishop Thomas] "Seckar," i.e., Secker. 4212.18 F* 2 v.

SCOTT, GEORGE LEWIS, 1708-1780, *see* Chambers, Ephraim

SCOTT, THOMAS, 1580?-1626. *Vox populi* ([London, 1620?]). Inv.4.52; 2.1.7.16; C25 <641212?, h> STC 22098 (B)

SCOTTI, GIULIO CLEMENTE, 1602-1669, trans. *La monarchie des solipses* (Amsterdam, 1722). Inv.10.43 (under Inchoffer); 4.3.8.41; not in C <680712, h> MLs 576.32*

SCRAFTON, LUKE. *Reflections on the government of Indostan* (London, 1770). Inv.13.49; 6.1.5.13; B22, C62 <700926, h> Designed and sponsored by TH. *EC75.Scr125.763rb

SEAGRAVE, ROBERT, 1693-1760? *The principles of liberty* (London, 1755). Inv.2.96 (part); 2.1.6.12; not in C <6410.., h> *EC75.H7267.Zz751t

SEAMAN, WILLIAM. *Grammatica linguæ turcicæ* (Oxford, 1670). 4.4.7.27; C53 <nd, h> *EC65.Se163.670g (B)

SECKER, THOMAS, 1693-1768.

> *An answer to Dr. Mayhew's Observations* (London, 1764). 2.4.6.2; C315 (under Mayhew) <nd, h> *AC7.M4587.B766m v.2
>
> *Eight charges delivered to the clergy of the dioceses of Oxford and Canterbury* (London, 1769). Inv.12.20; C191 <690818> Original Hollis gift not located.
>
> *Lectures on the catechism* (London, 1769). Inv.12.19; B21, C191 <690818, h> C 1345.32* 2 v.
>
> *A letter to the Right Honourable Horace Walpole* (London, 1769). Inv.14.56 (part); 6.1.6.22; B21, C332 <700926, h> *EC7.Se243.B769b (B)
>
> *Sermons on several subjects* (London, 1770). Inv.14.26; 6.1.5.22-28; B21, C291 <700926, h> Inventory records only 4 v. C 1345.15* 7 v.

The second part of Dr. Sherlock's Two kings of Brainford (London, 1690). 2.2.5.16; C251 (under Sherlock) <671209?, h> *EC75.H7267.Zz691t

The second part of the peoples antient and just liberties asserted .... tryals of Tho. Rudyard [et al.] ([London], 1670). 2.4.5.19; C229 (under Penn) Original Hollis gift rejected as a duplicate.

SEGUIN, PIERRE. *Selecta numismata antiqua* (Paris, 1684). 4.3.5.5; C130 <nd, h> Arc 1373.4*

SELBYE, THOMAS. ‡*A catalogue of the … collection of … coins* ([London, 1755]). 1.1.6.7; not in C <nd, h (boards)> A sale catalogue; TH marked desiderata. B 1827.401*

SELDEN, JOHN, 1584-1654.

> ‡*Mare clausum*, tr. Marchamont Nedham (London, 1635). Inv.16.83; 2.3.4.4; C86 <670511, r> On title page: "Ut spargam. T·H." At end of dedication: "Felicity is Freedom & Freedom in Magnanimity. Thucyd." On a2ᵛ: "Bradshaw," identifying an M.P. On g2ᵛ: "Marchamont Nedham, a man of good ability, natural and acquired; author of various treatises; writer of that remarkable State news-paper, in favor of the Commonwealth, intitled Mercurius Politicus. See his character in a·wood; but drawn in bitterness of wrath and anger." On back flyleaf: " The 'corrected, restored english copy by J. H. Gent.' Printed, London, 1662, in folio, is Marchamont Nedham's copy, under a new [copy] title, mutilated." STC 22175 (B)
>
> ‡*Of the dominion or ownership of the sea*, tr. Marchamont Nedham (London, 1652). Inv.6.6; 4.1.5.3; C86 <650817, h> On title page: "This edit. is very scarce." On flyleaf: "See, in the notes of the new edit. of A. Sydney's works, that curious letter of M. Sorbiere's, concerning the Dominion of the Sea. Among the medals which have been stricken in consequence of the premiums distributed by the Society, the noble Society instituted in London for promoting arts and commerce is one, on the naval and master victory over the French off Belleisle; in the exergue of the face of which is this signal inscription FRANCE RELINQUISHES THE SEA." *EC75.H7267.Zz652s
>
> *Opera omnia* (London, 1726). Inv.16.11; 2.2.2.7-12; C124 <670511, h> Typ 705.26.781 F 6 v.

A select collection of the most interesting letters (London, 1763-1764). Inv.7.20; 2.2.8.9-11; C146 <651010, h> Originally 4 v.; shelf-list states v. 4 was "lost in 1775." Br 2060.366* 3 v.

SENNERT, ANDREAS, 1606-1689.

Centuria canonum philologicorum, sive De idiotismis linguarum Orientalium (Wittenberg, 1657). 4.4.7.12; C237 <nd, h> 2255.13*

Dissertatio de Ebrææ S. S. linguæ ... origine etc. (Wittenberg, 1657). 4.4.7.12; C237 <nd, h> 2255.13*

SERAO, FRANCESO, 1702-1783. *Istoria dell'incendio del Vesuvio* (Naples, 1740). Inv.3.102, Inv.4.79; C126 (under Vesuvio) <641208, v> MCZ 781 Second copy not located.

SERLIO, SEBASTIANO, 1475-1554. *Libro primo d'architettura* (Venice, 1584). Inv.3.32; 2.4.4.12; C8 <641208, v> Typ 525.84.781

SERRES, JUAN DE, 1540?-1598. †‡*An historical collection, of the most memorable accidents, and tragicall massacres of France* (London, 1598). Inv.2.18; 4.4.4.1; C59 (under Massacres) & C112 (under France) <6410.., h> TH inserts extensive quotations from William Primatt and Andrew Marvell. STC 11275

SETTALA, MANFREDO, *see* Terzago, Paolo Maria

The several depositions concerning the late riot in Oxford (London, 1716). 2.1.7.4; C250 (under Oxford) <nd, r> *EC7.A100.717s2

SEWARD, THOMAS. *The conformity between popery and paganism* (London, 1746). 2.2.5.8; C231 <nd, h> *EC75.H7267.Zz745t

SHAFTESBURY, ANTHONY ASHLEY COOPER, EARL OF, 1671-1713. ‡*Several letters* (London, 1716). 4.2.7.18; C231 <nd, h> TH identifies author. *EC75.H7267.Zz730t

SHAKESPEARE, WILLIAM, 1564-1616. *Works*, ed. Alexander Pope (London, 1728). Inv. 12.33; 6.1.8.26-35; C131 <690818> Original Hollis gift not located; presumed worn out.

SHARPE, GREGORY, 1713-1771.

A dissertation upon the origin and structure of the Latin tongue (London, 1751). 4.4.6.14; B23, C237 <nd, h> 5264.8*

‡*A letter to the right reverend the lord bishop of Oxford* (London, 1769). 6.1.6.35; C332 <nd, h (sheep and marbled boards)> On title page: "Gregory Sharpe." Tr 405*

†‡*The origin and structure of the Greek tongue* (London, 1767). 4.4.6.2; B23, C136 <nd, h> On front flyleaf: "This copy of this very learned, valuable work, a present from the very excellent author of it to T·H, after decent decoration, is gladly bestowed by him on Harvard College, at Cambridge in N. E. And, from the great desire of promoting learning, that is every ingenuity, which is in him, he humbly submits to the grave consideration of the very learned President, Professors & Teachers of that College, whether it might not be advisable, to adopt the idea thrown out in it, of teaching the Greek before the Latin Tongue, to all such youths as seek and are intended to be bred up Scholars. The Young Nobleman is the Lord Ashley, Son of the Earl of Shaftesbury, a beneficent, good man. The Republic of Letters, owes great obligation to the Shaftesbury Family. Palmal, aug. 1, 1767." On title page: "Ut spargam T·H." *EC75.H7267.Zz767s

Seven letters containing a new and easy method of learning the Hebrew language (London, 1751). 4.2.6.25; not in C <670511, h> 1174.5*

‡*Two dissertations* (London, 1751). 2.1.5.24; C137 (under Sharpe, Granville) <nd, h> On flyleaf: "By the very learned and excellent Dr. Sharpe Master of the Temple." 1233.24*

[Another copy] Inv.16.100; 4.2.6.25; C137 (under Sharpe, Granville) <670511, h> 2274.4*

[Another copy] 4.4.6.8; C137 (under Sharpe, Granville) <nd, h> 2285.32*

SHELTON, MAURICE, 1683-1749. *An historical and critical essay on the true rise of nobility* (London, 1720). Inv.8.34; 2.3.5.9-10; C54 <661001, r> Br 5600.15* 2 v.

SHEPHERD, RICHARD, 1732?-1809. *Letters to Soame Jenyns, Esq.* (Oxford, 1773). 6.1.8.21; C333 <nd, h> *EC75.Sh487.759rb

SHERIDAN, THOMAS, 1719-1788.

    British education (London, 1769). Inv.12.57; 6.1.4.11; C124 <690818, h> Educ 817.69*

    A course of lectures on elocution (London, 1762). Inv.12.13; C149 <690818, h> 9280.759.10*

    A learned discourse on various subjects, viz., of the rise and power of parliaments (London, 1685). Inv.2.88; 2.2.8.13; B21, not in C <6410.., r> Br 139.2*

    ‡*A plan of education for the young nobility* (London, 1769). Inv.12.53; 6.1.3.30; C124 <690818, r> On p.62, last line, TH writes "pace" to replace "place." Gutman Library LB575.S5 A2

SHERINGHAM, ROBERT, 1602-1678.

    De Anglorum gentis origine (Cambridge, 1670). Inv.7.14; 2.2.6.26; not in C <651010, h> *EC75.H7267.Zz670s (A)

    ‡[Another copy] Inv.10.39; 2.2.6.25; not in C <680712, h> On title page: "rare." *EC75.H7267.Zz670s (B) A third copy, Inv.16.42 <670511>, not located.

SHERLOCK, WILLIAM, 1641?-1707. *The case of the allegiance owed to soveraign powers* (London, 1691). 2.2.5.16; C251 <671209, h> *EC75.H7267.Zz691t

SHIRLEY, WILLIAM, fl. 1739-1780. ‡*Electra, a tragedy* (London, 1765). Inv.7.2; 2.2.4.20; C131 <651010, h> On flyleaf: "William Shirley Esq. lately a Lisbon Merchant; an ingenious, public-spirited Gentleman." *EC75.Sh668.765e

A short account of Dr. Bentley's humanity and justice (London, 1699). Inv.9.23 (part); 6.1.8.14; C105 & C219 <680711, h> *EC65.B4465.B710b A second copy, Inv.14.34 <700926>, not located.

A short and faithful account of the life ... of Mr. Thomas Chubb (London, 1747). 4.2.7.35; C207 & C271 <nd, r> *EC7.C4705.B747t

[Another copy] 6.1.7.25; C207 & C271 <nd, xt> *EC7.C4705.W747s

†*A short and friendly caution to the good people of England* (London, 1766). Inv.16.38 (part); 4.1.7.22; C267 <670511, h> *AC7.Ot464.765ab (B)

†‡*A short narrative of the horrid massacre* [the Boston massacre] (London, 1770). Inv.14.37; 6.1.6.5; B18 (under Massacre), C106 (under Boston) <700926, r> On title page: "Felicity is Freedom and Freedom is Magnanimity. Thucyd." The edges are black, the remains of a "mourning" binding. *AC7.B6747.770sb

A short review of the controversy between Mr Boyle, and Dr. Bentley (London, 1701).
Inv.14.65; 6.1.7.31; not in C <700926, r> Gp 26.55*

SIDNEY, ALGERNON, 1622-1683.
†‡*Discourses concerning government* (London, 1751). Inv.1.13; 2.3.1.21; B24, C86 <631024, h>
Large paper, one of four copies with a suite of six different proofs of John Baptist
Jackson's chiaroscuro portrait of Sidney. The wood blocks were commissioned and
retained by TH. On flyleaf: the last six lines of Mark Akenside's "Ode VIII," beginning
"O fair Britannia, hail!" and "N.B. The Reader will least of all imagine that the Britannia
here described is that of Sidney's Days." With a long note on Jackson's prints, which
were based on a drawing by George Vertue after an oil by Justus ab Egmont. At some
point placed in the library of the President of Harvard College; bequeathed [*sic*] to the
College Library in 1875 by President James Walker.
f*EC75.H7267.Zz751s

[Another copy] C86 <641208, r> Gov 529.10.3 F*

†‡[Another edition] (London, 1763). Inv.3.68; 2.3.3.28; C84 (wrongly dated 1764)
<641208, h> On first flyleaf: "Thomas Hollis, an Englishman, a Lover of Liberty, his
Country, and its excellent Constitution, as nobly restored at the happy Revolution, is
desirous of having the honor to deposite [*sic*] this book in the public library of Harvard
College, at Cambridge in New England. Pall Mall, ap. 14, 1763." On second flyleaf:
"Felicity is freedom, and freedom is magnanimity! Thucyd." Designed and sponsored
by TH. f*EC75.H7267.Zz763s2

†*Letters* (London, 1742). Inv.2.83; 2.1.5.13; C148 <6410.., h> *EC65.Si143.742ℓ

SIGONIO, CARLO, 1524?-1584. *Emendationum libri duo* (Venice, 1557). 4.4.6.13; not in C
<nd, h> *IC5.Si263.557e

Silvarum libri quinque (London, 1728). 4.4.4.17; C20 (under Statius) <nd, h> KPG 372*

SIMEON, OF DURHAM, fl. 1130. *Libellus de exordio* (London, 1732). 4.2.6.1; C68 <nd, r>
Br 1055.101*

SIMPSON, JOSEPH, fl. 1764. *Reflections on the natural and acquired endowments requisite
for the study of law* (London, 1765). 4.4.6.27; C251 <nd, h (marbled boards)>
*EC75.B5628.752s

SINCLAIR, J. *Some remarks on a late letter to Thomas Burnet* (London, 1736). Inv.4.138
(part); 2.2.5.23; C213 (under Burnet) <641212?, h> *EC65.B9343.S736t

*Sir *'s speech upon the peace with Sp—n* (London, 1739). 4.2.3.22; not in C <nd, h>
f*EC75.H7267.Zz740p

SKINNER, THOMAS, 1629?-1679. *Elenchi motuum nuperorum in Anglia, pars III* (London,
1676). 4.4.8.19; not in C <nd, h> Br 1820.139.2*

SMART, CHRISTOPHER, 1722-1771. *Poems on several occasions* (London, 1752). Inv.16.75
(part); 6.3.2.14; C240 <670511, xt> 18448.42.14*

SMETIUS, JOANNES, 1599-1621.
‡*Antiquitates neomagenses* (Nijmegen, 1678). 4.3.6.15; C7 (under Smith) <nd, v> On
plate following p.126, one object marked and footnoted: "Penes T·H." Typ 632.78.798

Oppidum Batavorum ... liber singularis (Amsterdam, 1645). Inv.2.36; 2.1.7.2; C7 <6410.., h (paper wrappers)> *NC6.Sm394.644ob

SMITH, JOHN, 1630-1679. *The pourtract of old age* (London, 1676). 4.4.8.3; C193 <nd, h (rebacked)> Med 269.33.2*

SMITH, ROBERT, RAT-CATCHER. *The universal directory for taking alive and destroying rats* (London, 1768). Inv.12.64; 6.1.8.11; C124 <690818, h> *EC75.Sm644.768u

SMITH, THOMAS, 1638-1710.
De Græcæ ecclesiæ hodierno statu epistola (Utrecht, 1698). 4.3.7.19; not in C <nd, h> Tr 387*

Inscriptiones Græcae Palmyrenorum cum scholiis & annotationibus Edwardi Bernardi et Thomæ Smithi (Utrecht, 1698). 4.3.7.19; C208 (under Smith) <nd, h> Tr 387*

Septem Asiæ ecclesiarum et Constantinopoleos notitia (Utrecht, 1694). 4.3.7.19; not in C <nd, h> Tr 387*

SMITH, WILLIAM, M.D. *The student's vade mecum* (London, 1770). Inv.14.40; 6.1.7.3; B23, not in C <700926, h> Educ 7337.70*

SMYTH, GEORGE, 1689?-1746. *The Church of Rome's claim of authority* (London, 1735). Not in C <6506.., h> *EC75.H7267.Zz735s2

SNELLING, THOMAS, 1712-1773.
A view of the gold coin and coinage of England (London, 1763). Inv.2.12 (part); 2.2.3.22; not in C <6410.., h> f*EC75.H7267.Zz762s

A view of the silver coin and coinage of England (London, 1762). Inv.2.12 (part); 2.2.3.22; C129 <6410.., h> f*EC75.H7267.Zz762s

SOCIETY FOR THE PROMOTION OF MANUFACTURES, ARTS, AND COMMERCE, *see* Royal Society of Arts

SOLIS, ANTONIO DE, 1610-1686. *Histoire de la conquête du Mexique* (Paris, 1704). 4.2.8.14-15; C61 <nd, h> SA 3361.18.49* 2 v.

†*Some strictures on the late occurrences in North America* (London, 1766). Inv.16.38 (part); 4.1.7.22; C267 (under Strictures) <670511, h> *AC7.Ot464.765ab (B)

SOMERS, JOHN SOMERS, BARON, *see The judgment of whole kingdoms*

SOMNER, WILLIAM, 1598-1669. *Julii Caesaris portus Iccius illustratus* (Oxford, 1694). 4.2.8.36; C7 <nd, h> AH 816.76*

SORBIÈRE, SAMUEL, 1615-1670. *A voyage to England* (London, 1709). Inv.8.47; 2.3.7.10; C76 <661001, r> *FC6.So681.Eg709v

SPANG, WILLIAM. *Rerum nuper in regno Scotiæ gestarum historia* (Danzig, 1641). Inv.2.123; 2.1.8.47; C62 (under Scotia) <6410.., r> Br 8216.41*

SPANHEIM, EZEKIEL, 1629-1710. *Dissertationes de praestantia et usu numismatum antiquorum* (London, 1706). Inv.5.56; 2.4.1.14-15; C130 <6506.., h> Arc 1350.1 F* 2 v.

See also Julian, Emperor of Rome

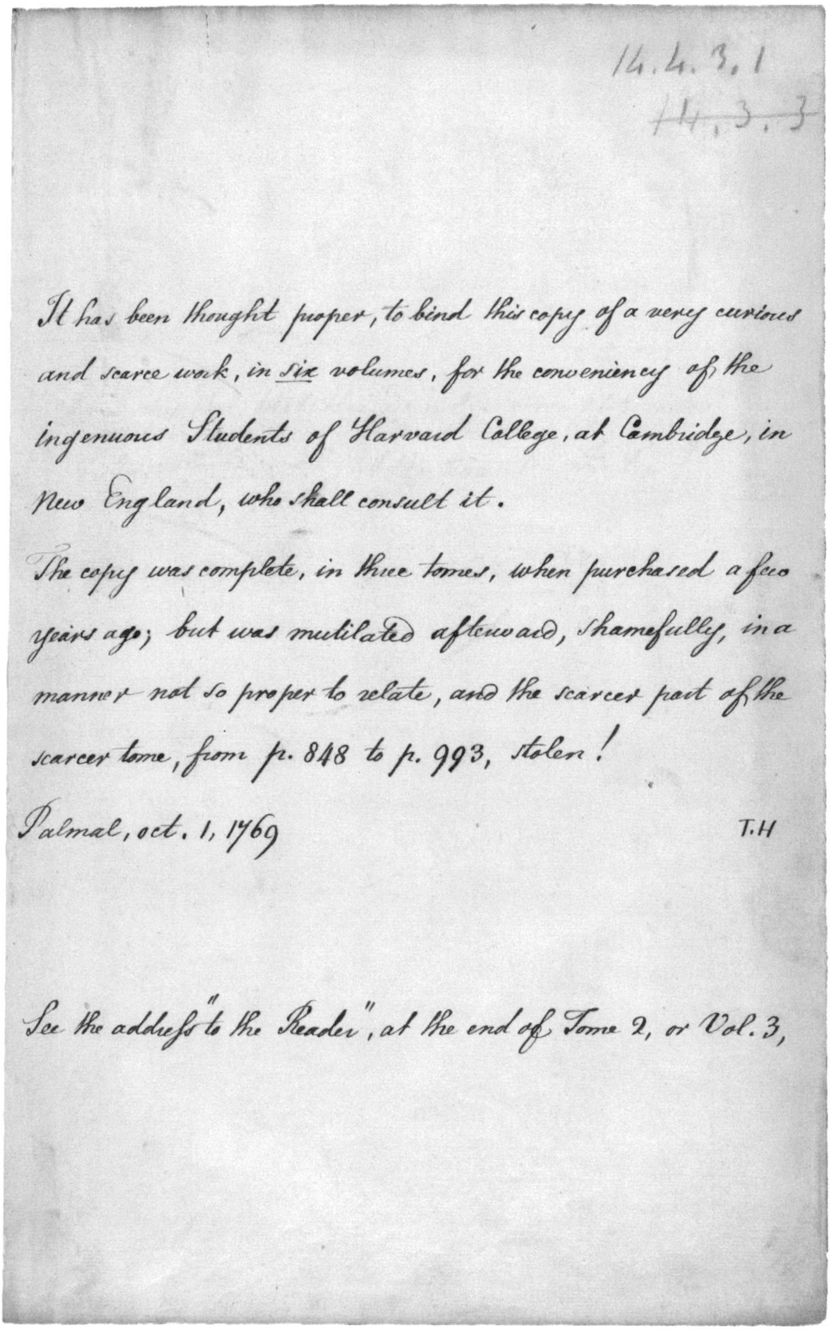

14.4.3.1
14.3.3

It has been thought proper, to bind this copy of a very curious and scarce work, in _six_ volumes, for the conveniency of the ingenuous Students of Harvard College, at Cambridge, in New England, who shall consult it.

The copy was complete, in three tomes, when purchased a few years ago; but was mutilated afterward, shamefully, in a manner not so proper to relate, and the scarcer part of the scarcer tome, from p. 848 to p. 993, stolen!

Palmal, oct. 1, 1769   T.H

See the address "to the Reader", at the end of Tome 2, or Vol. 3,

Figure 8. William Prynne, *An Exact Chronological Vindication* (London, 1666). On the first front flyleaf, TH recounts the complicated history of this damaged gift. See Introduction p. 20, and Checklist, p. 157.   f*EC65.P9567.666f 2 v. 33 cm.

Sparke, Joseph, 1683-1740, ed. *Historiæ anglicanæ scriptores variæ* (London, 1723). Inv.17.2; 4.4.2.25; not in C <68...., h> f*EC7.Sp264.723ha

Specimen of Dr. Burnet's behaviour in private cases (London, [17—]). Inv.4.138 (part); 2.2.5.23; C213 (under Burnet) <641212?, h> *EC65.B9343.S736t

‡*A speech in behalf of the constitution* (London, 1767). C252 < nd, xt> On title page, referring to the motto PER LEGEM TERRAE: "+ 'Per legem Terrae' is part of Lord Cmdn's motto—". *EC75.A100.759sb

The speeches and prayers of some of the late King's judges ([London], 1660). Inv.2.43; 2.3.8.14; B23, C108 (under Charles I) <6410.., r> *EC65.P4425.W660s

Speed, John, 1552?-1641. *The history of Great Britain* (London, 1611). Inv.5.63; 2.2.1.7; C62 <6506.., r> pf STC 23045

Speke, Hugh, 1656-1724?
    ‡*The case of Hugh Speke* ([London?, 1713]). 2.1.7.4; C231 (under Speake) <671209, xt> Two leaves supplied in TH's hand, reproducing the text of a printed petition by Speke. *EC7.Sp323.713c

    Some memoirs of the most remarkable passages (Dublin, 1709). 2.1.7.4; not in C <671209?, xt> *EC7.Sp323.713s

Spelman, Sir Henry, 1564?-1641. *Glossarium archæologicum* (London, 1687). Inv.16.64; 4.4.3.10; C205 <670511, h> Annotation by John Langdon Sibley: "This book was once sold as a duplicate – probably to Saml Phillips;. How it got back to the Library I know not. J. L. S[ibley]." 5291.4 F* A second copy, shelfmark 2.1.3.7, not located.

Spencer, John, 1630-1693. *De legibus Hebræorum ritualibus* (Cambridge, 1717). Inv.16.59; 2.1.3.1-2; C70 <670511> Original Hollis gift not located.

A discourse concerning prodigies (London, 1665). Inv.2.61; 2.1.7.37; C193 <6410.., h> *EC65.Sp336.663db

Spiltimber, George, d. 1749. *The weather-menders* (London, 1740). 4.2.3.22; C237 (under title) <nd, h> f*EC75.H7267.Zz740p

Spinoza, Benedictus de, 1632-1677. ‡*De jure ecclesiasticorum* ([n.p.], 1665). Inv.7.21; 2.2.7.44; C78 <651010, h> TH identifies the author, and notes: "Rariss." C 10266.65*

The spirit and principles of the Whigs and Jacobites compared (London, 1746). 4.2.7.11; C253 (under Whig's and Jacobite's) <nd, r> *EC75.C1527.747ℓ

Spon, Jacob, 1647-1685.
    The history of the city and state of Geneva (London, 1687). Inv.14.61; 6.1.2.9; C62 <700926, h> Swi 1105.1 F* (A)

    Miscellanea eruditæ antiquitatis (Leiden, 1685). 4.3.2.12; C8 (misdated 1683) <nd, v> On flyleaf: "The notes throughout this work, are in the handwriting of the very learned Masson." AH 816.85 F*

    Recherches curieuses d'antiquité (Lyons, 1683). Inv.14.5; 6.1.3.14; C8 <700926, h> Typ 615.83.805

    Voyage d'Italie (Amsterdam, 1679). Inv.14.4; 6.2.8.34-35; C76 <700926, h> Sold in 1769 by the British Museum as a duplicate. *FC6.Sp660.678vb 2 v.

SPOTTISWOOD, JOHN, 1565-1639.
The history of the Church of Scotland (London, 1655). Inv.3.85; C68 <641208, r> f*EC.Sp685.655h

[Another edition] (London, 1666). Inv.10.9; 4.3.4.14; C68 <680712, h> f*EC.Sp685.655hb

SPRIGG, WILLIAM, fl. 1657. ‡*A modest plea* (London, 1659). Inv.1.27 (under Osborne); 2.3.8.13; C85 (under Osborne) <631024, h> TH completed defective title page in MS. On back flyleaf: "In the title page of a Pamphlet called 'A perswasive to a mutuall compliance under the present Government. Together with a plea for a free state compared with Monarchy. Oxford, printed in the year 1652'. In quarto, is written, 'The Author of "Advise to a Sonn" is supposed to be the author of this book'. – That is Francis Osborn Esq. T.H. Osborne's works have been printed various times, but in every collection this tract hath been omitted." *EC65.Sp818.659m (B)

SPROTT, THOMAS, fl. 1270? *Chronica*, ed. Thomas Hearne (Oxford, 1719). 4.2.5.37; C5 <nd, h> Br 1460.14*

SQUIRE, SAMUEL, 1713-1766.
An enquiry into the foundation of the English constitution (London, 1752). 2.3.6.1; C86 <nd, r> *EC75.Sq587.745eb

Two essays [on Greek chronology and language] (Cambridge, 1741). Inv.12.58; 6.1.6.7; C35 <690818, h> *EC75.Sq587.741t

STAATLICHE MUSEEN ZU BERLIN (GERMANY). MÜNZKABINETT, *see* Beger, Lorenz

STADTBIBLIOTHEK BERN. ‡*Librorum typis editorum catalogus* (Berne, 1764). 4.3.7.36-37; C32 <680411?, h (calf & marbled boards)> On flyleaf: "There is a supplement to this work, intitled 'Catalogi Librorum Typis Editorum, qui in Bibliotheca Bernensis extant Supplementam.' Bernae, 1767, in thin octavo." B 1278.3.5* 2 v.

STANYAN, ABRAHAM, 1669?-1732.
‡*An account of Switzerland* (London, 1714). 2.1.6.38; B24, C63 (under Switzerland) <nd, r> On flyleaf: "Thomas Hollis of Pall Mall London, an Englishman, Citizen of the World, is desirous of having the honor to present this Book to the Public Library of Harvard College at Cambridge in N. England. Nov. 1, 1765." *EC7.St265.714a

[Another copy] B24, C63 (under Switzerland) <nd, h> *EC75.H7267.Zz714s

STANYAN, TEMPLE, 1677?-1752. *The Grecian history* (London, 1751). Inv.16.92; 2.1.5.26-27; B24, C62 <670511, h> *EC7.St266.707gc 2 v.

‡*State necessity considered as a question of law* (London, 1766). 6.1.7.20; C252 <nd, xt> On title page, with reference to the motto ET TU, BRUTE : "—alluding to Ld Cmdn—". *EC75.A100.766s2

[Another copy] 4.3.6.22; C252 <nd, h> *EC75.A100.767sb

The state of England in 1588 (London, 1746). 2.2.5.8; C223 (under England) <nd, h> Sometimes ascribed to Richard Leigh. *EC75.H7267.Zz745t

State tracts (London, 1692). Inv.16.56 (part); 2.3.1.14; C148 <670511, h> f*EC65.A100.B692sb

State tracts (London, 1693). Inv.16.56 (part); 2.3.1.15; C148 <670511, h> f*EC65.A100.B689s4b

STATIUS, *see Silvarum libri quinque*

STAVELEY, THOMAS, 1626-1684. ‡*The Romish horseleech* (London, 1769). Inv.14.67; 6.1.8.20; C124 <700926, h> On flyleaf: "a curious, valuable work." *EC65.St296.674rb

STAY, BENEDETTO, 1714-1801. *Philosophiæ versibus traditæ libri sex* (Rome, 1747). C144 <nd, v> MLs 876.30*

STEELE, SIR RICHARD, 1672-1729. *The D---n of W--------r still the same* (London, 1720). 6.1.5.41; not in C <700926, h> *EC7.Sy442.B725s

See also Cerri, Urbano

STENNETT, SAMUEL, 1727-1795. *Discourses on personal religion* (London, 1769). Inv.13.69; 6.1.6.8-9; B24, C194 <700926, h> C 1352.67.30* 2 v.

STEPHENS, WILLIAM, d. 1718.
An account of the growth of deism in England (London, 1696). 2.1.6.14; not in C <671209?, h> *EC65.C5614.681c

‡[Another edition] (London, 1709). Inv.3.54; 2.3.7.40; C151 (under title) & C279 (under Deism) <641208, h> On title page: "The editor Mr. Stephen's [*sic*] Trenchards friend." *EC7.St455.B709a (B)

STEUART, SIR JAMES, BART. , 1712-1780. *An inquiry into the principles of political œconomy* (London, 1767). 4.3.4.19-20; C148 <nd, r> *EC75.St468.767i 2 v.

STEVENS, JOHN, d. 1726.
An historical account of all the taxes (London, 1733). 4.2.7.28; C124 <nd, h> Original Hollis gift not located; noted by G. W. Cottrell Jr.

The history of the antient abbeys (London, 1722-1723). 4.1.3.3; not in C <nd, r> *EC7.St475.722h 2 v.

A new dictionary, Spanish and English (London, 1726). Inv.9.11; 4.3.5.4; C205 <680711, r> 7224.7*

STILLINGFLEET, BENJAMIN, 1702-1771. *An essay on conversation* (London, 1738). 4.2.3.22; C240 <nd, h> f*EC75.H7267.Zz740p

STILLINGFLEET, EDWARD, 1635-1699. *Origines britannicæ, or, The antiquities of British churches* (London, 1685). 4.3.4.10; C68 <nd, h> f*EC65.St545.685o

STONE, FRANCIS, 1738?-1813. *A short and seasonable application to the public* (London, 1768). 6.1.6.32; C320 (under Religious grievances) <nd, xt> *EC75.St713.768s

STOPPA, GIOVANNI BATTISTA. *A collection of the several papers* [concerning massacre of Protestants] ([London], 1655). 2.1.7.3; C148 (under Piedmont) <6410.., h> *FC6.St737.Eg655c

STOW, JOHN, 1525?-1605. *Survey of the cities of London and Westminster* (London, 1720). Inv.5.65; 2.3.1.19-20; C124 <6506.., h> Br 4369.20 F* 2 v.

STRABO. †*Rerum geographicarum libri XVII* (Amsterdam, 1707). 4.2.3.6-7; C20 <nd, h> Gs 53.115 F* 2 v.

STRAFFORD, THOMAS WENTWORTH, EARL OF, 1593-1641.

‡*The Earl of Strafford's letters and dispatches* (London, 1739). Inv.13.68; 6.1.2.3-4; not in C <700926, h> V. 1, on portrait frontispiece: "Floreat Libertas, Pereat Tyrannis! T·H." f*EC.St813.739ℓ 2 v.

The tryal of Thomas Earl of Strafford, ed. John Rushworth (London, 1680). Inv.16.36; 2.1.3.26; C148 <670511, h> f*EC.St813.680t

Strictures on an answer to the Pietas Oxoniensis (London, 1769). 6.1.4.30; C320 (under Chatham) <nd, xt> *EC75.A100.769s4

STRUTT, SAMUEL. ‡*A philosophical enquiry into the physical spring of human actions* (London, 1732). 4.2.7.15; C234 <nd, h> On title page: "very rare," and TH identifies the author. *EC75.H7267.Zz746t

STRYPE, JOHN, 1643-1737.

‡*Annals of the reformation* (London, 1725-1731). Inv.12.43; 6.1.1.14-17; C68 <690818, h> "T·H has now the honor to send Strype's publications, complete, to Harvard College. They are truly valuable, & are becoming scarce, good copies of them. Palmal, ap.14, 69." Br 1700.37.4* 4 v.

Ecclesiastical memorials (London, 1721). Inv.12.42; 6.1.2.6-8; C68 <690818, r> Br 1700.37 F* 3 v.

Historical collections of the life ... of ... John Aylmer (London, 1701). Inv.12.28; 6.1.7.29; C30 <690818, h> Br 1771.5*

‡*The history of the life and acts of ... Edmund Grindal* (London, 1710). Inv.12.46; 6.1.2.10; C30 <690818, r> On title page: "Strype." f*EC7.St905.710h

The life and acts of Matthew Parker (London, 1711). Inv.12.44; 6.1.2.11;. C30 <690818, h> f*EC75.H7267.Zz711s

The life and acts of the most reverend father in God, John Whitgift (London, 1718). Inv.12.45; 6.1.2.5; C30 <690818, r> Br 1793.14 F*

‡*The life of the learned Sir John Cheke* (London, 1705). Inv.12.60; 6.1.7.26; C30 <690818, h> On frontispiece portrait: "Homines sumus. T·H." On title page: "scarce, and very curious." *EC75.H7267.Zz705s

‡*The life of the learned Sir Thomas Smith* (London, 1698). Inv.12.66; 2.4.7.48; C29 (under Smith, Sir Thomas) <690818, r> On frontispiece portrait: "How glorious a Man! A Secretary." *EC75.H7267.Zz698s

Memorials of ... Thomas Cranmer (London, 1694). Inv.12.47; 6.1.2.12; C30 <690818, r> Br 1773.30.5 F*

STUART, GILBERT, 1742-1786. *An historical dissertation concerning the antiquity of the English constitution* (Edinburgh, 1768). Inv.11.6; 6.1.5.11; C86 <6809.., h> Br 1250.21*

STUART, JAMES, 1713-1788. *The antiquities of Athens* (London, 1762). Inv.1.2; 6.3.1.16; C8 <631024, h> Wrongly plated as gift of Nathaniel Rogers of Boston, but specially bound by Matthewman for TH, who was a subscriber but died before v. 2 appeared. Arc 705.5 PF* v. 1 only

STUBBE, HENRY, 1632-1676.

Campanella revived (London, 1670). 2.4.4.17; C231 <nd, r> *EC65.St935.B681t

A further iustification of the present war against the United Netherlands (London, 1673). 2.4.5.19; C252 <nd, xt> *EC65.St935.673f (B)

A justification of the present war against the United Netherlands (London, 1673). 2.4.5.19; C252 <nd, xt> *EC65.St935.672jb (B)

Legends no histories ([London, 1670]). 2.4.4.17; C231 <nd, r> *EC65.St935.B681t

‡*The plus ultra reduced to a non plus* (London, 1670). 2.4.4.17; C231 <nd, r> On flyleaf: "A volume of scarce tracts. See a long account of Henry Stubbe, in the 'Athenae Oxoniensis' of A. Wood, v. 2 [i.e., 3], p. 560." *EC65.St935.B681t

STUBBES, GEORGE, b. 1682 or 3.

A dialogue in the manner of Plato, on the superiority of the pleasures of the understanding (London, 1734). Inv.2.65 (part); 2.1.6.13; C231 <6410.., h> *EC7.St932.731d

A dialogue on beauty, in the manner of Plato (London, 1731). Inv.2.65 (part); 2.1.6.13; C231 <6410.., h> *EC7.St932.731d

A new adventure of Telemachus (London, 1731). Inv.2.65 (part); 2.1.6.13; C231 <6410.., h> *EC7.St932.731d

STUKELEY, WILLIAM, 1687-1765.

An account of Richard of Cirencester (London, 1757). Inv.2.32; 4.4.4.10; C8 <6410.., r> Br 1525.12*

A letter ... to Mr. Macpherson (London, 1763). Not in C <nd, xt> *EC75.B5754.763c

SWAMMERDAM, JAN, 1637-1680. *Ephemeri vita, or, The natural history of the Ephemeron* (London, 1681). Inv.4.15; 2.3.5.26; C72 <641212?, h> MCZ 809

SWIFT, JONATHAN, 1667-1745.

Good Queen Anne vindicated (London, 1748). 4.2.7.17 (part); not in C <nd, h> *EC75.H7267.Zz737t

A tale of a tub (London, 1710). Inv.10.24; 4.3.7.3; C125 <680712, r> *EC7.Sw551T.1710 (B)

[Another edition] (London, 1739). 4.4.8.2; C125 <nd, r> 16422.27*

SWINTON, JOHN, 1703-1777.

Inscriptiones Citieæ (Oxford, 1750). Inv.13.59 (part); 6.1.3.13; C208 <700926, h> *EC75.H7267.Zz750s

[Another copy] 4.2.5.3; C208 <nd, h> *EC75.H7267.Zz748h

Metilia (Oxford, 1750). Inv.13.59 (part); 6.1.3.13; C234 <700926, h> *EC75.H7267.Zz750s

[Another copy] 4.2.5.3; C234 <nd, h> *EC75.H7267.Zz748h

SYKES, ARTHUR ASHLEY, 1683 or 4-1756.

The authority of the clergy (London, 1720). Inv.13.23; 6.1.5.43; C195 <700926, h> *EC7.Sy442.720a

A brief discourse concerning the credibility of miracles (London, 1742). Inv.14.8; 4.4.7.38; C195 <700926, h> *EC7.Sy442.742b

[Another issue] Inv.13.15 (part); 6.1.5.36; not in C <700926, h> *EC7.Sy442.742ba

The consequences of the present conspiracy (London, 1722). Inv.13.15 (part); 6.1.5.41; not in C <700926, h> *EC7.Sy442.B725s

The Dean of Chichester's conduct considered (London, 1718). Inv.13.15 (part); 6.1.5.41; C339 <700926, h> *EC7.Sy442.B725s

A defence of the dissertation on the eclipse (London, 1733). Inv.13.29; 6.1.5.45; C340 <700926, h> C 1357.15.60*

[Another copy] 6.1.5.46; C340 <nd, h> C 1357.15.61* A third copy, shelfmark 6.1.5.34, not located.

A defence of the examination of Mr Warburton's account (London, 1746). Inv.13.42; 2.1.6.6; C340 <700926, h> C 1351.15.09*

A dissertation on the eclipse (London, 1732). Inv.13.28; 6.1.5.45; C339 <700926, h> C 1357.15.60*

[Another copy] 6.1.5.46; C339 <nd, h> C 1357.15.61*

‡*An enquiry how far papists ought to be treated here as good subjects* (London, 1763). Inv.2.87; 2.1.6.34; C340 <6410.., h> On front flyleaf, quotation from *Areopagitica*; on title page: "Ut spargam. T·H"; on back flyleaf, quotation from Thomas Hobbes. *EC75.H7267.Zz763s

[Another copy] 6.1.5.47; C340 <nd, h> *EC7.Sy442.746rb

†*An enquiry when the resurrection of the body ... was first inserted in the public creeds* (London, 1757). 2.1.5.39; C340 <6410.., h> *EC75.H7267.Zz752t

‡*An essay on the nature, design, and origin, of sacrifices* (London, 1748). Inv.13.30; 6.1.5.37; C195 <700926, h> TH identifies the author. *EC7.Sy442.648e

An essay upon the truth of the Christian religion (London, 1725). Inv.14.9; 6.1.5.39; C195 <700926, h> C 1357.15.52*

[Another edition] (London, 1755). Inv.13.31; 6.1.5.31; C195 <700926, h> C 1357.15.54*

‡*An examination of Mr. Warburton's account* (London, 1744). Inv.2.98; 2.1.6.6; C195 <6410.., h> On flyleaf, a table of contents. C 1357.15.09* A second copy, Inv.13.38, shelfmark 6.1.5.32 <700926>, not located.

‡*The external peace of the church* (London, 1716). Inv.13.24; 6.1.5.41; C339 <700926, h> TH identifies the author. *EC7.Sy442.B725s

The innocency of error (London, 1729). 2.3.7.4; C283 (under Error) <6410.., h> *EC7.Sy442.715ic

[Another copy] 6.1.5.40; C283 (under Error) <nd, h> EC75.H7267.Zz731t

[Another copy] 6.1.5.44; C283 (under Error) <70…., h> *EC7.Sy442.B729t

A letter to the reverend Dr. Sherlock (London, 1717). Inv.13.32 (part); 6.1.5.42; C339 <700926, h> *EC7.Sy442.B717ℓ

A second letter to the reverend Dr. Sherlock (London, [1717]). Inv.13.32 (part); 6.1.5.42; C339 <700926, h> *EC7.Sy442.B717ℓ

A third letter to the reverend Dr. Sherlock (London, 1717). Inv.13.32 (part); 6.1.5.42; C339 <700926, h> *EC7.Sy442.B717ℓ

A fourth letter to the reverend Dr. Sherlock (London, 1718). Inv.13.32 (part); 6.1.5.42; not in C <700926, h> *EC7.Sy442.B717ℓ

A letter to the Right Honourable the Earl of Nottingham (London, 1721). 6.1.5.41; C339 <nd, h> *EC7.Sy442.B725s

A paraphrase and notes [on the Epistle to the Hebrews] (London, 1755). Inv.13.41; 6.1.3.15; C195 <700926, h> *EC7.Sy442.755p

The principles and connexion of natural and revealed religion (London, 1740). Inv.13.43; 6.1.5.30; B24, C195 <700926, h> Phil 8598.21*

‡*The rational communicant* (London, 1754). Inv.13.40; 6.2.8.18; C195 <700926, h> TH identifies the author. C 1357.15.58*

The reasonableness of mending and executing the laws against papists (London, 1763). Inv.13.37; 6.1.5.47; C340 <700926, h> *EC7.Sy442.746rb

[Another copy] 2.1.6.34; C340 <6410.., h> *EC75.H7267.Zz763s

A reply to Dr. Waterland's Supplement (London, 1722). 6.1.5.41; C339 <nd, h> *EC7.Sy442.B725s

A second defence of the dissertation on the eclipse (London, 1734). 6.1.5.46; C340 <nd, h> C 1357.15.61*

A sermon preached in the Cathedral Church of Winchester (London, 1746). 6.1.3.15; not in C <nd, h> *EC7.Sy442.755p

A sermon preached Jan. 25, 1724 (London, 1725). 6.1.5.41; not in C <nd, h> *EC75.Sy442.B725s

The true foundations of natural and revealed religion asserted (London, 1730). 6.1.5.44; C339 <70…., h> *EC7.Sy442.B729t

‡*The true grounds of the expectation of the Messiah* (London, 1727). 6.1.5.44; C339 <70…., h> Inserted, a 3 page list of Sykes's works still lacking at Harvard in 1770. *EC7.Sy442.B729t

Two questions, previous to Dr. Middleton's Free inquiry (London, 1750). 2.3.7.4; C195 <6410.., h> *EC7.Sy442.715c

‡[Another copy] Inv.13.39; 6.1.5.33; C196 <700926, h> TH identifies the author. *EC75.H7267.Zz750s2

A vindication of the account of the double doctrine of the ancients (London, 1747). 2.1.6.6; C340 <700926, h> C 1351.15.09*

‡*Sylloge variorum tractatuum quibus Caroli* [I] *innocentia illustratur* ([n.p.], 1649). Inv.13.62; not in C <700926, v> On back flyleaf: "Floreat Libertas! Pereat Tyrannis! T·H." Br 1815.185*

Sylvæ, the second part of Miscellany poems (London, 1702). Inv.3.125 (under Dryden; part); B11, C141 (under Dryden) <641208, r> *EC65.D8474.B709m v. 2

SYMMONS, EDWARD.
A military sermon (Oxford, 1644). Inv.5.34 (part); 2.3.8.3; C252 <6506.., h> *EC65.Sy653.647vb

‡*A vindication of King Charles* ([London], 1648). Inv.5.34 (part); 2.3.8.3; C252 <6506.., h> In margins of pp.108-109: "Mark, Man of N. England, this foul passage! Rejoice in the Magnanimity of thy Ancestors, and thy own upright intentions; Abide thou and thy descendants steadfast in the principles of Liberty and the Revolution! T·H." *EC65.Sy653.647vb

T

TAAFE, NICHOLAS TAAFE, VISCOUNT, 1677-1769. *Observations on affairs in Ireland* (London, [1766]). 4.4.6.27; C232 <nd, h (marbled boards)> *EC75.B5628.752s

TACITUS.
†*Opera quæe extant* (Utrecht, 1721). Inv.8.32; 4.2.4.26-27; B24 (under Annales), C20 <661001, h> *EC75.H7267.Zz721t 2 v.

Works, tr. Thomas Gordon (London, 1728-1731). Inv.16.72; 2.3.2.6-7; C20 <670511, h> f*OLC.T118.Eg728 2 v.

TAISNIER, JEAN, b. 1509. *Opusculum perpetua memoria dignissimum, de natura magnetis* (Cologne, 1562). 4.4.6.2; C216 <nd, h> *FC5.M9425.559v

TALLENTS, FRANCIS, 1619-1708. *A view of universal history* (London, 1758). 6.1.1.1; C35 <nd, r> H 1907.58 F*

TANNER, THOMAS, 1674-1735. *Bibliotheca britannico-hibernica* (London, 1748). Inv.16.60; 2.4.2.6; C30 <670511, r> f*EC7.T1577.748b

TASSO, BERNARDO, 1493-1569. *Le lettere* (Venice, 1551). Inv.3.153; 4.4.8.38; C125 <641208, v> *IC5.T1852.549ℓb

TASSO, TORQUATO, 1544-1595. *La Gerusalemme liberata* (Cosenza, 1737). Inv.4.27; 2.4.4.18; B24, C144 <641212?, r> *IC5.T1853G.Eiz727cba

TASSONI, ALESSANDRO, 1565-1635. *De' pensieri diversi … libri dieci* (Venice, 1665). Inv.4.34; 2.3.5.23; C125 <641212?, calf (not TH?)> Ital 7987.41*

TAVERNIER, JEAN BAPTISTE, BARON D'AUBUDONNE, 1605-1687. *Nova, ed esatta descrizione del seraglio* (Milan, 1687). Inv.3.157; 2.4.8.28; C125 <641208, v> *FC6.T1987.Ei687b

TAYLOR, BROOK, 1685-1731, *see* Kirby, John Joshua

TAYLOR, JEREMY, 1613-1667. *Symbolon ethico-polemikon, or, A collection of polemical and moral discourses* (London, 1657). Inv.3.78; 2.2.3.23; C196 <641208, h> f*EC65.T2151.657s

TAYLOR, JOHN, 1694-1761.
An advertisement, offering to public notice … an Hebrew concordance ([London, 1745?]). 4.3.7.21; C237 (under Plan of a Hebrew concordance) <nd, r> *EC75.H7267.Zz7460

The Hebrew concordance, adapted to the English Bible (London, 1754-1757). 4.1.1.16-17; C38 <nd, r> Bi 580.2 F* 2 v.

TAYLOR, JOHN, 1704-1766.
Elements of the civil law (Cambridge, [1755]). 2.4.3.13; C77 <nd, h> *EC7.T2153.755e

Demosthenous, Aischinou [and other selected Greek texts, ed. Taylor] (Cambridge, 1769). Inv.13.56; 6.1.4.32-33; C14 <700926, h> Gd 15.370* 2 v.

TAYLOR, ZACHARY, 1653-1705. *The devil turn'd casuist* (London, 1696). 4.4.6.18; not in C <680930, h> *EC75.H7267.Zz698r

Teatro delle fabbriche piu conspicue in prospettiva della citta di Venezia ([Venice?, 17—?]). Inv.4.28; 4.4.6.44-45 (under Fabbrice); not in C <641212?> Declared lost.

TEMPLE, SIR WILLIAM, BART., 1628-1699. *The works* (London, 1740). Inv.16.67; 2.1.3.8-9; C125 <670511, r> f*EC65.T2475.C740w 2 v.

TERZAGO, PAOLO MARIA, d. 1695.
Musaeum Septalianum (Tortona, 1664). Inv.3.113; C124 (under Settala, Manfred) <641208> Original Hollis gift not located.

Museo o Galeria (Tortona, 1666). 2.4.5.36; not in C <641208, v> Typ 625.66.828

THEOPHILUS, ANGLICANUS, PSEUD. ‡*Protestant armour* (London, 1769). Inv.12.22; 6.1.5.5; C188 (under title) <690818, h> Faint offset of binder's instructions on verso of title page. *EC75.T3404.769p

THEOPHRASTUS. *History of stones* (London, 1746). Inv.5.24; 2.1.6.1; C20 <6506..> Original Hollis gift not located.

THIERRY, JEAN, *see Grammatici illustres XII*

THOMAS, OF ELMHAM, 1364-1440. *Vita & gesta Henrici quinti*, ed. Thomas Hearne (Oxford, 1727). 4.2.5.35; C27 <nd, h> Br 1575.9*

THOMASIUS, JACOB, 1622-1684. *Exercitatio de Stoica mundi exustione* (Leipzig, 1676). Inv.3.101; 2.1.5.34; C125 <641208, h> *GC6.T3696.676e (B)

THOMASSIN, LOUIS. *Glossarium universale hebraicum* (Paris, 1697). 4.2.2.18; C205 <nd, h> 2274.18 F*

THOMSON, JAMES, 1700-1748. *Works,* ed. Patrick Murdoch (London, 1762). Inv.1.11; 2.3.3.16-17; B25, C144 <631024, r> TH subscribed to this edition. 15467.9.3* 2 v.

THORESBY, RALPH, 1658-1725. *Vicaria Leodiensis* (London, 1724). Inv.4.86; 2.4.5.26; not in C <641212?, h> Br 5206.32.4*

THOU, JACQUES-AUGUSTE DE, 1553-1617.

†‡*Historiarum sui temporis tomus* (London, 1733). Inv.8.4; 4.2.2.6-12; C63 <661001, h> On title page of v. 1: "VT SPARGAM T·H." Fr 1202.2 F* 7 v.

Thuanus restitutus (Amsterdam, 1663). Inv.3.162; 2.2.8.57; C63 <641208, r> *FC6.T3997.663t

†*A thought relating to education* (London, 1732). 2.4.7.2; C222 (under Education) <6410.., h> *EC75.H7267.Zz734e

Thoughts on a question of importance proposed to the public (London, 1765). 4.1.7.19; C241 <66…., h> *EC75.A100.765t

Three important questions fairly debated (London, 1736). Inv.4.78; 2.3.7.18; C196 <641212?, h> C 1363.146*

THUCYDIDES.

Gli otto libri di Thucydide (Venice, [1550?]). Inv.3.151; 2.4.8.29; C21 <641208, v> *OGC.T421.Ei550b

Istorico greco (Verona, 1735). Inv.4.23; 2.4.4.23-24; C21 <641212?, v> KF 23378* 2 v.

THURLOE, JOHN, 1616-1668. *A collection of state papers,* ed. Thomas Birch (London, 1742). Inv.16.4; 2.4.2.16-22; not in C <670511, r> Br 1800.42 F* 7 v.

TILLEMONT, SÉBASTIEN LE NAIN DE, 1637-1698. *An account of the life of Apollonius Tyaneus* (London, 1702). Inv.4.124; 2.2.7.1; C30 <641212?, r> Ga 84.145*

TINDAL, MATTHEW, 1653?-1733.

‡*Christianity as old as the creation* (London, 1730). Inv.16.86; 2.4.4.7-8; C196 <670511, h> In v.2, half-title added in MS. by Hollis: "An IMPERFECT INTRODUCTION to the SECOND PART of CHRISTIANITY as old as the CREATION. Which was never printed. Purchased out of the Library of the late excellent Dʳ Ward. T·H. very rare." *EC7.T4921.730c 2 v.

[Another edition] (London, 1732). Inv.16.87; C270 <670511> Original Hollis gift not located.

A defence of The rights of the Christian church (London, 1709). Inv.4.199; 2.1.6.15; C211 <641212?, h> *EC7.T4921.709d

Four discourses (London, 1709). Inv.4.191 (under Works); 2.1.6.29; C211 (under Church) <641212?> Original Hollis gift not located.

‡*The rights of the Christian church asserted* (London, 1706). Inv.4.76; 2.2.6.13; C196 <641212?, h> On title page: "By Dʳ Tindal. No other Part publ." *EC7.T4921.706r

[Second edition] (London, 1706). 2.2.6.14; C196 <6506.., h> *EC7.T4921.706rb

Le tocsain, contre les massacreurs et auteurs des confusions en France (Reims, 1579). 2.1.8.26; C252 (under Toscain, M.) <671209?, h> Fr 1232.3.10*

TOLAND, JOHN, 1670-1722.

Anglia libera (London, 1701). Inv.9.37; 4.4.7.21; C86 <680711, h> Br 1985.44*

‡*The art of governing by parties* (London, 1701). Inv.9.38; 4.4.7.16; C148 <680711, r> TH identifies the author. *EC7.T5742.701a (B)

A collection of several pieces (London, 1726). 4.3.7.38-39; C125 <nd, r> Phil 2295.10* 2 v.

An historical account of the life and writings [of Toland] (London, 1722). Inv.9.34; 4.4.7.3; C207 & C341 <680711, h> Phil 2295.27*

‡*Letters to Serena* (London, 1704). 4.4.7.30; C125 <nd, h> On flyleaf: "There is a very curious & scarce collection of tracts relating to the Soul, in Harvard College." On title page: "Very scarce." Phil 2295.24*

†*The life of Iohn Milton* (London, 1761). Inv.2.103; 2.1.5.40; C30 <6410.., h> Designed and sponsored by TH. *EC7.T5742.699ℓb (A)

‡*The militia reform'd* (London, 1698). 2.2.5.7; C232 <671209?, h> On title page: "The author Mr. Toland." *EC75.H7267.Zz753t

Nazarenus, or Jewish, Gentile, and Mohammedan Christianity (London, 1718). 4.4.7.3; C341 <680711, h> Phil 2295.27*

Tetradymus (London, 1720). 4.4.7.3; not in C <680711, h> Phil 2295.27*

Vindicius liberius (London, 1702). Inv.9.41; 4.3.7.13; C125 (under Defence of himself) <680711, h> Phil 2295.75.2*

See also Schiner, Mathieu, Cardinal

Tomasini, Giacomo Filippo, 1595-1655.
De tesseris hospitalitatis (Amsterdam,1670). Inv.3.56 (part); not in C <641208, v> Ll 16.650*

Titi Livii Patavini vita (Amsterdam, 1670). Inv.3.56 (part); C30 <641208, v> Ll 16.650*

Tomkins, Martin, d. 1755? †*A sober appeal to a Turk* (London, 1748). Inv.2.104; 2.1.5.39; C153 (under Appeal) & C345 (under Trinity) <6410.., h> *EC75.H7267.Zz752t

Tonge, Ezerel, 1621-1680. *Jesuitical aphorismes, or, A summary account of the doctrine of the Jesuites* (London, 1679). 2.4.5.19; C232 <nd, xt> *EC65.T6135.679j

See also Morton, Thomas

Tooke, John Horne, 1736-1812. *An oration* (London, [1770]). Not in C <nd, xt> *EC75.T6176.770o

Toplady, Augustus, 1740-1778.
‡*The Church of England vindicated* (London, 1769). Inv.13.44 (part); 6.1.4.30; C342 <700926, h> TH identifies the author. *EC75.T6261.769c

A letter to the Rev. Mr. John Wesley (London, 1770). Not in C <nd, xt> *EC75.T6261.770ℓ

See also Zanchi, Girolamo

Touchet, Anselm, d. 1689? *Historical collections* ([London?], 1674). Inv.14.70; 6.2.8.4; not in C <700926, r> *EC65.T6426.674h

Toup, Jonathan, 1713-1785.
‡*Emendations in Suidas* (London, 1760-1766). 4.1.7.40-41; not in C <nd, h> In v. 1: "J. Toup, a divine of the Church of England, of good learning and excellence, hid in a little place in Cornwall!" Gs 58.83* 2 v.

Epistola critica (London, 1767). 4.4.6.34; not in C <nd, h> *EC75.H7267.Zz767t

TOURNEFORT, JOSEPH PITTON DE, 1636-1708. *Relation d'un voyage du Levant* (Lyon, 1717). Inv.8.36; 4.3.7.15-17; C76 <661001, h> Ott 3157.17* 3 v.

TOUSSAINT, FRANÇOIS-VINCENT, 1715-1772. ‡*Les moeurs* ([Lausanne], 1749). Inv.7.13; 2.2.7.47; C119 (under Moeurs) <651010, r> On front flyleaf: "Mons. Toussaint, Advocate at Paris, the ingenious author of this Book, having been troubled there for writing it, is now, in Asylum, in Berlin." *FC7.T6495.748mm

TOWGOOD, MICAIAH, 1700-1792.
A dissent from the Church of England (London, 1753). Inv.2.63; 2.2.7.35; C279 (under Towgood (Matt.) <6410.., h> *EC75.T6586.753d

The dissenting gentleman's answer to Mr. White (London, 1752). 2.2.7.35; not in C Original Hollis gift not located.

‡*Serious and free thoughts on the present state of the church* (London, 1755). Inv.2.65 (part); 2.1.6.12; C271 (under Church) <6410.., h> TH identifies author. *EC75.H7267.Zz751t

See also *A brief dissertation on funeral solemnities*

TOWNSON, THOMAS, 1715-1792.
A defence of the Doubts concerning the authenticity of the last publication of The confessional (London, 1768). 6.1.4.27; C275 (under Confessional) <nd, h> *EC75.H7267.Zz767pc

A dialogue between Isaac Walton and Homologistes (London, 1768). 6.1.4.27; C275 (under Confessional) <nd, h> *EC75.H7267.Zz767pc

Doubts concerning the authenticity of the last publication of The confessional (London, 1767 [i.e., 1768]). 6.1.4.27; C275 (under Confessional) <nd, h> *EC75.H7267.Zz767pc

Tradition des faites ([Paris?], 1753). Inv.4.163; 2.2.7.23; C111 (under Faites) <641212?, h> *FC7.C3974.753t

Tragicum theatrum actorum (Amsterdam, 1649). Inv.4.172; 2.2.8.36; C63 <641212?, h> Br 1869.16.9*

TRAPP, JOSEPH. *Lectures on poetry*, tr. William Bowyer (London, 1742). Inv.10.40; 4.3.8.42; B25, C125 <680712, r> Lit 1497.42*

A treatise on government (London, 1740). 2.3.7.38; C247 (under Government) <641208, h> *EC75.H7267.Zz735t

A treatise upon coal mines (London, 1769). Inv.13.3; 6.1.6.23; not in C <700926, h> Eng 1387.69*

TRENCHARD, JOHN, 1662-1723.
Cato's letters (London, 1748). Inv.16.21; 2.1.7.25-28; B9, not in C <670511> Original Hollis gift not located.

A collection of tracts by the late John Trenchard, Esq. and Thomas Gordon, Esq. (London, 1751). Inv.10.29; 4.3.8.30-31; C125 <680712, r> Br 2095.62* 2 v.

‡*A discourse of standing armies* (London, 1722). 2.2.5.7; C219 (under Army) <671209?, h> On title page: "Certainly Lord Molesworth's." *EC75.H7267.Zz753t

Essays on important subjects (London, 1755). Inv.16.46; 2.1.8.37; C125 <670511, h>
Br 2095.59*

A history of standing armies in England (London, 1739). 2.2.5.7; not in C <671209?, h>
*EC75.H7267.Zz753t TH gavc two copies, the second not located.

‡*The natural history of superstition* ([London], 1709). 2.4.5.4; C232 <nd, h> On flyleaf:
"The author Mr. Trenchard. very scarce" and corrections on p.40.
*EC75.H7267.Zz725m

‡*Several papers upon political subjects* (n.d., manuscript). Inv.2.9; 2.1.3.4; C89 <6410.., h>
On flyleaf: "Che trae l'uom' del sepolcro, ed in vita il serba. Petrarca." Bound with the
first printed edition (London, 1727) of the papers. Owned by John Milner; to Thomas
Gordon; to Richard Baron, who gave it to TH, June 16, 1755. fMS Eng 592

See also The independent Whig

A true and perfect copy of the whole disputation at the Savoy ([London], 1662). 6.1.7.35; C308
<700926, h> *EC65.A100.662t

*A true and perfect narrative of the late terrible and bloody murther of Sr. Edmondberry
Godfrey* ([London], 1678). 2.4.5.19; C224 Original Hollis gift discarded as a duplicate.

A true churchman's reasons for repealing the Corporation and Test-acts (London, 1732).
2.4.5.4; C221 (under Corporation) <nd, h> *EC75.H7267.Zz725m

The true interest of Great Britain, with respect to her American colonies (London, 1766).
4.1.7.19; C241 Original Hollis gift not located.

TRUMAN, JOSEPH, 1631-1671. *An endeavour to rectifie some prevailing opinions* (London,
1671). Inv.9.35 (under An endeavor); 4.4.8.17; C168 <680711, h> *EC65.T7715.671e

Tryal of King Charles I. of ever blessed memory (London, [1720?]). Inv.8.24; not in C
<661001> Original Hollis gift not located.

TUCKER, JOSIAH, 1712-1799. †*A letter from a merchant in London to his nephew in North
America* (London, 1766). Inv.16.38 (part); 4.1.7.2; C267 (under title) <670511, h>
*AC7.Ot464.765ab (B)

TUNSTALL, JAMES, 1708-1762. *Observations on the present collection of epistles* (London,
1744). 4.4.6.6; not in C <nd, h> *EC75.H7267.Zz742m v.2

TURNER, FRANCIS, 1638?-1700. *Animadversions upon a late pamphlet entituled The naked
truth* (London, 1676). 2.4.5.19; C211 (under Church) <nd, xt> *EC65.T8537.676ab

TURNER, JOHN, b. 1649 or 50. *A discourse concerning the Messias* (London, 1685). 4.3.8.4;
not in C <680711, xt> *EC65.T8545.685d

TURNER, THOMAS, d. 1679. *The case of the bankers and their creditors* ([London], 1675).
2.4.5.19; C210 <nd, xt> *EC65.T8618.674cd

TWYSDEN, SIR ROGER, 1597-1672. *Historiæ anglicanæ scriptores x* (London, 1652).
4.1.3.18-19; C52 <nd, h> Br 98.302 F* 2 v.

TYNDALE, WILLIAM, d. 1536. *The obedience of a Christen man* (Hesse, 1537). 2.2.8.56; C198
(under Whole works) <nd> Original Hollis gift not located.

TYRRELL, JAMES, 1642-1718.

Bibliotheca politica (London, 1691/2-[1694]). Inv.4.31; 2.4.7.16; C82 (under title) <641212?, h> *EC65.T9852.692b

[Another edition] (London, 1727). Inv.16.65; 2.2.3.9; not in C <670511, r> f*EC65.T9852.B727b

The general history of England (London, 1697-1704). Inv.16.66; 2.2.3.8-12; C63 <670511, h> *EC65.T9852.697g 3 v. in 5

Patriarcha non monarcha. The patriarch unmonarch'd (London, 1681). Inv.15.18; 6.1.8.36; C83 (under Filmer) <691129, h> Gov 530.9*

U

ULLOA, ANTONIO DE, 1716-1795. *A voyage to South America* (London, 1760). Inv.8.38; 2.4.5.12-13; C76 <661001, h> SA 907.35.12* 2 v. (v.2 only, v.1 presumed lost)

An universal history from the earliest account (London, 1736-1750). Inv.8.20; 4.3.3.1-8; C57 <661001, h> H 37.36 F* 8 v.

UNIVERSITY OF OXFORD. *Pietas in obitum Georgii III* (Oxford, 1761). Not in C <nd, h> Bookplate records "Emptus 1802," but remains of binding suggest a gift by TH. ML 117.61 F*

URBAN VIII, POPE, 1568-1644.

Poemata ([Rome, 1631]). 4.2.5.14; C140 (under Barberini) <nd, h> *IC6.Ur123.621pg

[Another edition] (Rome, 1643). 4.2.5.25; C140 (under Barberini) <nd, calf> *IC6.Ur123.621pn

USSHER, JAMES, ARCHBISHOP, 1581-1656.

Annales (Geneva, 1722). Inv.16.29; 2.2.2.20; C35 <670511, h> f*EC.Us750.B722a

Britannicarum ecclesiarum antiquitates (London, 1687). Inv.16.35; 2.1.3.13; C69 <670511, h> Br 326.39.2 F*

USSHER, JAMES, 1720-1772. *A free examination* (London, 1766-1768). 6.1.6.34; C324 (under Popery) <nd, h> *EC75.Us344.766f

UZTARIZ, GERONIMO DE, 1670-1732. *The theory and practice of commerce and maritime affairs*, tr. John Kippax (London, 1751). Inv.4.70; 2.1.5.30-31; C38 <641212?> Original Hollis gift not located.

V

VAILLANT, JEAN, *see* Foy-Vaillant

VALIERO, ANDREA, 1615-1691. *Historia della guerra di Candia* (Venice, 1629). Inv.3.26; 4.1.5.5; C63 <641208, h> *IC6.V2388.679h

VALLA, GIORGIO, 1430-1500, *see* Cleonides

Vanini, Giulio Cesare, 1585-1619.
Amphitheatrum æternæ providentiæ divino-magicvm (Leiden, 1615). Inv.7.7; 2.2.7.25; C126 <651010, h> Andover-Harvard Safe 17.35 Vanini

De admirandis naturæ reginæ deaque mortalium arcanis (Paris, 1616). 2.2.7.26; C126 <651010, h> Andover-Harvard Safe 17.35 Vanini

See also Durand, David

Varchi, Benedetto, 1503-1565. *L'Hercolano dialogo* (Venice, 1570). 2.4.5.34; not in C <641208, v> *IC5.V4227.570hb

Varenius, Bernhardus, 1612-1650. *A compleat system of general geography* (London, 1734). Inv.8.41; 4.2.7.9-10; B25, C49 <661001, r> S 6035.90.5* 2 v.

Varo, Salvator. *Vesuviani incendii historiæ libri tres* (Naples, 1634). 2.4.4.39; C126 <nd, contemporary Italian calf> MCZ 837

Vaslet, Louis. *Introduzzione alla scienza delle antichità romane* (Venice, 1732). Inv.4.109; 2.3.8.43; C8 <641212?, v> *FC7.V4434.Ei732i

Vattel, Emer de, 1714-1767.
Le droit des gens ou principes de la loi naturelle (Leiden, 1758). 4.2.4.14; C86 <65…., h> Int 2210.4*

The law of nations (London, 1759-1760). C86 <nd, r> Int 2210.10*

Vayrac, Jean de. *État present de l'Espagne* (Paris, 1718). Inv.4.67; C126 <641212?, h> Span 1710.3*

Velasti, Thomas Stanislas, b. 1717. *Dissertatio de litterarum græcarum pronuntiatione* (Rome, 1751). 4.1.5.6; C137 <nd, h> 4256.8*

Veneroni, sieur de, 1642-1708. *Le maître italien* (no edition cited). Inv.16.106 <670511> Original Hollis gift not located.

Venuti, Filippo, 1709-1769. *Duodenorum nomismatum antehac ineditorum … selegit ex gazophylacio Antonii Lefroy* (Leghorn, 1760). C130 <nd, v> Possibly the gift of Thomas Brand Hollis. Arc 1480.1*

Venuti, Niccolò Marcello, marchese, 1700-1755. ‡*Descrizione delle prime scoperte dell'antica citta d'Ercolano* (Venice, 1749). Inv.4.184; 2.3.8.11; B25, C8 <641212?, v> On flyleaf: "The Public, The Learned, are greatly obliged to the Family Venuti." *IC7.V5698.748dc

Venuti, Ridolfino, 1705-1763. *De dea Libertate* (Rome, 1762). 6.1.3.28; C209 <nd, h> *EC75.H7267.Zz769t

Vere, Sir Francis, 1560-1609. *The commentaries* (Cambridge, 1657). Inv.3.90; 2.3.4.18; C126 <641208, h (rebacked)> Neth 2325.1*

Vermigli, Pietro Martire, 1499-1562. *An epistle unto the right honorable and Christian prince, the Duke of Somerset*, tr. Thomas Norton (London, 1550). 2.2.8.38; C227 <nd, h> STC 4407.5

VERSTEGAN, RICHARD, ca. 1550-1640.
A restitution of decayed intelligence (London, 1628). 2.2.6.37; C8 <nd, h> STC 21362

†‡[Another edition] (London, 1634). Inv.5.40; 4.1.8.6; C8 <6506.., h> On flyleaf: "A curious & scarce Book." STC 21363

†‡[Another edition] (London, 1673). 4.4.8.1; C8 <nd, h> TH completes author's name on title page. Br 1250.17.12*

VESALIUS, ANDREAS, 1514-1564. ‡*De humani corporis fabrica* (Basel, 1555). Inv.1.4; 2.2.1.17; C2 <631024, r> On a bifolium inserted before the title page: "These prints from wooden blocks are very artistically executed & greatly admired. That of the Anatomical chamber is thought to be after a drawing of Titian's himself, who appears in it, a thin spare man, with a long beard & cap standing near the skeleton within the rails." f*FC5.V6305.543dc

VETTORI, PIETRO, 1499-1585. *Variarum lectionum libri xxv* (Florence, 1553). 4.3.4.9; not in C <nd, h> f*IC5.V6435.553v (B)

A view of the reign of King Charles the First (London, 1704). Inv.4.38 (part); 2.3.5.33; not in C <641212, xt> *EC7.A100.704v

VIGENÈRE, BLAISE DE, 1522-1596. *Traicté des chiffres* (Paris, 1586). Inv.3.36; 2.4.4.1; C126 <641208, r> *FC5.V6813.586t

VIGER, FRANÇOIS, 1590-1647. *De praecipuis græcæ dictionis et particulis* (London, 1695). 4.2.8.28; C137 <nd, r> *FC6.V6816.632dm

VIGNALI, ANTONIO. *Alcune lettere piacevole* (Siena, 1618). Inv.3.120 (under Palermo; part); 2.4.7.12; C227 (under Marzi) <641208, h> *IC7.A100.B752h

VIGNOLA, GIACOMO BAROZZIO, CALLED, 1507-1573. *Regola delle cinque ordine d'archittetura* (Rome, [1617]). Inv.3.6; 4.3.1.16; C8 <641208, v> FA 2800.208.7 F*

A vindication of the late Bishop Burnet (London, 1724). Inv.4.138 (part); 2.2.5.23; C213 <641212?, h> *EC65.B9343.S736t

A vindication of the memory of Mr. Thomas Chubb (London, 1747). 4.2.7.35; C271 <nd, r> *EC7.C4705.B747t

VIRGIL. *Antiquissimi Virgiliani codicis fragmenta … ex Bibliotheca Vaticana*, ed. Pietro Santi Bartoli (Rome, 1741). 4.3.1.6; C21 <nd, v> Typ 725.41.869 F (A)

VITA, GIOVANNI, 1708-1784. *Thesaurus antiquitatum Beneventarum* (Rome, 1754). Inv.3.3; 2.3.1.6; C3 <641208, Italian binding> Arc 720.205 F*

VITRUVIUS POLLIO.
De architectura libri dece (Como, 1521). Inv.3.4; 2.3.1.9; C8 <641208, v> f*OLC.V834.Ei521 (B)

Della architettura (Venice, 1590). Inv.3.19; 2.3.3.26; C8 (under Rusconi) <641208, h> Typ 525.90.872 F

I dieci libri dell' architettura (Venice, 1584). Inv.3.33; 2.4.4.3; C8 <641208, morocco> *EC75.H7267.Zz584v

See also Cleonides

VOET, JOHANNES, 1647-1713. *Commentaria ad Pandectas* (The Hague, 1731). 4.1.3.5-6; C77 <nd, h> AH 7203.138.6 F* 2 v.

VOLTAIRE, 1694-1778.
Panégyrique de Louis XV (Paris, 1748). 2.1.8.20; C207 <671209?, xt> *FC7.V8893.748pb

‡*Le philosophe ignorant* ([London?], 1766). 4.2.7.21; C126 <nd, h> On title page: "Par Mons. Voltaire." *FC7.V8893.766pb

VOLUSENUS, FLORENTIUS, 1504?-1546 or 7. *De animi tranquillitate dialogus* (Edinburgh, 1751). Inv.16.17; 2.2.8.6; C126 <670511, h> *EC.V8892.543dd

VOORBROEK, JACOBUS, *see* Perizonius, Jacobus

VORST, JOHANNES, 1623-1676. *De hebraismus Novi Testamenti commentarius* (Amsterdam, 1665). 4.4.6.20-21; C43 <nd, v> Andover Harvard S.C.R. 508 Vorst 2 v.

VOSSIUS, GERARDUS JOANNES, 1577-1649.
‡*De veterum poetarum temporibus libri duo* (Amsterdam, 1662). 4.4.7.9; C35 <nd, h> Verso of title page contains partly legible offset of directions to the binder. *NC6.V9367.654db

Etymologicon linguæ latinæ (Amsterdam, 1685). 4.4.2.17; C205 <nd, v> *f NC6.V9367.662ec

Opera (Amsterdam, 1695-1701). 4.4.2.18-23; C126 <nd, v> f*NC6.V9367.C701o 6 v.

VOSSIUS, ISAAC, 1618-1689. ‡*De poematum cantu* (Oxford, 1673). 4.3.7.31; not in C <nd, h> Verso of title page contains faint offset of directions to the binder. *EC65.V9373.673d

W

WACHTER, JOHANN GEORG, 1673-1757. *Glossarium germanicum* (Leipzig, 1737). 4.4.2.6-7; C205 <nd, h> 8211.3 F* 2 v.

WADDEL, GEORGE. *Animadversiones criticæ* (Edinburgh, 1734). 4.4.8.14; not in C <nd, h> Class 2247.34*

WAGENSEIL, JOHANN CHRISTOPH, 1633-1705. *Exercitationes sex* (Altdorf, 1687). 4.4.6.24; C232 <nd, v> *GC6.W1235.B692d

WAKE, WILLIAM, 1657-1737. †*A collection of several discourses against popery* (London, 1688). Inv.12.17 (part); 6.1.3.25-26; C198 <690818, 17th c. morocco> *EC7.W1377.B688c 2 v.

WALKER, CLEMENT, 1595-1654. *Relations and observations ... upon the parliament* ([London], 1648 [i.e., 1660]). 4.3.7.41, C60 & C147 (both under Parliament) <nd, r> *EC65.W1512.648hg (B)

WALKER, SIR HOVENDEN, 1656?-1728. *A journal: or Full account of the late expedition to Canada* (London, 1720). Inv.8.46; 2.4.5.37; B26, C63 <661001, r> Can 298.7*

Walker, Obadiah, 1616-1699. ‡*The Greek and Roman history* (London, 1692). Inv.5.46 *or* Inv.16.45; 2.1.7.33; C130 (misdated 1672) <6506.. *or* 670511, h> On flyleaf: "A pretty book, by a motley but ingenious Person, Obadiah Walker." *EC65.W1534.692g Second copy not located.

Waller, Edmund, 1606-1687. *Poems &c.* (London, 1711). Inv.3.126; 2.2.5.21; C144 <641208, r> 14455.52*

Wallerius, Johan Gottschalk, 1709-1785.
Elementa metallurgicæ (Stockholm, 1768). Inv.13.48; 6.1.6.44; C37 <700926, h> *QSC7.W1568.768e

‡*Mineralogie* (Paris, 1759). Inv.5.25; 2.2.5.18-19; C37 <6506.., h> On flyleaf: "The institution of a Professorship at Harvard College, of like kind to that held by the learned, excellent Wallerius, when a fund can be provided for it; it is apprehended, would be of greatest Benefit to New England." Geol 7257.59* 2 v.

Wallis, Edward. *Tentamen sophisticon* (London, [1767]). 4.3.6.9; C37 <nd, h> Chem 377.1*

Wallis, John, 1616-1703.
A defense of the Royal Society (London, 1678). 2.4.4.17; C232 <nd, r> *EC65.St935.B681t

†*Grammatica linguæ anglicanæ* (London, 1653). Inv.5.43; 2.2.8.24; C53 <6506.., h> *EC65.W1584.653g

‡†[Another edition] (London, 1765). Inv.5.18 & Inv.5.51; 2.1.5.11; C53 <6506.., h> On flyleaf: "Thomas Hollis, an Englishman, Citizen of the World, is desirous of having the honor to present this book to the Library of Harvard College, at Cambridge in N. England. Pall Mall, jan. 1., 1765." Designed and sponsored by TH. Second copy not located. *EC65.W1584.653gf

See also Great Britain. *A collection of all the publicke orders*; Great Britain. *An exact collection of all remonstrances*; Great Britain. *Speeches and prayers of this great and happy parliament*; May, Thomas, *The history of parliament*

Walpole, Horace, 1717-1797. ‡*Historic doubts on the life and reign of King Richard the Third* (London, 1768). Inv.10.19; 4.3.5.14; C63 <680712, r> Two newspaper cuttings laid down on back flyleaves: from *St. James's chronicle,* January 21 [nd], signed "N." protesting the story of Richard Plantagenet as the pretended son of Richard III, with note by TH: "Believed to have been written by the Rev. George North, Rector of Codicote, in Hertfordshire, an excellent antiquarie." From unidentified journal, unsigned: "Historic doubts …", a critique of *The winter's tale.* Br 1605.12*

Walton, Brian, 1600-1661
‡*The considerator considered* (London, 1659). Inv.14.7; 6.3.8.39; C43 <700926, h> On verso of front flyleaf: "Hollis." Andover-Harvard safe 303 1657 W239 1659

Introductio ad lectionem linguarum orientalium (London, 1655). 4.2.8.46-47; C205 <nd, h> 2255.11* 2 v.

See also Bible. Polyglot

WALWYN, WILLIAM, fl. 1646-1651. *Juries justified* (London, 1651). 2.4.5.19; C253 Original Hollis gift discarded as a duplicate.

WARBURTON, WILLIAM, 1698-1779. *An enquiry into the nature and origin of literary property* (London, 1762). C262 (under Literary property) <nd, xt> *EC75.A100.762c

WARD, JOHN, 1679-1758.
Ad viri reverendi Conier. Middletoni (London, 1727). Inv.13.21 (part); 6.1.7.18; not in C <700926, h> *EC7.W2137.728d

‡*De ratione interpungendi* (London, 1739). 2.1.8.23; C137 <nd, h> On title page: "+a curious Dissertation." *EC7.W2137.739d

‡*Dissertationis v. r. Con. Middletoni* (London, 1728). Inv.13.21 (part); 6.1.7.18; C127 <700926, h> TH identifies the author. *EC7.W2137.728d

Four essays upon the English language (London, 1758). 4.4.6.26; C237 <671209?, r> *EC7.W2137.758f

‡*The lives of the professors of Gresham College* (London, 1740). Inv.16.62; 2.1.3.12; B26, C30 <670511, r> On flyleaf: "Johannes Wardus LL.D. Rhet. Prof. Gresh. Reg. Et Ant. Soc SS. Sodal. Mus. Brit. Cur." Ward tutored TH at Gresham College. Educ 7460.612.5 F*

‡*A system of oratory* (London, 1759). Inv.1.19; 2.4.5.1-2; C150 <631024, h> TH quotes one page each of *Lycidas, Areopagitica,* and *Leviathan.* TH's gift copy was sold as a duplicate, ca. 1823, when three pages of his autograph notes were removed and inserted in this copy, given by Benning Wentworth of Vermont. *EC7.W2137.759s 2 v.

See also Birch, Thomas, *An account;* Cellarius, Christoph, *Notitia;* Celsi, Mino, *De haereticis capitali supplicio non afficiendis;* Kemp, John, *Monumenta vetustatis Kempiana;* Tindal, Matthew, *Christianity as old as the creation*

WARDER, JOSEPH, fl. 1680-1718. *The true Amazons* (London, 1765). 4.2.8.1; C72 <nd, h> *EC7.W2197.712tj

WARREN, ERASMUS. *No præexistence* (London, 1667). Inv.4.61; 2.2.6.12; C199 <641212?, h> Phil 665.5*

WARRINGTON, HENRY BOOTH, EARL OF, 1652-1684. *The works* (London, 1694). Inv.14.43; 6.1.7.50; C110 (under Booth) <700926, h> Br 1925.6.2*

WATSON, DAVID, 1710-1756. *A clear and compendious history of the gods and goddesses* (London, 1753). Inv.3.141; 2.1.8.13; C128 <641208, r> Class 7097.53*

WATSON, JAMES, d. 1722. ‡*The history of the art of printing* (Edinburgh, 1713). Inv.3.135 (under Mason); 2.1.8.5; C9 <641208, h > TH identifies the author. B 4487.13*

WATSON, JOHN, 1728-1783. *The apology of the Reverend John Watson* (London, [1755]). 2.2.5.22; C232 <nd, h> *EC75.H7267.Zz737h

WATSON, WILLIAM, ed. *Cyfreithju hywel dda ac eraill, sive Leges Wallicæ* (London, 1730). Inv.16.12; 2.2.2.5, C78 <670511, r> Br 6405.5.5 F*

WATTS, ISAAC, 1674-1748.
The improvement of the mind (London, 1761). 4.1.7.24; not in C <nd, h> Educ 7317.41.4*

Logick: or, The right use of reason (London, 1736). 4.2.7.23; C88 <nd, h> KE 16417*

‡*A new essay on civil power in things sacred* (London, 1739). 2.4.5.4; C221 (under Civil power) <nd, h> On title page: "Believe by Dr. Watts." *EC75.H7267.Zz725m

WEBB, DANIEL, 1718 or 19-1798.
An inquiry into the beauties of poetry (London, 1769). Inv.15.13; 6.1.8.4; C127 <691129, r> Fine Arts XFA3147.1.2

Observations on the correspondence between poetry and music (London, 1769). Inv.15.12; 6.1.8.5; C127 <691129, h> *EC75.W3815.769o

Remarks on the beauties of poetry (London, 1762). Inv.15.11; 6.1.8.6; C127 <691129, r> *EC75.W3815.762r

WEBB, PHILIP CARTERET, 1700-1770.
An account of a copper table (London, 1760). 2.1.8.20; C208 <6410.., h> *EC75.H7267.Zz763p

A short account of danegeld (London, 1756). 2.4.4.15; C208 <6410.., h> *EC75.H7267.Zz763p

‡*A short account of some particulars concerning Domes-day book* (London, 1756). Inv.2.33; 2.1.8.20; C208 <6410.., h> On flyleaf of tract volume: "These are all the Dissertations which have been printed hitherto by the Society of Antiquaries of London; for want of a sufficient fund to carry them on. T·H." *EC75.H7267.Zz756p

A week's preparation for solemnizing the thirtieth of January (London, 1718). Inv.4.115; 2.2.6.38; C115 (under January) <641212?, h> Br 2095.200*

WELDON, SIR ANTHONY, d. 1649?
A brief history of the kings of England (London, 1755). 2.1.7.22; C214 (under Welding) <671209?, h> *EC65.W4574.653cb (B)

[Another copy] 2.2.5.22; C214 (under Welding) <nd, h> *EC75.H7267.Zz737h

‡*A cat may look at a king* (Amsterdam [i.e., London], 1714). 2.1.7.20; C221 <671209?, h> At the end of the 3rd tract (*see* Burges, Cornelius): "N.B. The Notes are both clever & useful." *EC65.W4574.653cb (B) A second copy, 2.1.7.4, not located.

WELWOOD, JAMES, 1652-1727. *An answer to the late King James's declaration* (London, 1689). 2.2.5.16; C253 <671209, h> *EC75.H7267.Zz691t

WERENFELS, SAMUEL, 1657-1740. *Three discourses* (London, 1718). 6.1.7.9; C349 <700926, h> *EC7.H4317.B719h

WESLEY, JOHN, 1703-1791.
Dr. Free's edition of the Rev. Mr. John Wesley's first penny letter (London, 1759). 6.1.6.19; C290 (under Free) <690818, h> *EC75.H7267.Zz750f v.3

Dr.Free's edition of the Rev. Mr. John Wesley's second letter (London, 1759). 6.1.6.19; C290 (under Free) <690818, h> *EC75.H7267.Zz750f v.3

WESSELING, PETER, 1692-1764.
‡*Diatribe de Judæorum archontibus* (Utrecht, 1738). Inv.10.26; 4.4.6.37; not in C <680712, h> On front flyleaf: "All the works of <u>Wesseling</u> are greatly esteemed." Andover Harvard S.C.R. 232 Wesseling

Dissertatio Herodotea (Utrecht, 1758). 4.3.7.5; not in C <nd, h> Gh 44.505*

Observationum variarum libri duo (Utrecht, 1740). 4.3.7.6 (dated 1746); not in C Declared lost, October 2002.

Probabilium liber singularis (Utrecht, 1731). Inv.10.27; 4.3.7.4; not in C <680712, h> C 527.31*

WESTON, WILLIAM, 1710 or 11-1791. †*An enquiry into the rejection of Christian miracles* (Cambridge, 1746). Inv.2.85; 2.1.6.28; C199 <6410.., h> C 1391.47*

WHARTON, PHILIP WHARTON, DUKE OF, 1698-1731. *What of that?* (London, 1740). 4.2.3.22; C240 (under title) <nd, h> f*EC75.H7267.Zz740p

WHATELY, THOMAS, d. 1772.
Observations on modern gardening (London, 1770). Inv.14.27; 6.1.4.21; C1 <700926> Original Hollis gift not located.

The regulations lately made concerning the colonies (London, 1765). 4.1.7.23; C241 Original Hollis gift not located.

WHATLEY, STEPHEN, fl. 1712-1741. *A short account of a late journey to Tuscany* (London, 1741). Inv.1.32; 2.2.7.34; B15 (under Italy), C76 (under Rome, Tuscany) <631024, h> Ital 2147.41*

WHEARE, DEGORY, 1573-1647.
The method and order of reading both civil and ecclesiastical histories (London, 1685). 6.1.8.10; C127 <700926, h> H 6.60.12*

‡[Another edition] (London, 1698). Inv.12.30; 6.1.7.45; C127 <690818, r> On title page: "A valuable Book in the day of it." H 6.60.15*

Reflectiones hyemales, de ratione & methodo legendi utrasq; historias (Oxford, 1672). Inv.1.41; 2.4.8.32; not in C <631024, h> *EC.W5604.623de (B)

WHICHCOTE, BENJAMIN, 1609-1683. †*Select sermons* (London, 1698). Inv.2.82; 2.3.8.4; C199 <6410.., h (rebacked)> *EC65.W5758.698s

WHISTON, WILLIAM, 1667-1752. *The testimony of Phlegon vindicated* (London, 1732). 6.1.5.45; C349 <700926, h> C 1357.15.60*

WHITBY, DANIEL, 1638-1726.
Dissertatio de S. Scripturarum interpretatione (London, 1714). 2.4.6.41; C43 <nd, h> C 1391.31.55*

Disquisitiones modestæ in ... bulli Defensionem fidei Nicaenæ (London, 1720). 4.2.7.20; C200 <nd, h> *EC7.W5815.718da

Ethices compendium (London, 1713). Inv.2.72; 2.1.6.39; C47 <6410.., r> Phil 8897.15*

WHITE, JEREMIAH, 1629-1707. *The restoration of all things* (London, 1712). Inv.4.82; 2.3.8.6; C200 <641212?, h> Given by John Hollis (with his signature) to Thomas Hollis [IV?] in 1724. C 1391.42.30* 2 v.

WHITE, JOHN, 1590-1645. ‡*The first century of scandalous, malignant priests* (London, 1643). Inv.2.41; 2.1.7.8; not in C <6410.., h> On flyleaf: "John White was Burgess for Southwark, in the Parliament which began nov. 3, 1640. He was persuaded by his own Brethren from putting out a second Century for fear it should prove scandalous, & bring an imputation on the whole Body of the Clergy, Orthodox, Presbyterian, or Independent.' Athenae Oxoniensis of A. Wood, vol. 1, p.70, Also the preface to a new years gift to the high Church Clergy.—" (This last is a fragmentary pamphlet bound at the end of the volume.) *EC65.W5843.643fb

WHITE, THOMAS, 1593-1676.
‡*The grounds of obedience and government* (London, 1655). Inv.5.75; 2.2.8.55; C86 <6506.., h> Comments by TH about the author and his works on flyleaves at front and back of text. *EC75.H7267.Zz655w

‡[Another copy] Inv.14.48; 6.2.8.40; C86 <700926, h> TH writes 21 p. of notes and transcripts following the text. *EC75.H7267.Zz655w2

WHITEHEAD, PAUL, 1710-1774. *Manners: a satire* (London, 1739). 4.2.3.22; C240 <nd, h> f*EC75.H7267.Zz740p

WHITLOCKE, SIR BULSTRODE, 1605-1675 or 6.
Memorials of the English affairs (London, 1732). Inv.16.28; 2.2.2.21; C64 <670511, r> History Department Library Hist 1790.60

Notes upon the Kings writt (London, 1766). 4.1.4.19-20; C86 <nd, h> Br 150.7* 2 v.

WILDMAN, THOMAS, d. 1781.
A treatise on the management of bees (London, 1768). Inv.11.4; 6.1.2.25; C72 <6809.., h> *EC75.H7267.Zz768w (A)

[Another copy] Inv.12.75; 6.1.2.24; C72 <690818, h> *EC75.H7267.Zz768w (B)

WILKES, JOHN, 1727-1797, see *A complete collection of the genuine papers*

WILKINS, DAVID, 1685-1745.
Concilia Magnæ Britannicæ et Hiberniæ, a Synodo Verolamiensi (London, 1737). Inv.5.62; 2.3.1.15-18; C78 <6506.., r> Wrongly plated as the gift of the Society for the Propagation of the Gospel in Foreign Parts. Harvard Depository C 135.10.5 F 4 v.

Leges anglo-saxonicæ ecclesiasticæ et civilis (London, 1721). Inv.16.13; 2.2.2.6, 4.5.1.1; C78 <670511, r> Br 1035.21 F*

See also Bible. N.T. Coptic

WILKINS, JOHN, 1614-1672. *An essay towards a real character and a philosophical language* (London, 1668). Inv.1.10; 2.2.3.11; C137 <631024, r> *EC65.W6563.668e (B)

WILLIAM, OF NEWBURGH, 1136-1201. *Historia*, ed. Thomas Hearne (Oxford, 1719). 4.1.6.6-8; C5 <nd, h> Br 1345.90.4* 3 v.

WILLIAM, OF OCKHAM, ca. 1285-ca. 1349. *A dialogue betwene a knyght and a clerke* ([London, 1559]). C85 (under Oakham) <670815, h> STC 12511a

WILLIAMS, GRIFFITH, CAPTAIN. *An account of the island of Newfoundland* ([London], 1765). 4.1.7.19; not in C <nd> Original Hollis gift not located.

WILLIAMS, ROGER, 1604?-1683. ‡*The bloudy tenent, of persecution* ([London?], 1644). Inv.4.48; 2.1.6.48; C156 <641212?, h> On title page: "a curious tract." *AC6.W6754.644bb

WILSON, ARTHUR, 1595-1652. ‡*The history of Great Britain* (London, 1653). 4.3.4.25; C64 <nd, h> TH's directions to the binder offset on verso of title page. *EC65.W6911.653hb (B)

WILSON, JOHN, 1626-1696. *A discourse of monarchy* (London, 1684). Inv.14.68; C86 <700926, h> *EC65.W6946.684d

WINCKELMANN, JOHANN JOACHIM, 1717-1768. *Historie de l'art chez les anciens* (Amsterdam, 1766). 4.2.7.32-33; C9 <nd, r> Fine Arts X Cage XFA307.2.2 v.2 (v. 1 of Hollis's gift is missing and has been replaced by another copy)

WISE, FRANCIS, 1695-1767.
Further observations upon the White Horse (Oxford, 1742). 4.3.5.6; C209 <nd, h> *EC75.H7267.Zz738w

The history and chronology of the fabulous ages (Oxford, 1764). 4.3.5.6; C209 <nd, h> *EC75.H7267.Zz738w

A letter to Dr Mead (Oxford, 1738). 4.3.5.6; C209 <nd, h> *EC75.H7267.Zz738w

Nummorum antiquorum scriniis Bodleianis … catalogus (Oxford, 1750). Inv.16.71; 2.2.1.20; C131 <670511, h> Arc 1333.2 F*

Some enquiries concerning the first inhabitants … of Europe (Oxford, 1758). 4.3.5.6; C209 <nd, h> *EC75.H7267.Zz738w

WITTE, PETRUS DE, 1622-1669. *Catechizing upon the Heidelberg Catechisme* (Amsterdam, [1664]). 6.2.8.24; C201 <nd, h> *NC6.W7836.Eg664c

WODROW, ROBERT, 1679-1734. *The history of the sufferings of the Church of Scotland* (Edinburgh, 1721). Inv.10.1; 4.3.2.9-10; C69 <680712, h> Br 8217.21 F* 2 v.

WOLLASTON, WILLIAM, 1660-1724. *The religion of nature delineated* (London, 1738). Inv.16.85; 2.3.4.14; C47 <670511, h> *EC7.W8348.722rdac (A)

WOLTERECK, CHRISTOPH. ‡*Electa rei numeriæ* (Hamburg, 1709). Inv.5.17; 2.3.5.39; C129 <6506.., h> Very faint offset of TH's directions to the binder on the verso of the title page. Arc 1458.8*

WOMOCK, LAWRENCE, 1612-1685.
Arcana dogmatum anti-remonstrantium, or Calvinist's cabinet unlock'd (London, 1659). Inv.4.161 (under Apology); 2.1.8.52; not in C <641212?, h> *EC75.H7267.Zz658

The examination of Tilenus before the triers (London, 1658-1659). Inv.4.190; 2.1.8.54; C186 (under Tilenus) <641212?, h> *EC75.H7267.Zz658w 2 v.

WOOD, ANTHONY A, 1632-1695.
Athenæ Oxoniensis (London, 1721). Inv.16.49; C31 <670511, r> Wrongly plated as the gift of the Society for the Propagation of the Gospel in Foreign Parts. Educ 4000.2.3 PF*

Historia et antiquitates universitatis Oxoniensis (Oxford, 1674). 2.1.1.16-17; not in C <nd, r> f *EC75.H7267.Zz674w 2 v. in 1

See also Jones, Bassett

WOOD, ROBERT, 1717?-1771. *The ruins of Balbec* (London, 1757). 6.3.1.18; C3 Original Hollis gift not located.

WOOD, THOMAS, 1661-1722. *An institute of the laws of England* (London, 1763). Inv.6.3; 4.4.2.5; C82 <650817, h> Br 166.3.4 F*

WOODHEAD, ABRAHAM, 1609-1678, *see* R. H.

WOOLNOR, HENRY, d. ca. 1640. *The extraction of mans soul* (London, 1655). Inv.3.59; 2.2.8.40; C95 <641208, h (rebacked)> *EC.W8858.641taa

WOOLSTON, THOMAS, 1670-1733.
Note: on two occasions Hollis gave 5-volume sets of collected tracts by Woolston, recorded on C201 without listing contents. Only a few of the individual titles appear elsewhere in C.

An answer to Aristobulus's Two letters to Dr. Bennet (London, 1723). Inv.10.28 (part); 4.3.7.29 <680712, h> C 1397.19.08*

A defence of the Miracle of the Thundering Legion (London, 1726). Inv.10.28 (part); 4.3.7.30 <680712, h> C 1397.19.09*

A discourse on the miracles of Our Saviour (London, 1727). Inv.2.76 (part); 2.3.7.15 <6410.., h> C 1397.19.31*

‡[Another edition] (London, 1728). Inv.10.28 (part); 4.3.7.16 <680712, h> On front flyleaf: "These five Volumes make the completest Collection of Wolston's [*sic*] Pieces that I ever saw. T·H." C 1397.19.05*

Dissertatio de Pontii Pilati ad Tiberium epistola circa res Jesu Christi (London, 1720). Inv.10.28 (part); 4.3.7.30 <680712, h> C 1397.19.09*

The exact fitness of time, in which Christ was manifested in the flesh (London, 1722). Inv.10.28 (part); 4.3.7.30 <680712, h> C1397.19.09*

A fifth discourse on the miracles of Our Saviour (London, 1728). Inv.10.28 (part); 4.3.7.26 <680712, h> C 1397.19.05*

[Another copy] Inv.2.76 (part) <6410.., h> C 1397.19.31*

A fourth discourse on the miracles of Our Saviour (London, 1728). Inv.10.28 (part); 4.3.7.26 <680712, h> C 1397.19.05*

[Another copy] Inv.2.76 (part); 2.3.7.15 <6410.., h> C 1397.19.31*

A fourth free-gift to the clergy (London, 1724). Inv.2.79 (part); 2.3.7.13 <6410.., h> C 1397.19.50*

[Another copy] Inv.10.28 (part); 4.3.7.29 <680712, h> C 1397.19.08*

A free-gift to the clergy (London, 1722). Inv.2.79 (part); 2.3.7.13 <6410.., h> C 1397.19.50*

A letter to the Reverend Dr. Bennet (London, 1720). Inv.10.28 (part); 4.3.7.29 <680712, h> C 1397.19.08*

The moderator between an infidel and an apostate (London, 1725). Inv.2.77 (part); 2.3.7.12 <6410.., h> C 1397.19.40*

[Another copy] Inv.10.28 (part); 4.3.7.27 <680712, h> C 1397.19.06*

Mr. Woolston's Defense of his Discourses on the miracles of Our Saviour (London, 1729-1730). Inv.2.78 (part); 2.3.7.16 <6410.., h> C 1397.19.35* (2 parts in 1 v.)

The old apology for the truth of the Christian religion (London, 1705). Inv.2.75 (part); 2.3.7.14 <6410.., h> C 1397.19.45*

[Another copy] Inv.10.28 (part); 4.3.7.28 <680712, h> C 1397.19.07*

Originis Adamannij epistola secunda (London, 1720). Inv.10.28 (part); 4.3.7.30 <680712, h> C 1397.19.09*

Origenis Adamannij Renati epistola (London, 1720). Inv.10.28 (part); 4.3.7.30 <680712, h> C 1397.19.09*

A second discourse on the miracles of Our Saviour (London, 1728). Inv.10.28 (part); 4.3.7.26 <680712, h> C 1397.19.05*

A second free-gift to the clergy (London, 1723). Inv.2.79 (part); 2.3.7.13 <6410.., h> C 1397.19.50*

[Another copy] Inv.10.28 (part); 4.3.7.29 <680712, h> C 1397.19.08*

A second letter to the Reverend Dr. Bennet (London, 1721). Inv.10.28 (part); 4.3.7.29 <680712, h> C 1397.19.08*

A second supplement to The moderator between an infidel and an apostate (London,1725). Inv.2.76 (part); 2.3.7.12 <6410.., h> C 1397.19.40*

[Another copy] Inv.10.28 (part); 4.3.7.27 <680712, h> C 1397.19.06*

A sixth discourse on the miracles of Our Saviour (London, 1729). Inv.2.76 (part); 2.3.7.15 <6410.., h> C 1397.19.31*

[Another copy] Inv.10.28 (part); 4.3.7.26 <680712, h> C 1397.19.05*

A supplement to The moderator between an infidel and an apostate (London, 1725). Inv.2.77 (part); 2.3.7.12 <6410.., h> C 1397.19.40*

[Another copy] Inv.10.28 (part); 4.3.7.27 <680712, h> C 1397.19.06*

A third free-gift to the clergy (London, 1723). Inv.2.79 (part); 2.3.7.13 <6410.., h> C 1397.19.50*

[Another copy] Inv.10.28 (part); 4.3.7.29 <680712, h> C 1397.19.08*

WOTTON, SIR HENRY, 1568-1639.
Reliquiæ Wottonianæ (London, 1672). Inv.11.12; 4.4.7.50; C127 <6809.., calf> *EC.W9147.C672r (B)

[Another edition] (London, 1685). 4.3.8.23; C127 (misdated 1675) <nd, h> *EC.W9147.C685r (B)

WOTTON, WILLIAM, 1666-1727.
Miscellaneous discourses (London, 1718). Inv.4.133; 2.3.7.33-34; C70 <641212?> Original Hollis gift not located.

Reflections on ancient and modern learning (London, 1705). Inv.10.34 *or* Inv.15.9; 4.4.7.24 *or* 6.1.6.43; C127 <680711 or 691129, h> *EC7.W9142.694rc Second copy not located.

WREN, CHRISTOPHER, 1675-1747. ‡*A catalogue of the genuine and entire collection* ([London, 1749]). Not in C <nd, h> On flyleaf: "Che trae l'uom del sepolcro, ed in vita il serba. Petrarca." B 1827.401*

WRIGHT, JOHN MICHAEL, ca. 1617-ca. 1694. ‡*Raggvaglio della solenne comparsa … Conte dei Castlemaine* (Rome, [1687]). 4.3.3.14; C127 (under Writ) <nd, calf> On flyleaf: "Salus Populi suprema Lex esto! T·H." Typ 625.87.881 F

WRIGHT, SAMUEL, 1683-1746. *Scripture and tradition considered* (London, 1735). Not in C <6506.., h> *EC75.H7267.Zz735s2

WYNG, JOHN, fl. 1715-1730.
Reasons for discontinuing the observation of the thirtieth of January (London, [1730?]). 2.1.7.20; not in C <671209, h> *EC65.W4574.653cb (B)

Reasons humbly offered to Parliament (London, 1715). 2.1.7.20; C233 <671209?, h> *EC65.W4574.653cb (B)

X

XENOPHON.
De Cyri institutione libri octo (Oxford, 1727). 4.2.5.18; C21 <nd, r> KF 23380* v.1 only

Della vita di Cyro ([Florence, 1521]). Inv.3.156; 2.4.8.19; C21 <641208, v> Gx 9.770*

‡*Hieron*, tr. Pierre Coste [into French] (Amsterdam, 1711). Inv.17.39; 4.4.8.41; C21 <68…., h> On flyleaf: "The second edit. of Hiero, or the condition of a Tyrant, translated from the Greek into E[nglish] was printed at London, 1713, in 12°. Hiero, is a little, great work; was written by one of the most accomplished, excellent Gentlemen of all Antiquity, & cannot be too much read, valued, in all languages, by the ingenuous Youths of Harvard College, at Cambridge in New England. Palmal, dec. 7, 1767. T·H." *EC75.H7267.Zz711x

†*Opera*, ed. Henri Estienne ([Paris], 1581). 4.1.3.24; C21 <nd, h> Gx 9.112 F*

†[Another edition] ([Paris], 1596). 4.1.3.25; not in C <nd, h> Gx 9.112.2 F*

Le opere di Senofonte (Verona, 1736-1737). 2.3.4.25-27; C21 <nd, r> Harvard Depository KF 23390 3 v.

Y

YOUNG, ARTHUR, 1741-1820. *Letters concerning the present state of the French nation* (London, 1769). Inv.12.80; 6.1.4.10; C112 <690818, r> Fr 2007.69*

YOUNG, EDWARD, 1683-1765. *A vindication of providence* (London, 1731). 4.2.7.18; C353 <nd, h> *EC75.H7267.Zz730t

The young senator: a satyre (London, 1738). 4.2.3.22; C239 (under Senator) <nd, h> f*EC75.H7267.Zz740p

Z

ZABAGLIA, NICCOLA, 1674-1750.
　　Castelli e ponti (Rome, 1743).　4.3.1.5; C34　Original Hollis gift not located.

　　Contignationes, ac pontes (Rome, 1743).　6.3.1.34; C34　Original Hollis gift not located.

ZANCHI, GIROLAMO, 1516-1590.　‡*The doctrine of absolute predestination*, tr. Augustus
　　Toplady (London, 1769).　Inv.13.44 (part); C187 & C342 (under Toplady)　<700926, h>
　　On second front flyleaf: "The author the Rev. Mr Toplady."　*EC75.T6261.769d

ZANETTI, ANTONIO MARIA, 1680-1757.　†*Le gemme antiche* (Venice, 1750).　Inv.11.3;
　　4.3.1.24; C131　<6809.., h>　Typ 725.51.894 F (B)

ZIEGENBALG, BARTHOLOMÄUS, 1683-1719.　†*Thirty four conferences between the Danish
　　missionaries and the Malabarian Bramans*, tr. Jenkin Thomas Philipps　(London, 1719).
　　Inv.2.89 (under Phillips [*sic*]); 2.4.7.22; C120 (under Philipps)　<6410.., h>
　　*EC7.P5392.B750t

ZOESIUS, HENDRIK, d. 1627. *Commentarius ad Digestorum ... juris civili* (Brussels, 1718).
　　4.2.3.2; C77　<nd, h>　f*NC6.Z7330.645ce

ZUHAIR, KA'B IBN.　*Carmen panegyricum in laudem Muhammedis* (Leiden, 1748).
　　4.1.7.42; C134　<nd, h>　OL 23292.1*

ZURITA, JERONIMO, 1512-1580.　*Indices rerum gestarum ab Aragoniæ regibus* (Aragon,
　　1578).　Inv.3.22 (under Surita); C62　<641208>　Original Hollis gift not located.

Contributors

WILLIAM H. BOND was Librarian of Houghton Library (1965-1982) and Professor of Bibliography, Harvard University. His Sandars Lectures in Bibliography at Cambridge University in 1982 became the basis of his well-received monograph, *Thomas Hollis of Lincoln's Inn: A Whig and his Books* (1990). He also edited "Letters from Thomas Hollis of Lincoln's Inn to Andrew Eliot" for *Proceedings of the Massachusetts Historical Society* (1988). With Hugh Amory, he edited *The Printed Catalogues of the Harvard College Library, 1723-1790* (1996).

ALLEN REDDICK is Ordinarius Professor für Englische Literatur at the University of Zurich. He received his B.A. from the University of the South, his M.A. from Cambridge University and Ph.D. from Columbia University in New York. From 1985 until 1993, he was Professor of English and American Literature and Language at Harvard University.

Prof. Reddick's publications include *The Making of Johnson's Dictionary, 1746-1773* (Cambridge, 2nd rev. ed., 1996) and *Samuel Johnson's Unpublished Revisions to his Dictionary of the English Language* (Cambridge, 2005). At present, he is compiling a multi-volume descriptive bibliography, with accompanying analysis, of books (mostly republican and/or radical) donated by Thomas Hollis to institutions throughout England, Continental Europe, and the American Colonies. This project is supported through a grant from the Swiss National Science Foundation.